Praise for

Victor: The Final Battle of Ulysses S. Grant

Craig von Buseck is one of my favorite historical writers. You won't be disappointed.

~ Jerry Jenkins
Author of the Left Behind book series

Craig von Buseck is a gifted writer who paints a profoundly significant portrait in our nation's history!

~ Mitch Kruse
Host of The Restoration Road TV program
Author of *Restoration Road* and *Street Smarts from Proverbs*

Riveting! A must-read for military history aficionados. Dr. Craig von Buseck's fascinating biography captures the incredible leadership, courage, and perseverance of Ulysses S. Grant that few may know. Highlighting Grant's character and indomitable will, the author intertwines the toll of cancer's ravages on the general as he struggles to pen his Civil War experiences and finish his memoirs at the end of his life. Betrayal by others in war and peace fail to quell Grant's purpose in battle or the completion of his work. Dr. von Buseck bares the soul of the man who served his nation faithfully as the Union army's general in chief and as a two-term president of the United States. *Victor!* is a monumental work of gripping drama. Extensively researched. Make this required reading for military senior leaders.

~ Aaron M. Zook, Jr.
Colonel, US Army, Ret.

Victor! The Final Battle of Ulysses S. Grant by Dr. Craig von Buseck is a classic! Captivating and insightful, the reader is immediately swept into the world taking shape after the Civil War. The author masterfully brings to life not only the courageous general who saved the

Union and ended slavery but also a president dedicated to eliminating racial discrimination. The reader will gain new appreciation for someone who changed American politics forever and will get to know a caring husband and father who was inspired by a deep faith. I highly recommend this profound and insightful work.

~ **William J. Federer**
Best-selling author of *America's God*
and *Country Encyclopedia of Quotations*

With his usual mastery of investigation, as precise as it is complete and well executed, once again Dr. Craig von Buseck has given us something spectacular in his new book, *Victor! The Final Battle of Ulysses S. Grant*, on the post-Civil War post-presidential life of Ulysses S. Grant. Many of us are familiar with the image of the plainspoken, no-frills, cigar-smoking Union general with dust on his boots, including the legends that attend the name, but the author introduces us to a Grant we may not be aware of—the civilian Grant, the plainclothes Grant whose integrity and true largeness never wavered, whether in success or in failure. And, indeed, Grant failed spectacularly. But it is Grant's response to failure and ruin that is the real proof of the man. It is this astounding humanity that the author brings to the surface, that explores greatness of perhaps a higher kind. In an age of celebrity, when too often spectacle trumps substance and spin outshouts truth, this book provides proper medication and perspective. I also applaud Dr. von Buseck for how deliciously readable this book is.

~ **David Teems**
Best-selling author of *Majestie: The King Behind*
the King James Bible **and** *Tyndale: The Man Who Gave God*
an English Voice

In *Victor! The Final Battle of Ulysses S. Grant*, Dr. Craig von Buseck adds to the growing volumes of prose reestablishing Ulysses S. Grant as the great American hero that he truly was and that the nation he fought for has largely forgotten. *Victor!* is a touching account of Grant's final days where he demonstrated the same dogged determination to recover from financial ruin and care for his family that he did in defeating the Confederacy and preserving the Union.

~ Greg Roberts
U.S. Grant Birthplace, Point Pleasant, Ohio

I am excited to endorse Dr. Craig von Buseck's epic book *Victor! The Final Battle of Ulysses S. Grant*. The author opened my eyes to a chapter into General Grant's life that I had little awareness of before reading *Victor!* As a student of history and as a retired military officer (chaplain) for twenty-two years, I was aware of Grant's resilience and prowess as a leader. I was aware of his exploits in the Mexican-American War and his determination to provide for his family before the Civil War. I even knew about some of his other struggles both during and after his presidency. But after that season of his life, I was clueless—until I had a chance to look at Dr. von Buseck's new book. He takes the reader on a journey into the last chapters of Grant's epic journey, where we get to experience his grit, tenacity, resilience, and determination to provide for his family and leave a legacy of honor and integrity.

This is a much-needed resource. Rather than blaming others for his plight, Grant chooses to face the facts realistically. Rather than surrender to being a victim, he summons the strength and personal integrity to write his memoirs, thus securing his family's future and allowing us to see him for the man he was.

~ John Thurman
Author, Speaker, Counselor, and Chaplain (Major)
USAR, Ret.

In *Victor! The Final Battle of Ulysses S. Grant,* Dr. Craig von Buseck captures the tenacity, humility, and responsibility of General Grant as both supreme commander and beloved family man. The structure of the narrative—chronicling Grant's race against time in completing his memoirs while flashing back to reveal the general's tactics in some of the most consequential battles of the Civil War—draws the reader into the story in a most compelling way. By the book's poignant conclusion, I was cheering on Grant's final victory over enormous adversity while simultaneously mourning the absence of such a great servant-leader in our day.

~ Joel Natalie
Station Manager WZTE/TalkErie.com
and Host of The Joel Natalie Show

Perhaps you've heard of Ulysses S. Grant. His picture is on the fifty-dollar bill. He was the eighteenth president of the United States, and in the final year of the Civil War, he gave Robert E. Lee fits with a strategy of engagement and slide, engagement and slide that led to the fall of Richmond and the Confederacy. That's all many of us know about U. S. Grant. And yet his deep commitment to personal integrity, to doing the right thing when no one is watching, as well as his rare gift of humility make his last accomplishments the mark of true greatness. In an age where the prominent peak early and spend the rest of their lives chasing former glory, Grant peaked and fell greatly, only to live the remainder of his years as a common man of noble character. In my Civil War library, I place *Victor! The Final Battle of Ulysses S. Grant* alongside *Lee* by Douglas Southall Freeman as the bookends of this pivotal time in America's history.

~ **Eddie Jones**
Award-winning author and writers coach

Victor!

The Final Battle of
Ulysses S. Grant

Dr. Craig von Buseck

Birmingham, Alabama

LPCBooks
a division of Iron Stream Media
100 Missionary Ridge, Birmingham, AL 35242
ShopLPC.com

Cover design by Elaina Lee

Iron Stream Media serves its authors as they express their views, which may not express the views of the publisher.

Library of Congress Control Number: 2021932251

ISBN-13: 978-1-64526-315-9
E-book ISBN: 978-1-64526-316-6

To my son, Aaron.

You have been with me every step of the way

on this Grant project.

Thank you for your creativity, your critiques,

your encouragement, and your wisdom.

I'm proud of the man and the artist you have become—

and excited to see what you will create!

ALSO BY DR. CRAIG VON BUSECK

Forward: The Leadership Principles of Ulysses S. Grant

I Am Cyrus: Harry S. Truman and the Rebirth of Israel

Nobody Knows: The Harry T. Burleigh Story

Praying the News

Netcasters

Jesus at the Well

Seven Keys to Hearing God's Voice

Living the Christian Life

TABLE OF CONTENTS

FOREWORD

It is in looking into the past that we can see the future more clearly. The old adage of "those who forget the past are doomed to repeat it" is rooted deeply in the study of human nature. In the actions and events of the past, we can recognize the best and worst in our nature. Occasionally a figure will arise during a particularly tumultuous or pivotal moment that stands out among the rest—someone who captivates and inspires on the merit of their character and accomplishments. This individual may not be the archetype dashing hero or eloquent statesman, but something about their nature highlights the capacity for good and honor in humanity. Reading about such individuals provides an opportunity to better understand and appreciate the human experience.

Ulysses S. Grant remains one of the more enigmatic figures in American history. Despite his monumental contributions and accomplishments, his modesty coupled with misinformation has clouded his legacy for generations. The man who fellow general William T. Sherman claimed was a "mystery to himself" largely avoided writing about his experiences for most of his life.

Grant recognized the role of fate in life and resolved that the best one could do is simply fulfill their duty, regardless of the circumstances. Grant's unlikely rise from relative obscurity to become general in chief of the Union Army amidst the American Civil War was not due to fate alone. Grant's leadership traits were showcased clearly as he guided his nation first to military victory and then to the beginnings of reconciliation and peace.

One thing Grant keenly recognized throughout his life was inequality and oppression. He settled on the fact that not only individuals but also nations could suffer consequences for their transgressions. The cause of the Civil War he concluded "will have to be attributed to slavery." A man of peace at heart, Grant recognized, as Aristotle said, "It is not enough to win a war; it is more important to organize the peace." He knew this peace could not be achieved with inequality and division in the nation, and he worked as president to establish and protect the civil rights of African Americans. One of the greatest African-American leaders of the nineteenth century, Frederick Douglass, eulogized Grant as "a man too broad for prejudice, too humane to despise the humblest, too great to be small at any point. In him the Negro found a protector, the Indian a friend, a vanquished foe a brother, an imperiled nation a savior."

Although Grant resisted writing about the war, fate intervened in a series of tragic circumstances during his final years, which led him to create one of the finest literary works in American history. Facing financial failure and terminal disease only increased his resolve to complete the book for the sake of his beloved family in a final inspiring act of devotion. From this reserved, simple man poured forth a powerful narrative of a terrible war that helped define a nation. It is not simply in his words but also in his actions that we discover the personal character of Grant.

Dr. Craig von Buseck tells this inspiring story in *Victor! The Final Battle of Ulysses S. Grant*. The well-documented saga of the final year of Grant's life is laid out by the author, providing an opportunity for readers to peer directly into the past and meet a man at his most vulnerable but also his most valiantly determined. It is a story of tragedy and triumph that remains eminently relatable to us today. Looking past the glory and fame, we see a simple man fulfilling his final duty to his loving family with the same fierce determination and selflessness he devoted to his country decades before. The author weaves into the narrative the vivid scenes of war as though readers are entering the mind of the ailing general as he pens the words from his memory. The two stories, decades apart, intertwine together so well because readers can draw a consistent line that reveals Grant's steadfast, admirable traits.

For Grant, as with many veterans of his day, it was imperative not only to accurately remember their struggles and sacrifices but also to preserve what had been gained. Grant, in writing his memoirs, wanted to give an honest account at a time when a distorted narrative was being offered by Southern authors claiming a righteous "Lost Cause." Grant's friend, author Samuel Clemens (Mark Twain), published *Personal Memoirs,* and he employed Civil War veterans as salesmen in a final act of loyalty to their ailing commander. In an amazingly noble act of love, Grant completed his book, restored his family's fortune, and secured his final victory.

Today, as America continues to grapple with some of the same issues Grant and his contemporaries faced, Dr. von Buseck's work provides a powerful opportunity for reflection on who we were, who we are, and who we can strive to be. The struggle for racial equality, for unity, and for peace still remains, and looking back provides inspiration to continue forward toward a better future. We learn that America owes a great debt to Ulysses S. Grant. His immortal words, "Let us have peace" reach across the years to help guide his beloved nation forward.

Ben Kemp
U.S. Grant Cottage Historic Site Operations Manager
Mt. McGregor, Wilton, NY

Chapter One

WORLD TOUR

1878—CAIRO, EGYPT

Like a sentinel before the pyramids of the Pharaohs, the Sphinx stood with its lion's paws outstretched, as if digging into the sands of the Giza desert. In the ancient past, the painted face of a vaunted Pharaoh adorned the stone creature—half-lion and half-man. Then, over thousands of years, the human features of the king slowly vanished, whittled away by blowing sand, the scorching Egyptian sun, and the chisels of vandals. Surrounded by arid desert, the Sphinx once stood on the banks of the Nile, the glimmering white limestone pyramids rising in the background—the first of the ancient wonders of the world. Boats of all sizes and shapes carried pilgrims up a branch of the Nile into the harbor to pay homage at the feet of the Sphinx.

On this day in 1878, a modern pilgrim from a far-off land came to gaze on the wonders of Egypt and stand at the foot of the great Sphinx. He had been honored like a king in his own country, and now he was hailed around the world as a wise, just warrior and a political leader who did his best to bring peace to his people. As he prudently kept his counsel in times of crisis and trial, this man, Ulysses S. Grant, had been dubbed with the same moniker as the ancient statue—the Sphinx.

As a result of his strategic vision and leadership, Grant had become the savior of the Union at the head of the Federal armies of the United States. He had served first as General in Chief of the Army and then for two terms as president. After nearly two decades of military and public service, he decided to devote time to his beloved family. Because of his son Buck's wise investments on his behalf, Grant had made a small fortune from a silver mine in Nevada. So, when his second presidential term ended, he and his

1

wife, Julia, decided to see the wonders of the world and visit foreign heads of state along the way.

Grant studied people and their customs everywhere he traveled, but he was most interested in the antiquities, so he had come to the land of countless marvels. Seated on a camel, the hot desert sun blazing above, he stared into the weathered, vandalized face of the Sphinx—the human head out of proportion to the lion's body. "It looks as if it has kept on thinking through all eternity without talking too much," Grant exclaimed.[1]

Perhaps in the mythical creature Grant saw a reflection of himself.

At the US Ambassador's request, Ismail the Magnificent, the Khedive of Egypt, had placed a palace in Alexandria at the disposal of Grant and his party.[2] The entourage included General Grant; his wife, Julia; their twenty-year-old son, Jesse; and US Consul-General Elbert E. Farman. Chronicling the trip, at the request of the general, was thirty-seven-year-old journalist John Russell Young. During his presidency, Grant had been pleased by the work Young had done for him in Europe; therefore, Grant asked the reporter to serve as historian and send telegraphic dispatches to the *New York Herald* describing the journey so readers could follow the general's adventures around the globe.

Grant also invited three officers from the navy's USS *Vandalia*, which had brought his party to Alexandria at the order of President Rutherford B. Hayes. Farman brought his consulate's majordomo, Hassan, who dressed in Arab style, complete with turban and scimitar. The Khedive in turn sent his majordomo, Sami Bey, to ensure smooth passage for the general's group as they steamed up the Nile.

Another vital member of the excursion was Emile Brugsch, an official in the Egyptian Antiquities Department, serving as guide.[3] Considered the most distinguished living Egyptian scholar, Brugsch knew hieroglyphics as well as he knew his own German language. "What a blank our trip would be without Brugsch," Grant declared one day as the party returned from a fascinating ancient ruin.[4]

Grant and his party cruised up the Nile in the Khedive's personal yacht, visited Thebes, Abydos, the pyramids, and Memphis. They spent a month exploring ancient tombs, pyramids, and the great temple at Karnak.

To guard against the blazing desert sun, Grant covered his head in either a Turkish fez or a pith helmet wrapped in silk. At age fifty-six, the general displayed boundless energy and curiosity. His preferred mode of transport was a camel, though he mounted a donkey when necessary. One of the greatest horsemen in America, Grant easily adapted to the desert beasts. Although Julia had been an accomplished horsewoman in her younger years, she had a difficult time with her Egyptian mounts: "Your Ma balances on a donkey very well," Grant wrote to their son Fred, "when she has an Arab on each side to hold her, and one to lead the donkey."[5]

Grant was enamored with Egyptian history. "I have seen more in Egypt to interest me than in all my other travels," he wrote to Fred. "The ancient Egyptian was a cultivated man, but governed soul and body by a ruler. Without a thorough command of all the strength, muscle and mind of the inhabitants such structures could never have been built. Without talent, learning and training the inscriptions could not have been made. And without mechanical teaching the large blocks of granite and sandstone could never have been taken from the quarries to their present resting place nor dressed as they are."[6]

Yet he was transfixed by the Sphinx.

After allowing him to stare into its face for a long time, Brugsch finally rode his camel up next to the general's beast. "Magnificent, isn't it?"

Grant simply nodded.

Just then Julia rode up on her donkey followed by Jesse astride a camel. "Come, my good General," Brugsch cried out. "I will take you to the source. The beginning of all things Egyptian."

To the Source

The party set out on the long ride to the ruins of Abydos. Arriving hot and thirsty, they dismounted and entered the shade within the temple. "We should all take off our hats," said Brugsch, "for here is the cradle, the fountainhead of all the civilization of the world." Abydos, which sat amidst the sand in ruins, was the oldest city in Egypt, dating back to Menes, the first of the Egyptian kings who reigned in the centuries before the Jewish patriarch Abraham.

When asked whether the civilizations of China and India did not claim to antedate Abydos, Brugsch answered, "To be sure it did, but in China and India you have traditions; here you have monuments. Here, under the sands that we are crunching with our feet, here first flowed forth that civilization which has streamed over the world. Hebrew, Indian, Etruscan, Persian, Roman, Greek, Christian—whatever form you give it, whatever shape it takes—this is the fountain of it all.

"Here are the stones on which are written the names of the kings from Menes to Sethi I," Brugsch retorted dramatically. "Sethi built his temple somewhere about fourteen hundred years before Christ, and like a dutiful king he wrote the names of his predecessors, seventy-six in all, beginning with Menes."

Brugsch read the hieroglyphics on the stone carvings as easily as if he were reading the morning newspaper. "Here is the very stone, beautifully engraved, and, thanks to the sand, kept all these centuries as fresh as when the sculptor laid down his chisel. It was only found in 1865, and is perhaps the most valuable of the monuments, because it knits up the unraveled threads of Egyptian history and gives you a continuous link from this day to a day beyond that of Moses."

Brugsch encouraged the group to explore the rest of the city. Julia Grant rode along on her donkey while the rest of the party dispersed in different directions on foot. The general and Young climbed the highest of the sand mounds. When they reached the top, they could see into an excavation fifty feet deep with the remnants of a tomb and countless broken pottery fragments. "You could see the strata that age after age had heaped upon the buried city," Young observed. "The desert had slowly been creeping over it, and in some of the strata were marks of the Nile."

From that height, they could see endless rolling hills of burning sand. "As the shrinking eye followed the plain and searched the hills there was no sign of life," Young recorded. "Nothing except perhaps some careering hawk hurrying to the river. I have seen no scene in Egypt more striking than this view from the mounds of Abydos."

Brugsch then led them to Karnak, and finally to the grand ancient city of Thebes. "I cannot tell you when the Temple of Karnak was built," Young wrote. "Brugsch places the first building three thousand years before Christ. This seems to be a long time, but I wonder if we think how long ago it really was? You will remember reading how Abraham went down to Egypt because of the famine in the land, taking with him Sarah, his wife, who was fair, and whom he passed off as his sister. ... Well, if Abraham on that visit had visited Thebes, ... he would have seen a part of this very temple of Karnak, and he could have read on its walls the very inscription which Brugsch translates today, and which would have told him, as it tells us, of the glory of a king who had reigned before him."[7]

PILGRIMAGE TO JERUSALEM

From Egypt, Ulysses and Julia traveled to the Holy Land with great expectation, only to be disappointed by the barren countryside—a drastic contrast from the fertile land spoken of in the Bible.

"The utter absence of all civilization, of all trace of human existence, is the fact that meets and oppresses you," Young reported. "The hills have been washed bare by centuries of neglect, and terraced slopes that were once rich with all the fruits of Palestine are sterile and abandoned. The valley over which we have ridden strikes the eye of the general as one of the richest he has ever seen, and he makes the observation that the plain of Sharon alone, under good government, and tilled by such labor as could be found in America, would raise wheat enough to feed all that portion of the Mediterranean. It is an abandoned land, with barrenness written on every hillside."

Grant desired to enter Jerusalem during daylight, so the company pressed forward with great vigor. But as they approached the banks of the brook where David found his five smooth stones for Goliath, they were met by a large band of cavalry, which included Americans, Jews, Greeks, Armenians, and a representative of the Ottoman pasha. The American consul, Mr. Wilson, along with the pasha's lieutenant, rode forward to welcome the general to the Holy City.

This was a disappointment to Grant who had hoped to enter the city unrecognized. "We had expected to enter Jerusalem in our quiet, plain way," Young explained, "pilgrims really coming to see the Holy City, awed by its renowned memories." As usual, Grant's fame preceded him, dashing any hopes of anonymity.

The pasha offered the general his spirited white Arabian horse to ride into the city. The group followed the winding trail up toward Jerusalem, rising 2,500 feet above the sea as they ascended.

"We looked down the mountain's dizzy side and saw hill after hill sweeping like billows on toward the sea," Young explained. "We were thinking of the valley below, of events which have stirred the souls of Christian men for centuries, as the path of conquering armies—of Joshua and David—of Alexander and Vespasian—of Godfrey and Saladin. And here we were coming with banners and armed men, and at our head, riding side by side with the pasha's Turkish lieutenant, one whose name will live with that of the greatest commanders who ever preceded him over this rocky way."

"The general passes on with bared head," wrote Young, "for on both sides the assembled multitude do him honor. We see through the mist a mass of domes and towers, and the heart beats quickly, for we know they are the domes and towers of Jerusalem. We pass through a narrow gate that Tancred forced with his crusaders. We pass under the walls of the tower of David, and the flag that floats from the pole on the consulate tells us that our journey is at an end and that we are within the walls of Jerusalem."[8]

Grant was the first American president to visit Jerusalem.

During his stay, the general met with a delegation of American Jews who distributed relief to poverty-stricken Hebrews in Palestine. Grant promised to make their plight known to Jewish leaders in the United States.[9]

"Our visit to Jerusalem was a very unpleasant one," Grant wrote to Adam Badeau. "The roads are bad and it rained, blew and snowed all the time."[10] The snow and rain made for a slippery walk up the famed Via Dolorosa.

As they set out to see the holy sites, Julia, the granddaughter of a Methodist minister, took the lead. Entering an ornate sanctuary, Julia was moved by a sign at the door: "Anyone who will say a prayer for the soul of Pope Pius IX will receive absolution." Julia immediately dropped to her knees in prayer. "You see, Young," exclaimed the general, "Mrs. Grant is taking all the chances"—meaning every chance to enhance her standing in heaven.[11]

Young described the exploration of the Holy City in the midst of the snow and rain:

> We pass from our hotel on Mount Zion through a narrow, dingy street, paved with jagged cobblestones, rendered smooth by rain and mud. We make our way with difficulty. We stumble and slide rather than walk. ... We can readily see as we retrace our way up the Via Dolorosa that it must have been a rough and weary road to one rent, and torn, and bleeding, and crushed under the cruel burden of the cross. Even to us—free as we are—wayfarers, in full possession of our faculties, it is a tedious task to climb the hill of Calvary.[12]

From the Holy Land, the group traveled north in the Mediterranean on another US Navy vessel until they reached the Ottoman capital of Istanbul. The Turkish sultan was excited to show Grant his royal stables, and the general was impressed by the purebred Arabians. The magnanimous sultan immediately offered one of the stallions as a gift. "These horses, I am told, have their pedigrees kept for one or two hundred years back, and are of the purest blood," Grant wrote a friend. "It may be of some value to breeders in the United States to get some of this blood."[13] He arranged for his new horse to be transported to the recently built stables at his St. Louis farm.

On to Berlin

In Berlin, Young accompanied Grant to a meeting with Chancellor Otto von Bismarck at his residence. Grant shocked the staff by arriving not in a carriage, but on foot.

"The general saunters in a kind of nonchalant way into the courtyard," Young related. "The sentinels eye him for just an instant, perhaps curiously, and then quickly present arms. Somehow or other these grim soldiers recognize at once, as the salute is returned, that it comes from a man who is himself a soldier. His visit is expected, it is true, but it was supposed that an ex-President of the United States would have come thundering in a coach and six accompanied by outriders, and not quietly on foot."

"Of all the princes of the earth," Young exclaimed, "this Prince of Bismarck-Schinhausen is the most renowned. It is the prince who comes through the opening portals and with both hands extended welcomes General Grant. You cannot help but note that time has borne with a heavy hand on Bismarck within the past few years. The mustache and hair which but a short time ago were iron gray are now almost white; there is even some weariness in the gait, a tired look about the face."

"I am glad to welcome General Grant to Germany," Bismarck said in slow but precise English as he extended his hand to his guest.

"There is no incident in my German tour," Grant replied, "more interesting to me than this opportunity of meeting the prince."

Bismarck expressed surprise that Grant was only seven years his junior. "That shows the value of a military life," the Chancellor observed, "for here you have the frame of a young man, while I feel like an old one."

The general smiled and graciously replied, "I am at that period of life when I could have no higher compliment paid me than that of being called a young man."

The two world leaders sauntered into a library with walls of gray marble and simple furnishings, where the prince offered Grant a seat. An open window looked out on a private park of the Radziwill Palace, the June sun shining on Bismarck's Berlin home.[14]

Bismarck apologized for the absence of Emperor Wilhelm, who was nursing wounds from a recent attempted assassination. Grant conveyed his wishes for the emperor's recovery. "It is so strange, so strange and so sad," Bismarck replied. "Here is an old man, one of the kindest old gentlemen in the world, and yet they must try and shoot him!"

Grant agreed. The same thing had happened to Lincoln, he said. A man of the kindest and gentlest nature had been killed by a vengeful assassin.[15]

Bismarck explained that the emperor was sorry that he could not in person show General Grant a review, and that the crown prince would give him one. "The truth is I am more a farmer than a soldier," Grant replied. "I take little or no interest in military affairs, and although I entered the army thirty-five years ago and have been in two wars, in Mexico as a young lieutenant, and later, I never went into the army without regret and never retired without pleasure."

"You are so happily placed in America that you need fear no wars," Bismarck replied. "What always seemed so sad to me about your last great war was that you were fighting your own people. That is always so terrible in wars, so very hard."

"But it had to be done," Grant replied.

"Yes," said the prince. "You had to save the Union just as we had to save Germany."

"Not only save the Union, but destroy slavery," Grant answered.

Bismarck was taken aback by the comment. "I suppose, however, the Union was the real sentiment, the dominant sentiment."

"In the beginning, yes," Grant agreed, "but as soon as slavery fired upon the flag ... we all felt, even those who did not object to slaves, that slavery must be destroyed. We felt that it was a stain to the Union that men should be bought and sold like cattle."[16] Grant's views on the slavery issue had evolved as the war progressed, and he grew to respect and adopt Lincoln's policies. These views matured further during his time as president as he took a bold stand to protect Black civil rights.[17]

"I suppose if you had had a large army at the beginning of the war it would have ended in a much shorter time," Bismarck surmised.

"We might have had no war at all," Grant answered. "Our war had many strange features—there were many things which seemed odd enough at the time but which now seem Providential. If we had had a large regular army, as it was then constituted, it might have gone with the South. In fact, the Southern feeling in the army among high officers was so strong that when the war broke out the army dissolved. We had no army—then we had to organize one. A great commander like Sherman or Sheridan even then might have organized and put down the rebellion in six months or a year, or at the farthest two years. But that would have saved slavery, perhaps, and slavery meant the germs of a new rebellion. There had to be an end to slavery," Grant declared. "Then we were fighting an enemy with whom we could not make a peace. We had to destroy him. No convention, no treaty was possible—only destruction."[18]

Although Grant was not an abolitionist at the beginning of the war, he grew to oppose slavery on practical, military, and religious grounds. As early as the summer of 1861, he told an army chaplain that "he believed slavery would die with this rebellion, and that it might become necessary for the government to suppress it as a stroke of military policy."[19]

Grant's brother-in-law, Michael John Cramer, confirmed that "as the war progressed [Grant] became gradually convinced that 'slavery was doomed and must go.' He had always recognized its moral evil, as also its being the cause of the war ... hence General Grant came to look upon the war as a divine punishment for the sin of slavery."[20]

Grant had married into the slaveholding Dent family and had himself once owned a slave. But as the issue of slavery began to tear the country apart in the years just prior to the outbreak of war, Grant had freed his slave. This was during a time of extreme financial difficulty for Grant, and the sale of a slave could have brought in as much as one thousand dollars—a sum that would have relieved a great amount of pressure on his family. Yet Grant went ahead and emancipated his slave—a move that foreshadowed his growing antislavery sentiments.

In a letter to local congressman and chief political supporter, Elihu Washburne, soon after Lincoln issued the Emancipation Proclamation, Grant shared his belief that since slavery was the root cause of the war, its destruction had become the basis for settlement with the South. It was "patent to my mind early in the rebellion that the North & South could never live at peace with each other except as one nation, and that without Slavery. As anxious as I am to see peace reestablished I would not therefore be willing to see any settlement until this question is forever settled."[21]

"It was a long war," said Bismarck, "and a great work well done. I suppose it means a long peace."

"I believe so," Grant remarked with a slight smile.

The two men rose to their feet. "It is a pleasure to see a man who is so well known and so highly esteemed in America," Grant said.

"General," answered the prince, "the pleasure and the honor are mine. Germany and America have always been in such friendly relationship that nothing delights us more than to meet Americans, and especially an American who has done so much for his country, and whose name is so much honored in Germany as your own."

After shaking hands with Bismarck, the general said goodbye and passed into the square. The guard presented arms, Grant lit a fresh cigar, and Young joined him in a stroll to their hotel.[22]

After spending the Christmas season in Paris, the Grants spent two frigid weeks in Ireland. Named an honorary citizen of Dublin, Grant gave a brief speech. "I am by birth a citizen of a country where there are more Irishmen ... than there are in all Ireland. I have therefore had the honor and pleasure of representing more Irishmen and their descendants when in office than the Queen of England."[23]

HEADING EAST

From Ireland they set off on a relaxing three-week cruise through the Mediterranean, the Red Sea, and the Indian Ocean, arriving at

Bombay where they were greeted by the British rulers. Jesse Grant decided to return to America and his older brother, Fred, took his place.

With their eldest son's arrival, the Grants joined former Navy Secretary Adolph Borie on a visit to the Taj Mahal. "The effect of the Taj as seen from the gate," observed Young, "looking down the avenue of trees, is grand. The dome and towers seem to rest in the air, and it would not surprise you if they became clouds and vanished into rain. ... There is a row of fountains which throw out a spray and cool the air, and when you pass the trees and come to the door of the building its greatness comes upon you—its greatness and its beauty."[24]

While respectful, Julia was not overly impressed. "Everyone says it is the most beautiful building in the world, and I suppose it is. Only I think that everyone has not seen the Capitol at Washington!"[25]

THE ORIENT

Aboard the USS *Richmond*, the party sailed from India to China to see the famous Great Wall. "What impressed us was the infinite patience which could have compassed so vast a labor," Young observed. "The Great Wall is a marvel of patience. I had been reading the late Mr. Seward's calculation that the labor which had built the Great Wall would have built the Pacific Railways. General Grant thought that Mr. Seward had underrated its extent. 'I believe that the labor expended on this wall could have built every railroad in the United States, every canal and highway, and most if not all of our cities.'

"The Great Wall is a monument of the patience of the people and the prerogative of a king," Young explained. "It never could have been of much use in the most primitive days, and now it is only a curiosity. We walked about on the top and studied its simple, massive workmanship, and looked upon the plains of Mongolia, over which the dreaded Tartar came. On one side of the wall was China, on the other Mongolia."

As they finished their investigation of the Great Wall and returned to the ship, the small party was overcome with a sense that the two-year world tour would soon be coming to an end. "We were at the furthest end of our journey, and every step now would be toward home," Young recalled.[26]

The Grants made one final stop in Japan, where the general played the part of the diplomat, hammering out an agreement with the Chinese over the disputed Ryukyu Islands. After a two-month visit that included meetings with the emperor and top government officials, it was finally time to return to America.

Steaming out of Yokohama harbor, the USS *Richmond* was flanked by a Japanese steamer, escorting the Grants into the open ocean. After an hour at sea, the Japanese man-of-war fired twenty-one guns—the number designated to honor an American president. The Japanese sailors swarmed up the rigging to cheer and wave goodbye. The *Richmond* responded with her steam whistle as the Japanese vessel turned to head back, slowly drifting from view.

Ulysses S. Grant was returning to an uncertain future. No US president would receive a pension for another seventy years, and Grant had forfeited his retirement benefits when he resigned from the army to run for president.[27] Mining investments, like the famous Comstock silver mine bonanza, had funded his two-year world tour, but his son Buck reported that the money was running low.[28]

At the same time, the general's political backers were urging him to run for an unprecedented third term. Leading Republican Party bosses believed the nomination was his for the asking. If Grant were to win the nomination, no Democrat could beat him in November. After two years abroad, the heaviness of his former presidential burdens had lifted. At the same time, the pain of the scandals surrounding his administration in his second term had mostly been forgotten. After all, everyone knew that Grant himself had not been party to any of the scandals, and the public was willing to forgive.

But Grant was unsure if he wanted to reenter the arena.

As the general steamed toward California, the first problem to be solved was how the savior of the Union and two-term president would make a living.

Chapter Two

GRANT & WARD

1880—CHICAGO, ILLINOIS

In the end, Grant's heart was not in the presidential race of 1880. Yet he felt compelled to throw his hat into the ring, due to both the ongoing dangers facing the still fragile union and his political friends' predictions that he was by far the favorite to win the Republican nomination. Following the political traditions of that era, he hadn't campaigned for his first or second nomination; he decided not to campaign for a third one either.

On top of that, he refused to attend the Republican convention in Chicago despite Julia's pleas, who wanted to return to the White House. "Do you not desire success?" she prodded.

"Well, yes, of course, since my name is up, I would rather be nominated, but I will do nothing to further that end."

Julia was flabbergasted. "For heaven's sake, go—and go tonight. I know they are already making their cabals against you. Go, go tonight, I beseech you."

Grant then uttered the phrase used only when he and his wife could not come to an agreement in an argument. "Julia, I am amazed at you."[29]

He did not go to Chicago.

Grant received the majority of votes on every ballot but never enough to secure the nomination. On the thirty-fifth ballot, the tide turned against the former president. Two of the other leading contenders, James G. Blaine and John Sherman, threw their support behind the respected but relatively unknown Representative James Garfield of Ohio, even though he had not declared his candidacy. This move provoked a stampede for Garfield, giving him 399 votes to Grant's 306 and securing his nomination.

THE SEARCH FOR A HOME

Once again Grant faced the question of what he would do for a living.

Unlike other nations who lavished their military heroes with wealth and properties, the United States stripped the military pension from Ulysses S. Grant, the savior of the country. Recognizing this shameful state of affairs, some wealthy American citizens made sure that Grant and his family were cared for. He was given homes in Philadelphia and in Galena, Illinois. While he was president, Grant had also purchased a "summer cottage" in Long Branch, New Jersey, which was actually a large house overlooking the Atlantic Ocean.

But after eight years in the White House and two years traveling the world, the Grants had outgrown the small-town life of Galena, Illinois. They lived there temporarily after returning from their world tour only because they could not afford to live anywhere else. Two of their sons, Fred and Buck, were prospering in New York City, and Ulysses and Julia felt a growing desire to be near them in the country's premier metropolis.

Before Grant secured income for himself, however, he worked to get Garfield elected. He believed a win by the Democrats in the presidential election could undo the gains made possible by the war and by his efforts as president. For the first time in his life, Grant hit the campaign trail, promoting the Republican cause on a whistle-stop railroad tour.

Like so many other things that had seemed out of his reach in life, Grant learned to be a stump speaker. With practice, the Sphinx became a decent speechmaker, surprising everyone.

In October, northeastern Republicans welcomed Grant with torchlight parades and banquets. In Hartford, Connecticut, he was introduced on the stump by his old friend Mark Twain, a member of the welcoming committee. Earlier that day, on the train ride from Boston, Twain joked about the ex-president's wealth in a conversation with Fred Grant, who told him that the opposite was true. "It gradually came out," wrote Twain, "that the general, so far from being a rich man, as was commonly supposed, had not even income enough to enable him to live as respectably as a third-rate physician." Declaring "this was all so shameful and such a reproach to Congress," Twain determined to "take the general's straitened circumstances as my text in introducing him to the people of Hartford."

When he took the platform, Twain explained how the British had lavished riches and property on the Duke of Wellington after his triumph over Napoleon at Waterloo, honoring his "service with wealth and grandeur." Contrasting America's treatment of Grant, he turned to the general and declared, "Your country stands ready from this day forth to testify her measureless love and pride and gratitude toward you in every conceivable inexpensive way."[30]

When Grant came to the podium, he graciously replied that he had been sufficiently rewarded, declaring, "What they have given me is more valued than gold or silver." But Twain's critique hit its mark.[31]

Twain was determined to do whatever he could to honor and assist the man he believed was America's "great soldier, honored statesman, and unselfish citizen."[32] In the fall of 1880, he began to visit Grant regularly to share stories and cigars. Soon Twain broached a subject on the mind of many Americans: when Grant would write his memoirs.

Many generals on both sides of the conflict had published their account of the monumental struggle, including Grant's good friend William Tecumseh Sherman. Twain declared it was time to hear from the man who designed and executed the plans leading to the Union's triumph.

Grant politely refused, telling Twain that Young had published his book on the world tour and that his former aide, Adam Badeau, had just published his *Military History of Ulysses S. Grant*. The general did not believe the reading public wanted another book on his exploits during the Civil War.

Twain strongly disagreed, predicting that a book written by Grant himself would have an "enormous sale."

But the general insisted he did not need additional income and ended the discussion. He, of course, was not being completely honest with his literary friend. The Grants had a modest income, but they could not afford to mingle with the rich and famous in New York City.

CITIZENS OF NEW YORK

As the presidential campaign concluded, the Grants moved into rooms at New York's Fifth Avenue Hotel until they could decide where to go next.[33] But Ulysses and Julia could barely pay the low rent the hotel manager offered to the ex-president. Something had to be done soon to ease the financial burden.

In the summer of 1881, everything changed when Grant's friend and Long Branch neighbor, Philadelphia publisher George Childs, organized a group of wealthy businessmen to help correct the federal government's injustice.

Childs solicited funds from more than twenty of the nation's most powerful and wealthy men, including William H. Vanderbilt, Anthony J. Drexel, Jay Gould, John Mackay, and J. Pierpont Morgan. Together they raised enough money to establish a respectable trust fund of $250,000. From the interest on this gift, Grant and his family could draw enough income to live comfortably in New York.[34]

But these men were not finished. Knowing the Grants would need a proper home to entertain guests and dignitaries, the group raised an additional $100,000 for the purchase of a house. When Childs and Drexel presented the Grants with this generous gift, Julia was overjoyed. In her mind, such recognition by the country was long overdue. Having visited England on their world tour, Julia knew very well how the British had lavished gifts on Wellington for his victory at Waterloo. She had wondered then how their family would have been cared for had they been British citizens instead of Americans. After considering several options, the Grants purchased a new four-story brownstone at 3 East Sixty-Sixth Street, with bay windows offering a view of nearby Central Park.

"So I was to have a beautiful home, all my own," she later wrote in her *Memoirs*, "and how happy I was all that summer looking for a house and selecting paper, furniture, etc."[35]

The Grants moved into their new house and filled the first floor with war memorabilia and gifts lavished on them from heads of state and dignitaries during their trip around the world. Soon the entrance took on the appearance of a military museum, overflowing with flags, swords, uniforms, and weapons. This was complemented by an impressive library filled with more than five thousand books—also gifts from an admiring public.[36] With Fred and Buck, their wives, and all the grandchildren living nearby, 3 East Sixty-Sixth Street became the family gathering place Ulysses and Julia had always dreamed of.

At this stage of life, Grant was starting to think on a larger financial scale. Although his personal habits were not extravagant, he had children and grandchildren he wanted to support when necessary. Living among the powerful and wealthy of the Gilded Age, Grant acquired a taste for that lifestyle. He had triumphed as a military commander and political leader. Now he yearned to climb another ladder, so he investigated possible business ventures.

GRANT & WARD

Ulysses and Julia's second child, Ulysses S. Grant, Jr., known by everyone as Buck, was a successful lawyer and businessman. After working as an aide to his father in the White House, Buck launched an investment firm with a talented young man who had gained a reputation among financiers as "the young Napoleon of Wall Street," twenty-nine-year-old Ferdinand Ward.[37]

Buck and Ward approached the general and asked if he would join the firm to help attract more of "the carriage trade." After several days of discussions, Ulysses agreed to become an equal partner with Buck, Ward, and James D. Fish, president of the Marine National Bank. Ulysses trusted Fish, who had underwritten part of Grant's world tour, and considered him a respected businessman who could cover any shortfalls the firm might incur. Buck trusted Ward and, in time, so did his father.

General Grant invested $100,000 of his own money into the business. Buck borrowed another $100,000 from his millionaire father-in-law, former Senator Jerome B. Chaffee of Colorado, to secure his partnership.[38] Ward persuaded Chaffee, who had also settled in New York, to invest another $400,000 from his vast fortune.

In their negotiations, Grant made it abundantly clear to Ward that there should be no government contracts. "I had been President of the United States, and did not think it was suitable for me to have my name connected with government contracts, and I knew there was no large profit in them except by dishonest measures. There are some men who get government contracts year in and year out, and whether they manage their affairs dishonestly to make a profit or not, they are sometimes supposed to, and I did not think it was any place for me."[39]

Ward knew perfectly well that the general public had no clue how government contracts were issued or maintained. He deceitfully used Grant's connections with the government and the military as leverage in seeking investors. To tempt potential clients, he insinuated that the firm was loaded down with government contracts because of the general's connections.

Ward intimated that he and the Grants were willing to let certain favored clients invest in particularly promising deals. The firm was lending money on these contracts, he whispered, but they were doing so discreetly. He stealthily assured his customers that with the general's influence and contacts, their investments would yield handsome returns.[40]

The general and Buck knew nothing of this deceptive game.

To the Grant family, Ward talked only of railroad contracts and large rates of interest to subcontractors for temporary loans. He never mentioned leverage from phantom government contracts. The firm had on deposit approximately $1 million in Fish's Marine Bank, and from that lavish fund, Ward ran his schemes.[41]

General Grant was given an elegant office on the second floor of the Grant & Ward building at 2 Wall Street, where he also conducted business as the president of the fledgling Mexican Southern Railway. The former president arrived at the office by carriage each day to lend his influence, handshake, and sometimes his signature to Ward's various escapades.[42]

Every morning, Ward placed twenty-five thick Havana cigars on the general's desk. He also stopped by the senior Grant's office three or four times a day with papers for the general to sign, which Grant did, most often without reading them. At the end of each month, Ward answered any questions Buck or the general asked about the books. Grant informally perused the monthly statements. This was the extent of the general's oversight of the business. He never questioned the daily operation of the firm, although he thoroughly enjoyed the life of leisure it provided.[43]

Grant was eventually led to believe he was worth more than a million dollars. "As a family we are much better off than ever we were before," Ulysses wrote his daughter, Nellie.[44] Ulysses gave his wife, Julia, $1,000 a month to spend as she wished—an extravagant amount of money for the time. Julia employed a full staff of servants and stocked the kitchen with food. Ulysses attended weekly poker parties with the captains of politics, industry, and finance. The Grants purchased the best horses, ate at the finest restaurants, and attended festive parties around New York.[45]

Grant's trust in Ferdinand Ward had grown so much that he eventually had the two Arabian horses he received from the Ottoman sultan shipped to New York and housed in Ward's stables. The stallion he called Leopard, and the Barb, he named Linden Tree.[46] "All [Ward's] horses were of the most approved and purest blood," said Grant, "and there were about seventy horses in the stables I visited. I was told that the pedigrees of all of them ran back from five to seven hundred years (in breed)."[47]

Just as she had done as First Lady, Julia loved living the life of a socialite at the center of Gilded Age New York. The Grant home became a miniature version of the White House as they welcomed celebrities, politicians, and visiting heads of state. The Grants threw lavish parties for the crème de la crème of New York society. Julia was also a frequent visitor at theater premieres and the Metropolitan Opera.

The Grant family had arrived. Or so it seemed.

A SLIP AND A FALL

Fortunes turned sharply for the general, beginning on Christmas Eve 1883. After he arrived home from a number of social calls, Grant reached out to give his coachman a Christmas present and slipped and fell on the frozen street.[48] He ruptured a thigh muscle in the same leg he had injured when his horse fell on him years earlier after Vicksburg.[49]

"The general and I had anticipated a gay, bright winter," Julia later wrote of the incident. "We had sent out invitations for four large dinner parties in January. All had accepted. When this dreadful accident occurred, Dr. Fordyce Barker told me I must withdraw all my invitations, as the general would not be able to be present at dinner for a long time."[50]

At sixty-one years old and in seemingly good health, Grant was consigned to crutches and later a cane. Although admirers had presented him with many ornamental walking sticks over the years, the general preferred a plain hickory cane with a curved handle. The cane became his constant companion.[51]

Then, just as Ulysses was beginning to heal from his thigh injury, a much more ominous cloud appeared on the horizon.

A few days before the financial earthquake struck, the ever-optimistic Grant spoke about the future to his wife. "Julia, you need not trouble to save for our children. Ward is making us all rich—them as well as ourselves. I have been thinking how pleasant it would be for us to help some of our less-fortunate friends become independent. We could help to arrange for them to purchase comfortable little homes, and give them allowances to live upon. I would like to do this, and I am sure it would be a great pleasure to you."[52]

But on Sunday morning, May 4, Ferdinand Ward arrived unannounced at the Grant home. The general greeted his young partner pleasantly, almost like a member of the family.[53] A nervous-looking Ward explained that the city chamberlain of New York had made a sudden, unforeseen withdrawal from the Marine Bank. This move imperiled Grant & Ward's ability to conduct business.[54] Unless $400,000 could be raised immediately, the Marine Bank would not be able to open its doors for business on Monday morning.

Grant knew their partner, James D. Fish, was president of the Marine Bank, but he was having trouble making the connection. "Why are you concerned about the Marine Bank?"

"We have $660,000 on deposit there," Ward answered. "It would embarrass us very much if the bank should close its doors." He went on to say that he had rounded up commitments for $250,000, but if Grant could not come up with an additional $150,000 before the following morning, Grant & Ward would be in trouble.[55]

A suddenly sober Grant assured his young partner he would do what he could to help in this crisis.

Riding in his carriage, Grant called on several of his wealthy friends. These men were sympathetic but unable to help. Finally, he drove to the home of William H. Vanderbilt, head of the massive New York Central Railroad. The palatial Vanderbilt estate extended the entire block of Fifth Avenue between Fifty-First and Fifty-Second Streets. Grant explained the state of affairs as Vanderbilt listened graciously.

When the general concluded, Vanderbilt spoke frankly. "I care nothing about the Marine Bank. To tell the truth, I care very little about Grant & Ward. But to accommodate you personally, I will draw my check for the amount you ask. I consider it a personal loan to you, and not to any other party." Asking for nothing as collateral, Vanderbilt wrote the check.

Grant returned home and handed the check to Ward, who thanked him extravagantly. With Vanderbilt's check in hand, everything would be fine, Ward assured him.[56]

When a friend called on Grant that evening, the general was not at all bothered by the day's events. Grant invited him to a poker game that Tuesday night. "Ward is certainly coming, and the party is made."[57]

When word spread through Wall Street that Vanderbilt, a man with an estimated worth of $200 million, had provided $150,000 to cover a shortfall, Grant believed that everything would be all right. The following morning, Monday, May 5, that assumption seemed to be correct. Ward told Ulysses and Buck that he had deposited Vanderbilt's check at Fish's Marine Bank. Grant spent the day uneventfully, and went home in the afternoon thinking everything had returned to normal.[58]

Unknown to the general, that same day, a frantic Ward begged Buck to secure another $500,000 loan from William Vanderbilt. "I am very much afraid that the end has come and that, unless something is done to-night, everything will be over tomorrow. ... This is our last hope, Buck, so do all you can."

In reality, Ward had borrowed enormous amounts from Marine Bank, despite having nearly nothing on deposit there. When New York City pulled $1 million from its Marine National account, the bank called in its loans to Grant & Ward to cover the shortfall. Bank president James Fish frantically ran to the bank association armed with cash and securities to use as collateral as he begged for a colossal rescue loan.[59] But the deficit was too great.

On the morning of Tuesday, May 6, the Marine Bank failed, pulling Grant & Ward down with it.

When Ulysses S. Grant arrived at 2 Wall Street that morning, a group of angry, frustrated men stood at the doors of Grant & Ward and demanded entrance.[60] Confused, the general made his way into the building, still limping and using crutches from a fall on the ice the previous Christmas. Inside, irate customers were clamoring for their money and investment certificates.[61] Grant moved steadily on his crutches toward Ward's office, an unlit cigar in his mouth. In a gesture puzzling to Grant, people somberly lifted their hats when they saw him, as though mourning the loss of a friend.[62]

When he saw his father, Buck rushed to his side. "Father, you had better go home," he whispered into his ear. "The Marine Bank closed this morning. Ward has fled. We cannot find our securities."[63]

The enormous Ponzi scheme was finally exposed.

Without showing a hint of emotion, Grant limped past the staring crowd and climbed aboard the elevator. The reality of the situation was sinking in as he ascended to his second-floor office. Not only was he ruined financially, but so were all his children. Everything was gone—the life savings of all three sons, Julia's inheritance from her father's estate, even the meager savings of his two widowed sisters.

The scoundrel had destroyed the reputation Grant worked a lifetime to achieve. By trading on the general's good name, Ward had conned the titans of industry and the giants of Wall Street into investing in his pyramid scheme. But he also made off with the small pension checks of thousands of old soldiers who had trusted "Sam" Grant.[64]

When Adam Badeau visited Grant & Ward that afternoon, he found Grant alone in his office. "We are all ruined here," Grant lamented. "The bank has failed. Mr. Ward cannot be found. The securities are locked up in the safe, and he has the key. No one knows where he is."[65]

Later in the afternoon, George Spencer, a cashier for Grant & Ward, quietly entered the general's office to tell him that Buck had finally located the firm's securities. They were worthless. He also announced that the Vanderbilt check had been cashed by Ward, but the money had not been deposited in the Grant & Ward account. Everything was gone.

On a pad beside the general lay a penciled column of figures along with the names of friends and relatives whom Ward had deceived and robbed.[66] "Spencer," asked Grant, "how is it that man has deceived us all in this way?"[67]

Spencer could offer no explanation.

Grant's hands gripped the arms of the chair with white knuckles. "I have made it a rule of life to trust a man long after other people gave him up. I don't see how I can trust any human being again."

Clutching the ledgers containing Ward's fictitious and malicious entries, Spencer silently withdrew. As he left, he saw Grant bury his head in his hands.[68]

Grant left his Wall Street office for the last time at 2:15 p.m., offering no comment to waiting reporters. Buck followed, stopping to address the gathered press corps. "I cannot deny or corroborate the reports current," Buck explained. "We are nearly $500,000 short. Our safes are locked and until we can find Mr. Ward I cannot say how we stand." It was a telling statement. Buck admitted that he and his father lacked access to their own firm's safe.

On his way uptown, General Grant ran into his old friend James Fry, whom he had invited to his poker party that evening. "We will not have the meeting I fixed for tonight. I have bad news."

"Why, general, I hope it is nothing serious," Fry responded.

"Yes," Grant said, "the Marine Bank has failed or is about to fail. It owes our firm a large amount, and I suppose we are ruined. When I went downtown this morning I thought I was worth a great deal of money, now I don't know that I have a dollar; and probably my sons, too, have lost everything."

After telling Julia the shocking news, they both counted the money in their possession. Instead of being worth $1 million, Grant was suddenly worth $80 and Julia had only $130.[69]

LITERALLY WITHOUT MEANS

For the Grant family, Ward's treachery had tragic implications. Even the trust fund raised by Grant's wealthy friends had been raided by the scoundrel, leaving nothing for the Grants. Although he owned several properties, Grant did not have the cash to pay the staff's wages or the grocer's bills.

Once again, Grant was penniless.

Writing to his friend and neighbor, George Childs, he confessed, "The events of the last few days are much more disastrous than I supposed when the failure first occurred."[70]

The news of the scandal spread across the country in the newspapers. Soon individuals heard of Grant's plight and felt moved to help the general. The first to do so was Charles Wood of Lansingburgh, New York, who had fought with the Union Army in Virginia. A complete stranger to Grant, Wood nevertheless sent him five hundred dollars, "on account of my share for services ended April, 1865."[71]

"We were literally without means," Julia wrote, "when a gentleman from Lansingburgh, N.Y., sent the general five hundred dollars, saying, 'General, I owe you this for Appomattox.' The general acknowledged this and said to the gentleman, who was a stranger to us, that his timely thoughtfulness had been a great relief to him. The gentleman then sent a cheque for one thousand dollars, telling the general to consider it a loan to be repaid at his convenience."[72]

Help also came from Grant's old friend, Matias Romero, Mexico's ambassador to the United States, who had worked closely with the general on the Mexican Southern Railway. He paid a call on Grant, chatting with no mention of money. Then on his way out of the house, Señor Romero silently placed a check for a thousand dollars on a table near the door.

This total of $2,500 gave Ulysses and Julia some breathing room during which time she arranged to sell two small houses that she owned in Washington. That sale yielded slightly less than $6,000, but the payment would not reach them for several weeks. They knew this was only a stopgap. The general would need to find another source of income soon.

The crisis brought calamity to the entire family. Within a week of the Grant & Ward crash, creditors repossessed Fred's house in Morristown, New Jersey. Along with his wife, Ida, and their two children, he packed their belongings and moved in with his parents at 3 East Sixty-Sixth Street.

Buck was suddenly a pariah on Wall Street. No one would hire him. In the early days after the failure, no one knew if the Grants were innocent or guilty. Few people associated with Buck in those first months after the crisis. Broke and worried about possible legal action against him, he and his wife, Fannie, moved into a house owned by his father-in-law, Senator Chaffee near New Salem, forty-six miles from Manhattan.[73]

PAYING IT BACK

Grant vowed to repay every penny of his debt while also taking care of his wife and children. He took account of everything he owned, including the White Haven farm in Missouri, formerly owned by his father-in-law and purchased by Grant in the final years of the Civil War. It had been his dream to one day retire to this farm to raise thoroughbred race horses. He had designed and built an excellent horse stable on the property, although he rarely made it to St. Louis to work with his animals. The Grants also owned the homes in Galena and Philadelphia, the summerhouse in Long Branch, and two undeveloped parcels of land in Chicago.

The value of all these properties combined did not cover the $150,000 needed to repay Vanderbilt. So Grant collected both his wartime mementos and the gifts received on the world tour to help pay the debt. The family boxed up all Grant's war trophies, campaign maps, cigar boxes, gold medals, honorary commemorations, letters, notebooks, papers, uniforms, and boots.

Ulysses and Julia added to this collection all the cabinets, gold coins, jade, porcelain vases, teakwood cabinets, jewelry, and mementos from their world tour. All of this was calculated at precisely $155,417.20, which was $150,000 plus interest. These items were loaded into wooden crates and shipped to the Vanderbilt mansion.

William Vanderbilt had been out of the country on a trip to Europe and was perplexed when he returned and found the wooden crates stacked in his foyer. He dispatched his lawyer to call on the Grants and reassure them that they should not be concerned about the "personal loan." He considered the loan to Grant as a loss in the course of business and did not intend to press the matter. He asked that all the boxed-up items be returned.

But for Ulysses and Julia the debt's repayment was a matter of honor. Grant demanded that Vanderbilt lodge a judgment against him for the full amount of the loan. Vanderbilt argued the matter in vain. Finally, to satisfy the former president's dignity, he reluctantly agreed. In a moment of sad irony, two titans of the Gilded Age—one in business, the other in politics and the military—appeared in court, and the judgment was entered.

Vanderbilt was more embarrassed than Grant.[74]

In the midst of these uncomfortable negotiations, Vanderbilt suggested that he take title to the Grants' elegant house on Six-ty-Sixth Street to help cover the debt. He made it clear that they could continue living there rent free. To everyone's shock and be-wilderment, lawyers discovered that the Grants did not in fact own their house. They thought they had purchased it for $98,000 three years previous, but the man to whom they had entrusted that trans-action was none other than Ferdinand Ward. Instead of purchasing the house, Ward took the $98,000 the Grants had given him and arranged a mortgage for $48,000 that left the house in the hands of the original owners. He then deposited the remaining $50,000 in one of his own accounts.

Confronted with yet another theft on Ward's part, Vanderbilt reluctantly took title to the contents of the house—Grant's Civil War and presidential memorabilia, along with the gifts showered on him by heads of state during his trip around the world. With Vanderbilt's approval, Julia later gave all these objects and Grant's large collection of books to the federal government to be cared for by the Smithsonian Institute and the Library of Congress.[75]

In an effort to calm the relatives who also lost all in the Ward swindle, Grant wrote to his niece: "Your Aunt Jennie must not fret. … As long as I live she shall enjoy it [her home] as a matter of right; at least until she recovers what she has lost."[76]

As investigators probed into the details of the collapse, a Marine National director concluded, "The transactions of Grant & Ward constituted the most colossal swindle of the age."[77]

While Grant maintained a dignified outer appearance, inwardly he boiled with rage. "No one will ever know the extent of his anguish," wrote Senator Chaffee, "not even his own family, for he was the bravest in their presence. I was with him after the exposure of Ward. The general would suffer for hours in his large armchair, clutching nervously with his hands at the arm-rests, driving his fingers into the hard wood. One day he said to me; 'Chaffee I would kill Ward, as I would a snake. I believe I should do it, too, but I do not wish to be hanged for killing such a wretch.'"[78]

Ulysses and Julia had no choice but to give up the life of wealthy New Yorkers. She sadly paid the servants their final wages and sent them off with letters of recommendation. He sold all his horses and carriages and paid the coachman his final wages. Although he could barely afford his salary, Grant insisted on retaining the services of the man he called "Faithful Harrison," a Black valet named Harrison Terrell who had been with the family for three years.[79]

During these bleak days, Ulysses did not know how he would provide for his family. And the worst was yet to come.

Chapter Three

STUNG

Military memoirs were popular in the decades following the Civil War. Some were credible, making a helpful contribution to the history of the war, like the memoirs of William Tecumseh Sherman, James "Old Pete" Longstreet, or Philip Sheridan. But many were self-serving vanity pieces that minimized the faults of the author, embellished his accomplishments, and took potshots at political enemies.

Raised by his mother, Hannah Grant, to value humility, General Grant found many of these memoirs distasteful. As he did with Mark Twain's overture, Grant rebuffed every other attempt to persuade him to write his own reminiscence. "Oh, I'm not going to write any book," he told a St. Louis reporter not long after leaving the White House. "There are books enough already."[80]

Another suitor, Richard Watson Gilder, editor of *The Century Magazine*, tried to convince the general to write a series of articles on the war for his publication. Gilder, associate editor Robert Underwood Johnson, and company president Roswell Smith planned a series of articles titled, "Battles and Leaders of the Civil War," which they hoped would be written by various commanders.[81] *The Century*'s editors had earlier approached Grant, asking him to participate, but he adamantly refused.

"I have no idea of undertaking the task of writing any of the articles the *Century* requests," Grant wrote to his friend and former aid, Adam Badeau, in January 1884.[82] He was a soldier, not a literary man, he argued. "It is all in Badeau," Grant replied, referring to the recently released book, *Military History of Ulysses S. Grant*.[83] General Sherman then refused to write anything unless Grant did.

After the Grant & Ward bankruptcy, however, with his fortunes dramatically altered, Grant was forced to reconsider *The Century*'s offer. The general was also concerned with how he was viewed by the general public in the wake of the Grant & Ward swindle. He was especially sensitive to the opinions of old army comrades, some of whom had invested heavily in his firm.

The first test of his standing with the veterans came at a convention of army chaplains held at Ocean Grove, New Jersey, not far from Grant's summer home. The commander's fears subsided when his good friend, Dr. A. J. Palmer introduced him. "No combination of Wall Street sharpers shall tarnish the luster of my old Commander's fame for me." Everyone in the room sprang to their feet, affirming Palmer's sentiments with raucous applause.

This affirmation was repeated on June 11 when Grant traveled to Brooklyn to attend the annual reunion of the Society of the Army of the Potomac. Richard Gilder, the editor of *The Century Magazine*, witnessed the veterans' enthusiastic reception and decided to appeal to Grant once more.[84]

A few weeks later, thirty-one-year-old associate editor Robert Johnson[85] reached out to Adam Badeau. By this time, Grant's financial struggle had become public knowledge, and Johnson suggested that the sympathetic public would welcome an article by Grant. He assured Badeau that the endeavor would provide a source of financial relief for the general.

Johnson believed the public would welcome an article by the general "concerning a part of his honored career in which everyone takes pride." Badeau had recently resigned his consular appointment in Havana in order to expand his writing career. He was in the process of negotiating with *The Century* for a proposed article about the general to promote his own recently released book on Grant's Civil War campaigns.[86] Johnson asked Badeau to deliver a letter on his behalf.

It read in part: "The country looks with so much regret and sympathy upon General Grant's misfortune that it would gladly welcome the announcement and especially the publication of material relating to him or by him concerning a part of this honored career in which every one takes pride. It would be glad to have its attention diverted from his present troubles, and no doubt such diversion of his own mind would be welcome to him."[87]

Grant was moved by Johnson's kind words, but he and Julia were in the midst of dismissing their servants and closing up their home on East Sixty-Sixth Street to move to their summerhouse on the Jersey Shore. The *Century* people would have to wait.

A Strategic Retreat

As the Grants assessed their circumstances, they considered what they would do with their beach house in Long Branch, New Jersey—a seaside resort for the rich and famous thirty miles south of New York City. President Garfield had lived just down the street, and General Grant had been one of the first to personally offer his condolences to his neighbor, Mrs. Lucretia Garfield, after the president had been shot. Garfield had died in his Long Branch home, after being transported from Washington.

Julia called their vacation getaway "my little villa," but in reality it was a twenty-eight-room, four-story summerhouse on a dune that gently sloped down to the Atlantic. There the Grants sat on a porch or in a gazebo and chatted with family and friends. Julia used the popular term, *piazza,* to identify the setting. Across the avenue was the beach, where the family splashed in the ocean waves, and Grant either rode his horses or raced them, seated in a buggy. Nestled in nearby pine trees was a family playground and swing set where the grandchildren played with their friends.

Relating the anguished decisions they made after the failure of the investment firm, Julia later wrote of the house at Long Branch: "We decided at first to rent it," but the amount people were willing to pay "was so small that we decided to occupy it ourselves and have some of our family with us, a very happy arrangement for all."[88] Fred, Ida, and their children also moved to Long Branch for the summer.

As First Lady, Julia had the White House kitchen staff at her disposal; after the Grants left Washington, a host of servants had prepared their meals and served their guests. At Long Branch, Julia did all the cooking.[89]

Throughout his life, the general relished peaches, so Julia ensured that they were served with meals as often as possible. On June 2, Julia included a plate of them on the lunch table. After finishing his meal, Ulysses took a bite of a luscious peach. He shot up from the table in tremendous pain. "Oh my," he exclaimed, "I think something has stung me from that peach." He walked around the room in distress, and then stopped to rinse his throat again and again.

"He was in great pain," Julia later wrote, "and said water hurt him like liquid fire. This was the very beginning of his throat trouble. I always thought it was a sting from some insect in the peach."[90]

In the coming days, Grant's throat continued to be sensitive. Julia begged him to see a physician, but Ulysses refused. "No, it will be all right directly, and I will not have a doctor."[91] The pain diminished at times, but from that point forward, it never completely disappeared.

A New Hope

Once the Grants were settled in Long Branch, the general considered his options for securing much-needed income and the offer from The Century Magazine seemed more enticing. To their "surprise and joy," the editors of The Century received a note from Grant. If they still wanted him to write for the war series, they could send someone to discuss the matter.[92]

The general viewed the articles as an opportunity to remind the public of his contributions to the country, but the bottom line was that the war hero did not have the means to pay his household bills.[93] The magazine's war series presented the first steps out of poverty.

For Johnson, this was a priceless opportunity to meet a former president and the person he considered to be the greatest living figure of the Civil War. "This is one of the fortunate experiences of my life," he later wrote, "since it revealed to me the heroism and the integrity of a much misrepresented man."[94] Johnson happily traveled to Long Branch to discuss plans for the article.

Arriving at the seaside resort in mid-June, Johnson was welcomed at the door by the general himself. *The Century*'s editor paid little attention to the fact that on this warm June day Grant wore a heavy cape and draped a white silk scarf around his neck. After some discussion about *The Century*'s overall plans for a Civil War series, Johnson recalled that Grant "began to open his heart to me as to the situation in which he found himself as the result of the failure of Grant & Ward. In his direct and simple fashion he reviewed the debacle of his fortunes without restraint, showing deep feeling, even bitterness, as to his betrayal.

"He had been hurt to the quick in his proud name and in his honor," Johnson later wrote, "and the man [who was] stolid and reserved showed himself to me as a person of the most sensitive nature and the most human expression of feeling."

Grant explained his hesitancy about writing the articles, noting that he did not consider himself a writer. In addition, his military campaigns had already been examined and critiqued in many books and articles. He doubted he could add anything to the literature.

Johnson respectfully answered that an article from the commander of all the Union forces would be more interesting and informative than anything that had been written. The editor promised that Grant would be free to write as many articles as he desired on any subject from the Civil War. Johnson agreed to work with him to make the articles the best they could be and to ensure that they received the attention they deserved.[95]

Grant admitted that "his changed financial condition had compelled him to consider what resources might be offered by his pen." He worried about being bankrupt and continued to feel wounded and humiliated by the failure of Grant & Ward. He was also sensitive to the speculation about his role in the scandal.[96] Johnson added that Grant, who owed him no explanations, spent fifteen minutes giving the details of Ward's swindle "to clear the slate."[97]

"He told me, frankly and simply, that he had arrived at Long Branch almost penniless." Johnson was surprised and honored by the general's confidences and pictured Grant as "a wounded lion."[98]

The young editor suggested that Grant cover his major campaigns in four articles—Shiloh, Vicksburg, the Wilderness, and Lee's surrender. Grant agreed and said he could start on Shiloh at once.[99] Eventually the Battle of Chattanooga, or "The Battle above the Clouds," was substituted for Lee's surrender.[100]

"I told him that we should be glad to pay him five hundred dollars for each article," Johnson remembered, "and he said that it was entirely satisfactory."[101]

GRANT ON BEING GRANT

The general set to work on the Shiloh article almost immediately after Johnson's departure, setting up a white wooden table in a room facing the sea. The space was soon cluttered with maps, books, and military papers.[102] Grant worked diligently on his remembrances of Shiloh through June, averaging four hours of work each day.[103] To spark his memory, he referred to official reports and articles by other writers. His son Fred agreed to serve as editor and research assistant, working to retrieve necessary documents.

On July 1, Gilder received a handwritten first draft of Grant's Shiloh article in *The Century*'s offices. "Hurrah for Grant," he wrote to Johnson. For *The Century Magazine*, the article on a major aspect of Civil War history was a publishing coup.

Spirits dimmed when Johnson read the article and found that it was "substantially a copy of his dry official report of that engagement, as printed in the 'Rebellion Records,' with which we had already made ourselves familiar."The mood in the magazine's office turned from joy to dismay.[104]

The bland first draft, written on four single sheets of paper, provided a basic retelling of the battle but lacked emotional insights. Johnson realized he needed to coach Grant and help him understand what the public expected in these articles.[105]

With some coaching, Johnson believed Grant could provide the most insightful reflections anyone ever wrote on the Civil War. He hoped the general's recollections and conclusions might become some of the greatest writing a commanding general ever left to the nation.

"The general, of course, did not realize the requirements of a popular publication on the war," Johnson later wrote, "and it was for me to turn this new disaster of Shiloh into a signal success. This required all the tact that I could muster, that he should not be discouraged, and at the same time our project should be saved from the blight of the deadly official report, which is lacking in the personal touch that makes a great battle a vital and interesting human event."[106]

Johnson called again at Long Branch to tutor the general in the art of article writing. He thanked Grant for his first draft, and then humbly and graciously explained that there was still more work to do. He encouraged a rewrite of the article with the goal of adding more human touches. "This was not supposed to be a battle report," Johnson explained. "It is a story that comes complete with characters and a plot. It should be written as if the reader had never even heard of Shiloh."[107]

To help him grasp the understanding of the concept, the young editor questioned Grant about his thoughts and feelings during the monumental struggle. "General," Johnson respectfully probed, "you know of course that you have been criticized for not having intrenched against Albert Sidney Johnston at Shiloh; is this true?"

"Yes, at that stage of the war we had not yet learned to intrench," Grant admitted.[108]

With this admission, Johnson then inquired about other details. "What were your feelings at this juncture? Where was [General Don Carlos] Buell at such and such a time? After the first day's fight it was pouring rain and you had looked for shelter. Is that correct?"

Grant opened up under the kindly interrogation, revealing his perspective and feelings during the battle. "Yes, at first I had found shelter under a large tree. But the rain continued to pour down and so I had gone for shelter into an improvised military hospital. But I couldn't stand the amputations, and had to go out in the rain and sit for the most of the night against a tree."[109]

A skillful reporter and ghostwriter, Johnson took notes on a legal pad. Through his insightful questions and friendly manner, Johnson drew the general into vivid descriptions of one of the bloodiest engagements of this terrible war. "I then discovered that General Grant, instead of being a silent man, was positively loquacious. He spoke rapidly and long of the two days' battle."[110]

Grant, Johnson discovered, was expansive in his description of other generals and had a good eye for details. Surprisingly, he was also able to express his feelings well. The editor applauded this openness and praised Grant's ability to remember details. If such insights were included in the articles, Johnson explained, they would be enormously popular.

When the general answered him with interesting anecdotes or revelations, Johnson responded with enthusiasm: "Well, you should put that in the article."[111]

Before he left Long Branch, Johnson gave Grant his marching orders. "I told him that what was desirable for the success of the paper was to approximate such talk as he would make to friends after dinner, some of whom should know all about the battle and some nothing at all, and that the public was particularly interested in his point of view, in everything that concerned him, in what he planned, saw, said, and did. This was a new idea to him, and when I told him that I was convinced that he could do what was desired if he would not try too hard, he said that he would begin again."[112]

Johnson's advice was a revelation for Grant. Once he understood the expectations, he plunged into his work with renewed vigor.

INCREASING PAIN

Although he enjoyed the writing, the pain in his throat continued to increase. Grant's military discipline prevented him from speaking of the affliction until the soreness grew into stabbing pain.[113] After many days of quietly enduring the discomfort, he finally mentioned the irritation to his good friend and neighbor, George Childs, in early August.[114] The publisher suggested Grant consult a Philadelphia doctor named Jacob Mendez Da Costa, who was in town on a visit.

Da Costa arrived at the house, directed Grant to sit down on the porch in bright sunlight, and asked him to open his mouth. He observed a small growth, which troubled him. Sharing his concern, he wrote Grant a prescription and directed him to see his regular physician as soon as possible.[115]

Unfortunately, the general's family physician, Dr. Fordyce Barker, was traveling in Europe at that time. The general had known Barker since his days as a sanitary commissioner with the Union army. He trusted the man and decided to wait for his return instead of consulting another doctor.

Doctor Barker did not return from Europe until the middle of October, which gave the disease a head start of twelve weeks.[116] As he waited for Barker, Grant wrapped a silk scarf around his neck, worked on his articles, and kept smoking cigars.

The general threw himself into the work with the same vigor he had shown in every campaign. Speaking to Johnson, he exclaimed, "Why, I am positively enjoying the work. I am keeping at it every night and day, and Sundays." Fred Grant said his father had spoken of Mr. Johnson as his "literary tutor."[117]

The time had come for the Sphinx to share his story. His first published piece told the tale of one of the worst battles in American history—Shiloh, which in Hebrew means "place of peace."

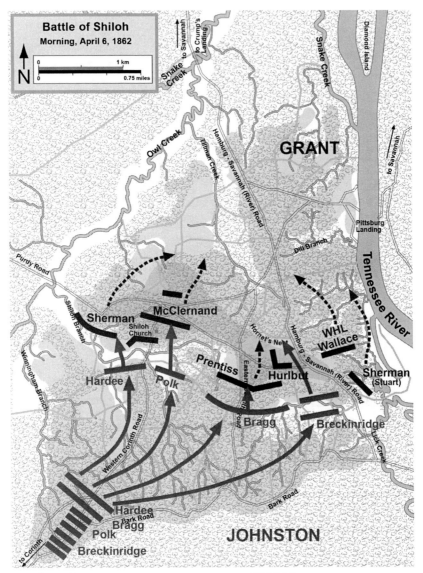

Battle of Shiloh
Morning, April 6, 1862

N

0   1 km
0   0.75 miles

to Crump's Landing
to Savannah
Snake Creek
Diamond Island
Snake Creek
Owl Creek
Tillman Creek
Hamburg · Savannah (River) Road
to Savannah
GRANT
Pittsburg Landing
Tennessee River
Dill Branch
Purdy Road
Shiloh Branch
Sherman
Shiloh Church
McClernand
Hornet's Nest
WHL Wallace
Winningham Branch
Hardee
Polk
Prentiss
Eastern Corinth Road
Hurlbut
Hamburg · Savannah (River) Road
Sherman (Stuart)
Western Corinth Road
Bragg
Breckinridge
Lick Creek
Hardee
Bark Road
Bragg
Polk
Bark Road
JOHNSTON
Breckinridge
to Corinth

Chapter Four

SHILOH

As he read through memoirs and books by people like William Tecumseh Sherman and Adam Badeau, then put pen to paper, Grant
discovered that he thoroughly enjoyed the writing process. Having
fully grasped the advice given by Robert Underwood Johnson, the
general and his son Fred added the personal touches to bring the
human dimension to the battlefield story.[118] Drawing on his powerful memory and official battlefield reports, Grant returned to those
two terrible days on the banks of the Tennessee River.

~

FROM *PERSONAL MEMOIRS*

At this time I generally spent the day at Pittsburg and returned to
Savannah in the evening. I was intending to remove my headquarters to Pittsburg, but General Don Carlos Buell was expected daily
and would come in at Savannah. I remained at this point, therefore,
a few days longer than I otherwise should have done, in order to
meet him on his arrival.

While I was at breakfast, however, heavy firing was heard in
the direction of Pittsburg Landing, and I hastened there, sending a
hurried note to Buell informing him of the reason why I could not
meet him at Savannah.[119]

~

APRIL 6–7, 1862—PITTSBURG LANDING, TENNESSEE

At seven o'clock on the fateful morning of April 6, Grant and his staff
gathered for breakfast on the veranda of the stately Cherry mansion

40

overlooking the wide Tennessee River. Grant's Army of the Tennessee was encamped four miles downriver at Pittsburg Landing, Tennessee, awaiting the arrival of General Buell and his Army of the Ohio. Buell was on his way from Columbia, eighty-five miles away, with forty thousand veteran troops and under orders from General Henry Halleck, the commander of the Department of the Mississippi at that time, to reinforce Grant at Savannah.[120] Grant planned to lead the combined forces to attack Albert Sidney Johnston's Confederate forces a little farther south in Corinth, Mississippi—that is, if Halleck did not appear and take over command in the field.

Lifting his cup of coffee to his lips, General Grant paused as a familiar, muffled, yet deadly sound broke through the morning air. The conversation among the staff officers came to an abrupt halt as they listened to the muted sound in the distance.

"General, that is the noise of cannon," said Colonel Joseph D. Webster, Grant's chief of staff.

"It very much sounds like it," the general replied.

"Where is it? Crump's Landing or Pittsburg?"

"That's what I am trying to determine." The battlefield noise steadily increased. "I think it is Pittsburg." Grant rose from his seat. His staff immediately stood in response. "Gentlemen, the ball is in motion. Let's be off."

Grant quickly wrote a dispatch to Buell. "Heavy firing is heard … an attack has been made on our most advanced positions. … This necessitates my joining the forces up the river instead of meeting you to-day as contemplated."[121]

Grant knew that Brigadier General William "Bull" Nelson, commander of Buell's leading division, was approaching Savannah. Grant fired off another dispatch, ordering Nelson to turn south and march to a point opposite Pittsburg Landing. From there, his troops could be ferried across the Tennessee River to the battlefield.

Grant had recently been injured when his horse slipped and fell in the rain, pinning the general's leg under the beast. Grant painfully hobbled on crutches as fast as he could from the veranda and down the hill to the dock. Boarding his flagship, the USS *Tigress*, Grant ordered the captain to steam forward to the sound of the battle.

As the *Tigress* approached Pittsburg Landing, the crackling of muskets and the booming of cannon became deafening. Grant and his staff arrived at 9:00 a.m. to a mixture of military gallantry and bedlam. On certain parts of the field, his troops bravely held the line against the Confederates, while at the same time hundreds of skulkers, who had run from the battlefield in terror, lined the bluffs of the river for half a mile.

Once ashore, Grant immediately coordinated the ammunition train to properly supply the troops at the front. Once this was accomplished, Webster hoisted the commander onto his horse. Lashing his crutches to his saddle, Grant rode forward into the battle.[122]

Arriving at the front, he found his division commanders, General John Alexander McClernand, General Benjamin Prentiss, and General William Sherman all fighting a pitched battle, having been surprised early that morning by Confederate Generals Albert Sidney Johnston and Pierre Beauregard. The Southerners caught the Union troops off guard as they prepared breakfast, throwing their six divisions at the drowsy Federal soldiers.

Grant flew into action, immediately organizing the Fifteenth and Sixteenth Iowa regiments, which had arrived the previous night, into a reserve to protect the landing and the ammunition train. He ordered the officers to shoot stragglers heading for the rear if they refused to engage in the battle. A colonel of the Fifteenth Iowa simply stared blankly at the rumpled man barking orders from atop his horse. In frustration, the commander finally blurted out, "I am General Grant," eliciting a sharp salute and immediate action.[123]

Despite his injury, Grant rode all over the battlefield, heedless of danger even in the midst of a shower of cannon and musket balls.

~

FROM *PERSONAL MEMOIRS*

The position of our troops made a continuous line from Lick Creek on the left to Owl Creek, a branch of Snake Creek, on the right, facing nearly south and possibly a little west. The water in all these streams was very high at the time and contributed to protect our flanks. The enemy was compelled, therefore, to attack directly in front. This he did with great vigor, inflicting heavy losses on the National side, but suffering much heavier on his own.[124]

~

Throughout the day, Grant calmly puffed on cigars, an action that had become an accidental trademark. Thousands of cigars arrived at Grant's headquarters by an admiring public after newspaper reports emerged of his smoking a stogie during the victory at Fort Donelson. What was not reported was that the general had forgotten his pipe and had bummed a cigar from a friend. Consequently, he had more cigars than he could smoke, so the pipe was packed away in his footlocker, and the general was rarely without his new aromatic vice.

When Grant's friend from Galena, John Rawlins, arrived on the Shiloh battlefield, he told a fellow officer looking for Grant, "We'll find him where the firing is heaviest."[125] Sure enough, that's where he was. As the general moved from one section of the fight to another, a bullet made a direct hit, bending the scabbard of his sword. Grant acknowledged the shot for only a second, and then returned his focus to the fight.[126]

The general raced from unit to unit, talking to regimental and brigade commanders, sometimes positioning troops himself as needed. At times he rounded up stragglers and led them back to the fight telling them, "Now boys pitch in."[127]

Nearly half his men had never seen combat. Some green recruits had received their weapons only a few days earlier. Despite the inexperienced troops, Grant had faith in the leadership skills of his lieutenants. This was especially true of his old friend from West Point, William Tecumseh Sherman, who commanded his right flank near a small clapboard church called Shiloh.

In the late afternoon, as a scout reported his findings to Grant, the messenger's head was blown off by an enemy shell, spattering the general with blood. Although always saddened by the loss of his men, in the heat of battle Grant didn't flinch at the gory sight.

"Not beaten by a damn sight," he responded and turned his horse to gallop off to the next division. [128]

Grant visited each of his major commanders several times during the day. He did not keep any of his forces in reserve—moving cavalry, artillery, and infantry, along with two naval gunboats to points of need. At Grant's urging, the navy shelled the enemy from their position in the middle of the Tennessee River throughout the day and all night long.

THE HORNET'S NEST

The division of Brigadier General Benjamin Prentiss was the first unit attacked early that morning, and its men had suffered greatly during the opening hours of that battle. After heavy fighting pushed him back, Prentiss reformed his command with reinforcements under the command of General W. H. L. Wallace and held the line in what became known as the "Hornet's Nest."

After Wallace was fatally wounded, Prentiss held on as wave after wave of Confederate soldiers rushed his position. Riding up in the heat of battle, Grant instructed Prentiss to "maintain that position at all hazards." For the next several hours, that is exactly what the men in the Hornet's Nest did.

Between 11:30 a.m. and noon, Prentiss's troops repelled a 3,600-man, four-brigade attack led by Confederate Brigadier General Alexander P. Stewart. Later, General Braxton Bragg ordered a series of four reckless charges that came no closer than sixty yards to the Hornet's Nest.

By midafternoon, however, Confederate attacks wore down the Union defenders in this critical spot on the battlefield. Two more rebel brigades made midafternoon assaults but were pushed back with great losses on both sides. Grant watched the action with Prentiss late in the afternoon expecting victory.

A PILLAR FALLS

Across no-man's-land, Confederate Commander Albert Sidney Johnston received a report that one of his brigades refused to advance against Union forces in a peach orchard. Rushing to the scene, Johnston rallied the men by leading the charge personally at 2:30 p.m. During the charge, Johnston was shot in his right leg, behind the knee, although he considered the wound insignificant. A similar wound twenty-five years earlier had left Johnston with permanent nerve damage, likely preventing him from recognizing how serious his injury really was.[129]

Returning from the charge with his boot heel flapping from a direct hit, Johnston declared, "They didn't trip me up that time."[130] He then told former Tennessee governor Isham Harris to pass on an order to Colonel Winfield S. Statham to charge another Union battery. Soon Harris observed Johnston sinking down in his saddle while leaning over to the left. "I instantly put my left arm around him pulling him to me saying 'General, are you wounded?' He said 'yes, and I fear seriously.' Capt. Wickham … and I lifted him from his horse, laid him upon the ground. I took his head in my lap. He never spoke after answering my question though continued to breathe for 25 or 30 minutes."[131]

Harris called for a medic, but earlier in the battle, Johnston had sent his personal surgeon to care for the wounded Confederate troops and Yankee prisoners. Harris ran to find medical assistance, but he failed to apply a tourniquet to Johnston's leg. Before a doctor could be found, Johnston bled to death from a torn artery as blood collected unnoticed in his riding boot.[132]

After Johnston's death, it became clear that the Confederates could not plow through the Hornet's Nest with infantry, so they changed their tactics. Brigadier General Daniel Ruggles assembled fifty-two pieces of artillery to smash the Yankee stronghold.

At the same time, Confederate infantry flanked the left end of the Union line, causing General Stephen A. Hurlbut's division to retreat toward Pittsburg Landing. The final Confederate assault on the Hornet's Nest included 10,000 Confederate troops, who incurred approximately 2,400 casualties.[133] Grant's line north of the Hornet's Nest finally caved as the Confederates outflanked Prentiss on both the left and right.

From *Personal Memoirs*

In one of the backward moves, on the 6th, the division commanded by General Prentiss did not fall back with the others. This left his flanks exposed and enabled the enemy to capture him with about two thousand two hundred of his officers and men. General Badeau gives four o'clock of the sixth as about the time this capture took place. He may be right as to the time, but my recollection is that the hour was later. General Prentiss himself gave the hour as half-past five. I was with him, as I was with each of the division commanders that day, several times, and my recollection is that the last time I was with him was about half-past four, when his division was standing up firmly and the general was as cool as if expecting victory. But no matter whether it was four or later, the story that he and his command were surprised and captured in their camps is without any foundation whatever. If it had been true, as currently reported at the time and yet believed by thousands of people, that Prentiss and his division had been captured in their beds, there would not have been an all-day struggle, with the loss of thousands killed and wounded on the Confederate side.[134]

~

Prentiss and his forces had held back the Confederate attack for more than twelve hours. After the mass surrender, the rebels let out a loud cheer. Prentiss responded to the Southern celebration: "Yell, boys, you have a right to shout for you have this day captured the bravest brigade in the United States Army."

When the news of Prentiss's surrender arrived, one of Grant's officers asked him if this was a sign of a rebel victory. "Oh, no," he answered confidently. "They can't break our lines tonight. It is too late. Tomorrow we shall attack them with fresh troops and drive them, of course."

"Do you think they are pressing us, General?" Rawlins asked nervously.

"They have been pressing us all day, John," replied Grant coolly, "but I think we will stop them here."[135]

HOLDING THE LINE

In midafternoon, the general directed his chief of staff, Colonel Webster, to create a line of defense for the Landing. For the next three hours, Webster assembled artillery pieces along the Dill Branch of Lick Creek near Pittsburg Landing. Gathering every gun he could find from the reserve artillery, and from any retreating units, Webster created a seventy-cannon line. This powerful defense included five 24-pounder siege guns that had been hauled up from the Landing. The Union gunners were assisted by the firing of 32-pounder cannonballs and 8-inch shells from the two Union gunboats, *Tyler* and *Lexington,* at the mouth of Dill Branch on the Tennessee River.

By 5:30 p.m., Grant maneuvered twenty thousand Union troops into position to face the eight thousand Confederates attempting to capture the Landing. As darkness descended, Grant's army held the line, pushing back the exhausted rebels. Both sides had lost between 8,000 and 8,500 casualties in the day's fighting, so they dug in for the night.

On the Union side, most of Prentiss's Division was killed or taken prisoner, and General William Wallace had been mortally wounded. Three divisions remained to Grant at the end of the day—Hurlbut on the left, McClernand in the center, and Sherman on the right.

~

FROM *PERSONAL MEMOIRS*

All three divisions were, as a matter of course, more or less shattered and depleted in numbers from the terrible battle of the day.[136]

~

By nightfall, Grant's army had backed up more than a mile from where it had been at dawn, but Grant remained optimistic. Lieutenant Colonel James B. McPherson asked whether the army should retreat across the Tennessee. "Retreat?" Grant responded. "No, I propose to attack at daylight and whip them."

By dusk, Buell's first five thousand troops under Bull Nelson were being ferried across the Tennessee River by steamboat. These footsore but otherwise fresh troops disembarked with their battle flags flying boldly and regimental bands playing familiar martial music. The battle-weary Northern troops who had endured intense fighting throughout the day cheered at the approach of Buell's reinforcements. As darkness fell, Grant rushed Nelson and his men toward the front to give fresh strength to his line.

On the right, General Lew Wallace—who had taken the wrong road and marched his troops through the woods most of the day— finally arrived with another five thousand men. Through the night, General Alexander M. McCook's and General Thomas L. Crittenden's divisions of Buell's army also joined Grant's forces.[137] Light faded into dusk and shooting became sporadic as Grant made his preparations to launch a massive counterattack early the next morning.

~

FROM *PERSONAL MEMOIRS*

So confident was I before firing had ceased on the 6th that the next day would bring victory to our arms if we could only take the initiative, that I visited each division commander in person before any reinforcements had reached the field. I directed them to throw out heavy lines of skirmishers in the morning as soon as they could see, and push them forward until they found the enemy, following with their entire divisions in supporting distance, and to engage the enemy as soon as found.[138]

~

When General Buell finally arrived and saw a large number of bloodied and terrified stragglers cowering beneath the bluff Pittsburg Landing, he asked Grant about the plan for retreat. The general coolly replied, "I haven't despaired of whipping them yet!"[139]

Throughout the night, the two ironclads, the USS *Tyler* and the USS *Lexington*, fired 8-inch shells relentlessly into the Confederate position, causing further destruction and hindering the enemy from getting much rest. Rain poured from the sky and lightning flashed, illuminating the horrific sight of hogs feeding on the dead. The cries of wounded men echoed across the battlefield and from the makeshift hospital.

On the Confederate side, Beauregard wired Richmond the news of what he assumed to be a glorious victory: "We this morning attacked the enemy in strong position in front of Pittsburg, and after a severe battle of ten hours, thanks be to the Almighty, gained a complete victory, driving the enemy from every position. Loss on both sides heavy, including our commander-in-chief, General A. S. Johnston, who fell gallantly leading his troops into the thickest of the fight."[140]

Beauregard received the incorrect report that Buell was not coming to join Grant. Convinced of victory in the morning, the Confederate commander allowed his exhausted troops to rest instead of reorganizing.

A BLOODY, RAINY NIGHT

Conversely, Grant conferred with each of his commanders and Buell to make sure everything was ready for the counterassault at dawn. When he was confident that all was in order, Grant hobbled in agony through the rain to an oak tree for shelter. During the heat of battle, he had not allowed himself to think about his injured leg. Once he dismounted, excruciating pain shot through his body. His leg was so inflamed that surgeons had to cut off his boot. Lying in the rain on a bed of wet hay, the roar of cannon from the gunboats and the throbbing of his injured leg prevented the general from getting much sleep.

Sometime after midnight, Grant decided to seek more comfortable lodgings. He limped on his crutches through the pouring rain until he reached a log house that had been converted into a field hospital. Inside the surgeons fought valiantly to save the lives of the wounded, amputating arms and legs and throwing them into piles in the corner. The general was overcome by the blood-soaked sight of wounded soldiers and the piles of rotting limbs.

In a twist of irony, the brave military commander could not stand the sight of blood once a battle was over. Indeed, Grant's aversion to blood was so strong that he insisted his meat be cooked almost to shoe leather before he would eat it.

~

FROM *PERSONAL MEMOIRS*

Sometime after midnight, growing restive under the storm and the continuous pain, I moved back to the loghouse under the bank. This had been taken as a hospital, and all night wounded men were being brought in, their wounds dressed, a leg or an arm amputated as the case might require, and everything being done to save life or alleviate suffering. The sight was more unendurable than encountering the enemy's fire, and I returned to my tree in the rain.[141]

~

General Sherman found Grant wincing in pain under that oak tree. Sherman had considered the idea of suggesting a retreat to his old friend, but something changed his mind as he approached the commander. "Well, Grant, we've had the devil's own day, haven't we?" Grant took several puffs on his cigar as he considered Sherman's words. "Yes," he finally replied. "Lick 'em tomorrow though."[142]

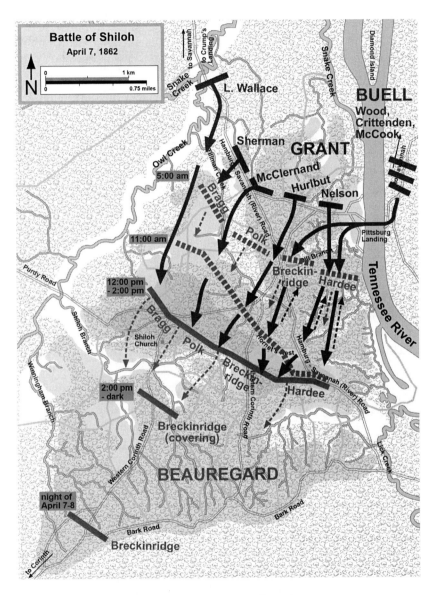

Battle of Shiloh
April 7, 1862

N

0   1 km
0   0.75 miles

to Savannah
to Crump's Landing
Snake Creek
L. Wallace
Owl Creek
Hamburg Savannah (River) Road
Shiloh Branch
Snake Creek
Diamond Island
to Savannah
BUELL
Wood,
Crittenden,
McCook
Sherman
GRANT
McClernand
5:00 am
Bragg
Hurlbut
Nelson
11:00 am
Polk
Pittsburg Landing
Purdy Road
12:00 pm
- 2:00 pm
Breckin-
ridge
Hardee
Tennessee River
Shiloh Branch
Bragg
Shiloh
Church
Polk
Hornet's Nest
Winningham Branch
Breckin-
ridge
Eastern Corinth Road
Hamburg Savannah (River) Road
Hardee
2:00 pm
- dark
Breckinridge
(covering)
BEAUREGARD
Western Corinth Road
Lick Creek
night of
April 7-8
Bark Road
Bark Road
Breckinridge
to Corinth

A New Day

With Buell's seventeen thousand men, along with Wallace's fresh division, forty thousand Union troops under Grant's command unleashed hell against Beauregard's twenty-five thousand. At first light, Grant issued orders to his division commanders: "Advance and recapture our original camps." Union soldiers launched a massive counteroffensive. Sherman called it "the severest musketry-fire I ever heard."[143]

Beauregard and his fellow Confederate officers were caught completely off guard. Not until 10:00 a.m. did the disorganized, scattered Confederate units patch together a solid defensive line. The Union onslaught pushed them steadily back.

Federal troops fought through a field covered with the dead and with the groaning wounded soldiers who had been abandoned on the battlefield overnight. Once again Grant rode back and forth in the midst of the fighting directing troop movements from his horse. At one crucial moment the commander personally organized two regiments, placed them in position, and shouted, "Charge!"[144]

Except for a few costly counterattacks, the Confederates were pushed back all day. Pressed by the overwhelming force from four of Grant's divisions and three of Buell's, the haggard Confederates fell back in a fighting retreat. By 2:30 p.m., Beauregard feared his army would disintegrate and ordered an immediate withdrawal. As the Southern troops fled into the deep woods, Union soldiers fell to the ground—exhausted, cold, and soaked by the persistent rain.

The rebel forces finally halted on the Corinth Road, five miles from Pittsburg Landing, where they made camp for the night.

Of more than one hundred thousand soldiers who fought in the Battle of Shiloh, more than twenty-four thousand were killed or wounded. The casualties from these two days of ferocious fighting eclipsed the total of the Revolutionary War, the War of 1812, and the Mexican War combined. Grant's losses came to thirteen thousand killed, wounded, and missing; the Confederates had lost close to twelve thousand.[145]

FROM *PERSONAL MEMOIRS*

Up to the battle of Shiloh I, as well as thousands of other citizens, believed that the rebellion against the Government would collapse suddenly and soon, if a decisive victory could be gained over any of its armies. But when Confederate armies were collected which not only attempted to hold a line farther south, from Memphis to Chattanooga, Knoxville and on to the Atlantic, but assumed the offensive and made such a gallant effort to regain what had been lost, then, indeed, I gave up all idea of saving the Union except by complete conquest.[146]

Chapter Five

OPPORTUNITY OF *THE CENTURY*

Grant's new draft of the Shiloh battle astonished and delighted *The Century*'s leadership. Johnson was so pleased with Grant's progress he immediately considered the possibility of convincing the general to write his memoirs. Johnson approached Gilder with the idea.

"Now that Grant is in the humor of writing would it not be worthwhile to think of getting him to write a book of his war experiences for subscription to go along side of our book?" Gilder agreed and pitched the idea to Century Company president, Roswell Smith.[147]

Johnson and Smith reached out to Grant to see if they could meet with him in Long Branch. Thankful for the income provided by the Shiloh article, Grant was more than happy to chat with the Century people.

Arriving in Long Branch, Johnson and Smith lunched with Grant and his neighbor, Philadelphia newspaper publisher George Childs. Although the day was warm, Grant's throat was wrapped in a scarf, and his voice was raspy. They sat in wicker chairs on the large veranda, the warm breeze whipping off the ocean.[148] Johnson introduced Smith, and then Grant introduced Childs.

Julia served a light lunch and the gentlemen settled down to business. Smith expressed his complete satisfaction with the Shiloh article, which greatly pleased the general. Then Smith brought up the idea of expanding the four articles Grant had already agreed to into an official memoir.

Grant was surprised by the proposal. "Do you really think anyone would be interested in a book by me?"

"General, do you not think the public would read with avidity Napoleon's personal account of his battles?" Smith replied.[149] Of course the question was rhetorical, and Grant was impressed by the offer.[150]

The general expressed his willingness to consider the possibility of writing a book and thanked the Century people for their visit. Childs did not offer any objections, so the general was left to ponder his options.

Johnson and Smith left with high hopes, knowing Grant was still in great need of financial assistance. To a certain degree, they felt as though they were coming to his rescue. To a large measure, this was an accurate assessment of the situation. Julia later wrote of that fateful time: "All that summer was spent by my dear husband in hard work: writing, writing, writing for bread."[151]

Weeks before, Grant had written to one of his wartime staff officers, William R. Rowley, that he intended to write and "probably will publish" something beyond his four articles, a work that would "finish all my connection with the war of the rebellion."[152]

Because of *The Century* editors' splendid reception to his Shiloh article and their suggestion that he write his memoirs, Grant was full of confidence and ready to write the next article about his military masterpiece—Vicksburg.

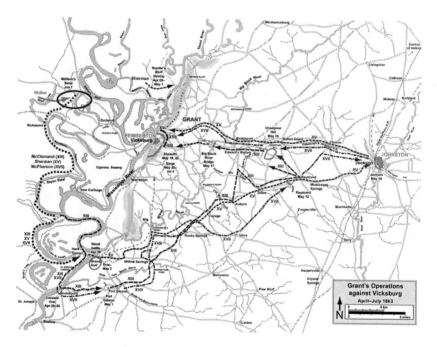

Map by Hal Jespersen, www.cwmaps.com © Hal Jespersen.
All rights reserved. Used with permission.

Chapter Six

VICKSBURG

Soon after sending the Shiloh article to Johnson, Grant jumped right into writing his article on the Vicksburg Campaign. The writing process alleviated the depression he suffered after the collapse of Grant & Ward. "I have now been writing on the Vicksburg Campaign two weeks, Sundays and all, averaging more than four hours a day," he wrote to Johnson on July 15. "Only now approaching [the Battle of] Champion Hill, I fear that my article will be longer than you want."[153]

On July 21, Grant wrote to Adam Badeau, explaining that the Vicksburg article would be "finished, ready for revision, to-morrow. If you feel like a change of mountain air to sea air for a while, I will be glad to see you here." Badeau had been writing his own article about Grant for *The Century*, and the general referred to it in his letter. "If you are not through with your article, you can finish it here."[154]

Badeau traveled to Long Branch to serve as an additional editor and researcher alongside Fred Grant. The team spread maps, military reports, books, and writing material on the white pine table that had been brought to an upstairs room from the kitchen. In the distance, ocean waves crashed along the New Jersey shoreline. Julia sat nearby in a wicker chair, watching them work with both curiosity and the satisfaction that her husband was active again.[155]

Grant focused his excellent memory on the battle that first revealed his military genius to the world.

MAY 18–JULY 4, 1863—VICKSBURG, MISSISSIPPI

One week after the bombardment of Fort Sumter by Southern forces, which marked the outbreak of the war, President Lincoln ordered a blockade of the rebel ports. To establish a strategy for the war, Lincoln met with his general in chief, Winfield Scott, who had gained fame in the War of 1812 and the Mexican War. Scott heartily agreed with Lincoln's blockade, so he proposed a strategy to cut off trade to the Confederacy and squeeze the life out of the rebellion.

Scott's proposal became known as the Anaconda Plan.

The plan called for a force of eighty thousand men to travel up the Mississippi River, taking cities along the way and dividing the Confederacy in two. The campaign would begin with an attack on the forts below New Orleans from the south, followed by a thrust at the cities along the river from the north. When these strongholds fell, the river would be in Federal hands from its source to its mouth, and the Confederacy would be divided.

The first great success in the plan came on April 24, 1862, when Admiral David Farragut ran his fleet past the forts that defended New Orleans, forcing the city to surrender.[156] After his ships were repaired, he sent them upriver, where they took Baton Rouge and Natchez.

After these conquests, the fleet was stymied when they attacked Vicksburg, where Confederate batteries sat on high bluffs, rendering the city impregnable to the navy's gunboats.

Called "the Gibraltar of the West," the Vicksburg garrison valiantly resisted Union control of the Mississippi. Other than Port Hudson, Louisiana, one hundred miles to the south, Vicksburg was the only remaining Confederate stronghold on the mighty river. Surrounded by nine major forts, Vicksburg was reinforced with 172 guns commanding all approaches by water and land. A garrison of thirty thousand protected the city.[157]

Having traveled the Mississippi by flatboat in his youth, President Lincoln knew its topography. Early in the war, Lincoln stressed Vicksburg's importance when he pointed to a national map and said, "See what a lot of land these fellows hold, of which Vicksburg is the key. The war can never be brought to a close until that key is in our pocket."[158]

THE RISE OF GENERAL GRANT

President Lincoln needed generals who were not afraid of a brawl. When some advisors urged him to drop Grant after the carnage at Shiloh, Lincoln answered, "I can't spare this man, he fights."[159]

Grant recognized that his next objective must be Vicksburg. During the winter of 1862–1863, he launched several experimental schemes against the stronghold with the dual purpose of seeking a breakthrough to the fortified city and also keeping his troops occupied. Union soldiers cut trees below the water line to open possible pathways for navy gunboats. Others built dikes and dams to raise or lower water levels. Another scheme proposed digging a new channel to divert the flow of the Mississippi. None of these experiments worked, but the labor kept the men physically fit and focused on the war effort.

As his soldiers toiled on, Grant devised a strategy for the coming spring campaign—a major push that would begin when the roads finally dried. Up to that point, Union forces threatening Vicksburg had been hindered by the enemy, by swamps and bayous, by topography, and by the great Mississippi itself. Grant knew he needed an audacious plan to end the stalemate.

Grant proposed to float navy ironclads and barges under intense fire past the Vicksburg batteries. Then he would march his army southward down the dry west bank of the Mississippi, moving below Vicksburg. From there, navy vessels would ferry his army across the Mississippi somewhere to the south of the Confederate stronghold.

Grant's subordinates—Sherman, McPherson, and General John A. "Black Jack" Logan—feared the scheme was too risky. Sherman strongly objected when Grant explained that once on the east side of the Mississippi, the army would move so fast it would be cut off from food and supplies and would have to survive off the land. This idea went against everything the officers had learned at West Point.

General Grant understood this, but he was a pragmatist—one of the reasons he had been somewhat half-hearted in his study of strategy at West Point. Grant had known then, as he understood fully now, that not all circumstances fit neatly into textbook theory.

Sherman preferred returning north to Memphis and moving south on the overland route through central Mississippi. But this would be a tactical retreat, and Grant didn't like to retreat. Though daring, Grant believed his plan would work.

"Grant is brave, honest, & true," Sherman concluded earlier that month, "but not a Genius."[160] Sherman handed Grant a written protest of the operation, making sure his concerns were placed in the official record. And Grant was okay with that.

In the end, Sherman went along with Grant's bold strategy. "Whatever plan of action he may adopt will receive from me the same zealous cooperation and energetic support as though conceived by myself."[161]

Grant respectfully noted Sherman's objections and went ahead with the plan anyway. As spring approached and the muddy roads dried, Grant was ready to move.

~

From Personal Memoirs

I had had in contemplation the whole winter the movement by land to a point below Vicksburg from which to operate, subject only to the possible but not expected success of some one of the expedients resorted to for the purpose of giving us a different base. This could not be undertaken until the waters receded. I did not therefore communicate this plan, even to an officer of my staff, until it was necessary to make preparations for the start.

My recollection is that Admiral Porter was the first one to whom I mentioned it. The co-operation of the navy was absolutely essential to the success (even to the contemplation) of such an enterprise. I had no more authority to command Porter than he had to command me. It was necessary to have part of his fleet below Vicksburg if the troops went there. Steamers to use as ferries were also essential. The navy was the only escort and protection for these steamers, all of which in getting below had to run about fourteen miles of batteries. Porter fell into the plan at once.[162]

~

Admiral David Dixon Porter prepared his ships for the hazardous passage in front of the Vicksburg guns. He made it clear to Grant that the ironclads could not return upstream against the strong Mississippi currents under fire from Vicksburg's artillery. Whatever vessels survived the gauntlet would remain south of the fortified city. To protect his vulnerable boilers, Porter directed his sailors to stack barriers of cotton, hay bales, and sacks filled with grain all around them.[163]

On April 16, as the moon shone brightly over the Mississippi, Porter's flotilla of gunboats and transport barges set out on their harrowing journey. Beginning at 10:00 p.m., Porter led seven iron-clad gunboats and four steamers downstream. Coal barges and ex-cess vessels were lashed to the sides of the main ships to provide additional protection and, later, extra room for transporting troops and supplies.[164]

General Grant's twelve-year-old son, Fred, had arrived in Lou-isiana at the end of March, which brought much joy to his father. Grant cherished his time with young Fred and even allowed the boy to ride along with him on a pony when the situation was not too dangerous.

Having the boy at his side reminded Grant of how much he missed his family, and he soon sent for Julia and their youngest son, Jesse, to join him as well. Julia arrived in time to witness the navy's running of the Vicksburg guns. Ulysses, Julia, and Fred, along with Grant's staff, boarded a steamer at Milliken's Bend, on the Louisi-ana side of the Mississippi. Near midnight, they dropped anchor at a safe distance just north of Vicksburg, close enough to view the engagement. As they watched, the ironclad gunboats closed in to engage the Confederate batteries.

When Porter's ships came into view in the bright moonlight, rebel lookouts alerted the garrison. Confederate cannons opened up on the Union boats, and Porter immediately returned fire. In the midst of the exploding cannon shells, houses and cabins along the Vicksburg shoreline soon burst into flame, providing even more light for Confederate gunners.[165]

Artillery shells arced through the sky in both directions as deafening explosions shook the earth. Union vessels pressed forward under Confederate bombardment for two hours. The Southerners fired 525 rounds, landing sixty-eight hits. Despite this hellish fire, only one steamboat was lost, after it took a direct hit to the engine room.[166] The other two steamers and most of the barges sustained only minor damage and no loss of life.[167]

On the night of April 22, a second collection of six steamers and twelve barges moved south to run the Confederate batteries. Grant's old headquarters boat, the USS *Tigress*, was the only steamer sunk by the rebels, although the entire crew survived. Half the barges passed the stronghold without damage. The vital army supplies were unharmed.[168]

Once the navy transportation was in place south of Vicksburg, Grant ordered General McClernand to move his troops thirty miles south and prepare for the crossing.

CROSSING THE MISSISSIPPI

Grant then issued Special Orders No. 110 for the march by his entire army. McClernand's Thirteenth Corps was to be followed by McPherson's Seventeenth, and then Sherman's Fifteenth. McClernand's four divisions set out first down the Louisiana side of the river to New Carthage. Construction of this narrow marching path was accomplished by digging canals to divert excess water; the men erected bridges where the water could not be drained and built roads where there had been none.

The Confederate commander in Vicksburg was General John C. Pemberton, a Pennsylvanian who had joined the rebellion at the urging of his Southern wife. As Grant set his troops in motion, he also dispatched four units to the north and east of Vicksburg to divert Pemberton's attention.

First, he sent Major General Frederick Steele's troops in transports one hundred miles northward up the Mississippi River toward Greenville, Mississippi. Observing this movement, Pemberton assumed Grant was retreating and ordered eight thousand rebel troops to be transferred from Mississippi back to General Bragg in Tennessee.

Grant then ordered a cavalry raid under the leadership of Colonel Benjamin H. Grierson. These dashing troopers traveled from Tennessee to Louisiana through the length of eastern Mississippi. On April 17, Grierson and his seventeen thousand horsemen rode out of La Grange, Tennessee, with a six-gun battery. Ignoring the massive troop movements in Louisiana, Pemberton instead sent his soldiers to block Grierson before he reached the railroad.

On April 27, Pemberton sent seventeen messages to Mississippi commanders about Grierson's raiders, but not a single dispatch concerning Grant's maneuvers on the west bank of the Mississippi River. By April 29, Pemberton had been so deceived by the false raid that he ordered his entire cavalry to pursue Grierson. At the same time, he inexplicably ignored panicked dispatches from lookouts south of Vicksburg who observed major troop movements on the western side of the river.

Grierson's dazzling raiders finally rode out of Mississippi on May 2, reaching the safety of Union lines at Baton Rouge. The raid was mainly a diversion, but it was so successful that the cavalry inflicted one hundred enemy casualties and captured more than five hundred prisoners, while suffering fewer than twenty-five casualties.

While Grierson caused panic in Mississippi, Colonel Abel D. Streight led what was called a "poorly mounted horse and mule brigade" from middle Tennessee into Alabama, diverting the attention of the bloodthirsty Confederate cavalry leader, Nathan Bedford Forrest.

Finally, Grant ordered Sherman and his troops to carry out a fourth diversion just to the north of Vicksburg in the same spot they had unsuccessfully attacked only a few weeks previous. While Grant moved south with McClernand and McPherson, Sherman's

Fifteenth Corps threatened Vicksburg from the bluffs northeast of the city. On April 29, while eight naval gunboats bombarded the Confederate forts at nearby Haynes Bluff, Sherman debarked ten regiments and feigned an assault.

At the same time, Confederate Brigadier General John S. Bowen could see the Union naval ships gathering across the river from Grand Gulf, a few miles south of Vicksburg, preparing to transport the Union troops. Bowen urgently requested reinforcements from Pemberton. But Grant's fourfold deception had completely fooled the Vicksburg commander, who remained focused on Grierson and Sherman. With fear of an invasion elsewhere, he refused to send reinforcements south toward Grand Gulf until late on April 29, but they arrived too late to halt the amphibious crossing.

~

FROM PERSONAL MEMOIRS

Sherman had not left his position above Vicksburg yet. On the morning of the 27th I ordered him to create a diversion by moving his corps up the Yazoo and threatening an attack on Haynes Bluff.

My object was to compel Pemberton to keep as much force about Vicksburg as I could, until I could secure a good footing on high land east of the river. The move was eminently successful and, as we afterwards learned, created great confusion about Vicksburg and doubts about our real design. Sherman moved the day of our attack on Grand Gulf, the 29th, with ten regiments of his command and eight gunboats which Porter had left above Vicksburg.

He debarked his troops and apparently made every preparation to attack the enemy while the navy bombarded the main forts at Haynes Bluff. This move was made without a single casualty in either branch of the service.[169]

~

Sherman's diversion worked, and his troops suffered zero casualties. On May 1, he withdrew from his position north of Vicksburg and led his soldiers down the west bank of the Mississippi to be ferried across the river with the rest of Grant's forces.

The operation began as Porter's eight gunboats attacked the Confederate batteries on the high bluffs at Grand Gulf. After a pitched battle that lasted five and a half hours, with the loss of eighteen killed and fifty-seven wounded, the Union fleet silenced the guns of Fort Wade. But it could not reach the guns of Fort Coburn, which stood forty feet above the river behind a massive parapet. Grant watched the battle from the relative safety of a small tugboat. Unable to silence the Confederate battery, Porter eventually halted the attack.

Grant acknowledged the setback and continued to look for a passage to the south. At this point, the Union forces were aided— as they often were—by a local Black man.

~

FROM *PERSONAL MEMOIRS*

When the troops debarked, the evening of the 29th, it was expected that we would have to go to Rodney, about nine miles below, to find a landing; but that night a colored man came in who informed me that a good landing would be found at Bruinsburg, a few miles above Rodney, from which point there was a good road leading to Port Gibson some twelve miles in the interior. The information was found correct, and our landing was effected without opposition.[170]

~

On the morning of April 30, Grant moved down the Mississippi to Bruinsburg and began the transport of his troops. McClernand's troops had marched unobserved across the top of a levee under cover of night. "By the time it was light the enemy saw our whole fleet," Grant recalled, "iron-clads, gunboats, river steamers and barges, quietly moving down the river three miles below them, black, or rather blue, with National troops."[171]

Troops were crammed aboard gunboats, river steamers, coal barges, and the occasional bayou flatboat. Even the *Benton*, Porter's flagship, served as a ferry. Porter and Grant oversaw the transports a division at a time. By dusk, McClernand's entire corps had completed the mile-wide crossing, as had a division of McPherson's corps. Grant had moved twenty-three thousand men across the river to begin the land-based assault on Port Gibson.[172]

With a strong foothold on the eastern side of the great Mississippi River, Grant experienced a rare moment of joy in the midst of the campaign.

~

FROM *PERSONAL MEMOIRS*

When this was effected I felt a degree of relief scarcely ever equaled since. Vicksburg was not yet taken it is true, nor were its defenders demoralized by any of our previous moves. I was now in the enemy's country, with a vast river and the stronghold of Vicksburg between me and my base of supplies. But I was on dry ground on the same side of the river with the enemy. All the campaigns, labors, hardships and exposures from the month of December previous to this time that had been made and endured, were for the accomplishment of this one object.[173]

~

PRESSING INLAND

Once ashore, Grant pushed McClernand two miles inland to high, dry ground and then onward toward the town of Port Gibson, where a bridge crossed Big Bayou Pierre, leading to Grand Gulf. Grant saw this small but strategic hamlet as the perfect supply base on the Mississippi.

As McClernand moved to take the bridge at Port Gibson, Grant oversaw the transport of troops and vital supplies across the Mississippi deep into the night. Aided by the light of huge bonfires,

McPherson's soldiers were transported until a 3:00 a.m. collision between two transports stopped the operation until daylight.

McClernand's troops had advanced inland until they collided with a Confederate force of five thousand men and the Battle of Port Gibson commenced.[174] Grant arrived shortly after with young Fred, who rode his excited pony. The general oversaw the battle as it raged from early morning until nightfall. After months of labor on Grant's various experiments, the Union forces were ready for a brawl. They soon pushed the Confederates back into the city.

When night fell, the exhausted rebels abandoned Port Gibson. The next morning, Grant and his soldiers occupied the deserted town. Grant sent a dispatch to Army Chief of Staff Halleck in Washington, informing him that the battle was waged "over the most broken country I ever saw ... a series of irregular ridges divided by deep and impassable ravines, grown up with heavy timber, undergrowth and cane."[175]

Grant moved to place his troops between Pemberton and any possible Confederate reinforcements. The strategy was to keep the rebel forces divided and then to defeat them. Grant doggedly followed the plan he had developed during the winter months, deploying his troops with what he called "celerity"—what a later generation called "blitzkrieg."

General Sherman counseled Grant to wait for the wagon trains, but Grant had come to understand that an army's speed made all the difference in a battle. "I do not calculate upon the possibility of supplying the army with full rations from Grand Gulf," Grant wrote to Sherman. "I know it will be impossible without constructing additional roads. What I do expect is to get up what rations of hard bread, coffee, and salt we can, and make the country furnish the balance."[176]

Grant's strategy proved correct. Choosing speed of movement over the security of his wagon trains, he directed his army to live off the fat of the Mississippi countryside.

After the Confederates were defeated at Champion Hill, they withdrew into their stronghold at Vicksburg. In three weeks of battle, Grant's men marched 180 miles, won five battles, and captured some six thousand prisoners, all the while fighting a combined rebel force larger than their own.[177]

THE SIEGE

On the morning of May 18, Grant crossed the Big Black River and met Sherman. Greeting each other with a knowing smile, they turned their horses and rode together toward the strategic position on the Yazoo River northeast of Vicksburg, where they could establish another base for supplies from the Mississippi.[178] This was the same hill above Haynes Bluff that Sherman's troops had failed to take back in December—and where he feigned an assault from below only days before.

Sitting on his charger next to Sherman, Grant savored the moment.

~

FROM PERSONAL MEMOIRS

In a few minutes Sherman had the pleasure of looking down from the spot coveted so much by him the December before on the ground where his command had lain so helpless for offensive action. He turned to me, saying that up to this minute he had felt no positive assurance of success. This, however, he said was the end of one of the greatest campaigns in history and I ought to make a report of it at once. Vicksburg was not yet captured, and there was no telling what might happen before it was taken; but whether captured or not, this was a complete and successful campaign.[179]

~

The two generals took a rare break from the battle to smoke cigars and gaze down from the rolling hills on the land below with the Mississippi River in the distance. "Well Grant," Sherman said with a smile, "you are entitled to every bit of the credit for this campaign.

I opposed it. Why hell, I wrote you a letter about it. But here we are. Until this moment I never thought your expedition a success," he told his longtime friend. "I never could see the end clearly until now. But this is a campaign. This is a success, if we never take the town. Well done, General."[180]

The expression in Grant's face remained mostly unchanged, other than a slight lift of one side of his smile and a twinkle in his eyes—signs those closest to the general recognized as an outward hint of delight. "Sherman, your untiring energy and great efficiency during the campaign entitles you to a full share of all the credit due for its success," Grant replied.[181]

With his army encircling the beleaguered city, Grant informed Admiral Porter that the reduction of Vicksburg was underway. "My men are now investing Vicksburg. Sherman's forces run from the Mississippi River above the city two miles east. McPherson is to his left, and McClernand to the left of McPherson." Grant informed Porter that the Confederates were severely weakened by the recent battles. "The enemy have not been able to return to the city with one half of his forces. If you can run down and throw shell in just back of the lower part of the city, it would aid us and demoralize an already badly beaten enemy."[182]

For insurance against the concentration of Confederate forces, Grant posted Sherman in his rear with six divisions to arrest any move toward Vicksburg by General Joseph E. Johnston, whose army stood off a distance to the east. Johnston had urged Pemberton to give up the city and keep his army intact. Instead, Pemberton followed the advice of Confederate President Jefferson Davis and fought to the end to preserve the strategic garrison. Without adequate forces to attack, Johnston could do nothing but watch the inevitable unfold.

By June 11, Union forces blocked the last road between the two Confederate generals. Neither Johnston nor Pemberton were strong enough to break through the Union forces that divided them. "I am too weak to save Vicksburg," Johnston confessed to the besieged commander. "Can do no more than attempt to save you and your garrison. It will be impossible to extricate you unless you co-operate." Johnston sent the dispatch on May 29, but the messenger could not find a way through the Union stranglehold until June 13.

In the midst of incessant shelling, Pemberton replied on June 15, explaining that his troops were greatly fatigued but could hold out for another twenty days. "What aid am I to expect from you?"

For Johnston, the writing was on the wall. He had only thirty thousand men, minimal artillery, and limited transportation. At the same time, Grant's forces numbered about eighty thousand. On June 22, Johnston informed Pemberton that all roads leading to Vicksburg were blocked and he could do nothing to relieve the city. Grasping at straws, Johnston suggested that Pemberton attempt to escape across the Mississippi. But Porter's navy flotilla made such a maneuver impossible.

Withdrawing his forces, Johnston sent an explanation to Richmond. "The defeat of this little army would at once open Mississippi and Alabama to Grant."[183]

Pemberton was on his own.

THE NOOSE TIGHTENS

All food and supplies were cut off from the citizens of Vicksburg, who were reduced to eating dogs, cats, and mules. As the siege continued into late June, people trapped and ate the rats that filled the port city. Soldiers shared small rations of mule and horse meat, along with handfuls of rice, corn, and peas. In their weakened condition, rebel troops contracted scurvy and other maladies. As June turned into July, half of Pemberton's troops were taken out of commission by illness.[184]

Nonstop Union shelling from all directions forced Vicksburg residents underground into cellars or man-made caves carved out of the hillsides. Compelled by hunger and disease, Confederate soldiers surrendered on a daily basis.

On June 28, rebel deserters told one of Grant's division commanders there were only six days' rations left in the town. Pemberton, they said, had his eye on the Fourth of July. He planned to fire a salute to the Confederacy on Independence Day, then surrender. Grant believed them.

Grant resolved that if Pemberton did not quit by then, he would end the siege his own way. The Union commander had well-fed, rested soldiers, 220 artillery pieces, dozens of mortars, and boatloads of ammunition. Porter's gunboats would join in the barrage from the river. If Pemberton failed to surrender, the army would assault the stronghold on July 6.

By July 1, Pemberton's last hopes vanished. "Unless the siege of Vicksburg is raised, or supplies are thrown in," he warned his commanders, "it will become necessary very shortly to evacuate the place." With his garrison verging on mutiny, Pemberton reluctantly concluded he could not withstand the rumored assault.

Pemberton later wrote in his report: "If it should be asked why the 4th of July was selected as the day for surrender, the answer is obvious. I believed that upon that day I should obtain better terms. Well aware of the vanity of our foe, I knew they would attach vast importance to the entrance on the 4th of July into the stronghold of the great river, and that, to gratify their national vanity, they would yield then what could not be extorted from them at any other time."[185]

With only one day of rations remaining and his men too weak or sick to attempt a breakout, Pemberton finally yielded. At 10:00 a.m. on July 3, white flags appeared all along Confederate lines. Pemberton sent a message to Grant, asking for an armistice and the appointment of three commissioners from each side, who would negotiate the terms of capitulation. "I make this proposition to save the further effusion of blood."

Grant sent back much the same reply he had given General Simon Bolivar Buckner more than a year earlier at Fort Donelson. "The useless effusion of blood you propose stopping can be ended at any time you choose, by the unconditional surrender of the city."

Pemberton continued to seek better terms through the night, but Grant knew the Southerners were beaten. He issued an ultimatum: If the town did not surrender by 9:00 a.m. on July 4, he would consider his demands rejected.[186]

The besieging Union troops were eating breakfast the next morning when a messenger arrived at Grant's tent. The general sat at a table, writing. Fred sat on his army cot, nursing a leg wound. Grant opened the note the messenger handed to him, read it, sighed deeply, and looked up at his son. "Vicksburg has surrendered."[187]

Later, on that steamy Mississippi morning of July 4, 1863, Pemberton surrendered thirty-one thousand men and 172 pieces of artillery.

As Grant climbed up to the verandah on which the Confederate commander sat, Pemberton remained seated with his staff. A foreign observer, Comte de Paris, recorded his thoughts of the confrontation: "As victory put Grant in a position to be indifferent to this, he affected not to notice it, and, addressing Pemberton, asked him how many rations were needed for his army."[188]

Union quartermasters quickly distributed food to the famished Confederate troops. Food sources hoarded by certain Vicksburg citizens were also broken open and the contents dispersed throughout the city.

Charles A. Dana, Assistant Secretary of War and observer for the War Department, wired to Secretary of War Edwin Stanton: "Grant was received by Pemberton with marked impertinence. ... He bore it like a philosopher."

At 10:00 a.m., Pemberton ordered the Stars and Stripes hoisted over the Vicksburg battlement. Regiment after regiment marched out of the city to lay down their arms, with flags flying and bands playing.[189] The Union troops stood in respectful attention as the Confederate soldiers deposited their arms in stacks, then retreated to their lines. In all, more than forty-three thousand Southern men were taken prisoner from the time of the river crossing until the fall of the city.[190]

~

FROM *PERSONAL MEMOIRS*

At the appointed hour the garrison of Vicksburg marched out of their works and formed line in front, stacked arms and marched back in good order. Our whole army present witnessed this scene without cheering. Logan's division, which had approached nearest the rebel works, was the first to march in; and the flag of one of the regiments of his division was soon floating over the court-house.[191]

~

At noon Grant rode to the levee to meet Admiral Porter whose new flagship, the USS *Black Hawk*, was ablaze with multicolored banners and streamers. The crew had donned their dress white pants and blue jackets. Porter opened his wine locker to toast the victory, and Grant joined briefly in the celebration.

Soon the general quietly strolled to a corner of the vessel where he sat alone, calmly enjoying a fresh cigar. Years later, Porter remembered the poignant scene. "No one, to see him sitting there with that calm exterior amid all the jollity ... would ever have taken him for the great general who had accomplished one of the most stupendous military feats on record."[192]

The United States rewarded Ulysses S. Grant for the victory at Vicksburg by promoting him to the rank of major general in the regular army, the highest honor the nation could bestow.[193] When Lincoln heard of the fall of Vicksburg on July 7, he rejoiced as he proclaimed, "Grant is my man, and I am his, the rest of the war."[194]

Chapter Seven

IS IT CANCER?

As summer ended, William Vanderbilt encouraged the Grants to return to 3 East Sixty-Sixth Street. By early October, the Grants moved back into their former home, along with their son Fred and his family. Ulysses and Julia had separate bedrooms on the second floor. The third floor was occupied by Fred; his wife, Ida; Julia's namesake, Julia Dent Grant, age eight; and three-year-old Ulysses S. Grant III.

Soon Buck also moved in with his wife, Fannie, and their daughter, Miriam, who was two months younger than her cousin Ulysses.[195]

When the Grants arrived back in New York, Ulysses asked Adam Badeau to continue his work with Fred as an editor and researcher. The general offered Badeau a spare room in the house where "he would always be welcome." After everyone was settled, Grant asked Badeau to look over "the remaining articles for the *Century*."[196]

On the morning of October 20, 1884, four months after Grant first noticed the soreness of his throat, he went to see his family physician, Dr. Fordyce Barker, who had finally returned from Europe. Grant told Barker about his nagging throat pain and the difficulty of eating. The doctor conducted a preliminary examination of Grant's throat and noticed a suspicious swelling at the back of the general's tongue. But Barker did not want to make a diagnosis; instead, he gave the general his business card and sent him to see Dr. John Hancock Douglas, one of America's foremost throat specialists.[197]

Douglas had taken care of General John Rawlins, Grant's former military chief of staff, throughout his losing fight with tuberculosis. Douglas had also served as associate Secretary of the United States Sanitary Commission throughout the Civil War. He had met Grant at Fort Donelson, before the general became a national figure.[198]

Two days later, on October 22, General Grant walked into Doctor Douglas's office, observing the medical proprieties of the day by handing his army acquaintance the card from Doctor Barker. Douglas was a barrel-chested man with a full head of white hair and a beard like Thomas Nast's Santa Claus.

Grant could have gone to Douglas as soon as the problem emerged at Long Branch, but the general was aware of the well-known rules of professional etiquette among medical practitioners. Family and close friends knew Grant was particular about proprieties, especially where the feelings of other people were concerned.[199]

Holding the card from Dr. Barker in his hand, Douglas asked, "In what way can I be of service?" The general told him of the growing pain in his throat and the difficulty of swallowing certain foods and liquids. Douglas asked his patient to sit, then used a reflecting mirror for a detailed examination. Douglas later described Grant's throat tissue as a "dark, deep congestive hue, a scaly squamus inflammation, strongly suggestive of serious epithelial trouble." The tongue was somewhat rigid at the base on the right side.[200]

The cause of the pain was actually at the base of the tongue. In the tissue on the right side, Douglas found a dark swollen inflammation, some of it crusty, and the gland beneath the tissue was enlarged. He also identified some ulceration on the right tonsil. Checking the roof of his patient's mouth, he found an irritated area that appeared to be three small suspicious growths.[201]

Grant could read the result in the doctor's facial expression. "Is it cancer?" the general inquired.

"The question having been asked," Doctor Douglas later wrote, "I could give no uncertain, hesitating reply. I gave that which I believed, qualified with a hope. I realized that if he once found that I had deceived him, I could never reinstate myself in his good opinion. 'General, the disease is serious, epithelial in character, and sometimes capable of being cured.'"[202]

To ease the pain, Dr. Douglas coated Grant's throat and tongue with a solution of cocaine and water, which brought immediate relief. Although Douglas could give the general temporary freedom from the pain for the first time in weeks, he knew Grant's condition would grow worse. The pain would return more frequently until it became constant and excruciating.[203]

Douglas told Grant, whose house was two miles from the doctor's office, that he would have to come to him twice a day for treatment.[204] In addition to the cocaine water, Douglas would use iodoform as a disinfectant, which would aid in healing the ulcerated and inflamed tonsil. These daily treatments would temporarily allow Grant to sleep and to eat.[205]

From this preliminary examination, Douglas had already concluded that Grant's inflammation was cancerous. He believed the general's disease was malignant and would likely kill him. The carcinoma at the base of Grant's tongue would soon spread into his neck. In time it would become nearly impossible for the general to eat and, later, to breathe. After enduring excruciating pain, Grant would eventually die of hemorrhage, starvation, or strangulation.[206]

Douglas's carefully chosen words, "epithelial in character, and sometimes capable of being cured," meant only one thing to Grant—cancer, and most likely, a death sentence. Deep down, Grant knew it.

SECURING THE FUTURE

After receiving the shocking diagnosis, Grant and his valet, Harrison, boarded a public horse-drawn streetcar—to the surprise of the other passengers. Grant traveled across town to the offices of The Century Company's president, Roswell Smith. Grant knew his time was short, and he wanted to get his financial house in order as quickly as he could. During the meeting, Grant told Smith that he was ready to write his memoirs and hinted that more than one volume might be involved.

Grant understood that if he passed away before he could secure an income for Julia, she would struggle for the rest of her life. It was a race against the tolling bell of death, and on that day, the bell tolled loudly.

On the spot, Grant and Smith agreed to a verbal contract of a 10 percent royalty on each copy of his memoirs, with projected sales of twenty-five thousand copies. Smith promised Grant that a formal agreement would be drawn up, and in the interim Grant should finish the four articles they had already agreed to. These pieces could be later expanded for the final book.

Smith was overjoyed. "General Grant has just been in," he told his colleagues at the Century, "spent some time and wants us to publish his book or books." Smith went to work on a draft agreement for the book.[207] The Century Magazine's editor, Richard Watson Gilder, told Robert Johnson that Grant "ought not to be permitted to get too high an idea of immediate sales and profits. We have never had such a card before as Grant ... and we mustn't let that slip!"[208]

Adam Badeau observed that when the general returned from his visit to Douglas he seemed serious but not overly alarmed. The physician "had told him that his throat was affected by a complaint with a cancerous tendency," Grant explained, then went back to work on the next Century article.[209]

TREATMENT BEGINS

The next day General Grant gathered his crutches and with his ever-present shadow, Harrison, climbed aboard a public streetcar to go to his appointment with Dr. Douglas. The passengers were startled to be on the bus with the former president of the United States, but Grant could no longer afford private carriages.[210]

The general did not inform Julia of the physician's diagnosis for several days, but she grew suspicious of her husband's departures at the same time every day. Confronting Harrison, she learned of her husband's daily visits with Dr. Douglas.

Accompanied by Fred, Julia went to see the throat specialist herself. In a gentle tone, Douglas explained that their loved one

had cancer, that it was painful, and that it would become excruciating. He charted the likely course of the disease. He told them
that many patients rallied in mid-course, but then suffered setbacks
as the cancer continued to invade the body. He also warned that
Grant's emotional state would shift from depression to hope and
back again.[211]

"I then went myself to the specialist and learned the dreadful
truth but still could not believe the malady was a fatal one," Julia
later wrote. "I asked again and again if it were not curable and was
answered that there had been instances when it had been cured.
Then hope returned to me. My husband was healthy, temperate,
strong. Why should he not be well and strong again? ... Down in
my heart, I could not believe that God in his wisdom and mercy
would take this great, wise, good man from us, to whom he was so
necessary and so beloved. It could not be, and I surely thought he
would recover."[212]

The doctor instructed Julia and Fred on how to apply the pain-
killers and warned them how to avoid irritating the throat even
further. At the end of their visit, Douglas told Julia and Fred that
the disease would take a long course but that, in the end, Grant
would die.[213]

Inconsolable, Julia left the office in tears. Fred stayed behind a
few minutes to thank Dr. Douglas for his aid and to assure him that
they would do whatever necessary to care for his father.

During the next two months, the general's pain and congestion
temporarily diminished with the added care of the doctor and his
family. Although he visited Douglas almost daily, Grant continued
to work diligently on his memoirs.[214]

A DEFINING DIAGNOSIS

Over the next few weeks, Douglas consulted with Grant's personal
physician, Dr. Fordyce Barker, and with two other specialists, Dr.
Henry Sands and Dr. T. M. Markoe. All three agreed with Douglas's
diagnosis, confirming his initial thoughts about Grant's condition
and the needed medical treatment.

To arrive at a definitive diagnosis, Douglas froze a portion of Grant's ulcerated throat and snipped a sample. He sent the specimen to one of the country's leading microbiologists, Dr. George Shrady, for a biopsy. To guard against influencing Shrady's opinion, Douglas did not identify his patient.[215]

After examining the tissue, Shrady met with Douglas. "This specimen comes from the throat and base of the tongue and is affected with cancer," Shrady announced clinically.

Douglas replied, "Are you sure?"

"Perfectly sure. This patient has a lingual epithelioma—cancer of the tongue."

"This patient is General Grant," Douglas said.

Shrady paused to process this revelation, then answered with a note of sadness: "Then General Grant is doomed."[216]

As the disease quickly spread through the general's throat and neck, his doctors gathered for a formal consultation. They planned to examine the patient and then discuss the option of an operation to remove the cancerous tissue with the goal of buying time.[217] Those present included Grant's family physician and long-trusted friend, Dr. Barker, along with Dr. Douglas, Dr. Shrady, and Dr. Sands.

Grant was clearly anxious as the consultation began, so Shrady looked for a way to ease the tension: "Each in turn made a very formal and careful examination of the throat of the patient," Dr. Shrady later wrote, "using for the purpose the ordinary circular reflecting mirror fastened to the forehead by a band around the observer's head. Very few words were exchanged by the little group. There seemed to be a strain about the procedure which plainly affected the patient. Dr. Sands, as well as the others present, duly appreciated this and were evidently desirous of diverting the patient's mind from the real object of the visit. Accordingly, when he handed me the mirror, he remarked in his quiet off-handed manner, that whenever I followed him in such an examination, it was necessary to enlarge the head loop to give extra accommodation for thickness of hair.

"As an opportunity was thus afforded to start a conversation of some sort between us, I ventured to suggest that hair did not always make the difference, nor the mere size of the skull, as sometimes the best brains were very closely packed in very small quarters. At this the general gave a faint smile for the first time during the meeting."[218]

After the examination ended, the doctors met in private to share their conclusions. Shrady advised against operating on Grant, explaining that the cancerous tissue at the back of his tongue was already growing, had ruptured and spread cancer through the surrounding area. An operation would do the patient absolutely no good and would only increase Grant's discomfort. Shrady believed that over the next months, Grant would go through periods of excruciating pain, relieved by short spells of exhaustion. The end would come soon, within a year at the most, perhaps much sooner. Douglas agreed with Shrady's diagnosis.[219]

"With the first formal consultation of the surgical staff, the advisability of an operation was thoroughly discussed, and arguments were made against any such efforts to relieve him," Shrady later wrote. "Thus the treatment of the case was narrowed to such efforts as might be necessary to guard against possible complications and to make him as comfortable as possible by assuaging his pain and keeping his throat clear of an accidental accumulation of secretions. ... The wisdom of such a decision was manifested in sparing him unnecessary mutilation and allowing him to pass the remainder of his days in comparative comfort. Relatively, however, it meant suffering for him until the end."[220]

THE SLOW DECLINE

Fearing for his wife's financial future, Grant had numerous discussions with George Childs on his thoughts of what the prospective sale of the memoirs might bring. Barely covering their monthly bills, the Grants gave up their pew at their Madison Avenue church, telling friends he was forced to do so "because of my inability to pay the rent."[221]

In recruiting his friend and former aide Adam Badeau to become his editor and research assistant, Grant had promised him $5,000 out of the first $20,000 that the book earned, then $5,000 out of the next $10,000. Grant sheepishly told Badeau that he was bankrupt and could not offer more. Badeau was reluctant to agree, fearing the general's memoirs would overshadow his own recent three-volume work. He was finally worn down by his loyalty to Grant.

The general made it clear that Badeau would provide research and editing services, but that Grant himself would be the one and only author. "I am going to do it myself," he told a visitor one day. "If I do not do it myself it will not be mine."[222]

After several weeks of working side by side with the general, Badeau described Grant's physical condition as debilitated but still tolerable. "He was crippled and unable to move without crutches, but he walked out alone, and he had driven me once or twice at Long Branch behind his own horse. He gave up driving, however, after his return to town. But he was cheerful; his children and grandchildren were a great solace to him; many friends came in to see him and to testify their undiminished respect."

Within a few weeks of Douglas's diagnosis, Grant's health and strength started to fade. Badeau soon revised his estimate of Grant's health, saying that "he complained constantly of pains in his throat."[223]

Grant wrapped a shawl around his neck, both for comfort and to hide the growing cancer that had become visible. To stay warm and to fight bouts of neuralgia, he often covered his head with a simple knit cap, the kind people wear while skating on a frozen pond.

On most days, Grant worked from the early morning until well into the evening in the room at the head of the stairs on the second floor of his New York City home. Two windows looked out onto Sixty-Sixth Street, which provided the light for his work and a soothing view of beautiful Central Park just down the street. His bedroom was connected by a doorway at the back of the library, and beyond it was Julia's room. The general labored at a small desk filled with piles of notes Badeau and Fred compiled for him.[224] "He worked often five, and six, and seven hours a day," Badeau observed.[225]

The second floor of 3 East Sixty-Sixth Street became a literary assembly line. As Ulysses wrote in the front room near the light of the window, Fred and Badeau edited or compiled research materials in the next room from books written on the Mexican War and the Civil War. Badeau also used his own work as a reference.[226] Badeau and Fred placed a series of maps, arranged in chronological order, on a nearby folding table so Grant could refer to them as needed. The general also kept a copy of *The Memoirs of General William T. Sherman* at his desk for reference.[227] In the beginning, Grant wrote his memoirs in his own hand on sheets of lined loose-leaf paper.[228]

In the evening and overnight hours, Grant made notes to remind himself of small details and anecdotes from his life and his campaigns to work on the next day. Badeau compiled a stack of his own notes. Then the two discussed how these ideas would fit into the evolving outline of the book. After that, Grant decided on the direction of the book. Most days he wrote with quiet determination, unless the pain became too great. Only the general knew how much pain he was in, as he masked it from others—especially his wife.[229]

FAMILY STRENGTH

Julia spent much of each day in her bedroom, knowing that her Ulys was fully aware of her presence. When he wrote a passage that particularly pleased him, he called to Julia in his weakening voice, asking her to come in and let him read it to her.[230]

At the conclusion of each writing session, he forwarded the pages he had written to be edited or revised. Fred and Badeau both made comments, and then the general either included or rejected the additions in the next session. In the evening, Grant reviewed the day's work and, with Badeau and Fred, planned for the next.[231]

Occasionally, Badeau became argumentative about the general's decisions. At that point, Grant simply stopped talking to him and turned his attention back to his writing. After a moment, the short-tempered Badeau stormed from the room.[232]

As they had done for many years in their marriage, Ulysses read aloud to Julia toward the end of the evening as long as his voice held out.[233] General Grant's voice was soft, deep, and distinct, and his speech deliberate, quiet, and even-toned.[234] Julia cherished this time alone with the man she had called "Victor" ever since his triumph at Vicksburg, and occasionally she offered suggestions.[235]

STEADY DECLINE

While Grant worked diligently for hours at a time, the cancer's effect on his strength was apparent. His cough worsened, his throat seemed always aflame, and his voice failed from time to time.[236] Swallowing solid food became nearly impossible, so Harrison brought the general milk on a tray twice each day to help maintain his strength. Julia and Harrison insisted that he drink it, as it was one of the few sources of nourishment he received—but even drinking milk had become excruciating.

Family meals, once the highlight of the day in the Grant household, became depressing episodes for the general. Adam Badeau later wrote, "I shall always recall his figure as he sat at the head of the table, his head bowed over his plate, his mouth set grimly, his features clinched in the endeavor to conceal the expression of pain, especially from Mrs. Grant, who sat at the other end. He no longer carved or helped the family, and at last was often obliged to leave before the meal was over, pacing the hall or the adjoining library in his agony. At this time he said to me that he had no desire to live if he was not to recover. He preferred death at once to lingering, hopeless disease."[237]

Harrison became a silent sentinel, sitting in a corner a few yards from where the general worked. He often sensed what his employer needed and rose quietly to attend to him. He readjusted the shawl that Grant kept constantly wrapped around his throat as needed and then resumed his quiet vigil. He continued to accompany Grant on his visits to the doctor's office and assumed the duty of keeping track of when and in what quantity Grant's medicines were to be taken. Becoming more of a nurse than a valet, he added the swabbing of Grant's throat with cocaine water to his other duties.

By November, Grant was in constant pain. In addition to his throat ailment, he had a severe attack of neuralgia, causing extreme pain in his cheek, jaw, teeth, and gums. To relieve this new source of pain, the dentist extracted several teeth without anesthesia. Harrison made sure the general—in agony after the procedure—returned home safely.[238] At least the ordeal of the extractions made it easier for Dr. Douglas to clean the general's throat during his daily appointments.[239]

Grant stubbornly refused Julia's advice that he take a carriage instead of a horse-drawn public carriage for his daily visits to Dr. Douglas. That changed with the coming of colder weather. In his weakened state, Grant was much more susceptible to disease in the winter months. Both Dr. Douglas and Dr. Shrady decided it was best to make daily calls to the Grant home. These visits were brief and formal, since both doctors understood the importance of the general's writing and did not want to divert his attention from the work for too long.

They stayed only when he insisted. Over the weeks, Grant grew to enjoy their company. He looked forward to the daily diversions and often shared his thoughts on the war and other subjects of interest. Talking about the Civil War became a way for him to both refresh his memory and to think through the reasons for his decisions at the time.[240]

The effects of the disease multiplied. When he lay down to sleep, he was overcome with a sensation of strangulation, so he was forced to sleep sitting up in a leather armchair with his legs resting in another armchair facing him.[241] He retained the soldierly fashion of merely covering the lower portion of his body.[242] The uncomfortable position coupled with his growing pain made it difficult for him to sleep through the night.[243] Added to his other maladies, exhaustion amplified the challenge of completing his memoirs.

Despite these hardships, Grant was determined to finish the work that would provide income for his family after his death. The speed of his writing had increased, partly because Grant gained confidence as a writer but also because he was driven to complete the task before he became incapacitated by illness.

Writing the introduction to *Personal Memoirs*, Grant explained, "The first volume, as well as a portion of the second, was written before I had reason to suppose I was in a critical condition of health. Later I was reduced almost to the point of death, and it became impossible for me to attend to anything for weeks. I have, however, somewhat regained my strength, and am able, often, to devote as many hours a day as a person should devote to such work. I would have more hope of satisfying the expectation of the public if I could have allowed myself more time."[244]

As he soldiered on, time became a wraith, hovering over him as he wrote during the day and haunting him during his sleepless, pain-filled nights. When he became too exhausted to write, Grant scribbled notes on what he wanted to accomplish the following day—knowing every day could be his last.

Chapter Eight

MARK TWAIN

NOVEMBER 1884—NEW YORK CITY

Like most Americans, Mark Twain watched the fall of Grant & Ward with astonishment. A personal friend of the general, Twain often visited the Sixty-Sixth Street house to pass time talking and smoking a cigar. Ferdinand Ward's crime against the entire Grant family infuriated the famous author.

He did not know, however, that Grant was also fighting a battle with cancer.

Twain's new book, *Huckleberry Finn*, would be released in December from the publishing company he established to control his work—Charles L. Webster and Company, named after the husband of Twain's niece. Webster was also the firm's business director. But there was a buzz in the air regarding a book by Grant, and Twain advised young Webster to compete for the general's memoirs if the opportunity arose.[245]

To promote *Huckleberry Finn* and to raise money for the struggling publishing house, Twain performed at New York's Chickering Hall early in November 1884. As he and his wife were leaving the building that night, he bumped into Richard Watson Gilder, who invited them to a late supper at his house. Twain had struck a deal to publish portions of *Huckleberry Finn* in *The Century*, so he was delighted to dine with the editor.

"We were there an hour or two," Twain later remembered, "and in the course of the conversation Gilder said that General Grant had written three war articles for the *Century* and was going to write a fourth. I pricked up my ears."

Gilder went on to describe how General Grant had entertained the proposition to write. He explained "... how poor he evidently was and how eager to make some trifle of bread and butter money and how the handing him a check for $500 for the first article had manifestly gladdened his heart and lifted from it a mighty burden."

Twain was flabbergasted.

"Admirable man as Gilder certainly is," he wrote in his autobiography, "and with a heart which is in the right place, it had never seemed to occur to him that to offer General Grant $500 for a magazine article was not only the monumental insult of the nineteenth century, but of all centuries. He ought to have known that if he had given General Grant a check for $10,000 the sum would still have been trivial; that if he had paid him $20,000 for a single article the sum would still have been inadequate."[246]

Gilder was so delighted with what he believed was a literary coup that he explained the whole arrangement to Twain, who was himself a publisher of books. What Gilder did not know is that Twain—like so many others—was interested in securing a contract with Grant. The famous author was not only prepared to publish Grant's memoirs but also eager to do so.

A Meeting of Titans

The following morning Samuel Clemens called at 3 East Sixty-Sixth Street to "smoke a cigar." "I went straight to General Grant's house next morning and told him what I had heard. He said it was all true."[247]

"General, if, as I have heard, you are writing a book I hope you make a good sum for yourself and family." Twain then explained his long, painful experience in bookmaking and publishing. "If there would be no impropriety in his showing me the rough contract I believed I might be useful."

Grant had no objection to showing Twain the contract, since the arrangement with The Century Company had proceeded no further than a mere consideration of its details without promises given or received on either side. He added that he supposed that the Century offer was fair and right and that he had been expecting to accept it and conclude the bargain.[248]

Fred had entered the room during the conversations and agreed to read the proposed terms aloud. When he came to a stipulation that Grant would get 10 percent of the sales price of each copy sold, Twain stopped him. "Strike out the ten per cent and put twenty per cent in its place. Better still, put seventy-five per cent of the net returns in its place."

Both Ulysses and Fred Grant were dumbfounded by the suggestion, and the general shook his head. "The Century Company would never go along with that."

"General," Twain replied, "while the Century people know how to sell magazines, they do not understand that the way to sell a book like yours is by advertising it for sale by subscription—with the readers committing themselves in advance to buying their copies—rather than just printing books and placing them on the shelves of bookstores. There is not a reputable publisher in American who would not be very glad to pay twenty percent or even seventy-five percent for a book by such a colossus as General Grant."

Reading on, Clemens was also bewildered by an "offensive detail" buried in the Century contract. Part of Grant's 10 percent would be withheld for, as Twain said, "clerk hire, house rent, sweeping out the offices, or some such nonsense as that." He insisted that Grant should have three-fourths of the profits, with no deductions.[249]

"I didn't know whether to cry or laugh," Twain later wrote. He was amazed that The Century Company had the audacity to offer a two-term former president and the savior of the Union such an offer. If Samuel Clemens knew anything, he knew the publishing business. He was confident that Grant's memoirs would sell hundreds of thousands of copies.

"If I had not been acquainted with the Century people I should have said that this was a deliberate attempt to take advantage of a man's ignorance and trusting nature, to rob him," Twain wrote. "But I do know the Century people and therefore I know that they had no such base intentions as these but were simply making their offer out of their boundless resources of ignorance and stupidity."

That day in the general's home, Twain said, "General Grant, the Century offer is simply absurd and should not be considered for an instant." He repeated his recommendation that Grant cross out the 10 percent and write in 75 percent of the net returns in its place. "If you place these terms before the Century people they would accept them."[250]

"My dear Mr. Clemens," Grant interrupted. "I can't imagine the Century people accepting these terms."

"Well, if they are afraid to accept them, you will simply need to offer them to any great publishing house in the country." He paused to let the Grants comprehend the notion. "And not one would decline them," he concluded.[251]

Grant challenged Twain to be specific and to name a publisher who would, in fact, give him everything that Twain said he could get. "Frank Bliss's American Publishing Company would doubtless jump at this chance," Twain responded.[252]

Grant was shocked at these numbers and asked if Twain could prove his position. Twain answered that he could furnish the proof by telegraph in six hours.

Fred Grant was impressed. He knew that the American Publishing Company had profitably released several of Twain's books. He did not want his father to be hoodwinked again, and he warmed to Clemens's proposal.

General Grant, however, fell back on his military code of loyalty, telling Twain that he had been dealing with one or another of The Century Magazine's staff for months. By backing out, he "did not want to be thought of as dishonest or as a thief, a 'robber of a publisher.'"[253]

"If you regard that as a crime it is because your education has been neglected," Twain responded with a slight laugh. "It is not a crime, and it is always rewarded in heaven with two halos."[254]

Grant was impressed by Twain's argument. "But I am distressed at the idea of not giving the book to the people who had first suggested it."

"In that case, it belongs to me," Clemens replied with a smile, "for you will recall that long ago I urged you to write your memoirs."[255]

In January 1881, Samuel Clemens had paid a visit to Grant at his 2 Wall Street office, accompanied by his friend, author, editor, and literary critic William Dean Howells. During the conversation, Twain suggested that Grant write a book about his life and career.[256]

"The same suggestion you make has been frequently made by others," Grant responded, "but never entertained for a moment. In the first place I have always distrusted my ability to write anything that would satisfy myself, and the public would be much more difficult to please. In the second place I am not possessed of the kind of industry necessary to undertake such a work."

Adam Badeau was currently writing his three-volume work on Grant's wartime experiences. John Russell Young, the *New York Herald* reporter who had followed Grant around the world, had recently published a book on that journey. "It would be unfair to them for me to do anything now that would in any way interfere with the sale of their work," he told Clemens. "Then too they have done it much better than I could if I was to try."

At that time, Grant could see that Clemens was disappointed, so he tried to mollify his friend in a note. "If I ever settle down in a house of my own I may make notes which some one of my children may use after I am gone." He would do nothing before then, however. "I am very much obliged to you for your kind suggestions and for the friendship which inspires them and will always appreciate both."[257]

Now, three years later, and in the wake of the Grant & Ward failure, the general was beginning to understand the scale of what Clemens was talking about. Julia faced a life of struggle if Grant died in his present financial condition. But the general was still conflicted by a sense of loyalty to the Century people. Fred tried to ease his mind. "Father, nothing could be lost by considering the matter for another twenty-four hours."

Grant agreed.[258]

A PLAN OF BATTLE

Overnight, Clemens developed his business plan. He would sell the Grant memoir by subscription, requiring readers to pay in advance of publication and enlisting subscription agents to go door-to-door. The plan diminished the risk to the publisher, while it was ideal for an author like Grant, who was already well known. Many people would buy the book simply because they liked Grant and his history. Twain understood that more than a million men had served under Grant, and millions of others had voted for him. From this pool, several hundred thousand would undoubtedly want to buy his book.[259]

"I wanted the general's book and I wanted it very much," Twain wrote later, "but I had very little expectation of getting it. I supposed that he would lay these new propositions before the Century people, that they would accept immediately, and that there the matter would end, for the general evidently felt under great obligations to the Century people for saving him from the grip of poverty by paying him $1,500 for three magazine articles which were well worth $100,000. He seemed wholly unable to free himself from this sense of obligation."

Twain went back to Grant's home the following morning, finding the general in a good mood but still not persuaded by his arguments. Twain then unveiled a new proposal. "Give me the book on the terms which I have already suggested that you make with the Century people."[260] Grant was skeptical. He had talked to his friend, General Sherman, who said he had made $25,000 from his memoir. Grant doubted he could do that well. Clemens asked why. Grant said he had offered to sell his memoir for that amount to the Century people and Roswell Smith had nearly fainted.

Clemens saw his opportunity. "Sell me the memoirs, General. I am a publisher. I will pay double the price. I have a checkbook in my pocket. Take my check for fifty thousand dollars now and let's draw the contract." He went on to say that he could make an initial $100,000 on the book in six months. Somewhat bemused, Grant told Twain that he regarded him as a friend and did not want him to lose money on a risky venture.[261] He said the book might be a failure, and he did not want him to carry all the risk.

Clemens once again explained the subscription model and how it reduced the risk. Again he specified his terms: "Seventy-five per cent of the profits on the publication goes to you, I to pay all running expenses such as salaries, etc., out of my fourth."

Grant asked what Clemens thought would be left out of his fourth. "A hundred thousand dollars in six months," Clemens replied confidently.[262]

"Take my check for fifty thousand dollars now, and let's draw the contract."[263]

It took Grant some time to comprehend both the wisdom and the fairness of Twain's offer.

Clemens sweetened the deal by offering to give the general living expenses as he composed the book. He went on to offer the unemployed Jesse Grant a job with Charles L. Webster and Company. Grant was consumed with worry over the future of his three sons, who had not been able to find gainful employment since the collapse of Grant & Ward, and so Twain's offer was very meaningful.[264]

Grant ruminated on this astounding offer. Finally he looked up and said that he would consult with George Childs, whose lawyer had already studied a version of the Century contract. Childs would do a study of the leading competitors to see who could do the best job for the general. And Fred would go along to oversee the entire investigation.

Twain agreed that this was just what Grant should do.

TELL US YOUR BEST OFFER

After three days of further contemplation, Grant wrote to Childs: "On re-examining the contract prepared by the Century people I see that it is all in favor of the publisher, with nothing left for the Author. I am offered very much more favorable terms by the Charles L. Webster and Company."

He then added, "Mark Twain is the Company."[265]

Colonel Fred Grant, a longtime friend of Twain, could see that his was the superior offer. After hearing Twain's argument, he became strongly opposed to letting the Century people have the book and favored Twain's proposal instead.

The general's first magazine article on the Battle of Shiloh had immediately added 50,000 names to *The Century Magazine*'s list of subscribers. This confirmed Twain's claim that the Century people would still have made a profit if they had paid General Grant $50,000 for the articles. They could expect to keep most of these subscribers for several years, which would reap a profit from them in the end of at least $100,000.

Besides this increased circulation, the number of *The Century Magazine*'s advertising pages doubled—a huge addition to the magazine's cash income. Recognizing the obvious growth as a result of Grant's article, *The Century*'s editors eventually added to the original check of $1,500 a check for $1,000, knowing they were going to make a fortune out of the first of the three articles.

"This seemed a fine liberality to General Grant, who is the most simple-hearted of all men," Twain wrote, "but to me it seemed merely another exhibition of incomparable nonsense, as the added check ought to have been for $30,000 instead of $1,000." When it came to business, Twain, like so many others, saw Ulysses S. Grant as a "babe in the woods."

While the Grants negotiated with the Century people and Charles Webster, Twain headed out west to promote *Huckleberry Finn* through a lecture tour. While he was away, propositions from publishers poured into the Grant home almost daily, confirming Twain's predictions concerning interest in the general's memoirs.

All the proposals shared a common clause: "Only tell us what your best offer is and we stand ready to make a better one."

Chapter Nine

WINTER OF DISCONTENT

As Dr. Douglas predicted, with the onset of debilitating painful symptoms, Grant experienced severe depression. He stopped working on the memoirs; instead, he sat in his armchair, hands folded, staring blankly into space.[266] The general may have been overwhelmed not only by the battle with the pain but also by the thought that the 1884 holiday season would likely be his final Christmas with Julia and the family.

Rarely moving, he didn't smile or talk, and he was unable to work. Sometimes he looked out the front window onto East Sixty-Sixth Street at nothing in particular. Julia checked on him from time to time and rearranged his pillow.

General Sherman visited that December, finding Ulysses in a state of apathy. Julia was beside herself, worrying about her husband's withdrawal "into a silent moody state looking the picture of woe." To cheer her, Sherman reminded Julia that this was exactly the way Grant behaved during the Civil War as he planned each battle. He sat for hours under the flap of his tent in deep contemplation as battles raged about him.

Sherman assured Julia that her husband would emerge from this stage and be ready to celebrate Christmas with the family, then he climbed the stairs to meet with his fellow warrior. The visit cheered Grant, who valued their friendship.

During this dark period, both Fred Grant and Adam Badeau were forced to wait as they watched the general's mood swing back and forth. "In December his pains became still more excruciating," Badeau later wrote. "He could not swallow without torture, and his sufferings at table were intense."[267]

When George Childs invited the Grants to visit him in Philadelphia for a week, Grant gracefully declined. "The doctor will not allow me to leave until the weather gets warmer. Nothing gives me so much pain as swallowing water.[268] If you can imagine what molten lead would be going down your throat, that is what I feel when swallowing."[269]

Badeau joined Julia in wondering if Grant had given up. "[He] often sat for hours propped in his chair, with his hands clasped, looking at the blank wall before him. It was like a man gazing into his open grave. He was in no way dismayed, but the sight was to me the most appalling I have ever witnessed—the conqueror looking at his inevitable conqueror; the stern soldier to whom so many armies had surrendered, watching the approach of the enemy before whom even he must yield."[270]

Grant was gripped by violent coughing spells. At times he coughed so hard that he could barely breathe. As night approached, his coughing and wheezing continued until, in a state of exhaustion, the general mercifully fell asleep.[271]

Dr. Douglas had warned Julia to expect the worst, and she was ever mindful that her husband's despondency was another aspect of his illness. Grant would sometimes feel like giving up, the doctor had said. He would refuse to eat, be unable to sleep, reject his work, and become fatalistic. This was normal mental preparation for a terminally ill patient. Eventually, Douglas believed, Grant would accept the inevitability of his illness and work through the pain.[272]

A DEFEATED GENERAL

In all the battles of the Civil War, Grant had never appeared defeated. So Julia, Fred, and Badeau were shaken to see Ulysses being overwhelmed by the advent of this death sentence.

Douglas knew that Grant's descent into depression would either lead to his quick death or that he would revive and use his impending demise as motivation to complete his memoirs.[273] Grant looked forward to the daily visits of Dr. Douglas and Dr. Shrady. The general quickly bonded with these two men and soon the doctors became his confidants.

"When I first visited him," Shrady later wrote, "he was somewhat reduced in flesh and had a decidedly sick and dejected look, which told of his mental and physical suffering. He was seated in a leather arm-chair in one corner of his library in his house at No. 3 East Sixty-Sixth Street, New York, and he wore a loose, woolen morning gown and an ordinary smoking-cap of the same material.

"It was not until he bared his head and showed his broad, square forehead and the characteristic double-curved brow-lock that his actual presence could be realized. The difference in the respect between the lower and the upper part of his face was to me most striking and distinctive. There was the broad and square lower jaw, and close-cropped full beard, the down-curved corners of the firmly closed mouth, the small, straight nose with the gradual droop at its tip, the heavily browed and penetrating deep-blue eyes."[274]

Shrady recognized Grant's struggle with depression. "He had a great burden to bear in the contemplation of the ultimate doom that awaited him. Although he defiantly and bravely awaited the final termination of his sufferings, there were many occasions when he became mentally depressed. At such times he was ominously silent, and would sit gazing abstractly into space, and be in essence and substance the silent introspective man.

"When attempts were made to arouse him from such depressing reveries he would merely reply in monosyllables, as if desiring in a courteous way to be left to himself. Often in apparent desperation, he would take to a game of solitaire, and for hours would be quietly fighting a battle with himself."[275]

In the depth of his depression, Grant was unable to focus on the book project. Sometimes he would start writing, only to find he did not have the energy or will to continue. After an ineffectual effort, he gave up in despair.

"What seemed to annoy him most was the teasing pain in his throat and his difficulty in swallowing," Shrady observed. "When these symptoms were prominent, the mental depression was proportionately pronounced. His only concern was lest he might choke in his sleep. This possibility was so constantly in his thoughts that it was frequently necessary to comfort him with positive assurances to the contrary. His 'choking spells' so often mentioned in the bulletins were nevertheless very distressing, and, although temporarily demoralizing to his pluck, were never attended with immediate danger of absolute suffocation."[276]

Always a fighter, Grant finally concluded that he could wallow in self-pity or face his foe and do what needed to be done to save his family from its desperate financial condition. As he had done so many times, he pulled himself out of the doldrums and determined to fight.

A FINAL CHRISTMAS

As Christmas approached, Grant slowly emerged from the darkness. "His wonderful self-control, which seldom deserted him, not only made him the least complaining, but the most dutiful, of patients," Shrady observed:

> The study of his different moods in his long wait for death was a revelation in resignation which could never go unheeded.
>
> To fit oneself to the burden of sickness requires time and patience. It was at first hard for him to submit to the inevitable. View the situation as he might, there was still the ominous shadow over his immediate future. The willing submission to fate strains the strongest philosophy. Still, like others under like circumstances, he resolved to face the enemy, and trust to adapting himself to new conditions.
>
> This explained his deep gloom when the real nature of his malady was first announced to him. It was this discipline that was necessary for the few working days left to him. The only relief in the situation was to make the most of the remaining opportunities, and stubbornly persist to the end.
>
> Then came the reaction that readjusted the burden. Becoming more used to the mental depression, it was the more easily borne. He admitted that fact, and bravely trudged along under heavy marching orders. It thus became his necessity to devote himself afresh to the completion of his memoirs.[277]

Grant made it clear he intended to fight, declaring to Badeau, "I am not going to commit suicide."[278] He went back to work and found renewed joy in his writing life. Soon he was once again devoting four or five hours daily to his memoirs.[279]

"He liked to have his pages read aloud to the family in the evenings," Badeau recalled, "so that he might hear how they sounded and hear their comments." This was often done by Julia, a reverse of the habit from most of their marriage where Ulysses had read to his wife in the evening hours, although Fred, Ida, or others would also do the reading at times.

The grandchildren were the other tonic for Grant. "Daily about one o'clock he was interrupted by his grandchildren who stopped as they passed to their lunch," wrote Badeau. "They came, indeed, like a burst of light into the sick man's study, three of them, dancing, gamboling, laughing—as pretty a brood of merry, graceful grandchildren as ever a conqueror claimed for descendants, or looked upon to perpetuate his name."[280]

"I shall never forget the frolic with the little ones on Christmas Day," Badeau remembered. "They all came to dinner, and the two youngest sat on each side of him. He was comparatively free from pain." The children led the conversation with glee at the day's festivities. "When their mamas endeavored to check them, the general interposed and declared that this was their day. So they prattled across their grandpapa, and made preposterous attempts at jokes … and no one [laughed] more heartily than the great warrior, their progenitor. It was a delicious morsel of sweet in the midst of so much bitter care, a gleam of satisfaction in the gloom of that sad winter, with its fears, and certainties, and sorrows."[281]

CORRECTING THE RECORD

After the holidays, the general was back to work in his small study. His goal in writing the memoirs was to reveal the true history rather than to embellish his own reputation as so many other military histories had done. Grant was a stickler for the facts. This often slowed the process as Ulysses, Fred, and Badeau scanned the records looking for exact details.

Once Grant set to work on the book, he determined to make it as readable and accurate as possible. His style of writing was clear and concise. His time was limited, so he did not waste time on anything unnecessary. As a result, his writing improved as he went on.[282]

While the general was motivated to provide for his wife and family after his death, he also had a larger vision for the book itself. He knew he needed to address the myths and outright lies that had grown concerning the Civil War and what became known as Reconstruction.

Since the 1870s, when as president he led the fight to silence the Ku Klux Klan and protect the former slaves throughout the South, Grant had become the target of the "Lost Cause" school of historians and writers. This group of Southern sympathizers were embarrassed to admit that the Civil War was about slavery, so they tried to change the narrative, saying the war was about states' rights and tariffs. Regarding the true cause embraced by the Confederate States of America—slavery—Grant declared it was "one of the worst for which a people ever fought, and one for which there was the least excuse."[283]

At the same time, the Lost Cause writers worked both to build the reputation of their general, Robert E. Lee, into what was called "the marble model" and to dismiss the accomplishments of Ulysses S. Grant. Instead of recognizing that Grant was the strategic genius who orchestrated the surrender of three rebel armies and ultimately the defeat of the Confederacy through a national concerted effort, conceived and directed by him, the Lost Cause writers labeled Grant a "butcher" who mindlessly wore down the South with overwhelming northern resources and men.

After the assassination of Abraham Lincoln, Grant took up the torch of freedom for all Americans.

When it came to civil rights, Grant was decades ahead of his time. In the 1868 presidential election, as a Republican, Grant won the office with the slogan, "Let Us Have Peace." Republicans also won a majority in Congress. With control of all three branches of government, the Republicans pushed through the Fifteenth Amendment, guaranteeing the right to vote to Black men throughout the country. Grant had pushed hard for its passage, telling delegates from the first national Black political convention in Washington that as president he would ensure that "the colored people of the Nation may receive every protection which the law gives them."[284]

Grant also championed the creation of the new Justice Department and gave it the mandate to crush the Ku Klux Klan and similar white supremacist groups. Many Northerners, disgusted by Klan violence, lent their support to the Fifteenth Amendment and to the First Reconstruction Act of 1867, which placed harsher restrictions on the South and closely regulated the formation of its new state governments.

Grant supported other legislation that attacked the Klan more directly. Between 1870 and 1871, Congress passed the Enforcement Acts, which made it a crime to interfere with registration, voting, office holding, or jury service of Blacks. In 1871, Congress also passed the Ku Klux Klan Act, which allowed the government to act against terrorist organizations. Grant had lobbied hard for the bill's passage, and he traveled up Pennsylvania Avenue to sign the law with congressional allies on Capitol Hill. Under the leadership of Grant and Attorney General Amos Akerman, federal grand juries—many interracial—brought 3,384 indictments against the KKK, resulting in 1,143 convictions.[285]

By 1872, both legally and militarily, the Ku Klux Klan had been almost completely destroyed in the South.[286]

Another triumph was the Civil Rights Act of 1875, which Grant endorsed and signed into law. It outlawed racial segregation in public accommodations, schools, transportation, and juries.[287] Sadly, in 1883, the Supreme Court ruled the Civil Rights Act of 1875 unconstitutional, thereby sanctioning the notion of "separate but equal" facilities and transportation for the races. With that decision, the nation descended into eighty years of Jim Crow segregation. Not until the Civil Rights Act of 1964 were many of the 1875 Act's protections for Blacks restored.[288]

The overturning of the Civil Rights Act in 1883 was the beginning of the perfect storm for Ulysses S. Grant. The following year brought the collapse of Grant & Ward and the diagnosis of terminal throat cancer. The time had come for him to fight back.

Writing his memoirs gave Grant the opportunity to correct the errors that had begun to be communicated by the Lost Cause school of writers, historians, and professors. In the closing of his memoirs, Grant planned to make it clear that the war was about slavery—from beginning to end.

SHARING HAPPY MEMORIES

Occasionally, the general took a break from writing to share a story—mainly from the Civil War. According to Dr. Shrady, "The general seemed always ready in his communicable moods to refer to some peculiarity of the martyr president which showed simplicity of demeanor and directness of purpose. His esteem for him was unbounded."

"The first time I saw President Lincoln," Grant recalled, "I was profoundly impressed by his modesty, sincerity, and earnestness. He was justice, humanity, and charity all in one."

Grant often described Lincoln's odd, innocent mannerisms. Shrady explained that the general's comments reflected his loving spirit, which was the natural and instinctive outgrowth of an unquestioned admiration for "the greatest man he had ever known." According to Grant, Lincoln never laughed at his own stories. At most, there was a mere twitching of the corner of the mouth and a merry twinkle in the watchful eye.[289]

One rare afternoon when his pain had subsided, Grant was in a talkative mood. He told Doctor Shrady about an occasion years previous when he had walked in the rain to a reception given in his honor. A stranger joined him in the use of an umbrella.

"I have never seen Grant," said the stranger, "and I merely go to satisfy a personal curiosity. Between us I have always thought that Grant was a very much over-rated man."

"That's my view also," replied the general.[290]

When the verbal storytelling was done, Grant went back to telling stories with his pen. As he labored, his mind went back to one of the most monumental days in his life—when he became lieutenant general with command of all the armies of the United States.

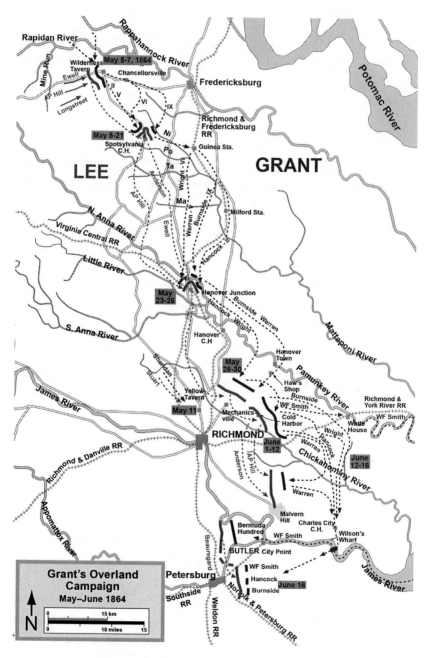

Map by Hal Jespersen, www.cwmaps.com © Hal Jespersen.
All rights reserved. Used with permission.

Chapter Ten

THREE STARS

MARCH 1864—WASHINGTON, DC

~

FROM *PERSONAL MEMOIRS*

The bill restoring the grade of lieutenant general of the army had passed through Congress and became a law on the 26th of February. My nomination had been sent to the Senate on the 1st of March and confirmed the next day (the 2d). I was ordered to Washington on the 3d to receive my commission, and started the day following that.[291]

~

Ulysses S. Grant had galloped from one victory to the next during his meteoric rise in the western theater of the Civil War. From Fort Donelson to Shiloh to Vicksburg and then to Chattanooga, Grant achieved glorious success against the Confederate armies. Lincoln was determined to bring him east so the North's premier general could be pitted against the South's greatest general—Robert E. Lee.

When the new Congress convened in December 1863, Grant's local congressman and main supporter in the legislature, Elihu Washburne, introduced a bill authorizing the president to revive the rank of lieutenant general, last held permanently by George Washington. He proposed to confer this high honor on the commander "most distinguished for courage, skill, and ability."

Everyone knew the identity of the candidate for this honor, but Washburne still made a speech in Congress calling on President Lincoln to name Ulysses S. Grant as the first three-star general since Washington. "Look at what this man has done for his country, for humanity and civilization. He has fought more battles and won more victories than any living man. He has captured more prisoners and taken more guns than any general of modern times."[292]

Grant was humbled by the gesture, and he wrote his thanks to Congressman Washburne: "I feel under many obligations to you for the interest you have taken in my welfare. But recollect that I have been highly honored already by the Government, and do not ask or feel that I deserve anything more in the shape of honors or promotion. A success over the enemy is what I crave above anything else."[293]

At first, Lincoln was nervous about Washburne's proposal. With a presidential election looming in the coming year, Lincoln did not wish to create an unbeatable political opponent. The president met with Washburne, Grant's greatest supporter on Capitol Hill, to discuss the matter. The congressman suggested that Lincoln dispatch Grant's friend, J. Russell Jones, to discover where the general stood on the matter. Jones talked to Grant, and then hurried to Washington with a letter he had received from the general for Mr. Lincoln. In the letter, Grant assured him that his only desire was to see the rebellion crushed and Lincoln reelected. "Nothing could induce me to think of being a presidential candidate, particularly so long as there is a possibility of having Mr. Lincoln re-elected."

Greatly relieved after reading the letter, Lincoln told Jones: "My son, you will never know how gratifying that is to me. No man knows, when that Presidential grub gets to gnawing at him, just how deep it will get until he has tried it; and I didn't know but what there was one gnawing at Grant."[294]

With this reassurance, Lincoln expressed his support of the promotion. Congress passed the bill and Lincoln immediately announced Grant's upcoming advancement to the rank of lieutenant general.

SUCH A GREAT MAN

With her husband being spoken of as a future presidential candidate, Julia Grant realized that she too was becoming something of a public figure. Suddenly self-conscious of her strabismus—the condition of crossed-eyes that she had from birth—Julia consulted an old medical acquaintance to see if surgery could correct the problem.[295]

"I had often been urged in my girlhood by Dr. [Charles A.] Pope, the most distinguished surgeon in the country at that time, to permit him to make a very simple operation on my eyes," Julia wrote. "I had never had the courage to consent, but now that my husband had become so famous I really thought it behooved me to try to look as well as possible. So I consulted the Doctor on this, to me, most delicate subject, but alas! he told me it was too late, too late. ... I told the general and expressed my regret."

Grant was surprised by the notion. "What in the world put such a thought in your head, Julia?"

"Why, you are getting to be such a great man," Julia responded, "and I am such a plain little wife. I thought if my eyes were as others are I might not be so very, very plain, Ulys; who knows?"

Ulysses drew Julia to himself and said gently, "Did I not see you and fall in love with you with these same eyes? I like them just as they are, and now, remember, you are not to interfere with them. They are mine, and let me tell you, Mrs. Grant, you had better not make any experiments, as I might not like you half so well with any other eyes."[296]

MARCH 8, 1864

Grant arrived in Washington by train late in the afternoon of March 8, accompanied by his son Fred, going on fourteen, and two of his aides, Brigadier General John A. Rawlins and Lieutenant Colonel Cyrus B. Comstock.[297] To pay their respects, the troupe called on General Halleck in his office and then at his Georgetown home. Finding that the general was not in, they walked to Willard's, the famous Washington hotel where the most important visitors to the city found lodging.[298]

The travel-weary Grant entered the lobby of the famous hotel, followed by Fred. The general wore a plain linen overcoat, which hid most of his uniform, including the two stars on his shoulder straps.

The clerk, who had seen multiple generals come and go through Willard's, was professionally courteous but aloof and unimpressed. He said that maybe he could let the general have a small room on the top floor of the hotel. Grant, in his quiet, modest way said that would be just fine and signed the register. When the clerk swung the book around to write down the room number after the name, he saw the entry: "U. S. Grant and son, Galena, Ill." He suddenly snapped into action, remembering that Parlor 6 was reserved for the general on the second floor—the same luxurious suite President Lincoln stayed in when he arrived in Washington for his inaugural.[299]

The clerk came bustling out from behind the desk to carry the general's bag upstairs to his room.[300] Noticing the clerk's sudden change of behavior, people in the lobby realized that the man under the dusty woolen coat was General Grant, and they took notice of his appearance. Among the hotel guests that day was the novelist Richard Henry Dana. Writing to his wife, Dana gave his first impression of the vaunted commander:

> A short, round-shouldered man, in a very tarnished major general's uniform come up ... There was nothing marked in his appearance. He had no gait, no station, no manner, rough, light-brown whiskers, a blue eye, and rather a scrubby look withal.
>
> A crowd formed round him; men looked, stared at him, as if they were taking his likeness, and two generals were introduced. Still, I could not get his name. It was not Hooker. Who could it be? I inquired of the bookkeeper.
>
> "That is General Grant."
>
> I joined the starers. I saw that the ordinary, scrubby-looking man, with a slightly seedy look, as if he was out of office and on half pay, and nothing to do but hang around the entry of Willard's, cigar in mouth, had a clear blue eye, and a look of resolution, as if he could not be trifled with, and an entire indifference to the crowd about him. Straight nose, too. Still to see him talking and smoking in the lower entry of Willard's in that crowd, in such times—the generalissimo of our armies, on whom the destiny of the empire seemed to hang.

He gets over the ground queerly. He does not march, nor quite walk, but pitches along as if the next step would bring him on his nose.[301]

Grant misplaced the key to his trunk and was forced to wear the same plain, dust-covered uniform in which he had traveled that day. A Washington newspaper had announced that Grant would attend the reception, so the White House was packed with spectators eager to catch their first glimpse of the victorious commander. Grant arrived at the White House around 9:30 p.m. and entered the Blue Room.[302]

Lincoln had prepared for the meeting by studying a Grant portrait by John Antrobus that hung in the Capitol, showing him on Missionary Ridge in Chattanooga.[303] At six feet four, President Lincoln stood head and shoulders above the crème de la crème of Washington society, so he saw the general enter the room.

Wearing a collar one size too large and a necktie "rather broad and awkwardly tied," Lincoln stepped forward, his hand outstretched, a smile on his face. Grant walked toward him with no expression whatsoever. A White House secretary observed it was "a long walk for a bashful man, the eyes of the world upon him."[304]

Beaming with delight, the president reached out his hand to the popular general. "It is General Grant, is it not?"

Grant replied simply, "Yes."[305]

The president shook the general's hand with enthusiasm. "Why, here is General Grant," he said while continuing to look into his face. "Well, this is a great pleasure, I assure you!"

Lincoln was taller than Grant by eight inches, and he beamed down on the general with great satisfaction. Grant looked up at the president with an unchanged expression, his right hand grasping the lapel of his uniform coat.[306] The president introduced Grant to Secretary of State William H. Seward, who immediately whisked him off to present him to Mrs. Lincoln. The president's wife expressed her pleasure at meeting the general, and she and Grant chatted for several minutes.

A few minutes later, Seward led the general into the East Room where the crowd waited. When Grant entered the room, people cheered and pressed forward to shake his hand or touch him. The five-foot-eight Grant disappeared in the throng. Seward, realizing the people in the back could not see the guest of honor, persuaded Grant to stand on a sofa—partly to ensure he could shake the hands that were thrust at him and partly to avoid being trampled under-foot. The people broke into brisk applause and wave after wave of cheers, chanting "Grant! Grant! Grant!"[307] Secretary of the Navy Gideon Welles considered the raucous scene "rowdy and unseemly."

Grant was forced to stand on the sofa for almost an hour, shak-ing hands and greeting strangers.[308] One observer noted that for once the president "was not the chief figure in the picture. The lit-tle, scared-looking man who stood on a crimson-covered sofa was the idol of the hour."[309]

Julia later recounted the affair: "He went to Washington, and what glorious accounts came back of his enthusiastic reception there. The papers said that when General Grant was announced at one of the President's levees, the guests became wildly excited, mounting on sofas, chairs, and even tables, to get a look at Grant. When Ulys told me of this afterwards, he said, 'Really, it was very embarrassing. I heartily wished myself back in camp.'"[310]

Seward finally announced that the show was over and, with the help of several officers and ushers, shepherded Grant back to a drawing room where President Lincoln and Secretary Stanton waited. The president explained that Grant must return to the White House the next day for a special ceremony—the formal pre-sentation of his commission as lieutenant general.[311]

March 9, 1864

Ulysses S. Grant and his son Fred, along with his aides, gathered at the White House the next day at 1:00 p.m. for the formal cer-emony. In recognition of the occasion's importance and to garner maximum publicity for the ceremony, Lincoln gathered members of his cabinet and the press. President Lincoln and General Grant took their positions, standing face to face, then Lincoln read a pre-pared statement.

~

FROM PERSONAL MEMOIRS

The President in presenting my commission read from a paper—stating, however, as a preliminary, and prior to the delivery of it, that he had drawn that up on paper, knowing my disinclination to speak in public, and handed me a copy in advance so that I might prepare a few lines of reply. The President said:

"General Grant, the nation's appreciation of what you have done, and its reliance upon you for what remains to be done in the existing great struggle, are now presented, with this commission constituting you lieutenant-general in the Army of the United States. With this high honor, devolves upon you, also, a corresponding responsibility. As the country herein trusts you, so, under God, it will sustain you. I scarcely need to add, that, with what I here speak for the nation, goes my own hearty personal concurrence."[312]

~

Grant had written his reply out in pencil the previous night, and he held the draft in his wavering hand. The general did not seem to take in enough air as he began to speak, and the first few words were barely audible. The general paused, took a deep breath, and gripped the paper with both hands, top and bottom. He stopped, advanced his left foot, and continued in a loud, distinct voice:

> Mr. President, I accept this commission with gratitude for the high honor conferred. With the aid of the noble armies that fought on so many fields for our common country, it will be my earnest endeavor not to disappoint your expectations. I feel the full weight of the responsibilities now devolving on me and know that if they are met it will be due to those armies, and above all to the favor of the Providence which leads both Nations and men.[313]

Although Julia could not attend the ceremony, Ulysses kept her informed on the details of the occasion. Julia later wrote that when she expressed her delight at this honor, the general said he had but one regret at receiving it. In answer to Julia's astonished "Regret?"

he said, "Yes, regret, for this means my station henceforth will be in Washington, and I had hoped when the war was over I might have my choice of stations. ... My choice is the Pacific slope, but (with a sigh) this breaks that all up."[314]

When the festivities concluded, the president sat down with Grant for a strategy session. "I have never professed to be a military man," Lincoln confessed. He explained that he had no desire to interfere or meddle in military strategy, and that he had reluctantly done so in the past from necessity only. Grant later wrote of the conversation, explaining that Lincoln "did not care to know what I was to do, only to know what I wanted; that I should have all I required. He wished me to beat Lee, how I did it was my own duty. He said he did not wish to know my plans or to exercise any scrutiny over my plans; so long as I beat the rebel army he was satisfied."[315]

Grant was forty-two years old when he became general in chief of the armies of the United States. *The New York Times* provided a description: "He is a man of plain exterior, light hair, blue eyes, ... plain and retiring in his manners, firm and decisive in character, esteemed by his soldiers, never wastes a word with any one, but pays strict attention to his military duties. His personal bravery and dash is undoubted. He is one of the hard-fighting school of generals."[316]

One of Grant's chief aides, Horace Porter, offered his own vivid description of Grant's appearance when he first met him in October 1863, prior to the Battle of Chattanooga:

> Many of us were not a little surprised to find in him a man of slim figure, slightly stooped, five feet eight inches in height, weighing only a hundred and thirty-five pounds, and of a modesty of mien and gentleness of manner which seemed to fit him more for the court than for the camp. His eyes were dark-gray, and were the most expressive of his features.
>
> Like nearly all men who speak little, he was a good listener; but his face gave little indication of his thoughts, and it was the expression of his eyes which furnished about the only response to the speaker who conversed with him. ... The firmness with which the general's square-shaped jaws were set when his features were in repose was highly expressive of his force of character and

the strength of his will-power. His hair and beard were of a chestnut-brown color. The beard was worn full, no part of the face being shaved, but, like the hair, was always kept closely and neatly trimmed.

His face was not perfectly symmetrical, the left eye being a very little lower than the right. His brow was high, broad, and rather square, and was creased with several horizontal wrinkles, which helped to emphasize the serious and somewhat careworn look which was never absent from his countenance. This expression, however, was in no wise an indication of his nature, which was always buoyant, cheerful, and hopeful. . . .

His voice was exceedingly musical, and one of the clearest in sound and most distinct in utterance that I ever heard. It had a singular power of penetration, and sentences spoken by him in an ordinary tone in camp could be heard at a distance which was surprising. His gait in walking might have been called decidedly un-military. He never carried his body erect, and having no ear for music or rhythm, he never kept step to the airs played by the bands, no matter how vigorously the bass drums emphasized the accent. When walking in company there was no attempt to keep step with others.

In conversing with others he usually employed only two gestures; one was the stroking of his chin beard with his left hand; the other was the raising and lowering of his right hand, and resting it at intervals upon his knee or a table, the hand being held with the fingers close together and the knuckles bent, so that the back of the hand and fingers formed a right angle. When not pressed by any matter of importance he was often slow in his movements, but when roused to activity he was quick in every motion, and worked with marvelous rapidity.[317]

Porter explained that unlike the feisty General George Gordon Meade, Grant was civil to all who came in contact with him. He "never attempted to snub any one, or treat anybody with less consideration on account of his inferiority in rank."[318]

COMMANDER OF THE ARMY OF THE POTOMAC

Grant was eager to finalize his plans to confront Lee and the Army of Northern Virginia. He was equally impatient to escape what he saw as the carnival atmosphere of Washington, DC. On March 10, Grant departed for the headquarters of the Army of the Potomac at Brandy Station to talk with that army's commander, Major General Meade.[319]

Meade showed respect for the new lieutenant general by dispatching a Zouave regiment, beautifully attired with the unit's red fezzes and exotic flowing trousers, to salute him as a band struck up "The General's March." It rained heavily as Grant's train pulled into Brandy Station, but the regiment of Zouaves still snapped to a salute as the army band enthusiastically belted out its tune.[320]

Meade was fighting a nagging cold, so he sent his chief of staff, General A. A. Humphreys, to meet Grant at the rainy train depot. Grant's horse was brought from the rear of the train, and he was led to Meade's headquarters.

Meade was tall and thin with a balding head and a trimmed beard. The gaunt look on his face, highlighted by the bags under his eyes, reflected his notorious short temper. These attributes resulted in a nickname from his men that he could not shake—"that goggle-eyed snapping turtle."

As the lieutenant general approached, Meade emerged from his tent, extending a friendly handshake while Grant was still on his horse. The two men had last met during the Mexican War as young lieutenants. In the coming days, they would face one of the greatest generals in military history.[321]

~

From *Personal Memoirs*

I was a stranger to most of the Army of the Potomac, I might say to all except the officers of the regular army who had served in the Mexican war. There had been some changes ordered in the organization of that army before my promotion. One was the consolidation of five corps into three, thus throwing some officers of rank out of important commands. Meade evidently thought that I might want to make still one more change not yet ordered. He said to me that I might want an officer who had served with me in the West, mentioning Sherman specially, to take his place. If so, he begged me not to hesitate about making the change. He urged that the work before us was of such vast importance to the whole nation that the feeling or wishes of no one person should stand in the way of selecting the right men for all positions. For himself, he would serve to the best of his ability wherever placed. I assured him that I had no thought of substituting any one for him. As to Sherman, he could not be spared from the West.

This incident gave me even a more favorable opinion of Meade than did his great victory at Gettysburg the July before. It is men who wait to be selected, and not those who seek, from whom we may always expect the most efficient service.[322]

~

"He spoke so patriotically and unselfishly that even if I had had any intention of relieving him, I should have been inclined to change my mind after the manly attitude he assumed in this frank interview," Grant later explained.[323]

He and Meade hit it off immediately. Grant later discovered from the president that he had been misinformed about the Lincoln administration's view of General Meade, as neither Lincoln nor Stanton desired to see him removed from his position as head of the Army of the Potomac.[324]

Grant asked Meade to remain in command and said he had ordered Phil Sheridan, "Little Phil," to take over the cavalry. Sherman would be promoted to lead the western armies—a surprise to some, as General George Henry Thomas outranked him. Grant would make his headquarters in the field and travel with the Army of the Potomac, while Meade handled the daily administrative work of commanding the eastern forces. Grant would issue broad orders; Meade would take care of the details to ensure they were executed.[325]

Grant shared his vision with Meade as he had with Sherman. All the armies were to move together and toward one common objective—defeating the Confederate forces. After explaining what the other armies were going to do, he gave Meade specific instructions: "Lee's army will be your objective point. Wherever Lee goes, there you will go also."[326]

And Grant would come along—overseeing all the armies but giving his main focus to the Army of the Potomac.

TIRED OF THIS SHOW BUSINESS

On his return to Washington, General Grant became an object of curiosity, continuously surrounded by admiring crowds on the street and even in his hotel. The general could not understand why he was the center of so much attention. Eventually, the adulation became irksome, and he longed to return to the field with the soldiers.

When the president extended an invitation to dine with him and Mrs. Lincoln that evening, Grant begged to be excused. If he stayed in Washington he would lose a whole day, which he could not afford at that critical stage of the war. "Besides," he added, "I have become very tired of this show business."[327]

President Lincoln, of all people, understood the tedium of Washington society functions and graciously withdrew the invitation.

Grant's primary objective was to crush Lee in Virginia, while Sherman moved against General Joseph Johnston's forces in Georgia. Above everything else, Grant's goal was to make sure that all the Union forces worked in harmony. "Oh yes, I see that," Lincoln exclaimed when Grant explained his plan. "As we say out West, if a man can't skin he must hold a leg while somebody else does."[328]

Lincoln and Grant both understood that Lee's army was the main force defending the Confederacy. The death of Lee's command would naturally lead to the death of the rebellion.

Grant intended to advance on five fronts with the two central armies, led by Meade in the east and Sherman in the west, supported by three smaller armies. Franz Sigel would drive his army south up the Shenandoah Valley and apply pressure on Richmond from the west. Benjamin Butler, with the Army of the James coming up from Fortress Monroe, would push toward Richmond from the south. Grant saw the Army of the James as the left wing of the Army of the Potomac. Butler would attack south of Richmond, the Confederate capital, to keep the rebel forces divided and to attempt to cut Lee from his base of supplies.[329]

Grant directed Sherman's army to push southeast through Georgia to capture Atlanta: "You I propose to move against Johnston's Army, to break it up and get into the interior of the enemy's country as far as you can, inflicting all the damage you can against their War resources."[330] Nathaniel Banks would seize Mobile, Alabama, and then drive north to unite with Sherman.

"It is my design," Grant wrote to Sherman, "if the enemy keep quiet and allow me to take the initiative in the Spring Campaign to work all parts of the Army together, and, somewhat, towards a common center."

As usual, Grant and Sherman were on the same page. Sherman enthusiastically replied, "That we are now all to act in a common plan, converging on a common center looks like enlightened war."[331]

In mid-April, Grant added General Ambrose Burnside's Ninth Corps alongside the Army of the Potomac. To circumvent the awkwardness of positioning Meade over Burnside, who outranked him, Grant instructed Burnside to report directly to him. Meade had only been a division commander when Burnside was commander of the entire Army of the Potomac, so Grant was in reality coordinating two armies on the field at the same time.

Burnside's most discussed division was the Fourth—seven regiments of African American troops drawn from both north and south. Led by White officers, the US Colored Troops later became the first African American troops in the Army of the Potomac.

Grant's strategy was one of unrelenting attack. The siege of Vicksburg had reinforced his belief that Richmond was fortified so well "that one man inside to defend was more than equal to five outside besieging or assaulting." His first objective was to attack Lee's army, confident that with its capture, Richmond "would necessarily follow."

On March 24, 1864, Grant left Washington, DC, for Culpeper, Virginia, six miles beyond Meade's headquarters at Brandy Station, about midway between the two important rivers of the region, the Rappahannock and the Rapidan. He traveled light. As general in chief, he had a staff of fourteen officers, two of whom were left behind in Washington. Initially, headquarters was established in a small brick house on the outskirts of Culpeper.

Once in the field, the headquarters of the Army of the United States consisted of three tents: a large hospital tent, where the mess was housed; a slightly smaller one for business; and a very small one where Grant slept. Its only furniture consisted of a portable cot made of canvas stretched over a light wooden frame, a tin washbasin that stood on an iron tripod, two folding camp chairs, and a plain pine table. The general's baggage consisted of a single trunk, which contained underclothing, toilet articles, a suit of clothes, and an extra pair of boots.[332]

Meals were casual and informal. Officers sat where they wished at the table, coming and going as their duties required, and the conversation "was as familiar as that which occurs in the household of any private family."[333]

Grant ate less and talked less than anyone else. His usual breakfast consisted of a cup of coffee and a sliced cucumber doused with vinegar. If he ate meat, it was roasted black and tough as shoe leather. He never ate fowl. He was just as happy to eat the old army standbys: pork and beans or buckwheat cakes.

Grant ate lightly but smoked heavily. When he started his rounds each morning, he loaded his pockets with cigars and carried with him a small silver tinderbox, which contained a flint and steel with which to strike a spark, and a coil of fuse that was easily ignited and unaffected by the wind.

Grant was a simple man, but he enjoyed one luxury—his horses. At forty-two, Grant remained one of the best horsemen in the United States. His most famous mounts included Jack, a cream-colored stallion, used at Donelson; Fox, a powerful roan gelding, used at Shiloh; and Kangaroo, a thoroughbred, used at Shiloh and Vicksburg. Jeff Davis, a pony liberated from the Davis plantation in Mississippi, was another favorite. Grant enjoyed the horse's easy gait and always used him when traveling a long distance. Grant's most famous charger, Cincinnati, an enormous animal of seventeen and a half hands, was the fastest four-mile thoroughbred in the country.[334] Grant mostly rode Cincinnati and Jeff Davis for the rest of the war.

Under General Grant, army reviews were not social occasions, as in the old days, but true inspections. Grant was not interested in parades. He preferred to ride down the lines, looking intently at the soldiers in the ranks, as if he wanted to see the faces of the men who were going to fight for him.

"Yesterday the 6th Corps was reviewed by Lieutenant General U. S. Grant," wrote Elisha Hunt Rhodes in his diary. "He is a short, thick-set man, and rode his horse like a bag of meal. I was a little disappointed in his appearance. But I liked the look of his eye."[335]

Grant also liked what he saw. As a result, his natural optimism rose. As preparations neared completion, he wrote to Halleck: "The Army of the Potomac is in splendid condition and evidently feel like whipping somebody."[336]

THE LEGEND OF LEE

The somebody Grant focused on whipping more than anyone else was Robert E. Lee.

After hearing multiple officers repeat the mantra, "Grant hasn't faced Bobby Lee," Chief of Staff John Rawlins wrote in frustration to his wife: "There is a habit contracted among officers of this army anything but praiseworthy, namely, of saying of western successes: 'Well, you never met Bobby Lee and his boys; it would be quite different if you had.' And in speaking of the probabilities of our success in the coming campaign: 'Well, that may be, but, mind you, Bobby Lee is just over the Rapidan.'"[337]

To defeat the rebellion, Grant knew he had to exorcise the specter of General Lee from the mind of Federal soldiers and officers. From his experience in Mexico, Grant had observed the vaunted Southern commander in the Mexican War and believed he could be beaten. Grant later wrote: "I knew Lee was mortal."[338]

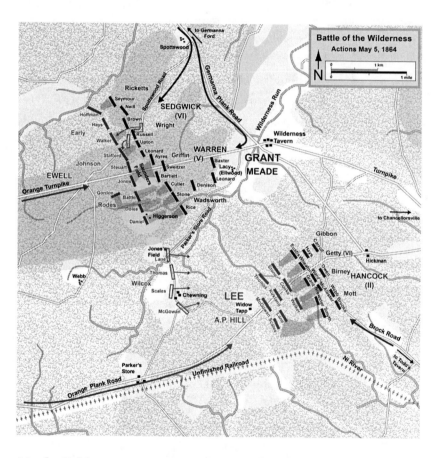

Chapter Eleven

GRANT AND LEE

DECEMBER 1884—NEW YORK CITY

Having heard of Grant's illness, his wartime aide and lifelong friend, Horace Porter, came to visit him in New York in early December 1884. The general, still fighting depression, was happy to see his comrade, and the two exchanged news about their families. Toward the end of their long, pleasant conversation, Grant confided to Porter that he was suffering from cancer and it was likely fatal. This sad news shocked Porter.

The conversation turned to reminiscences of the Battle of the Wilderness, where Grant first confronted Lee.[339] Porter reminded the general of how he gave the final orders on the second night of the battle, then entered his tent and threw himself down on his camp bed in exhaustion. Ten minutes later, Porter brought alarming reports from the right side of the line, where Lee had pushed back Major General John Sedgwick's forces.

"I looked in your tent and found you sleeping as perfectly as an infant," Porter said. "You immediately concluded that it was a gross exaggeration. Since you had already made every provision for meeting any renewed attempts on the right, you turned over in your bed and quickly fell asleep again."

Grant smiled, thinking back to those momentous events twenty-one years earlier. "Ah yes," he responded. "It seems strange that I, who always slept so well in the field, should now pass whole nights in the quiet of this peaceful house without being able to close my eyes."

After a few more minutes of conversation, Porter rose and bid his commander farewell, leaving him with thoughts of the first clash of the titans in the American Civil War.

MAY 1864—VIRGINIA

~

FROM PERSONAL MEMOIRS

Soon after midnight, May 3d–4th, the Army of the Potomac moved out from its position north of the Rapidan, to start upon that memorable campaign, destined to result in the capture of the Confederate capital and the army defending it. This was not to be accomplished, however, without as desperate fighting as the world has ever witnessed.[340]

~

MAY 3, 1864

On the night of May 3, General Grant assembled his eight senior staff members in the little front room of his headquarters at Culpeper to receive their final instructions. The general sat at his desk, preparing some final notes. When he finished, he turned to his men, crossed one leg over the other, lit a fresh cigar, and shared his thoughts on the movement of the Army of the Potomac, which would begin in the early hours of the next morning.

"I weighed very carefully the advantages and disadvantages of moving against Lee's left and moving against his right," Grant began. "The former promised more decisive results if immediately successful. It would best prevent Lee from moving north to make raids. But it would also deprive our army of the advantages of easy communication with a water base of supplies and compel us to carry such a large amount of ammunition and rations in wagon-trains, and detach so many troops as train guards, that I found it presented too many serious difficulties."

He paused and took a long drag on his new cigar. "When I considered the suffering of the wounded in being transported long distances overland, instead of being carried by short routes to water, where they could be comfortably moved by boats, I had no longer any hesitation in deciding to cross the Rapidan below the position occupied by Lee's army, and move by our left.

"This plan will also enable us to cooperate better with Butler's forces, and not become separated too far from them." He then repeated what he had shared with them individually and with each of the separate army commanders. "I shall not give my attention so much to Richmond as to Lee's army, and I want all commanders to feel that hostile armies, and not cities, are to be their objective points."

The lieutenant general believed that Lee would fall back to Richmond in case of defeat and place himself behind its fortifications. In his instructions to Meade, Grant declared, "Should a siege of Richmond become necessary, ammunition and equipment can be got from the arsenals at Washington and Fort Monroe."

Grant rose from his seat, stepped up to an impressive military map hanging on the wall, and with a sweep of his forefinger created an arching semicircle around Richmond, stopping at Petersburg. "When my troops are there, Richmond is mine. Lee must retreat or surrender."[341]

~

FROM *PERSONAL MEMOIRS*

From an early period in the rebellion I had been impressed with the idea that active and continuous operations of all the troops that could be brought into the field, regardless of season and weather, were necessary to a speedy termination of the war. The resources of the enemy and his numerical strength were far inferior to ours; but as an offset to this, we had a vast territory, with a population hostile to the government, to garrison, and long lines of river and railroad communications to protect, to enable us to supply the operating armies.

The armies in the East and West acted independently and without concert, like a balky team, no two ever pulling together, enabling the enemy to use to great advantage his interior lines of communication for transporting troops from East to West, reinforcing the army most vigorously pressed, and to furlough large numbers, during seasons of inactivity on our part, to go to their homes and do the work of producing, for the support of their armies. It was a question whether our numerical strength and resources were not more than balanced by these disadvantages and the enemy's superior position.[342]

~

"I want you to discuss with me freely from time to time the details of the orders given for the conduct of a battle," Grant told his staff, "and learn my views as fully as possible. ... I expect to send you to the critical points of the lines to keep me promptly advised of what is taking place. ... In cases of great emergency, when new dispositions have to be made on the instant, or it becomes suddenly necessary to reinforce one command by sending to its aid troops from another, and there is not time to communicate with headquarters, I want you to explain my views to commanders, and urge immediate action, looking to cooperation, without waiting for specific orders from me."

General Grant reminded them that emergencies might arise in which he himself would have to give immediate direction to troops when actually engaged in battle. Grant would locate his headquarters near Meade and communicate his instructions through him to the troops. He would send separate orders to Burnside.

The discussion did not end until long past midnight. As usual on the eve of a battle, before the general retired he wrote a letter to Mrs. Grant and then went to bed.[343]

Grant would be the seventh Union commander to try to defeat the Confederacy in Virginia and bring the rebellion to an end. In 1861, Irvin McDowell was defeated at First Manassas, and his troops "skedaddled" back to Washington in a panicked retreat. In 1862, George McClellan was within sight of the spires of Richmond when Robert E. Lee took command of the Southern troops. McClellan was immediately out-generaled and pushed back down the Virginia Peninsula to the James River. John Pope was routed at

Second Manassas. Ambrose Burnside led the disaster at Fredericks-
burg. In 1863, Joe Hooker's pride preceded his fall at Chancellorsville.

While General Meade defeated Lee at Gettysburg in Pennsylvania, he failed to follow up on the victory, raising Abraham Lincoln's
ire and allowing Lee to cross his army back over the Potomac into
the safety of Virginia. Late in the year, Meade called off a hopeless
attack on Lee's fortified position at Mine Run and pulled his Union
troops back across the Rapidan into winter camp.

Many in the South believed Grant would simply be the seventh name added to the list of failed Yankee generals. So far, the
Southerners weren't impressed with the Northern commander.
Confederate General Evander M. Law declared the "universal verdict" among rebel soldiers asserted that Grant "was no strategist
and that he relied almost entirely upon the brute force of numbers
for success."[344]

On the evening the Confederacy received news that Grant
intended to give personal direction to the Army of the Potomac,
General James Longstreet had a conversation on the subject at
Lee's headquarters. One officer present spoke confidently of being
able to easily whip the western general who had been brought east
to confront the Confederates under Robert E. Lee.

General Longstreet knew better.

"Do you know Grant?" Longstreet asked. The braggadocious officer did not. "Well, I do," Old Pete replied. "I was in the corps of
cadets with him at West Point for three years. I was present at his
wedding. I served in the same army with him in Mexico. I have observed his methods of warfare in the West, and I believe I know him
through and through. And I tell you we cannot afford to underrate
him and the army he now commands. We must make up our minds
to get into line of battle and stay there, for that man will fight us
every day and every hour till the end of this war. In order to whip
him we must outmaneuver him, and husband our strength as best
we can."[345]

CROSSING THE RAPIDAN

Just across the Rapidan, Grant waited until dark to ensure maximum secrecy before issuing the final orders that set five Federal armies in motion.

Before dawn on the morning of May 4, Sheridan's cavalry raced forward under cover of darkness, drove off the enemy's pickets, then secured Germanna Ford on the Rapidan and also Ely's Ford, six miles below. Before 6:00 a.m., Federal engineers laid pontoon bridges at both locations. As the infantry began their approach to the fords, the cavalry passed to the south side of the river. General Gouverneur K. Warren's corps crossed at Germanna Ford, followed by General John Sedgwick's, while General Winfield Scott Hancock's corps made the passage at Ely's Ford.[346] Most infantrymen lifted their weapons and waded across waist-high water, while cannon and supply wagons rolled across the pontoon bridges.

The general's staff officers were surprised to see their boss break from his usual attire of a private's simple riding jacket. On this historic occasion, Grant donned a uniform frock coat over a blue vest, three-star shoulder straps, a black felt hat adorned with a gold braid, a gold midriff sash, and his battle sword. Instead of the usual buckskin gauntlets, Grant wore gold thread gloves. General Grant had never worn thread gloves before, and most of the staff assumed they were a gift from Julia.

Riding his famous bay, Cincinnati, Grant and his staff galloped toward the Rapidan.

Adam Badeau believed that Grant dressed in full regalia that day because "he seemed to consider the occasion one of peculiar dignity.[347] At his command, 120,000 men stepped out in formation to confront Lee on the soil of old Virginia.

Congressman Elihu Washburne asked to ride at Grant's side as they crossed Germanna Ford on their way to confront Lee. The politician was dressed from head to toe in black, leading some of the soldiers to ask if General Grant had enlisted his own minister or mortician, just in case.

Horace Porter described how fast-stepping soldiers with lusty shouts greeted their new commander as he passed. As General Grant was rarely communicative, he gave no indication of his feelings that day; he merely nodded in acknowledgment from time to time.

"A sun as bright as the 'sun of Austerlitz' shone down upon the scene," Porter later wrote, describing the scene. "Its light brought out in vivid colors the beauties of the landscape which lay before us, and its rays were reflected with dazzling brilliancy from the brass field-pieces and the white covers of the wagons as they rolled lazily along in the distance. As far as the eye could reach the troops were wending their way to the front. Their war banners, bullet-riddled and battle-stained, floated proudly in the morning breeze. The roads resounded to the measured tread of the advancing columns, and the deep forests were lighted by the glitter of their steel. The quick, elastic step and easy, swinging gait of the men, the cheery look upon their faces, gave proof of the temper of their metal [sic], and the superb spirit which animated their hearts."[348]

A newspaper reporter, with whom the general was acquainted, stepped up to him as he surveyed the scene. "General Grant, about how long will it take you to get to Richmond?" The general replied with a slight twinkle in his eye: "I will agree to be there in about four days—that is, if General Lee becomes a party to the agreement; but if he objects, the trip will undoubtedly be prolonged." The joke brought hearty laughter from the staff and a look of confusion from the correspondent.[349]

Grant rode to the top of the bluff overlooking the crossing, dismounted, and established temporary headquarters in an abandoned farmhouse. The general in chief watched anxiously from the porch as Sedgwick's corps crossed the ford. A courier rode up with news that Winfield Scott Hancock's Second Corps had successfully cleared the Ely Ford. "Everything is across," Hancock reported, bringing great relief to the Northern commander.

"It removed from my mind the most serious apprehensions I had entertained, that of crossing the river in the face of an active, large, well-appointed and ably commanded army."[350]

LEE ON THE MOVE

Grant turned to his aides and remarked that Lee was probably aware that the Army of the Potomac was in motion, but he doubted if the Southern commander realized the full extent of their movement. "We shall probably soon get some indication as to what he intends to do."

Grant did not have to wait long.

Just after one o'clock in the afternoon, Meade sent a dispatch. Intercepted rebel signals revealed that Lee had left his entrenchments and was moving east with at least one corps.

"That gives just the information I wanted," Grant responded with enthusiasm. "It shows that Lee is drawing out from his position, and is pushing across to meet us." Grant called for writing material and, placing the book on his knee, wrote a dispatch to General Burnside at Rappahannock Station. "Make forced marches until you reach this place. Start your troops now in the rear the moment they can be got off, and require them to make a night march."[351]

Soon another message arrived from Meade. "The enemy have appeared in force on the Orange Pike, and are now reported forming line of battle in front of [General Charles] Griffin's division, Fifth Corps. I have directed General Warren to attack them at once with his whole force. Until this movement of the enemy is developed, the march of the corps must be suspended. I have, therefore, sent word to Hancock not to advance beyond Todd's Tavern for the present. I think the enemy is trying to delay our movement, and will not give battle, but of this we shall soon see. For the present I will stop here, and have stopped our trains."

Grant sent Meade this reply: "Your note giving movement of enemy and your dispositions received. Burnside's advance is now crossing the river. I will have Ricketts' division relieved and advanced at once, and urge Burnside's crossing."[352]

Lee understood the advantages of fighting in the Wilderness—a tangled thicket of second-growth forest that he had used to his advantage to defeat Hooker one year earlier. In earlier times, the region had been covered by iron ore mines. The original forest had been cut down to provide fuel for smelters. An unruly mass of twisted trees and underbrush had grown up in its place, aptly called "the Wilderness."

"It was uneven, with woods, thickets, and ravines right and left," Union General Alexander Webb explained. "Tangled thickets of pine, scrub-oak, and cedar prevented our seeing the enemy, and prevented anyone in command of a large force from determining accurately the position of the troops he was ordering to and fro."

Lee had only sixty-four thousand men versus Grant's 120,000—a difference that could be fatal to Lee in an open field confrontation. In the tangled maze of the Wilderness, however, the Union's advantage would disappear. For this reason, Lee made no effort to thwart Grant's crossing of the Rapidan. He planned to spring his trap once the Federals were deep into the Wilderness.[353] He would hit Grant hard and fast before his army could get beyond the dense briar patch of a forest.

To cut off Grant's approach, Lee ordered one corps eastward under General Richard S. Ewell down the Orange Turnpike and another under General A. P. Hill down the Orange Plank Road.[354]

Meade's original plan called for the infantry to march throughout the day, with the goal of bringing the infantry through the Wilderness before sunset. Grant and Meade hoped Lee would be taken by surprise and react slowly, keeping the initiative with the Army of the Potomac. But the problem was the massive wagon train of the Yankee army. The infantry could clear the Wilderness by nightfall, but it would be impossible for General Rufus Ingalls's wagons to do so.

With Grant's approval, Meade halted the march in the early afternoon to allow the wagons to catch up. Hampered by the necessity of protecting the army's supplies, Union commanders were forced to accept battle in the Wilderness.[355]

Grant clearly understood this, but he had no choice—he had to protect his supplies. He hoped to get his army through the Wilderness with the goal of confronting Lee's army in the open field. If Lee brought on a battle in the Wilderness, however, Grant would engage, knowing that every battle would whittle down the forces of the enemy—troops Lee could not replace.

TIME TO ATTACK

In reply to Meade's report, Grant urged him to attack: "If any opportunity presents itself for pitching into a part of Lee's Army do so without time for disposition."

General Grant directed his staff to mount and move forward with him along the Germanna Road. After riding a mile, Lieutenant Colonel Thomas W. Hyde of Sedgwick's staff approached at a gallop. He halted to report: "General Meade directed me to … say that the enemy is still advancing along the turnpike, and that Warren's and Sedgwick's troops are being put in position to meet him."

Grant moved forward at an accelerated pace and met General Meade who stood at the crossing of the Orange Turnpike. The commanding general dismounted to discuss the situation. "It was now evident that the enemy intended to give battle in the heart of the Wilderness," Porter later wrote, "and it was decided to establish the headquarters of both generals near the place where they were holding their present conference."

Just east of the crossroads stood the abandoned Wilderness Tavern, a deserted building slowly being consumed by the surrounding forest. A few hundred yards to the west was a knoll from which the old trees had been cut. This small hill was high enough to afford a short-range view but was limited in all directions by the almost impenetrable forest.

Porter described the terrain. "The ground upon which the battle was fought was intersected in every direction by winding rivulets, rugged ravines, and ridges of mineral rock. Many excavations had been made in opening iron-ore beds, leaving pits bordered by ridges of earth. Trees had been felled in a number of places to furnish fuel and supply sawmills."

Headquarters for both Grant and Meade was established on low ground at the foot of the knoll, while the two men climbed to the top of the hill, joined by Warren, who communicated the latest news from his front. "As soon as General Grant learned the situation," Porter recalled, "he followed his habitual custom in warfare, and instead of waiting to be attacked, took the initiative and pushed out against the enemy."

Warren was directed to move out in force on the Orange Turnpike. The division led by General George W. Getty of Sedgwick's corps was put into position on Warren's left. Word soon came that the enemy was advancing on the Orange Plank Road, and orders were sent to Hancock to hurry his troops and take up a position on the left of Getty.

Once the orders were given, General Grant lit a cigar, sat down on the stump of a tree, took out his penknife, and began to whittle a stick. He did not remove his golden-thread gloves once during the entire day.

Near noon, the stillness was suddenly broken by the sharp rattle of musketry and the roar of artillery as Warren encountered Ewell's corps. The Battle of the Wilderness had begun.

Union forces drove the rebels nearly a mile, but they soon fell back to restore the connection with other divisions. It quickly became clear that the infantry would have to fight with minimal aid from the artillery. The thick, tangled woods made it impossible to move many batteries to the front, and the artillery fire was mostly ineffective in the deep forest.[356]

Grant was aware that Longstreet's corps was some distance behind Ewell and Hill. If Lee planned to confront the Army of the Potomac, Grant hoped to gain the advantage before Longstreet arrived. Although Lee had a total of sixty-six thousand troops at his disposal, he had put himself at a distinct disadvantage because of Longstreet's location so far back at Orange Court House. Lee was fighting with only two-thirds of his troops when the Wilderness conflict erupted on May 5.

Longstreet's men did not start marching toward the Wilderness until 11:00 a.m. on May 4, several hours after Grant's troops started crossing the Rapidan. As a result, Longstreet would not arrive on the battlefield until midmorning on May 6.

Confederate General Edward Porter Alexander found Lee's positioning of Longstreet puzzling in light of Lee's statement on May 2 that he expected Grant to turn the Confederates' right flank. "The first day, naturally, offered us far the greatest chances," Alexander later wrote. "Grant's army was not all in hand, and had had no time to make breastworks. It was at a great disadvantage in the Wilderness and could not use its superiority in artillery. We had here the one rare chance of the whole campaign to involve it in a panic such as ruined Hooker on the same ground. ... What proved a drawn battle when begun by three divisions reinforced by two more after six hours and by three more 18 hours later might have proved a decisive victory if fought by all eight from the beginning."[357]

~

FROM *PERSONAL MEMOIRS*

At six o'clock, before reaching Parker's store, Warren discovered the enemy. He sent word back to this effect, and was ordered to halt and prepare to meet and attack him. Wright, with his division of Sedgwick's corps, was ordered, by any road he could find, to join on to Warren's right, and Getty with his division, also of Sedgwick's corps, was ordered to move rapidly by Warren's rear and get on his left.[358]

~

Warren's Union Fifth Corps attacked Ewell's Confederate Second Corps at Saunders' Field. Griffin's division went swinging forward on both sides of the Turnpike, striking Ewell's advance brigade, which was splintered and routed and its brigadier killed.

Griffin's men ran forward for three-quarters of a mile through the saplings and underbrush beside the road. They were so successful in this maneuver that they soon found themselves isolated from the rest of the army. Meade had ordered General Horatio Wright's division of Sedgwick's corps to advance on Griffin's right, and Warren had two of his own divisions trying to come up on the left, but none of these troops could cut through the underbrush. Griffin's men could see nothing at all because, in addition to the thick forest growth, their vision was clouded by powder smoke. This was intensified as the dead leaves on the forest floor caught fire, filing the woods with even more smoke.

One officer remarked that this was a fight of invisibles against invisibles. When Ewell counterattacked, the whole Federal division retreated back to its starting point. From there, Griffin rallied his men and set them to work building breastworks.[359]

The fighting quickly spread south to Higgerson's Field and north along Culpeper Mine Road, continuing into the evening with tremendous casualties on both sides.

A division from Major General John Sedgwick's Sixth Corps initially delayed Hill's approach. At the same time, Hancock worked to reverse his course on the Brock Road and get back to the Plank Road to stop Hill. Hancock's corps began arriving at the strategic intersection at 3:00 p.m. His troops launched their major assault down the Orange Plank Road near 4:30 p.m.[360]

At the same time, General A. P. Hill ordered all of his men into action. Conditions for a Federal offensive along the Plank Road were deteriorating by the minute. By midafternoon, Meade sent a staff officer to tell Getty to attack without waiting for Hancock. Just then, the head of Hancock's column was coming up, with General Hancock himself in the lead. While Getty and Hancock examined the situation, Hancock's leading troops formed a line along the length of the Brock Road, just south of the Plank Road. Getty ordered his men forward, and Hancock managed to bring in two divisions to help. The battle flared into an inferno.[361]

CONSUMED BY THE FLAMES

Within an hour, Hancock had repulsed the movement of Hill's forces. In the midst of this new attack, the woods burst into flames, multiplying the horror of the battle.[362] The fire crept through the underbrush, igniting matted dead leaves and fallen trees all across the front. Added to the sounds of battle, a growing chorus of wounded men begged to be rescued before they were burned to death.

Wooden breastworks also burst into flame, increasing the confusion and mayhem. Many wounded soldiers chose suicide over burning to death; swirling smoke asphyxiated soldiers on both sides.[363] In front of General James Wadsworth's division, where many dead and wounded of both armies lay in the path of the flames, a dying Confederate kept calling out: "My God, why hast Thou forsaken me!"[364]

Porter described the scene of unutterable horror: "At times the wind howled before the tree-tops, mingling its moans with the groans of the dying, and heavy branches were cut off by the fire of the artillery, and fell crashing upon the heads of the men, adding a new terror to battle. Forest fires raged; ammunition trains exploded; the dead were roasted in the conflagration; the wounded, roused by its hot breath, dragged themselves along with their torn and mangled limbs, in the mad energy of despair, to escape the ravages of the flames; and every bush seemed hung with shreds of blood-stained clothing. It seems as though Christian men had turned to fiends, and hell itself had usurped the place of earth."[365]

In front of the Fifth Maine, a wounded Union soldier screamed for help as the flames reached him. Two of his comrades left their entrenchment in an effort to save their friend. Both were shot down. As the fire approached the wounded man, a sergeant, who dared not leave the breastworks, took aim with his musket and shot the soldier, putting him out of his misery.[366]

Vicious fighting continued long after darkness fell. Hill had been stopped and potential disaster averted. Lee now left Hill's battered troops exposed in an advanced position on the Orange Plank Road. Despite Hill's request to withdraw his forces under cover of darkness, the rebels remained in place, their flanks exposed, with Longstreet nowhere in sight.[367]

The fires raged all night, providing light to the troops as they prepared for the next day. Across the battlefield, the forest was alive with the sound of axes and falling trees as soldiers worked desperately to build additional, higher breastworks. Everyone understood the need for defense against the fighting that was sure to erupt with first light.[368]

That night when General Grant's staff gathered at the mess table, they discussed the day's events. Each staff officer related to the general details of the particular portion of the front that he had visited.

As the fighting subsided, staff members made a campfire of dry fence rails in front of the headquarters tents. General Meade walked over to Grant's headquarters after dinner and sat on a folding camp chair by the fire. He and General Grant discussed the day's events and planned for the next day's fighting.

The general in chief offered Meade a cigar, but the blowing wind caused some difficulty in lighting it. Grant then offered Meade his flint and steel lighter, which overcame the difficulty.[369] As they talked, Grant received a series of telegrams informing him that Sherman had advanced in Georgia, Butler was ascending the James River, and Sigel's forces were moving up the Shenandoah Valley.[370]

General Grant expressed anxiety about the care of the wounded. He directed the medical officers and the commanders to make every possible effort to find the injured and transport them to the field hospital. Those who had been slightly wounded made their own way. With the fires still raging, intensive efforts were made to gather the seriously injured.

"As Burnside's corps, on our side, and Longstreet's, on the other side, have not been engaged, and the troops of both armies have been occupied principally in struggling through thickets and fighting for position, today's work has not been much of a test of strength," Grant remarked to Meade. "I feel pretty well satisfied with the result of the engagement; for it is evident that Lee attempted by a bold movement to strike this army in flank before it could be put into line of battle and be prepared to fight to advantage; but in this he has failed."

They agreed that Hancock and Wadsworth would attack Hill before Longstreet arrived to reinforce him. Burnside, who would arrive early in the morning with three divisions, was to send the troops of General Thomas G. Stevenson to Hancock, and place his other two divisions between Wadsworth's and Warren's troops to attack Hill in flank. At the same time, Warren and Sedgwick would attack along their fronts, inflicting all the damage they could.

Before eleven o'clock, Grant announced he was going to bed. "We shall have a busy day to-morrow, and I think we had better get all the sleep we can to-night. I am a confirmed believer in the restorative qualities of sleep, and I always like to get at least seven hours of it, though I have often been compelled to put up with much less."[371]

A young reporter, Henry Wing from the *New-York Daily Tribune*, approached the general in chief near the fire. Wing said he would leave in the morning to take dispatches from the battle to Washington for his newspaper. Did Grant have anything he would like to add?

"Well, yes," said Grant emphatically. "You may tell the people that things are going swimmingly down here."

Having witnessed some of the horrors of the day, Wing gave the general a quizzical look. Not sure how to respond, the reporter slowly took out his notebook and wrote down what Grant had said. Tipping his hat, he expressed his thanks, then turned to walk away from the fire. After a few paces, the young man realized Grant was walking behind him.

Once he was sure the other officers couldn't hear him, Grant placed his hand on Wing's shoulder. "You expect to get through to Washington?" Wing nodded, then said that was his objective. "Well, if you see the President," Grant said quietly, "tell him from me that whatever happens, there will be no turning back."[372]

The fires kindled during the afternoon were stoked by the evening breeze and spread through the underbrush, trapping many of the wounded within the flames. The screams of these pitiful soldiers as they were consumed combined with the stench of burning flesh. Any sleep that came to those who survived that monstrous night was both tortured and far too short.[373]

Every man on both sides understood that the worst of the fighting was yet to come.

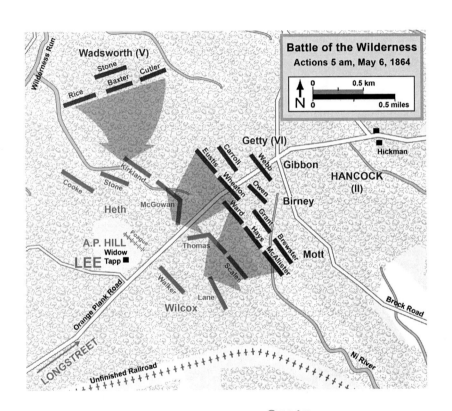

Map by Hal Jespersen, www.cwmaps.com © Hal Jespersen.
All rights reserved. Used with permission.

Chapter Twelve

THE WILDERNESS: DAY TWO

MAY 6, 1864—THE WILDERNESS, VIRGINIA

~

FROM *PERSONAL MEMOIRS*

Fighting had continued from five in the morning sometimes along the whole line, at other times only in places. The ground fought over had varied in width, but averaged three-quarters of a mile. The killed, and many of the severely wounded, of both armies, lay within this belt where it was impossible to reach them. The woods were set on fire by the bursting shells, and the conflagration raged. The wounded who had not strength to move themselves were either suffocated or burned to death. Finally the fire communicated with our breastworks, in places. Being constructed of wood, they burned with great fury. But the battle still raged, our men firing through the flames until it became too hot to remain longer.[374]

~

Headquarters staff was awakened at 4:00 a.m. on the second day of battle by the sound of Burnside's men moving along the Germanna Road. General Grant rose with his staff and ate his usual quick breakfast of a cucumber doused in vinegar. Rising from the table, the commander filled his pockets with two dozen fresh cigars. After lighting his first stogie of the day, he strolled back over to the knoll and walked slowly back and forth, listening for Hancock's attack on the left. At exactly 5:00 a.m., Hancock's signal gun broke the silence, and more than thirty thousand Federals stepped forward to engage the enemy.[375]

To everyone's surprise, suddenly there was also the sound of heavy firing on the right, as the enemy attacked Sedgwick and Warren.

Hancock's forces opened a fierce attack of cannon and musket fire. By 7:00 a.m. the enemy's line was broken, and Hancock's forces drove the rebels back in confusion for more than a mile.

Colonel Porter rode to the Orange Plank Road to meet Major General Hancock and tell him of Burnside's arrival on the field. He found Hancock actively directing his troops and reorganizing the confused alignment caused by the tangled forest and the desperate fighting.

"His face was flushed with the excitement of victory," Porter recalled, "his eyes were lighted by the fire of battle, his flaxen hair was thrust back from his temples, his right arm was extended to its full length in pointing out certain positions as he gave his orders, and his commanding form toward still higher as he rose in his stirrups to peer through the opening in the woods."[376]

"We are driving them, sir!" Hancock exclaimed. "Tell General Meade we are driving them most beautifully."[377]

After waiting for some time for word on Burnside's assault, Porter said he would ride over to explain fully the situation on the left and urge Burnside to make all possible haste. When he reached Burnside, he found the general experiencing great difficulty moving his men into position through the thicket. Porter explained the vital importance of coming to Hancock's relief. Porter and Colonel Comstock worked diligently to help Burnside find an opening to lead the troops through the woods, but their efforts were in vain. Porter returned to General Grant to notify him of the impasse, telling him that an attack from that quarter would not be possible until they could navigate through the forest.

ORDER UP SOME ARTILLERY

The battle raged directly in front of general headquarters as Warren's troops were driven back by the enemy. Stragglers emerged from the woods as they made their way to the rear. Suddenly rebel shells began falling on the knoll where General Grant was seated on the stump of a tree. He rose slowly to his feet to monitor the situation but said nothing.

An officer approached with a look of great anxiety. "General, wouldn't it be prudent to move headquarters to the other side of the Germanna Road 'till the result of the present attack is known?" The general took a few puffs on his cigar, then replied quietly, "It strikes me it would be better to order up some artillery and defend the present location." The officer saluted and turned to tend to the order. Soon a battery was brought up to defend the knoll. The enemy, however, was checked, and the Federal forces pushed them away from the general's position.[378]

Grant went back to his whittling.

Hancock attacked along Orange Plank Road from the east, while James Wadsworth's Fourth Division of Warren's Fifth Corps confronted A. P. Hill's defenses from the north. In furious fighting, Hill's forces buckled, then slowly retreated.

At that critical moment, someone heard Lee wonder aloud: "Where is Longstreet?"[379]

Then, just as Hill's forces seemed to be overrun, Longstreet's First Corps appeared, double-timing it onto the Orange Plank Road. "Old Pete's" fresh troops arrived at the front in line of battle to confront the Union forces that had become disorganized after fighting for hours in the overgrown forest. Longstreet's counterattack reversed the tide of the battle, pushing Hancock's troops back in confusion.

By midmorning, Grant's offensive had been checked by Longstreet's arrival. Sedgwick and Warren were stalled as they fought Ewell from their trenches. Burnside, who was supposed to be Grant's ace in the hole, still could find no path through the dense thicket.[380] The momentum now shifted to the Confederate side.

Everyone on the right was on the alert and eager to hear particulars about the fighting on the left. It was General Grant's policy to send out aids continuously throughout the day on any battlefield to ensure that commanding officers were updated on what was taking place at various points along the line.[381]

Suddenly, the fortunes of war turned dramatically in favor of the Union again. Lee had ordered Longstreet to counterattack around the exposed southern flank of the Union forces on an abandoned railroad bed. Longstreet initially surprised the Union defenders and, as Hancock later expressed it, "rolled me up like a wet blanket." Longstreet was driving back the Second Corps, but when he swept across the front of his troops, he was struck and severely wounded by bullets his own men fired. His serious throat and shoulder wounds brought the attack to an immediate halt.[382] For the Confederate soldiers, this seemed like a tragic repeat of the nightmare on this same ground one year before when friendly fire brought down Stonewall Jackson.

~

FROM PERSONAL MEMOIRS

The Confederate General Micah Jenkins was killed and Longstreet seriously wounded in this engagement. Longstreet had to leave the field, not to resume command for many weeks. His loss was a severe one to Lee, and compensated in a great measure for the mishap, or misapprehensions, which had fallen to our lot during the day.[383]

~

As medics picked up the wounded Longstreet and placed him on the stretcher, they placed his hat over his face to block the blazing sun. When Confederate soldiers saw them carrying the listless commander from the field, rumor quickly spread that he was dead. Longstreet could hear the comments of the fearful soldiers. To encourage his men, he raised his hat with his uninjured arm and waved it to show he was still alive. The rebel troops cheered at the gesture, though the momentum of the attack was completely checked by the incident.[384]

With the lull in the fighting, Grant and Meade met to discuss how to take advantage of the tide of battle that had again turned in their favor. Grant believed the only way forward was a coordinated attack by both Hancock and Burnside. He assumed Burnside could work his troops into position to unite in such an assault. Hancock's soldiers had been in the heat of the battle since early morning, so Grant ordered him to entrench and give his men rest during the afternoon hours. Hancock and Burnside could resume the attack at 6:00 p.m.[385]

THE REBEL COUNTERATTACK

But just after 4:00 p.m., the woods in front of Hancock erupted in enemy fire. Directed by Lee in person, the rebels made a desperate assault with a thirteen-brigade frontal assault against Union fortifications along Brock Road.

The forest once again burst into flames that quickly engulfed Hancock's log breastworks and the abatis of slashed timber. The wind blew the inferno toward the Federal forces. Smoke blinded the men as the fire swept down on them. For a time, Hancock's troops heroically maintained their position, fighting both the raging flames and the advancing enemy. But the heat and smoke from the flames around the breastworks became so intense that the troops were forced to fall back.

The Southerners rushed forward with cheers, planting battle flags on breastworks that had not yet caught on fire.

Finding a clearing, Hancock and his officers worked diligently to reorganize and rally the men, who were soon led back to the front. The gallant troops of Colonel Samuel S. Carroll's brigade dashed forward to retake the line of entrenchments that had been lost. Cheering as they ran, the troops swept everything before them, and soon regained possession of the works.[386] At nearly every point of attack, rebel troops were stopped by deadly musketry and cannon fire.[387]

By 5:00 p.m., Lee had been completely repulsed and fell back, leaving his dead and wounded strewn across the field.[388] Hancock and his well-rested troops proved too much for Lee's brigades. For the first time in this battle, Lee overreached himself.[389]

GRANT ON THE BATTLEFIELD

The general remained cool while the most critical movements were taking place, quietly whittling sticks with a penknife down to nothing, creating a pile of woodchips at his feet. This nervous occupation brought a sad ending to the thread gloves. Before nightfall several holes had been worn in them, from which his fingernails protruded. After that, the gloves disappeared, and the general wore the usual buckskin gauntlets when on horseback.[390]

Grant remained near Wilderness Tavern in the center where his commands—and his air of confidence—could be communicated to the greatest number of his troops, as he believed he could be located more readily and issue orders more promptly if he remained there almost the entire day. At times, he walked up and down the knoll, gazing toward an invisible battlefield, hearing telltale sounds from the direction of the fight, but seeing only the tangled thicket before him and the smoke rising from the forest. Most of the day he sat on the stump, or on the ground with his back leaning against a tree smoking his cigars—lighting a new one as soon as the previous had been consumed.

Grant gave orders to staff officers and messengers, who dashed off to different hot points along the line. "His speech was never hurried," Porter recalled, "and his manner betrayed no trace of excitability or even impatience. He never exhibited to better advantage his peculiar ability in moving troops with unparalleled speed to the critical points on the line of battle where they were most needed, or, as it was sometimes called, 'feeding a fight.' ... There was a spur on the heel of every order he sent, and his subordinates were made to realize that in battle it is the minutes which control events."[391]

At one point in the day, Grant was sitting with Meade beneath a tree when an aide came thundering into headquarters with the news that General David B. Birney's line, ahead of Hancock's on the left, had been broken. Without moving, the general in chief answered in his deep, strong voice, "I don't believe it."[392]

When he felt he was needed somewhere on the battlefield, Grant swung himself into the saddle without a word, then rode off at top speed with his staff following as best they could. Roads were unnecessary for this master horseman. He had a sense for finding shortcuts, splashing through streams or squeezing through hedges.[393]

He rode out to important points of the line twice during the day, accompanied by General Meade and two staff officers. Grant was always affected when he viewed the wounded soldiers, especially by the sight of blood. "He would turn his face away from such scenes," said Porter, "and show by the expression of his countenance, and sometimes by a pause in his conversation, that he felt most keenly the painful spectacle presented by the field of battle."[394]

THE CONFEDERATES' FINAL ATTACK

Late in the day, Confederate General Ewell ignored eyewitness information from Brigadier General John B. Gordon that the Union right flank was in the open and vulnerable to attack. When this information was finally communicated to Lee, he superseded Ewell and ordered a late-afternoon attack around the Union right flank.[395]

Just at that time, General Grant had asked his aides for a map to study the surrounding area. Joined by General Rawlins, Colonel Orville E. Babcock, and Colonel Porter, Grant got down on the ground, his legs tucked under him, tailor fashion, to study the map. After a moment, he said, "I do not hope to gain any very decided advantage from the fighting in this forest. I did expect excellent results from Hancock's movement early this morning, when he started the enemy on the run, but it was impossible for him to see his own troops, or the true position of the enemy, and the success gained could not be followed up in such a country."

Focused on the map, he continued. "I can certainly drive Lee back into his works, but I shall not assault him there. He would have all the advantage in such a fight. If he falls back and entrenches, my notion is to move promptly toward the left. This will, in all probability, compel him to try and throw himself between us and Richmond, and in such a movement I hope to be able to attack him in a more open country, and outside his breastworks."

By sundown, the sounds of battle, which had thundered from early dawn, had grown quiet. Then, without warning, the stillness was disrupted by loud, continuous volleys of musketry on the extreme right. Lee had unleashed his attack on Sedgwick. In a lightning-fast movement, Confederate General Gordon outflanked Sedgwick and began driving the Federals back, while taking a large number of prisoners.

Meade had strolled over to Grant's headquarters, and they stood together on the knoll discussing the day's events. Suddenly staff officers and couriers came galloping into Meade's headquarters with word confirming that the attack was directed against the extreme right, and that part of Sedgwick's line had been driven back in some confusion.

Grant and Meade hurried to Meade's tent and heard reports of increasing disaster. A messenger then reported that General Shaler and part of his brigade had been captured. Then word came that General Truman Seymour and several hundred of his men had fallen into the hands of the enemy. Another courier reported that Sedgwick's right had been turned, and General Edward Ferrero's division was cut off and forced back to the banks of the Rapidan.

Darkness had set in, but the firing continued as General Grant took the matter in hand. Aides continued to gallop in from the right, giving the most exaggerated reports of the engagement. One declared that a large force had broken and scattered Sedgwick's entire corps. Others insisted the enemy had turned the Union right completely and captured the wagon train. One courier asserted that both Sedgwick and Wright had been captured.

"In the darkness of the night," Porter recalled, "in the gloom of a tangled forest, and after men's nerves had been racked by the strain of a two days' desperate battle, the most immovable commander might have been shaken. But it was in just such sudden emergencies that General Grant was always at his best. Without a change of a muscle of his face, or the slightest alteration in the tones of his voice, he quietly interrogated the officers who brought the reports; then, sifting out the truth from the mass of exaggerations, he gave directions for relieving the situation with the marvelous rapidity which was always characteristic of him when directing movements in the face of an enemy. Reinforcements were rushed to the point attacked, and preparations were made for Sedgwick's corps to take up a new line, with the front and right thrown back."

His orders given, General Grant slowly walked back to his own camp, seated himself on a stool in front of his tent, and lit a fresh cigar. Couriers continued to bring messages and reports from the right. Grant acknowledged these dispatches, calmly puffing on his tobacco and staring into the campfire.

Suddenly an officer came thundering into the firelight from his command on the right. Leaping from his horse, he spoke rapidly with considerable excitement. "General Grant, this is a crisis that cannot be looked upon too seriously. I know Lee's methods well by past experience; he will throw his whole army between us and the Rapidan, and cut us off completely from our communications."

It was time for General Grant to exorcise the specter of Robert E. Lee.

In a most uncharacteristic manner, the general rose to his feet, took the cigar out of his mouth, and for the first time since taking command of the Army of the Potomac, raised his voice in reply. "Oh, I am heartily tired of hearing about what Lee is going to do. Some of you always seem to think he is suddenly going to turn a double somersault, and land in our rear and on both of our flanks at the same time. Go back to your command, and try to think what we are going to do ourselves, instead of what Lee is going to do."

Officers and aides from both headquarters stopped to marvel. No one spoke. The officer from Sedgwick's corps stood stunned before his commander for a long moment. Then, without saying a word, he slowly and methodically mounted his horse and trotted off into the darkness.[396]

Grant sat down again in his camp chair, picked up a stick, and commenced whittling, while the startled officers and staff quietly resumed their business.

Everything remained relatively quiet until 8:00 p.m. when Hancock galloped into headquarters to have a conference with the general in chief and General Meade. Although known as a talkative man, Hancock showed signs of fatigue after a busy day on the front. General Grant offered him a cigar but to his surprise found only one left in his pocket. "Deducting the number he had given away from the supply he had started out with in the morning showed that he had smoked that day about twenty," Porter observed, "all very strong and of formidable size. He never afterward equaled that record in the use of tobacco."

It had been an exhausting, stressful day for everyone on the battlefield. After giving final orders providing for any emergency that might arise, General Grant entered his tent and collapsed on his camp bed. Ten minutes later, another alarming report was received from the right. Colonel Porter carried the message over to General Grant's tent and found him sound asleep. "I waked him, and communicated the report," Porter wrote. "His military instincts convinced him that it was a gross exaggeration, and as he had already made every provision for meeting any renewed attempts against the right, he turned over in his bed and immediately went to sleep again."[397]

After two days of horrific fighting in the Wilderness, Grant had lost almost eighteen thousand men, while Lee lost more than eleven thousand. Grant, however, had lured Lee's army out from behind its trenches, and he would hold on with bulldog tenacity. Grant lost 15 percent of his soldiers, but these were troops the North could resupply. Lee lost 20 percent of his strength, and the South had no new troops to give him.

Lee no longer had the manpower to launch daring campaigns like those he had waged in 1862 and 1863. For the duration of the war, he was forced to remain on the defensive; only rarely was he able to launch a counterattack.[398]

From a purely tactical perspective, the battle of the Wilderness was a draw. Because Union forces suffered more casualties, some even said Grant may have lost. Yet from a strategic standpoint, this was a vital victory for Grant.[399]

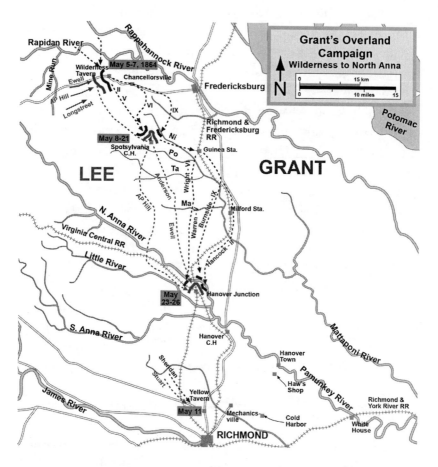

Map by Hal Jespersen, www.cwmaps.com © Hal Jespersen.
All rights reserved. Used with permission.

Chapter Thirteen

By the Left Flank

May 1864—Central Virginia

~

From *Personal Memoirs*

More desperate fighting has not been witnessed on this continent than that of the 5th and 6th of May. Our victory consisted in having successfully crossed a formidable stream, almost in the face of an enemy, and in getting the army together as a unit. We gained an advantage on the morning of the 6th, which, if it had been followed up, must have proven very decisive. In the evening the enemy gained an advantage; but was speedily repulsed. As we stood at the close, the two armies were relatively in about the same condition to meet each other as when the river divided them. But the fact of having safely crossed was a victory.[400]

~

May 7, 1864

General Grant was up early, refreshed by a night of deep sleep. He seated himself at the campfire at dawn and looked out at the woods in front of the knoll. Dense fog, combined with smoke from the smoldering forest fires, made it difficult to see any great distance, even where openings appeared in the forest.

A little after 6:00 a.m., some artillery fire was heard from Warren's batteries, leading Grant to believe that the enemy might be moving against the left. General Warren soon sent a courier to inform Grant and Meade that he had been firing at skirmishers who had pushed in too close to his entrenchments.

As soon as things calmed down again, the general in chief issued his orders to prepare for a night march.

While the commanders may not have fully grasped the gravity of what took place in the Wilderness, the men certainly did. To them the battle felt like another Chancellorsville—the same effect, the same emotions, in the exact same place. And Chancellorsville had been a humiliating defeat.

During the Battle of the Wilderness, Hancock and Warren had been repeatedly pushed back. Burnside spent most of the battle looking for a way to actually get into the fight, much to the other commanders' frustration. Sedgwick's line had been pushed back in humiliating fashion. The cavalry and artillery had been neutralized in the tangled thicket. Nearly eighteen thousand Northern troops had been killed and wounded. As they prepared to march, the air was filled with the sickening smell of burnt and rotting flesh.

Nearly every soldier in the Army of the Potomac thought he knew what orders Grant would issue that day. The Union troops had fought to a standstill in the twisted thicket, and Lee had retreated into his fortifications at Mine Run. From past experience, they knew it would be suicide to attack him there. So the troops assumed the next order would be another retreat across the Rapidan—heading north toward Washington, DC, to refit and resupply, yet again.[401]

Grant issued orders for the day, but only the corps commanders and key staff knew what those orders were.

Once his commands were communicated, the general in chief lit a cigar and took his seat on a wooden folding chair in front of his tent. The headquarters staff gathered around, each pulling up a chair. Grant explained his satisfaction with the result of the previous two days of battle. "While it is in one sense a drawn battle, as neither side has gained or lost ground substantially since the fighting began, yet we remain in possession of the field. The forces opposed to us have withdrawn to a distance from our front and taken up a defensive position. We cannot call the engagement a positive victory, but the enemy have only twice actually reached our lines in their many attacks, and have not gained a single advantage."[402]

Moving the Army of the Potomac

When all preparations for the night march were completed, the wagon trains moved out at 4:00 p.m., to get a start on the infantry. The cavalry had already been thrown out in advance; the infantry began to march at 8:30 p.m.[403]

That afternoon, as the artillery prepared to move out, the troops believed their suspicions had been confirmed. The army was pulling back, and the artillery was moving first. Soon after dark, the order came down from the corps commanders for the infantry to march. Warren and Sedgwick led the way, while Hancock held his position to guard against an attack from Lee. As they had done so many times before, the men slung their packs onto their shoulders and gloomily formed their marching columns.[404]

An eerie scene met the troops as darkness fell on the crowded Brock Road—the only roadway available to the Army of the Potomac. Beams of moonlight cut through the mixture of fog and smoke as flickering flames of orange and red still licked at trees and breastworks in the forest. The smell of burned and rotting corpses left behind on the battlefield filled the air. Men covered their noses with handkerchiefs or their sleeves.

"The men seemed aged," observed an artillerist. "They were very tired and very hungry. They seemed to be greatly depressed."[405]

All along the west side of the road for more than a mile, Hancock's soldiers remained in their combat positions, defending the movement. Most were trying to steal a little sleep after two exhausting days of fighting, but they were roused by the clatter of the moving troops.

Warren's corps was out in front, although the troops did not know where they were going. Mixed into the columns was an occasional ambulance, its wounded occupants crying out in agony whenever the wagon wheel sunk into a rut or bumped a stone or log in the roadway.[406] The Federal wagons that had moved out first raised a huge cloud of dust off the dry Virginia roads. The cavalry threw even more powdery dirt into the air, and then the infantry added its share of dust to the air above the crowded Brock Road.

Long before nightfall, Lee knew that the Army of the Potomac was on the move, but he did not know their destination. Now the infantry was adding its share of dust to the air above the crowded Brock Road.

Soon after dark, the dispirited troops were surprised as a large group of officers galloped past them on the Brock Road. Staff officers rode ahead shouting, "Give way to the right. Move to the left. Clear a path."

Suddenly a realization dawned on the weary troops. The horsemen were Grant on his massive bay, Cincinnati, and Meade on the familiar Baldy.[407] Every soldier looked up to see the movement at the fork in the road up ahead beyond the ruins of the Chancellor mansion. If Grant turned left, they were following the same pattern and retreating across the Rapidan toward Washington, DC. After three years of retreats, most of the soldiers anticipated yet another backward march.

Then, to everyone's astonishment, the soldiers watched as Grant turned to the right![408]

The commanding general was clearly heading south. The Army of the Potomac was advancing, not retreating! Spontaneous cheers arose from the troops. "On to Richmond! Huzzah for Grant! We will whip the Rebs now!"

It wouldn't be as it was with all the other commanders. Despite the dismal battle in the Wilderness, Grant was pushing forward to fight another day.

Word passed rapidly along the column that the general in chief was moving forward toward Richmond. As their officers confirmed the command to move by the left flank, which would take them south, the troops realized Grant's strategy was different than their previous offensives. This campaign had just begun![409]

The cheers grew to a crescendo.

Forgetting their weariness and wounds, Hancock's soldiers sprang to their feet and rushed to the roadside. Wild cheers echoed through the forest. Men set pinecones and branches on fire and waved them, illuminating the scene with a hypnotic, flickering glare.[410]

The cheers and shouts of excitement spooked the horses, which soon became restive. Grant's large horse, Cincinnati, prancing and whinnying with excitement, became difficult to control—something that rarely happened. After some maneuvering, the general mastered the grand animal. "This is most unfortunate," Grant declared. "The sound will reach the ears of the enemy, and I fear it may reveal our movement."

As he suspected, the rebels heard the celebration, rushed to their weapons, and responded with a cannonade in the direction of the revelry. The artillery shells fell harmlessly, far short of the Union columns. Grant ordered the staff officers to disperse and urge the men to keep quiet. But the cheering did not cease until the general in chief had finally ridden out of sight.

Grant appreciated the cheers, however, even if he tried to stop them.[411]

"The previous history of the Army of the Potomac had been to advance and fight a battle, then either to retreat or lie still," noted Charles Dana, of the War Department, who traveled with the Army of the Potomac and sent constant updates to Secretary of War Stanton and President Lincoln. "Grant did not intend to proceed in that way. As soon as he had fought a battle and had not routed Lee, he meant to move nearer to Richmond and fight another battle. ... As the army began to realize that we were really moving south, and at that moment were probably much nearer Richmond than was our enemy, the spirits of men and officers rose to the highest pitch of animation. On every hand I heard the cry: 'On to Richmond!'"[412]

"Our spirits rose," wrote a Pennsylvania soldier. "We marched free, and the men began to sing."[413]

On that narrow road, in that pitch-black night, amid the putrid stench of horrible carnage, the Army of the Potomac received a new birth of freedom.

They were all too aware of the horrors and hardships that awaited them down that road. Many of them would not live to see the end of the war. But all of that was up ahead—in the direction they were moving. "I do not know that during the entire war," declared one soldier, "I had such a real feeling of delight and satisfaction as in the night when we came to the road leading to Spotsylvania Court House and turned right."[414]

The night march had become a triumphal procession for the new general in chief. The demonstration was the emphatic verdict pronounced by the troops upon his first battle in the East.[415] Long afterward, veterans of the Army of the Potomac repeated that, for them, the march was the high point of the war.[416]

~

From *Personal Memoirs*

With my staff and a small escort of cavalry I preceded the troops. Meade with his staff accompanied me. The greatest enthusiasm was manifested by Hancock's men as we passed by. No doubt it was inspired by the fact that the movement was south. It indicated to them that they had passed through the "beginning of the end" in the battle just fought. The cheering was so lusty that the enemy must have taken it for a night attack. At all events it drew from him a furious fusillade of artillery and musketry, plainly heard but not felt by us.[417]

~

Grant made camp at Todd's Tavern just after midnight. As it was late and they still had some miles to travel the following day, the general and his staff decided to bivouac on the ground. The night air had turned cold, and fires were lit to give some warmth. Exhausted, Grant lay down next to one of the fires and quickly fell asleep.

At daybreak, the soldiers woke and noticed a pungent odor hung in the morning air. They had made camp next to a pigpen, although the pigs were gone—likely eaten by the Union cavalry the day before. The stench of death was mixed with odor coming from the pigpen, and as the sun rose, they saw the dead of both armies strewn across the field, victims of the cavalry clash the previous day.

Grant joined his staff in a breakfast of soldier's rations, then mounted and traveled with General Meade two miles down the road to Piney Branch Church, where they both set up their headquarters. A drum corps passing by caught sight of the general, and at once struck up a popular camp-meeting tune. Everyone but the general in chief laughed, and Rawlins cried, "Good for the drummers!"

"What's the fun?" Grant asked innocently.

"Why, they are playing 'Ain't I glad to get out of de wilderness!'" Rawlins replied.

The general smiled at the musicians' wit. After a moment, he divulged why he didn't grasp the comedy of the moment. "With me a musical joke always requires explanation. I know only two tunes: one is 'Yankee Doodle,' and the other isn't."[418]

ON TO RICHMOND

From the Wilderness, it was a race to the next important crossroads, Spotsylvania Court House. Lee knew the building would be Grant's strategic objective, and he ordered Longstreet's corps, under the command of General R. H. Anderson, to start for that location the next morning. Finding much of the forest on fire, with no good place to go into camp, Anderson kept his troops awake and moving. Marching throughout the night, the rebels arrived first at Spotsylvania early in the morning. When Yankee troops under General Warren arrived on May 8, they found the Southern troops already entrenched. Warren attacked, but made no real progress.[419]

By May 9, Lee was in firm possession of Spotsylvania. If Grant's goal was to push Lee back to Richmond, then he had to stop and fight the rebels here. The general in chief ordered his commanders to prepare for an assault and every corps was placed.

Hancock, the last to leave the Wilderness as he defended the rear of the Federal army, moved south and formed a line of battle half a mile short of the Po River. Warren and Sedgwick dug trenches and gun emplacements. Burnside moved in a wide arc to the left.

The line in front of Warren and Sedgwick was hot with long-range skirmishing all day. During the morning, Grant and Porter met with Sedgwick to make sure all his troops were prepared for the coming assault. After the meeting, Sedgwick and his aides rode forward to an elevation near the center of his position to inspect the progress. Sedgwick was amused by the nervous troops, who ducked and bobbed with the sound of the gunfire from sharpshooters on the enemy side. Chuckling, Sedgwick chided his men and assured them there was nothing to worry about. "They couldn't hit an elephant at this distance—"[420] Before he completed the sentence, a rebel bullet hit him in the face just under his left eye, and he fell to the ground dead.[421]

The fighting at Spotsylvania reached a new level of barbarity as both sides sensed that the campaign would likely decide the war. At the infamous "bloody angle," a brigadier in Wright's corps said that in a space measuring no more than fifteen by twelve feet, he counted 150 bodies. According to one Pennsylvania officer, at places along the line dead men were sprawled eight or ten bodies deep. Some rifle pits were filled with dead bodies as though they were mass graves.

A member of the Fifth Maine found one of his officers whose body had been so mangled by rifle fire that "there were not four inches of space about his person that had not been struck by bullets."

A rebel soldier from Louisiana observed, "We have met a man this time who either does not know when he is whipped, or who cares not if he loses his whole Army, so that he may accomplish an end. ... I have as you know been in a good many hard fights, but never saw anything like the contest of the 12th."[422]

During the worst part of the battle, Congressman Washburne, who had been at headquarters, was leaving for Washington and asked if he could relay a message to the President and Secretary of War. Grant considered a moment, then said he preferred to write a report as usual to Halleck, but Washburne could carry it back with him. Grant stepped to the field table inside his tent and wrote words that would echo down through time:

Hon. E. M. Stanton,
Sec. of War. Washington D. C.

We have now ended the sixth day of very heavy fighting. The result to this time is much in our favor. But our losses have been heavy as well as those of the enemy. We have lost to this time eleven General officers killed wounded or missing, and probably twenty thousand men. I think the loss of the enemy must be greater. ... I propose to fight it out on this line if it takes all summer.[423]

Chapter Fourteen

THE BOOK CONTRACT

Just after the New Year, General Grant received his first royalty check of $1,000 from the Century Company for his article on the Battle of Shiloh. Without hesitation, Grant mailed a check for $1,000 to Charles Wood of Lansingburgh, New York—the first person who had stepped forward and provided financial assistance when news of the Grant & Ward failure appeared in the newspapers.

"I wish to state to you," the general wrote in an enclosed note, "how great was the relief afforded by your timely loan. At the time I had not a hundred dollars in my pocket." Grant also explained that he planned to mail him another check as repayment for the rest of the money Wood had sent him. "It affords me greater pleasure from the fact that I have earned this from my own work," Grant added.[424]

Wood donated the money to charity in Grant's name.[425]

In her memoirs, Julia Grant wrote of how she fulfilled the general's promise: "The five hundred dollars sent by Mr. Wood I paid from the first proceeds of my husband's book."[426]

By the end of January, Grant's mood had greatly improved. He was encouraged by the payment for his writing, and he enjoyed receiving ten copies of *The Century Magazine* issue that contained his article on Shiloh.[427] The prospect of writing a complete account of his military exploits invigorated him.

Grant once again adopted the habit of rising early each morning, draping himself in a shawl, and writing for several hours. Occasionally, he stopped his work for a few minutes to receive family or visitors. After a brief rest, he continued with his task.

Whenever he swallowed anything, however, Grant was overcome with agony. After eating, he took opiates for the pain, but the drugs clouded his mind and hindered his writing, so he decided to endure extended periods of thirst and hunger as he labored over his manuscript. When the pain became unbearable, Harrison sprayed his throat with cocaine water, which brought temporary relief.

Grant feared drug addiction, so he resisted morphine or opiates during the day. "I suffer pain all the time, except when asleep," he told his doctor. Speaking to a reporter, Grant confessed that "when the suffering was so intense ... he only wished for the one great relief to all human pain."[428]

As Dr. Douglas had predicted, General Grant's spirits revived. The melancholy of early winter dissipated, and he dove into the writing project with renewed vigor. Of course, the doctor had witnessed this pattern with many other patients. He surmised that the general had finally come to terms with the reality of his impending death and plowed forward with his memoirs to ensure that his family would be financially cared for after he was gone.

The soldier had reached an understanding of his enemy and what he needed to do to win this final battle.

Grant worked on his memoirs at an extemporized table with folding legs, which could be easily moved from one part of the room to another. He had all he needed within his reach—his pad, his notes, and a few sheets of plain manila paper. According to Dr. Shrady, the general was a slow and painstaking composer, "his aim being to make himself clear to the reader. After a long and studied effort in framing a descriptive sentence, he would read it to his friends with all the modesty of a school-boy reciting a lesson. A pertinent question from them would give him the hint he required."[429]

At times Grant breezed through sections of text, but mostly he spent hours carefully crafting a description of a complicated battle or encounter. Each day he added piece by piece to the work, providing the gift of his perspective and memories to the annals of the American Civil War.[430]

Like Dr. Douglas, Dr. Shrady saw the book project as a blessing for Grant. He was glad the general had once again become thoroughly absorbed in its authorship. "It opened him to an entirely new field for diversion, and enabled him to get away from himself and for a time to forget the advance of his relentless malady."[431]

By midwinter, Grant had finished Volume I of his memoirs, at an astonishing 180,000 words. His self-discipline pushed him forward, and soon he was well along in Volume II, which was to be of even greater length.[432] He actually worked faster as the pain in his throat grew more intense and the choking more frequent.

CONSIDERING THE CONTRACT

In light of increased competition by publishers for Grant's memoirs, the Century leadership finally accepted the terms Twain had proposed, but they offered nothing better. The American Publishing Company of Harford offered the general 70 percent of the profits and hinted they would increase the percentage if required.

These reports began to have their effect on Grant. To Fred's great relief, his father realized that he had narrowly escaped being hoodwinked in the original book deal. "Now he began to incline toward me," Twain later explained, "for the reason, no doubt, that I had been the accidental cause of stopping that bad bargain."[433]

After George Childs completed his investigation and examined the evidence with Fred Grant's help, Childs confidently told Grant, "Give the book to Clemens."[434]

TWAIN RETURNS

After a successful lecture tour throughout the West to promote *Huckleberry Finn*, Mark Twain called on Grant on February 21. "No agreement had at that time been reached as to the contract," Twain remembered, "but I called at General Grant's house simply to inquire after his health, for I had seen reports in the newspapers that he had been sick and confined to his house for some time. ... The last time I had been at his house he told me that he had stopped smoking because of the trouble in his throat, which the physicians had said would be quickest cured in that way. But while I was in the west the newspapers had reported that this throat affection was believed to be in the nature of a cancer."[435]

On the morning of Twain's arrival in New York, the newspapers had quoted Grant's physicians, saying the general was a great deal better and was getting along very comfortably.

Twain greeted his friend warmly and told him he was cheered by the news that his threatening symptoms had disappeared. "I took for granted the report," Twain wrote, "and said I had been glad to see that news. General Grant simply smiled and replied, 'Yes—if it had only been true.'"[436]

Twain was shocked at the response, but tried to not let it show on his face.

Grant chatted for a short time about Twain's tour and the success of *Huckleberry Finn*. Soon the conversation turned to the issue of the memoirs. The general confirmed to Twain that he, his son, and George Childs had been busily negotiating the details of a contract with Charles Webster. "I mean you shall have the book—I have made up my mind about that," Grant announced.

Twain beamed and nodded his approval. They talked for a time about Grant's writing, about the progress he had made over the last three months, and about what yet needed to be done.

Grant's frail appearance disturbed Twain. The general looked exhausted and spoke with difficulty, barely above a whisper. He was noticeably thinner and appeared weaker. At times, Twain noticed, Grant clutched at his throat, clearly in pain.[437]

Dr. Douglas, who had also entered the room, overhead Twain's statement about Grant's health. He replied that the general's affliction could not be attributed altogether to smoking, but far more to his distress of mind and the grief of his financial disaster. This observation—a matter of doubt and debate at a later time—prompted General Grant to comment on his broken relationship with Ferdinand Ward.[438]

Colonel Fred Grant also entered the room and chimed in to the conversation. "Father is letting you see that the Grant family are a pack of fools, Mr. Clemens."

The general objected to this statement. He argued that facts could be produced that would show that when Ward laid siege to a man, he was certain to turn out to be a fool, as much of a fool as any of the Grant family. "Nobody could call the president of the Erie Railroad a fool, yet Ward had robbed him of eight hundred thousand dollars." He cited another man whom no one could call a fool who had invested in Ward to the extent of half a million, losing everything.

Grant shared the story of a Grant & Ward customer who had grown wealthy by being sharper and smarter than other people. Yet Ward convinced him to buy a portion of a mine belonging to ex-Senator Chaffee—a property that was not for sale, which Ward could produce no authority for selling—yet he got out of that man $300,000 in cash, without the passage of a single piece of paper or a line of writing, to show that the sale had been made.

"This man came to the office of Grant and Ward every day for a good while and talked with Ward about the prospects of that rich mine," Grant recalled, "and it *was* very rich, and these two would pass directly by Mr. Chaffee and go into the next room to talk. You would think that a man of his reputation for shrewdness would at some time or other have concluded to ask Mr. Chaffee a question or two; but, no: Ward had told this man that Chaffee did not want to be known in the transaction at all, that he must seem to be at Grant and Ward's office on other business, and that he must not venture to speak to Chaffee or the whole business would be spoiled."[439]

General Grant mentioned yet another man who came into the office one day and said, "'Ward, here is my check for $50,000, I have no use for it at the present, I am going to make a flying trip to Europe; turn it over for me, and see what you can do with it.' Some time afterwards I was in the office when this gentleman returned from his trip and presented himself," Grant explained. "He asked Ward if he had accomplished anything with that money? Ward said 'Just wait a moment,' went to his books, turned over a page, mumbled to himself a few moments, drew a check for $250,000, handed it to this man with the air of a person who had really accomplished nothing worth talking of! The man stared at the check a moment, handed it back to Ward, and said 'That is plenty good enough for me, set that hen again,' and he went out of the place. It was the last he ever saw of any of that money."[440]

After this defense, Grant wished Twain a good day. Twain thanked the general and said his goodbyes.

Fred Grant and Dr. Douglas followed Twain into the hallway and closed the door to Grant's study. "Of course I was both surprised and discomfited," Twain later wrote, "and asked his physician, Dr. Douglas, if the general were in truth not progressing as well as I had supposed." Douglas responded that the reports were rather rose-colored and that this affection was no doubt cancer. In hushed and somber tones he confirmed that the general's condition was serious, and then added that it would worsen.[441]

Talking about details that had yet to be cleared up in the publishing contract, Fred Grant walked with Twain toward the front door. When they reached the bottom of the stairs, Fred turned to Twain for a final word. "My father is gravely ill," he said, "and he is not expected to recover. His doctors believe he might have only a few weeks to live."[442]

"Colonel Fred Grant went down stairs with me, and stunned me by telling me confidentially that the physicians were trying to keep his father's real condition from him," Twain later wrote, "but that in fact they considered him to be under sentence of death and that he would not be likely to live more than a fortnight or three weeks longer."[443]

Twain had difficulty hiding his shock. He had revered the savior of the Union for two decades and was shaken to know that a man of such caliber could be stricken so quickly. Fred attempted to calm him. Twain should not be concerned about his father's illness, he said, or worry about how it might affect his work. The writing was proceeding as planned, and his father was diligently laboring on it each day. "The first volume of the *Memoirs* was finished," Fred announced with a weak smile. "Work on the second volume was well under way." Twain nodded, although he was clearly upset by the report on Grant's health. Shaking Fred's hand, he turned and left for his office.[444]

Signing the Deal

The fact that Twain signed the book contract a few days later is a testament to his courage—but also his friendship. The memoirs were far from finished, despite Fred's assurances.[445]

Twain's offer to General Grant was magnanimous. He promised to give Grant a 20 percent royalty on every copy sold. The honorable Grant protested. He was afraid Twain was being too generous. Doubling the standard royalty, as Twain had proposed, could mean publishing the book at a loss. Over time, Twain could sink his own publishing firm. To avoid this, Grant opted for 70 percent of the profits. With this agreement, if the book failed, Twain would not have to pay him anything.

Nearly a year after the failure of Grant & Ward, Ulysses feared the creditors would go after any profits from the book. General Grant asked George Childs to investigate the question with J. G. Rosegarten, Childs's personal lawyer.

"An unpublished manuscript," Rosegarten reported, "has no market value." If Grant wanted to give the rights to the manuscript to Julia, the creditors could not stop him. She could then sell her rights to the manuscript to Charles L. Webster. This is exactly what she did. The contract included a transfer of the book to General Grant's wife, and then the transfer from her to the publisher for the consideration of $1,000.[446]

Charles Webster met at the offices of Grant's personal lawyer, Frederick W. Seward, the son of the former Secretary of State, to sign the contract for the memoirs. As Webster was preparing to leave, he mentioned that the $1,000 was a mere formality, which meant nothing. Mr. Seward took him aside and said quietly: "No, it means just what it says, for the general's family have not a penny in the house and they are waiting at this moment with lively anxiety for that small sum of money."

Webster was astonished. He drew a check at once for $1,000. Mr. Seward gave it to a messenger boy, and told him to take it swiftly—by the speediest route—"to General Grant's house, and not let the grass grow under his feet."

"It was a shameful thing that the man who had saved this country and its government from destruction should still be in a position where so small a sum—so trivial an amount—as $1,000, could be looked upon as a godsend," Twain lamented. "Everybody knew that the general was in reduced circumstances, but what a storm would have gone up all over the land if the people could have known that his poverty had reached such a point as this."[447]

TWAIN TAKES COMMAND

Grant's memoirs would be published on the subscription basis Twain had recommended. Samuel Clemens became so engrossed in the practical side of the venture that he cancelled a planned lecture tour of England and Australia.[448] Taking on the personage of a general himself, Twain barked orders at Webster and the rest of the staff. He assembled one of the best subscription departments of the day. The bulk of the salesmen were former veterans who wore their old blue uniforms as they went door to door.[449]

Within weeks of signing the contract, Twain dispatched his ten thousand subscription agents across America to sell *Personal Memoirs of Ulysses S. Grant*.

The former soldiers' uniforms sported meritorious and commemorative medals from battles such as Shiloh, Vicksburg, the Wilderness, and Gettysburg. They knocked on doors in cities, towns, and villages across America, asking if there was a veteran in the house.[450] When the man of the house appeared, the interaction was not the typical back-and-forth of salesman and customer, but a friendly conversation of soldier to soldier, veteran to veteran. In their youth, these men had fought for a cause—for the salvation of their country and the destruction of slavery. This was a new cause. The general they loved and respected was dying, and at the same time he was writing his memoirs to provide for his wife and family.

As the memories flowed from the pen of General Grant in his small study in New York City, the memories also arose in tens of thousands of doorways across America. The veterans reminisced of campaigns and battlefields, marches, campgrounds, and old friends—some still living, but many had passed on.

The agent could sense when the time was right. He did not have to cajole to make the sale. He just pulled out the black leather-bound subscription book, the writing case with a steel-nib pen, and a small ink bottle from the pocket of his coat. "Here's where you sign. A two-volume set, only $3.50 for both volumes. Pay $1 down, the balance on delivery, a memorial to pass on to your children and your children's children."[451]

Twain borrowed $200,000 to underwrite the printing and publishing of Grant's book. He insisted on overseeing every part of the operation, from ordering the paper to reading the galleys, and then ensuring that the book was properly printed, marketed, advertised, and sold.[452]

Knowing the general was racing against time, Twain spoke to Grant about hiring a stenographer to speed up the writing. Grant requested a man he knew and trusted—Noble Dawson, who had served as his secretary during one of his post-presidential trips to Mexico. Dawson had been working as a stenographer for the Senate Interstate Commerce Committee, but when Grant requested his services, he was immediately released to go to New York.

Dawson and Grant picked up their friendship where they had left off. The stenographer arrived at Grant's house early in the morning, where Julia, Fred, and Ida greeted him warmly. He ascended the stairs to the general's study and worked for most of the day, setting down in shorthand what Grant said. Then Dawson read the dictated text back to Grant, making corrections as the commander directed.

"General Grant dictated very freely and easily," Dawson said of their sessions. "He made very few changes and never hemmed and hawed. Mr. Mark Twain was shown the manuscript of the first volume during one of my dictation sessions with the general. Mr.

Twain was astonished when he looked at it and said that there was not one literary man in one hundred who furnished as clean a copy as Grant. The general's sentences rarely had to be revised in any way."

Twain was initially motivated to secure Grant's memoirs because of the anticipated financial bonanza. But as he read through the completed first volume, it became clear that the book was a literary and historical masterpiece.

Twain concluded that Grant's writings were on par with Caesar's Commentaries. "The same high merits distinguished both books—clarity of statement, directness, simplicity, manifest truthfulness, fairness and justice toward friend and foe alike and avoidance of flowery speech. General Grant's book is a great, unique, and unapproachable literary masterpiece. There is no higher literature than these modern, simple memoirs. Their style is flawless—no man can improve upon it."[453]

While Grant busied himself daily, as much as his strength would allow, Twain was concerned that the general was losing valuable time on fact checking. "Only one-half or two-thirds of the second and last volume was as yet written," Twain later wrote. "However, he was more anxious that what was written should be *absolutely correct* than that the book should be finished in an incorrect form and then find himself unable to correct it."

"His memory was superb," Twain marveled, "and nearly any other man with such a memory would have been satisfied to trust it. Not so the general. No matter how sure he was of the fact or the date, he would never let it go until he had verified it with the official records. This constant and painstaking searching for the records cost a great deal of time, but it was not wasted. Everything stated as a fact in General Grant's book may be accepted with entire confidence as being thoroughly trustworthy."[454]

Everything that could be done to speed along the process had been done. Twain concluded that he had to trust Grant's will to finish and win this race with death. Like Dr. Douglas and Dr. Shrady, Twain realized that the will to complete the book and restore his family's financial security was actually keeping Grant alive. This became abundantly clear as Grant grew weaker.

In the evening, Grant often meditated and made notes. "He never dictated at night," his daughter-in-law Ida remembered, "as he was much too weak, but several of us would look through books to verify dates and little bits of fact. Sometimes Colonel Fred Grant and I would do this together."[455]

For Grant the struggle was no longer simply to provide an income for his family after the bankruptcy of Grant & Ward. The writing of his memoirs gave him reason to soldier on in ways he could not have imagined when he began. As his body weakened, Grant became aware of how his writing gave him a reason to continue living.

He spoke of this in a letter to his daughter, Nellie: "It would be very hard for me to be confined to the house if it was not that I have become interested in the work which I have undertaken. It will take several months yet to complete the writing of my campaigns. If you ever take the time to read it you will find out what a boy and man I was before you knew me. I do not know whether my book will be interesting to other people or not, but all the publishers want to get it, and I have had larger offers than have ever been made for a book before."[456]

His next task was to reach back in his memory to recall and describe one of the darkest days in the war—and then, one of the most glorious.

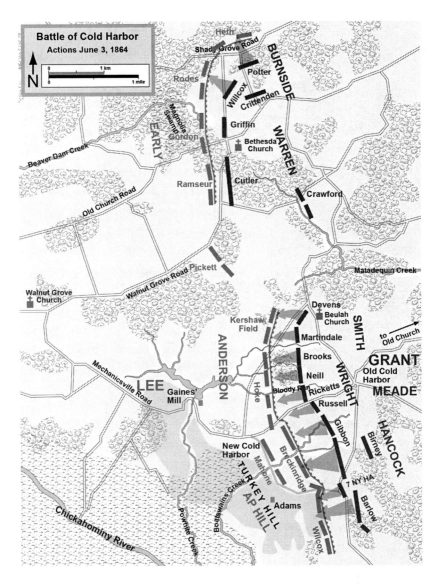

Map by Hal Jespersen, www.cwmaps.com © Hal Jespersen.
All rights reserved. Used with permission.

Chapter Fifteen

COLD HARBOR

WINTER 1885—NEW YORK CITY

In early 1885, as rumors spread throughout the New York City media that Grant was suffering from cancer of the tongue, *The New York Times* dispatched reporters to confirm the truth of these reports. Dr. Barker worked to protect the general's privacy, explaining that the pain which had given rise to the rumors had been greatly relieved. "The general is cheerful and comfortable, and spends a great part of his time at home writing the history of his military life, which is to be published by a prominent house as soon as it is completed."

Barker's words quelled the media frenzy temporarily and refocused the attention on the book project. There had never been a promised work of literature more widely heralded or more eagerly awaited than *Personal Memoirs of Ulysses S. Grant*. The public longed to see the great and terrible Civil War through the eyes of the victorious commander.

What also appealed to the sympathy of the American people was the known motive for the task—the general's desire to lift his family above their financial distress. What most did not know yet was that Grant's completion of the memoirs was a race against death.

"During it all he was bravely working against time by making the most of the life so soon to end," Dr. Shrady later remembered. "He was getting away from himself by a forced interest in work, although it was a race against reason, strength, and hope."

In the final months of his illness, General Grant was primarily confined to his bedchamber and the adjoining apartment. This cloistered existence was occasionally relieved by a short drive in

Central Park on pleasant days. Another relief came from his growing friendship with Douglas and Shrady.

"He greatly felt the need of something to occupy his thoughts," Shrady later wrote in an article for *The Century Magazine*, "and the preparation of his memoirs was in this respect a welcome relief. For hours he would sit at an extemporized table oblivious to his surroundings. When abstracted or engaged in anything that took his attention, no one ventured to interrupt him. That he was not disturbed by the presence of others was often proved by a polite motion to sit down, while he would unconcernedly go on with his work."[457]

The general soon felt enough of a kinship with Dr. Shrady that he began sharing intimate thoughts with him—some that he did not feel at liberty to share even with his family.

In one of these conversations, Grant confided that before every battle he calculated the dreadful cost in killed and wounded. For him, it was the price to be considered before the bargain could be closed. "He more than once informed me that the carnage in some of his engagements was a positive horror to him," Shrady recalled, "and could be excused to his conscience only on the score of the awful necessity of the situation."

"It was always the idea to do it with the least suffering," Grant explained, "on the same principle as the performance of a severe and necessary surgical operation. It was the proportion of the killed and wounded that was the main thing to take into account. A severe and decisive engagement prevented much subsequent and useless slaughter."

Shrady asked if his military responsibilities had not at times rested heavily on him. "He significantly answered that, having carefully studied his plan, it then became a bounden duty to the Government to carry it out as best he could. If he then failed, he had no after regret that this or that might have been done to alter the result."[458]

The characterization of Grant as a "butcher" was ironic for a man who couldn't stand the sight of blood. This was a man who shied away from a military career. In fact, his greatest ambition on graduating West Point was to become a mathematics professor. "I never went into a battle willingly or with enthusiasm," he remarked. "I was always glad when a battle was over."[459]

This was never more true for Grant than during the crucible of Cold Harbor.

MAY 31, 1864

~

FROM *PERSONAL MEMOIRS*

New Cold Harbor was important to us because while there we both covered the roads back to White House (where our supplies came from), and the roads south-east over which we would have to pass to get to the James River below the Richmond defenses.[460]

The enemy well knew the importance of Cold Harbor to us, and seemed determined that we should not hold it. He returned with such a large force that Sheridan was about withdrawing without making any effort to hold it against such odds; but about the time he commenced the evacuation he received orders to hold the place at all hazards, until reinforcements could be sent to him. He speedily turned the rebel works to face against them and placed his men in position for defense.[461]

~

The Federal soldiers were perplexed by the name of the little crossroads only ten miles from Richmond—Cold Harbor. With Virginia summer temperatures rising above one hundred degrees and no water for miles, the place was neither "cold" nor was it a "harbor." They assumed that someone in the early history of Virginia had made a mistake. The Federals soon discovered that the name came from England, where a "cold harbor" was an inn where a traveler could have overnight accommodations but no hot meals.[462]

After the battle of Spotsylvania, Northern and Southern troops raced to the next strategic crossroads. Once again the Southerners, with knowledge of the country and shorter interior lines, arrived ahead of the Yankees. But when General Sheridan swooped in on May 31 with two cavalry divisions, he moved forward to take the crossing. Rebel cavalry held the position with a handful of infantry, but Sheridan's men now carried the newly issued Spencer repeating rifles, capable of shooting up to twenty rounds per minute. Southern forces facing this new technology referred to the sixteen shooter as "that damned Yankee rifle that you load on Sunday and shoot all week."[463]

Sheridan's men dismounted and attacked the Confederates, pushing them back and securing the crossing. The rebels counterattacked with reinforcements, and soon Sheridan sent word to headquarters that he would be forced to retreat unless supplied with fresh troops. Meade ordered the cavalry commander to hold that crossroads at all hazards.

General Wright's corps was pulled out of the far right of the Union line and sent on an all-night forced march to reinforce Sheridan. On the morning of June 1, Wright's infantry streamed into the trenches and relieved Sheridan's weary horsemen. Ten thousand troops of General "Baldy" Smith's Eighteenth Corps, sent up from Bermuda Hundred to reinforce Grant, filed in next to Wright. Early that evening, Wright and Smith attacked, opening up a full-scale battle with the Confederates. Despite the loss of 2,200 men, the Union troops successfully drove the Southerners from their first line, taking several hundred troops as prisoners.[464]

On May 29, General Lee had replaced the ailing and ineffective General Ewell with General Jubal Early as commander of his Second Corps. When Union General Warren crossed Totopotomoy Creek that same day, Lee saw an opportunity to cut off and destroy that isolated corps. He sent an order to Early: "Send out a brigade and see if those people are in force."

Lee also made a prophetic statement to Early that revealed one of his biggest fears: "We must destroy this Army of Grant's before he gets to James River. If he gets there it will become a siege, and then it will be a mere question of time."[465]

General Grant's intention was to attack early in the morning in a vigorous effort to break Lee's right flank. Lee's fears increased when he learned of the arrival of Baldy Smith's troops. Everything was in place for a full-pitched battle.

Grant had established headquarters near Old Cold Harbor to be near the main point of attack. The general in chief hoped to bring his army through Cold Harbor, turn on Lee's right, and pin the Confederates in a vulnerable spot against the Chickahominy River. Grant believed that Lee's men were growing weaker, while his own soldiers remained strong. "Lee's Army is really whipped," he wrote at the time. "The prisoners we now take show it, and the actions of his army shows it unmistakably. A battle with them outside of intrenchments cannot be had. Our men feel they have gained the morale over the enemy and attack with confidence. I may be mistaken but I feel that our success over Lees [sic] Army is already assured."

By June 3, approximately 59,000 well-entrenched Confederates faced 108,000 Yankees across a seven-mile front at Cold Harbor.[466]

PINNING THEIR NAMES

Colonel Horace Porter responded to critics in Washington and in the press who charged that the men had become demoralized by the many assaults of the Overland Campaign, losing much of their spirit. "This is a gross slander upon the troops," Porter countered, "who were as gallant and subordinate as any forces in the history of modern warfare—although it is true that many of the veterans had fallen, and that the recruits who replaced them were inferior in fighting qualities."

On the night before Cold Water, while transmitting some final orders, Porter observed an incident to demonstrate what he called "the deliberate and desperate courage of the men."

"As I came near one of the regiments which was making preparations for the next morning's assault, I noticed that many of the soldiers had taken off their coats, and seemed to be engaged in sewing up rents in them. This exhibition of tailoring seemed rather peculiar at such a moment, but upon closer examination it was found that the men were calmly writing their names and home addresses on slips of paper, and pinning them on the backs of their coats, so that their dead bodies might be recognized upon the field, and their fate made known to their families at home. ... These were veterans who knew well from terrible experience the danger which awaited them, but their minds were occupied not with thoughts of shirking their duty, but with preparation for the desperate work of the coming morning."[467]

WAITING FOR BATTLE

Grant's plan to attack at 5:00 a.m. on June 2 was delayed because Hancock's corps did not arrive until 6:30 a.m. So the general in chief moved the attack to 5:00 p.m. This was once again postponed until 4:30 a.m. the following day due to the exhaustion of Hancock's men. These unfortunate delays gave the Confederates precious time to dig in and build breastworks for defense—a recipe for disaster, and the Yankee troops knew it.

Positioned only ten miles from Richmond, however, Grant believed he had no choice but to attempt to break Lee's army and perhaps win the war. When the bugles blew for the attack at 4:30 a.m., more than sixty thousand closely packed Union troops belonging to the Second, Sixth, and Eighteenth Corps dashed forward, striking at three points along the center and right-center of the rebel line. The battle lines swung up to the skirmishers, scattered them, and moved on toward the main body of the rebel forces. Up ahead, two miles of Confederate troops rose from their trenches and let loose a hail of deadly lead.[468]

Hundreds of rifles went off every second. The Confederate artillery then entered the fight, cutting down swaths of Federal troops with shell, solid shot, and canister. The well-entrenched defenders gunned down nearly every exposed Union soldier.[469]

In approximately seven minutes, the rebels shot down more than seven thousand Union soldiers.[470] Along most of the front, the charge collapsed almost as soon as it had begun. Some of the troops advanced only a short distance before they dropped to the ground under the rebel barrage. Using bayonets and tin cups, many carved out shallow rifle pits to try to protect themselves.[471]

Hancock's leading troops attacked a salient of the enemy's works. After intense fighting they captured it, taking a couple hundred prisoners, three guns, and a stand of colors. Turning the captured guns on the enemy, they soon drove them from that part of the line into the main works, a short distance in the rear. Hancock's second line, however, did not move up in time to support the first, which was finally driven back and forced out of the works it had captured. The men fell back and took advantage of the crest of a low hill fifty yards from the captured works. They quickly threw up enough cover to allow them to hold that position.

Another division had rushed forward in column, but an impassable swamp divided the troops as they came under the blistering fire of rebel artillery and musketry. Although a portion of them gained the enemy's entrenchments, their ranks were scattered by the enemy fire and forced to retreat.

Wright's corps had moved forward and carried the rifle pits in its front; they then assaulted the main line. But the Confederate defenses were too strong, and the Union troops were forced to fall back. They finally established a line only thirty yards from the enemy and protected it as best they could.[472]

~

FROM PERSONAL MEMOIRS

Wright's corps moving in two lines captured the outer rifle-pits in their front, but accomplished nothing more. Smith's corps also gained the outer rifle-pits in its front. The ground over which this corps (18th) had to move was the most exposed of any over which charges were made. An open plain intervened between the contending forces at this point, which was exposed both to a direct and a cross fire. Smith, however, finding a ravine running towards his front, sufficiently deep to protect men in it from cross fire, and somewhat from a direct fire, put General John H. Martindale's division in it, and with General William T. H. Brooks supporting him on the left and General Charles Devens on the right succeeded in gaining the outer—probably picket—rifle-pits. Warren and Burnside also advanced and gained ground—which brought the whole army on one line.[473]

~

General "Baldy" Smith drove the enemy's skirmishers before them, and carried the rifle pits. But the same cross fire from which Wright had suffered made further advances extremely hazardous. Smith's troops were so cut up that there was no prospect of carrying the works in his front unless the enfilading fire on his flank could be silenced.

Burnside had captured the advance rifle pits in front of Early's left and had taken up a position close to the enemy's main line. Warren's line was stretched thin, and as a result his troops were not able to make an assault.

Messages coming from the front conflicted as the attack proceeded. Staff officers hurried information from every important point on the battlefield to Meade and Grant, but events were changing faster than could be properly reported.[474]

Confederate rifles and artillery picked away relentlessly at the Yankee troops, creating growing piles of fallen men. Along most of the line, the attack was stopped in its tracks. General Meade sent a message to Grant: "I should be very glad of your views as to continuance of these efforts, if unsuccessful."

Grant sent the only reply he could make. "The moment it becomes certain that an assault cannot succeed, suspend the offensive, but when one does succeed push it vigorously." Shortly after scribbling this note, Grant set off to inspect the battlefield for himself.[475]

On receiving Grant's message, Meade ordered that the attack be relaunched. This time Smith refused to send his corps forward. Other Union officers rejected the idea outright. "I will not take my regiment in another such charge if Jesus Christ himself should order it," responded one New Hampshire captain.[476] Across the battlefield, many Union soldiers recognized the futility of the situation and either refused to move or shot their guns into the air as they lay on the ground.

By 11:00 a.m., the attack had ground to a halt. Grant rode out to speak directly to each of the corps commanders, gauging their opinions. Hancock reported that the position in front of him could not be taken. Wright said he might be able to secure an opening, but nothing would be gained by it unless Hancock and Smith advanced at the same time. The general in chief became convinced that no further attack upon the enemy's works would succeed. At 12:30 p.m., he wrote to General Meade: "The opinion of the corps commanders not being sanguine of success in case an assault is ordered, you may direct a suspension of farther advance for the present. Hold our most advanced positions, and strengthen them."[477]

Grant returned to his tent, dismounted, and sat on a stone marker beside the road with his head down. Julia's cousin, William W. Smith, had been visiting the past few days and recognized the sobriety in the general's face. "What's the situation?" asked Smith.

"Bad," sighed Grant. "Very bad."[478]

Union losses were staggering. Grant's casualties for the day totaled more than thirteen thousand, most of them during the first half hour. Lee lost less than twenty-five hundred troops that day.[479]

After the battle, the diary of a Massachusetts soldier was found spattered with blood. Its final entry read: "June 3rd, 1864, Cold Harbor, Virginia—I was killed."[480]

That evening, when the staff officers assembled at headquarters after much hard riding and hot work during the day, they discussed the battle with General Grant. "I regret this assault more than any one I have ever ordered," Grant told his staff. "I regarded it as a stern necessity, and believed that it would bring compensating results; but, as it has proved, no advantages have been gained sufficient to justify the heavy losses suffered."[481]

Costly as the battle was, Grant had no intention of pulling back or relaxing his grip on Lee. Success, he told his staff, "was only a question of time."[482]

After Cold Harbor, the commanding general became an easy target for those who called him "Butcher Grant." Even Mary Todd Lincoln criticized the lieutenant general. "Grant is a butcher and not fit to be at the head of an army. He loses two men to the enemy's one. He has no management—no regard for life. I could fight an army as well myself."[483] This criticism came despite the fact that Robert E. Lee had been equally reckless with men's lives. Pickett's hopeless charge at Gettysburg, bloodily repulsed by Hancock's troops, was nearly as costly in lives as Grant's failure at Cold Harbor.

Yet Cold Harbor came in the midst of the Overland Campaign, where the Army of the Potomac suffered fifty thousand casualties—half as many as had been lost by that army in the whole war up to this time.[484]

The losses at Cold Harbor, according to many war statisticians, were not out of proportion for an attacking force; but much was made of them by the pacifist element in the North. The "butcher" title was also used for political purposes by the opposition party in the presidential election as they pushed their slogan that "the war is a failure."[485]

Samuel Beckwith, the telegraph officer working for General Grant, noticed that after Cold Harbor, the face of the general in chief developed "a careworn expression that indicated sleepless nights and wearisome days." When he delivered a message to the general's tent, Grant read the telegram and then sighed. "Beckwith," he said, "the hardest part of this General business is the responsibility for the loss of one's men. I can see no other way out of it, however; we've got to keep at them. But it is hard, very hard, to see all these brave fellows killed and wounded. It means aching hearts back home."[486]

The criticism bothered Grant for the rest of his life. "They call me a butcher," he said to an old friend after the war. "But do you know, I sometimes could hardly bring myself to give an order for battle. When I contemplated the death and misery that were sure to follow, I stood appalled.[487]

~

FROM *PERSONAL MEMOIRS*

I have always regretted that the last assault at Cold Harbor was ever made. ... No advantage whatever was gained to compensate for the heavy loss we sustained.[488]

~

The previous battles of Grant's Overland Campaign had been inconclusive. Cold Harbor, however, was a decisive victory for Lee. Cold Harbor culminated a month of nonstop brutal battle for both armies. Grant lost 41 percent of his forces. At the same time, Lee lost 50 percent of his troops, which he was unable to replenish. Although the Union had an almost limitless supply of equipment and personnel, these losses were a devastating blow to Northern morale.

Grant's casualties from the six-week campaign were now pouring back into Washington by the boatload. The wounded men filled twenty-one Washington-area hospitals.[489] In this election year, many in the North were so thoroughly tired of this war they were ready to vote for a candidate who would promise peace, no matter what the cost.

THINKING OF HOME

The day after the terrible battle at Cold Harbor, Grant did what many of the other soldiers did that day—he wrote home.

Nellie Grant, the general's eight-year-old daughter, was in school with her two older brothers in St. Louis. The Sanitary Commission had recently sponsored a fair, and Nellie had played the part of the Old Woman Who Lived in a Shoe. She had recently written to her father to bring him up-to-date on the events in her young life. Before he wrote the orders that directed the Army of the Potomac toward their next destination, Grant sat down in his tent and wrote a letter to his much-beloved daughter.

> My dear little Nellie:
>
> I received your pretty well written letter more than a week ago. You do not know how happy it made me feel to see how well my little girl not yet nine years old could write. I expect by the end of the year you and Buck [her eleven-year-old brother] will be able to speak German, and then I will have to buy you those nice gold watches I promised. I see in the papers and also from Mama's letters that you have been representing "the old Woman that lived in a Shoe" at the Fair; I know you must have enjoyed it very much. You must send me one of your photographs taken at the Fair.
>
> Be a good little girl as you have always been, study your lessons, and you will be contented and happy.[490]

A CHANGE IN STRATEGY

Ever since the Union troops had crossed the Rapidan, the war had been conducted nonstop. Besides the carnage, Cold Harbor became a turning point where defensive fortifications, siege warfare, and daily fighting became the norm in the Eastern Theater.[491]

~

FROM *PERSONAL MEMOIRS*

This assault cost us heavily and probably without benefit to compensate: but the enemy was not cheered by the occurrence sufficiently to induce him to take the offensive. In fact, nowhere after the battle of the Wilderness did Lee show any disposition to leave his defenses far behind him.[492]

~

The bloodletting at Cold Harbor caused Grant to reconsider his strategy for cornering Lee and capturing Richmond. "I now find, after more than thirty days of trial, the enemy deems it of first importance to run no risks with the armies they now have," he wrote Halleck. "They act purely on the defensive, behind breastworks, or feebly on the offensive immediately in front of them and where, in case of repulse, they can instantly retire behind them. Without a greater sacrifice of human life than I am willing to make, all cannot be accomplished that I had designed outside of the city."

A changed was required. Grant now moved forward with plans he had in mind from the beginning of the Overland Campaign—to boldly move his army across the James River. "Once on the south side of the James River, I can cut off all sources of supply to the enemy except what is furnished by the canal"—the James River Canal, to Richmond's west. Grant planned to attack the vital railways supplying Richmond from the south and west, then he would attack the canal and complete the encirclement of Lee's troops.[493]

The Army of Northern Virginia seemed to have acquired a new respect for the courage, endurance, and soldierly qualities of the Army of the Potomac. They no longer wanted to fight them "one Confederate to five Yanks," as they had boasted earlier in the war. Cold Harbor revived rebel hopes temporarily, although they seemed to have given up the idea of gaining any advantage in the open field.

The ramifications on the Army of the Potomac were in some ways temporary. When the soldiers learned that Grant planned to break loose of the Confederate army and head for the James River, most of the negative attitudes about Cold Harbor disappeared.

1

2. John Rawlins, Grant's Galena friend who became his chief of staff. Rawlins, along with Julia Grant, helped Ulysses stay sober through most of the Civil War.

2

1. This portrait was taken shortly after Grant was named brigadier general in 1861.

3

3. General William Tecumseh Sherman, Grant's West Point friend who became his chief military subordinate.

5. Colonel Horace Porter, trusted member of Grant's army staff and later a close friend and supporter. Porter became president of the Grant Monument association and led the drive to finish the fundraising and begin construction of Grant's tomb.

4. General George Gordon Meade, the final commander of the Army of the Potomac.

6. General Winfield Scott Hancock, one of the most talented and aggressive generals in the Army of the Potomac.

8. Grant's good friend and publisher, Mark Twain.

7. General Philip H. Sheridan, the cavalry commander of the Army of the Potomac and one of Grant's most trusted lieutenants

9. Julia Grant, after the Civil War.

10. The Grant family at their summer cottage at Long Branch, New Jersey, 1870.

11. Frederick and Ida Grant in their later years.

12. Ulysses S. "Buck" Grant, Jr., in his later years.

13. Grant's beloved daughter, Nellie.

14. Ulysses and Julia's youngest son, Jesse Grant.

15. Dr. George F. Shrady became one of Grant's friends and confidants during the final year of his life.

16. Dr. John Hancock Douglas first diagnosed the cancer at the base of Grant's tongue. Dr. Douglas became a close friend of Grant and his family throughout his illness.

17. Some members of the Grant family with Dr. John Hancock Douglas at Mt. McGregor in June, 1885, only weeks before the death of Ulysses.

18. Ulysses S. Grant writing and editing his memoirs only days before his death at Mt. McGregor, New York, summer, 1885. A towel covers the large cancerous growth on his neck.

Chapter Sixteen

RACE WITH DEATH

The New York newspapers had finally uncovered the fact that Grant's health was not as rosy as they had been led to believe. Doctors Barker and Douglas did their best to guard the general's medical privacy. Both doctors knew the general was a voracious reader of the newspapers. He would eventually see anything they said to the press, so they were especially careful with their public pronouncements. At first Douglas refused to discuss Grant's condition with the press. But when the word *cancer* appeared in the papers, the doctor felt it was time to respond. "General Grant has not cancer of the tongue," Douglas told the press. "The difficulty is in his mouth, and it is of an epithelial character. The irritation has now been greatly relieved, and that is all I feel at liberty to say."[494]

Somehow, however, his true condition was eventually leaked to the press. At the end of February, the *New York World* was first to paint a gloomy picture concerning the general's condition: "Not withstanding the rose-colored report of Gen. Grant's health, recently given in a medical journal, the truth is that Gen. Grant is a very sick man, and his death apparently not far distant."

The paper reported that the condition of the general's mouth and tongue gave evidence of a malignant, fatal disease. They mentioned that his injured hip still caused him pain, and he was also suffering terribly from neuralgia. "He works every day with bandaged head and an unremitting pain to finish his military autobiography or history of the war and hopes to complete it this spring."[495]

The doctors realized they could no longer withhold the facts. Somehow the *World* had obtained the results of the biopsy that had been done. "The conclusion was reached," the paper reported, "that the disease was an epithelioma, or epithelial cancer of the malignant type, that was sure to end fatally."

Then the bombshell dropped on March 1. Opening *The New York Times* that morning, General Grant was shocked by the bold headline on page 2:

SINKING INTO THE GRAVE

GEN. GRANT'S FRIENDS GIVE UP HOPE

DYING SLOWLY FROM CANCER—WORKING CALMLY ON HIS BOOK IN SPITE OF PAIN

SYMPATHY FROM EVERY SIDE

There was a consultation of the physicians on February 19, at which it was agreed that the trouble from which the general was suffering was cancer, and the only difference of opinion was as to the probable rapidity of its development.[496]

Although Grant had been informed by his doctors that the disease was quite serious, reading the terminal diagnosis in *The Times* was difficult:

> The cancer, Dr. Douglas said, was a malignant cancer. If it were in any other part of the body it could be held in abeyance. The consulting physicians had all agreed that an operation would be of no use.
>
> The doctors, of course, make no predictions as to the rapidity with which the disease will progress, but their opinion seems to be that the gallant old warrior has at the most only a few months to live, and that his death may occur in a short time.[497]

Once again General Grant came face-to-face with the reality of how little time he had left and, worse still, the general public also knew. "That his days were numbered was an intimation for which he was not prepared," wrote Adam Badeau.[498]

Unlike the immobilizing depression he suffered prior to Christmas, this jolt served as motivation to win his race with death and finish *Personal Memoirs*.

Within twenty-four hours after the *Times* article was published, all the New York metropolitan papers dispatched reporters to camp out across the street from the Grant family home on East Sixty-Sixth Street. Within a week, journalists from as far away as San Francisco and Los Angeles had joined the death watch.

Doctors Douglas and Shrady decided it would be best to hold regular consultations and issue formal bulletins to the press as needed. Three bulletin boys were stationed in the main hall of the house, representing Western Union, the Associated Press, and the United Press. As the crisis deepened, the press became much more aggressive in gathering information. A general clearinghouse for news was established in the basement of a nearby house on Madison Avenue. From there, all the metropolitan newspapers connected special telegraph wires to their downtown offices.

One reporter even feigned a love affair with a chambermaid across the street to secure a good observation window. Reporters took turns on the deathwatch twenty-four hours a day in all weather. Any unusual light emanating from the house brought raised binoculars and strained necks. Visitors and members of the family leaving the house were pounced on for a statement.[499]

Long accustomed to being in the public eye, Grant viewed the situation as routine. He dispassionately read the often-exaggerated accounts of his condition in the papers. To meet the urgent demand for details, he cooperated with a decision to issue bulletins to the press—the only way the truth could be told.

On one occasion when Twain came to visit, Grant greeted him with a note of surprise. "You would think the newspapers could get my weight right. While I was out riding, the thought occurred to me that I would like to be weighed. When I got to a store, I got out and slipped on the scales, which balanced at 146. Well, I read six newspapers this morning. No two of them have the same figures and no one of them is right."[500]

THE DAILY PRESS RELEASE

The preparation of the press release became a matter of daily excitement with the medical staff. "Bearing in mind the many mistakes made in the case of President Garfield, in which contradictory and misleading bulletins were published, it was deemed imperative to state exact facts," wrote Dr. Shrady, "with the full sanction of the medical men in attendance and also that of the family." The arrangements for the distribution of these dispatches were elaborate and systematic.

"Reporters 'covering the case' were so constantly on guard in the street that it seemed impossible for anything of importance to occur in the house without their knowledge," Shrady remembered. "At the end of every consultation there was a group of anxious interviewers, who plied the medical men with questions. As there was never any other disposition than to tell the plain truth of the situation, all necessary satisfaction regarding the true import of the bulletins was easily obtained." The doctors were besieged even in their own homes. There was no limit to the probing imposition of the news-gatherers.[501]

"For obvious reasons no unfavorable change in symptoms was discussed in the presence of the general," Shrady explained, "and it was only after the official bulletins were published that he had knowledge of the fact. As he insisted on reading his favorite papers, there was no way of keeping him in desirable ignorance of his actual condition."[502]

Grant was often amused by the stories told of him, of his habits, plans, and moods. Having been president of the United States, he understood the daily news cycle and was mostly willing to forgive the newsmongers for their fictions.

At other times, the general was saddened by the gloomy prognosis reported in the various papers. After reading one of the bulletins, he remarked to Shrady: "Doctor, you did not give a very favorable account of me yesterday." The doctors walked a delicate balance between informing the public and preventing alarm in the general and his family regarding his actual condition.[503]

SOLDIERING ON

After leaving the White House, General Grant enjoyed a short period of private life as an ordinary citizen. With the publication of his health struggle, he was again an object of interest across the country and around the world. Letters and telegrams of sympathy from common citizens up to Queen Victoria poured into the Grant residence.

Grant continued writing and dictating as he worked on volume two. He wore a shirt that had become one or two sizes too big for him along with the ever-present scarf around his neck. Any cold air on his head brought on terrible headaches, so the general often wore his knit skating cap. Both day and night, he curled up in his two large, overstuffed black leather armchairs, bending forward during the day to write on a board set across the space above his thighs. At night he leaned back against his pillows as he slept to keep from choking on the phlegm and dead tissue that accumulated in his throat.[504] His greatest fear was choking to death.

Watching the man who had saved his nation from rebellion endure excruciating pain with patience and grace, Dr. Shrady developed a profound admiration for Grant. The general who once gave orders to a million men now had to take orders himself—and he did so with dignity and grace.

NELLIE RETURNS

In early March, Nellie Grant Sartoris arrived in New York from Europe with her children to help care for her father. Ulysses had written telling her simply that he was not well but that he was busy writing his memoirs. Nellie, however, knew the true situation thanks to her older brother Fred, who had written a letter to inform her that their father was dying.

Nellie's arrival in March greatly cheered Grant, who had missed his only daughter. He insisted on traveling to the steamship pier on that cold day to meet her.[505] The excitement of her arrival, the embraces and the tears, all weakened the general, but his heart was full of joy at her arrival.[506]

Nellie had always been special to Ulysses, possibly closer to him even than his sons. Grant was proud that Nellie, the first daughter of a president married in the White House, had become a charming, respected woman. Nellie had endured a tragic marriage to the Englishman Algernon Charles Francis Sartoris, who was both an alcoholic and a notorious womanizer.[507] Grant had wept after Nellie's wedding and departure to England, so he was thrilled to have her and the grandchildren with him in the large New York City townhouse.

As the weather warmed, Grant and Nellie took pleasant rides together through Central Park in a carriage Senator Chaffee had loaned to the family. Sometimes the senator and the general's friend Matias Romero of Mexico accompanied Grant and his daughter. At other times, the tall, white-bearded Dr. Douglas joined them on these excursions. Romero said that Grant was so overjoyed by Nellie's presence that it sometimes robbed him of sleep at night.[508]

On one such occasion, when the general had passed a restless night, he could not shake a feeling of melancholy the following day. Dr. Shrady noticed Grant's depression and orchestrated an innocent ruse to brighten his spirits.

Julia and Nellie had waited outside Ulysses' room during one of Dr. Shrady's morning visits. When the doctor stepped into the hall, they asked their usual questions: how had the general slept; how was he feeling; was there any area of concern? Shrady explained that Ulysses had a restless night and awoke in a depressed condition. The ladies glanced at each other with increased anxiety. The doctor asked them if they would help him cheer their husband and father. They eagerly agreed.

Shrady told them his plan and then knocked on the door to reenter Grant's study. "General, two ladies have called, and have asked if they can see you. They are very anxious to know how you are, but have promised not to disturb you by useless questions."

"But—" Grant paused, trying to remain polite, "can't you tell them my condition?"

"They insist upon seeing you themselves, if it is possible," the doctor answered in a serious manner.

"What did you say to them?"

"That they might see you if they promised to allow me to speak for you."

"Well," he said wearily, "you may invite them in."

Shrady went to the door and invited Julia and Nellie into the room. They entered, doing all they could to conceal their smiles. Dr. Shrady introduced them with mock formality and stated the object of their visit. He promised the smiling general that both ladies had made a solemn promise not to engage him in any conversation whatsoever.

Ulysses immediately joined in the fun. With a gleam in his eye and a suppressed smile, he deliberately said, "Ladies, the doctor will tell you all that you wish to know."

Then, as if they had been strangers to him, Shrady simply replied to the ladies that the general did not wish to be troubled with useless questions. "He desires to say that he is feeling reasonably comfortable, that he fully appreciates the honor of your visit, and is correspondingly grateful for your sympathy."

By this time, Grant's despondency had disappeared, and he couldn't help smiling. Both Julia and Nellie then bowed and turned to leave the room. Before they closed the door, the general called to them with his weak voice, and they returned giggling and lavishing him with affectionate hugs and kisses.[509]

GO TO SLEEP

On one particularly difficult night, Grant suffered searing pain, gasping with every breath. The general called out for Shrady, hoping he had not left for the evening. The doctor rushed in from the adjoining room, not knowing that Julia had quietly followed him and was watching with concern from the doorway.

"What shall I do?" Grant asked in meek desperation.

Quickly taking stock of the situation, Shrady realized Grant was not only in pain but also fearful of the suffering to come in the hours ahead. He promised Grant that he would feel better if he would change the way he was positioned on the chairs.

"Allow me to arrange your pillow and turn it on its cooler side, while you imagine yourself a boy again," he gently instructed. "Now, curl up your legs, lie over on your side, and bend your neck while I tuck the cover around your shoulders."

Grant followed the doctor's direction. Shrady then leaned in and quietly whispered to the former president of the United States and general in chief: "Now go to sleep like a good boy."[510] Within a few minutes, the man who had been gasping for air and racked with pain was peacefully asleep.

Shrady slowly walked from Grant's bedside and turned the light down low. As he approached the door, he noticed Julia silently standing in the darkened doorway to the anteroom. Shrady stepped into the room and closed the door behind him. Somewhat embarrassed, the doctor fumbled for words. "I'm sorry, Mrs. Grant," he said quietly. "I didn't mean any disrespect. I wanted only to give him some rest." He paused, looking back at his sleeping patient. "I'm afraid that the general will not like that kind of treatment. He may think it inconsistent with his dignity to be treated like a child, and may not understand the real motive."

"There is not the slightest danger of that," Julia replied as they exited the room. "He is the most simple-mannered and reasonable person in the world, and he likes to have persons whom he knows treat him without ceremony."[511]

Closing the door to the general's study, Shrady thanked her for her kindness. Julia nodded and bid the doctor a pleasant evening.

Chapter Seventeen

The General Returns

When the question of reinstating Grant to his position as lieutenant general on the retired list was raised, many in Congress wondered why they should give more money to the ex-president when he was already being taken care of by his wealthy friends. They entirely missed the point that Grant's friends felt compelled to help him because Congress did not give honor to whom honor was due.

The members of Congress were also unaware that the money raised by Grant's wealthy friends had been stolen by Ferdinand Ward. The general no longer received a penny from the trust fund that was intended to pay him $15,000 a year. Grant had also signed over all his property to William H. Vanderbilt to pay off the $150,000 loan. The ex-president was truly without means, other than the income from two small Washington houses Julia had sold and the money from *The Century* articles.

Grant, of course, was too proud to divulge the true nature of his financial situation.

But the general had some heavy hitters on his side. Fighting for Grant's reinstatement were friends such as William Tecumseh Sherman, Joseph W. Drexel, George Childs, and former Secretary of State Hamilton Fish. These men and others exerted influence to see a bill passed in Congress that would have guaranteed a lieutenant general's salary to Grant. Then at his death, Julia would receive a pension of $5,000 per year.[512]

The Senate passed the bill. Then, after heated debate, where some of Grant's enemies rose against him, the House did not.

On February 16, 1885, the House of Representatives voted 158 to 103, sixteen less than the two-thirds needed to place Ulysses S. Grant on the retired list of the US Army. Southern members of

Congress were joined by one of Grant's political enemies, William Rosecrans, in defeating the measure. A classmate of Grant's at West Point, Rosecrans was serving as a congressman from California. He had never forgiven Grant for his part in demoting him during the Civil War, and he saw the defeat of the reinstatement as his opportunity for revenge.

Grant made no comment when he heard the news from Washington that the bill failed to pass, but Dr. Douglas noticed a heightened state of melancholy.[513] In their first bulletin to the press on Grant's condition, his physicians wrote: "The action of Congress in refusing to pass the bill restoring him to his honors has been very depressing."

Adam Badeau wrote that the general had considered the bill partial reparation for the injury his reputation had sustained in the failure of Grant & Ward. "When the reparation was withheld," Badeau observed, "he suffered proportionately."[514]

THE ILLNESS REVEALED

Then the news of General Grant's illness hit the papers. When members of Congress learned Grant was dying and had lost the private trust fund in the Grant & Ward swindle, hearts softened. With this news reverberating throughout the country, one more attempt was made to push the reinstatement through Congress.[515]

The bill was reintroduced to authorize President Chester Arthur to restore Grant's highest rank and then retire him with full pay. In addition to the pension of $19,000 a year, there would be "commutations for forage, rations, the care of horses," that would probably add between $4,000 and $5,000 to this retirement fund.

This time, *The New York Times* eloquently endorsed the proposed pension in an editorial that placed Grant's military strategy and victories above Lincoln's leadership in terms of what had defeated the Confederacy and brought about the reunification of the nation: "The plain fact is that it [the country] was saved by him, and that, humanly speaking, this great people owes its existence, with its vast achievements and wonderful possibilities as a united nation, to him more than any one man."[516]

Childs wrote an editorial supporting the bill in his Philadelphia newspaper, declaring that it was not only possible to reward a national hero, but it was also customary. Adding to the momentum, the New York State Assembly instructed its congressional delegation to vote unanimously for any bill reinstating General Grant.[517]

Representative Samuel J. Randall, the Democratic Speaker of the House, told both Sherman and Childs that he would reintroduce the bill. Randall reassured them that it would somehow pass.

But time was against them as March 4 was the last day of the session. If Randall could not get the bill passed, it would have to be taken up by the next Congress and the incoming president, Grover Cleveland. With Grant's health failing fast, there was no guarantee that he would live long enough for Congress to act on his behalf when it reconvened.

Having been president himself, Grant was not optimistic of the bill's passage with all the other legislation being considered by Congress. When he learned that the House had adjourned the night before the inauguration without taking action on his behalf, he was pessimistic. He told Childs, who was in town visiting: "You know during the last day of a session everything is in turmoil. Such a thing cannot possibly be passed. If anyone in the world could pass such a bill, I think Mr. Randall could. But I don't think it is at all likely, and I have given up expectation."[518]

The Constitution mandates a brief congressional recess to occur before a new president is inaugurated. At noon on March 4, the presidency of Chester Arthur would end, and Grover Cleveland would be sworn in.[519] Grant did not believe the bill could be passed in the short morning session before the inauguration.

A POLITICAL MIRACLE

But Speaker Randall had given Grant his word, and he was determined to push the measure through. He reconvened the House and ordered the clerk to date all business as having been transacted on the previous day. He then quickly plowed through the necessary parliamentary procedures, moving to pass agenda items that had not been completed. With this necessary housekeeping finished, at precisely 11:00 a.m. he surrendered the chair and asked his replacement for a suspension of the rules to consider the Grant reinstatement bill.

To his chagrin, however, the new chair overruled him, arguing that the House had not yet considered the matter of the disputed Iowa election. Randall knew this detour could derail his bid to see Grant reinstated, but he now had no power to stop it.

The dispute—between George Frederick, who had been certified by the Iowa Board of Elections, and James Wilson, the incumbent Republican, who was not certified by the board—was a difficult partisan question that could consume hours of debate. Wilson had claimed that the Iowa board had wrongly certified his challenger and that he, not Frederick, was the rightful holder of Iowa's congressional seat. The issue had reached an impasse, and there did not seem to be sufficient time to deal with it before the required recess.

Then to everyone's surprise, at the last minute Wilson rose from his chair and announced that he would withdraw his objection to the Iowa election results if the House would immediately move to consider the Grant bill. The statement was met with stunned silence. Then the chamber erupted with enthusiastic applause. In an act of compassionate patriotism, Wilson had given up his congressional seat so Grant could receive his pension. Within minutes, the Grant bill was passed.

Back in the game, Randall rushed from the House chambers and ran through the Capitol rotunda, where senators were congregating for Cleveland's inauguration. Randall loudly called their names and implored them to return to the Senate chamber to vote on the Grant bill.

The senators walked briskly to the chamber and filed into their seats. Outgoing President Chester A. Arthur waited impatiently in one of the nearby Senate offices to sign the bill for Grant's reinstatement—if it passed before he was no longer president. Arthur had made Grant's successful reinstatement one of his administration's primary goals and intended to fulfill his promise.

Time was not on his side. In fact, time had run out. The clock at the front of the Senate chamber had just passed noon, and by law the Congress was required to adjourn.

But as in the day when Joshua prayed for the sun to stand still so he could finish his battle, on this day in 1885, time once again stood still. At the order of the leaders of that august body, a clerk scaled a ladder in front of the Senate chamber and turned back the clock so the Senate could legally consider the Grant bill. In this moment of supreme political theater, the bill reinstating General Grant to the rank of General of the Army on the retired list was passed by the Senate and rushed to President Arthur for his signature.

In his final act as president, Chester A. Arthur directed the president pro tempore of the Senate to send Grant a telegram telling him of his reinstatement. With that, Arthur and Speaker Randall finally joined the procession escorting Grover Cleveland to his inauguration. Behind them, the Senate clock tolled noon. It was twenty minutes slow.[520]

A GENERAL ONCE MORE

That afternoon, Grant sat chatting with his son Fred, Mark Twain, George Childs, and Adam Badeau. Julia was in the next room. Noon had come and gone, and everyone assumed that, for whatever combination of reasons, the bill had failed to become law. Suddenly there was a knock at the door. A telegram had been delivered for Mr. Childs. The publisher read the note, and handed it to Grant. The general looked at it for a long moment, then looked up at his family and friends and declared: "I am grateful the thing has passed."

Julia rushed in from her room down the hall beaming with joy as she exclaimed, "Hurrah! Our old commander is back!"[521]

Mark Twain described the momentous scene. "Every face there betrayed strong excitement and emotion—except one, General Grant's. The volume of his emotion was greater than all the other emotions there present combined, but he was able to suppress all expression of it and make no sign."[522]

Upon receiving the news, Grant told Childs that it was vitally important that he immediately write a letter to Cleveland accepting the reinstatement. "The law," he insisted, "is to date the commission from the time one accepts. In the early part of the war I saw in the newspapers I was appointed to a higher rank and I wrote at once and accepted on the strength of the newspaper report. In about two months' time, through red tape, I got my appointment, but I got my pay from the time I wrote."[523]

The next morning, the new president, Grover Cleveland, made the reinstatement official by signing Grant's commission. The papers were presented to him by Robert Lincoln, the martyred president's son, and the outgoing secretary of war. Cleveland signed the papers and suggested that Lincoln also affix his signature—after all, Cleveland said, Lincoln's father was the man who had promoted Grant. It would be only fitting if Lincoln's son reconfirmed that rank. But Lincoln declined the honor, saying that this duty was best left in the hands of the new secretary of war. Cleveland reluctantly agreed.

For the first time since the collapse of Grant & Ward, Grant worried less about his financial condition and more about finishing his memoirs to secure Julia's future.[524]

That night Mark Twain sent a telegram to his wife saying that when Grant read the message about his pension, "The effect upon him was like raising the dead."[525]

Chapter Eighteen

CROSSING THE JAMES

JUNE 1864—JAMES RIVER, VIRGINIA

As Grant reminisced about the high and low points of the struggle, his focus was drawn to one of the most strategic and majestic days of the entire Civil War. Crossing the James was his most audacious plan—possibly the most dangerous maneuver undertaken by either army—and the one time when Robert E. Lee was completely out-generaled.

~

FROM *PERSONAL MEMOIRS*

Lee's position was now so near Richmond and the intervening swamps of the Chickahominy so great an obstacle to the movement of troops in the face of an enemy, that I determined to make my next left flank move carry the Army of the Potomac south of the James River. Preparations for this were promptly commenced. The move was a hazardous one to make: the Chickahominy River, with its marshy and heavily timbered approaches, had to be crossed; all the bridges over it east of Lee were destroyed; ... the Army of the Potomac had to be got out of a position but a few hundred yards from the enemy at the widest place.[526]

~

The night before the Army of the Potomac crossed the Rapidan River and engaged the Army of Northern Virginia in battle, Ulysses S. Grant had gathered his staff to give them final instructions. At one point, he stood and walked to a map on the wall. Using his finger, he drew an imaginary crescent from their present location,

around the eastern side of Richmond heading south and then crossing the James River. Tapping that spot south of the James, Grant
declared, "When my troops are there, Richmond is mine. Lee must
retreat or surrender."[527]

After two months of some of the most brutal fighting in human
history, Grant had one final obstacle to get his troops "there"—but
it was monumental.

From Cold Harbor on June 5, he wrote to Halleck at Washington concerning his strategy for victory:

> My idea from the start has been to beat Lee's Army, if possible,
> north of Richmond, then after destroying his lines of commu-
> nications north of the James River to transfer the Army to the
> south side and besiege Lee in Richmond, or follow him south if
> he should retreat.
>
> I will continue to hold substantially the ground now occu-
> pied by the Army of the Potomac, taking advantage of any favor-
> able circumstance that may present itself until the cavalry can be
> sent west to destroy the Virginia Central Railroad from about
> Beaver Dam for some twenty-five or thirty miles west. When
> this is effected I will move the army to the south side of the
> James River, either by crossing the Chickahominy and marching
> near to City Point, or by going to the mouth of the Chickahomi-
> ny on [the] north side and crossing there. To provide for this last
> and most possible contingency, several ferry-boats of the largest
> class ought to be immediately provided.[528]

Since the beginning of the war, the Army of the Potomac had
positioned itself primarily on the eastern side of Richmond so that
while fighting the battles against the rebels, they could still defend
Washington, DC. This position also allowed them to transport supplies, troops, and the wounded by the various rivers flowing south-
eastward toward the Chesapeake Bay and then on to Washington or
Fortress Monroe.

Grant understood the importance of defending the capital, but
he was also completely focused on defeating Lee's army. He comprehended, like many other commanders had not, that to defeat the

Army of Northern Virginia was to defeat the Confederacy. And the only way to weaken Lee's army to the point where it could be driven to its knees was to do what he had done in Vicksburg—cut off all supplies to the enemy. Those goods flowed into Richmond nearly unhindered from the south and the west—the opposite side of where the Army of the Potomac had focused its efforts up to that time.

Grant believed that Lee would defend Richmond first and foremost, rather than pulling away to attack Washington. So if Grant could engage the Army of Northern Virginia—and the other Union forces could keep the smaller rebel armies in check—Lee would have no forces available to attack Washington. Grant could then move around to the southern and western side of Richmond to begin the siege that would eventually choke off the supplies and defeat the rebel army.

"We can defend Washington best by keeping Lee so occupied that he cannot detach enough troops to capture it," Grant declared.[529]

Some of the troops sensed Grant's intentions. Two days after the battle at Cold Harbor, Union cavalry Captain Charles Frances Adams told Richard Henry Dana Jr., "I think Grant will be forced to adopt his Vicksburg tactics—he will have to uncover Washington, cross the James, move up the south bank and then throw himself on the Confederate line of communications and supplies."[530]

Grant could hold enough troops around Washington to keep it safe from any small rebel force that Lee might send against it. In a crisis, he could rush more troops from south of Richmond by water down the James River, around Old Point Comfort on the Chesapeake Bay, and then up the Potomac River to Washington. In the meantime, he would lay siege to the Army of Northern Virginia—and as General Lee warned Jubal Early, "then it would only be a mere question of time."[531]

THE LOOMING ELECTION

As Grant planned his next military move, he was also fighting the battle of public opinion regarding the war. It was an election year, and unless Federal troops could demonstrate success on the battlefield, there was a growing likelihood that the public would tire of the conflict and pick a candidate running on a so-called "peace platform."

Northern hospitals were teaming with Union casualties, while cemeteries were being filled to capacity with the dead. The expense of the war had reached nearly $4 million a day. And there were constant rumors that if the war continued much longer, European powers might recognize the Confederacy and provide materials, perhaps even military assistance.[532]

The Union Armies needed a significant victory if Lincoln was to be reelected.

Grant was convinced that Petersburg, the railway hub and supply depot twenty miles south of Richmond, was the key to the Confederate capital. He hoped to capture Petersburg by assault, and then take the other railroads and canals bringing supplies from the west, which would cut off Lee's lifeline and make it impossible for him to remain in Richmond. Grant would then pursue the fleeing Army of Northern Virginia, meet it in open battle somewhere outside of Richmond, and defeat it, finally bringing the war to a close.[533]

CROSSING THE JAMES

General Grant's first move toward his objective was to march his army south and then cross the formidable James—a tidal river more than eighty feet deep. He had already called for pontoon bridge materials to be sent from Fortress Monroe at the mouth of Chesapeake Bay. He also asked the navy to send vessels from all directions to help in ferrying troops and supplies to the south side of the river.

To gain a night's march before its absence was discovered, the Army of the Potomac had to be withdrawn quietly from its position at Cold Harbor. In some places, the rebel lines were only thirty to forty yards away, making the evacuation an exceedingly delicate task. In preparation for the operation, roads had to be constructed over the marshes leading to the lower Chickahominy and bridges built to allow the troops to cross.

Getting across the Chickahominy was the relatively easy part. After that, the army would move forty to fifty miles south to cross the mighty James.

On June 5, Grant called in Colonels Porter and Comstock from his staff and asked them to ride ahead and scout the banks of the James looking for the best possible place to cross.[534] Both men had served under General George McClellan in the Peninsula Campaign and were familiar with the terrain. They set out for the James and soon found what they believed was the best place for a crossing. Both men were strongly in favor of a location known by locals as Fort Powhatan, about ten miles below City Point.

"Several roads led to the point selected for crossing both on the north and the south side of the James," Porter explained, "and it was found that they could be made suitable for the passage of wagon-trains by repairing and in some places corduroying them." The army had become proficient at the construction of "corduroy" roads—a process whereby logs were split down the middle and then laid side by side over muddy ground to allow horses, loaded wagons, and heavy artillery to pass.

Another significant advantage was that Fort Powhatan was the narrowest point that could be found on the river below City Point, being twenty-one hundred feet in width from Wilcox's Landing on the north side to Windmill Point on the south side.

General Grant waited anxiously for the return of this scouting party and busied himself with preparations for the delicate operation required for the army's withdrawal. When Comstock and Porter arrived, he called them immediately into his tent to present their recommended route.

"While listening to our verbal report and preparing the orders for the movement which was to take place, the general showed the only anxiety and nervousness of manner he had ever manifested on any occasion," Porter recalled. "In giving him the information he desired, we could hardly get the words out of our mouths fast enough to suit him. He kept repeating, 'Yes, yes,' in a manner which was equivalent to saying, 'Go on, go on'; and the numerous questions he asked were uttered with much greater rapidity than usual. This would not have been noticed by persons unfamiliar with his habit; but to us it was evident that he was wrought up to an intensity of thought and action which he seldom displayed."[535]

CREATING A DIVERSION

Just as he had done at Vicksburg, Grant now sent out his cavalry to divert the attention of the enemy commander. The other objective of this move was to sever the railroads and canal supplying Richmond. Grant sent orders to General Meade directing him to dispatch Sheridan:

> The object of the cavalry expedition to Charlottesville and Gordonsville is to effectually break up the railroad connection between Richmond and the Shenandoah Valley and Lynchburg. ... It is desirable that every rail on the road destroyed should be so bent or twisted as to make it impossible to repair the road without supplying new rails.[536]

On June 7, Sheridan set out on the raid around Richmond with the goal of destroying much of the Virginia Central Railroad, a key supply route from the Shenandoah Valley to Richmond. He was then to connect with General David Hunter, whose troops were ordered to destroy the James River Canal at Lynchburg.

Both Sheridan and Hunter failed in these assignments. Confederate cavalry commanded by Wade Hampton kept Sheridan from reaching Gordonsville and drove him to retreat at the Battle of Trevilian Station on June 11 and 12. Jubal Early and the Second Corps arrived from Richmond in time to save Lynchburg from Hunter and drive him into West Virginia.

A positive result of Sheridan's expedition—and the most important to Grant at the time—was that by drawing Hampton away from Richmond, Lee was deprived of the eyes of his cavalry for the critical period while Grant moved his army to the James.

On June 9, a Federal detail was set to work fortifying a line to the left and rear on ground overlooking the Chickahominy. Engineers worked to bridge the necessary points on the river, and a large force worked to repair and corduroy the roads through the swampy bottoms.[537]

All this activity could have suggested one of Grant's now famous moves by the left flank. The problem as Lee saw it was that Grant was running out of room. If he moved much further left, he would be forced to confront the Confederates straight on, using the same roads McClellan had used two years earlier.

Lee did not know, however, that the navy had deployed a small armada of ships well out of his sight on the lower James, including ironclad gunboats to guard against rebel raiders. The pontoons Grant ordered arrived at Wilcox's Landing from Fortress Monroe, along with a large supply of bridging lumber.

MOVING OUT

As the Confederate army hunkered down in its Cold Harbor entrenchments, bracing for another Union attack, Grant gave the order for his army to move in the opposite direction.[538] At dusk on June 12, the legendary march to the James began. General Grant had acted with his usual secrecy, sharing his detailed plans with only a few officers. Orders for the movement were delivered to commanders in the strictest confidence.

Behind a massive screen of Federal cavalry and Warren's Fifth Corps, Grant evacuated his line corps one at a time.

~

FROM *PERSONAL MEMOIRS*

Attaching great importance to the possession of Petersburg, I sent back to Bermuda Hundred and City Point, General Smith's command by water, via White House, to reach there in advance of the Army of the Potomac. This was for the express purpose of securing Petersburg before the enemy, becoming aware of our intention, could reinforce the place.[539]

~

W. F. Smith's Eighteenth Corps began the march on the night of June 12, quietly leaving their trenches and moving east to White House Landing. From there the troops were loaded onto navy steamers and traveled down the Pamunkey and York rivers to the Chesapeake Bay, through Hampton Roads and back up the James River to Bermuda Hundred, where they finally arrived on June 14. Smith's corps was familiar with the terrain on the south side of the James, and Grant wanted it in position to attack Petersburg on his command.

As Smith's men moved out, the Union cavalry division not with Sheridan crossed the Chickahominy in a feint toward Richmond to mask Grant's move from rebel scouts. Warren's Fifth Corps followed behind the cavalry to add heft to the maneuver and also to protect the exposed Union flank if Lee should grow wise to Grant's plans.[540]

The portion of Wilson's division of cavalry that had not accompanied Sheridan pushed forward to Long Bridge on the Chickahominy, fifteen miles below Cold Harbor. The enemy had destroyed all the bridges on that part of the river, and the cavalry had to dismount and wade across the muddy stream. They soon reached the opposite bank with enough force to drive away the enemy's cavalry pickets. A pontoon bridge was then rapidly constructed over the Chickahominy, allowing Warren to stay close to the cavalry. On the morning of June 13, his entire corps crossed the bridge.

Warren moved out some distance on the Long Bridge Road to watch the routes leading toward Richmond and hold the bridge across the White Oak Swamp. He made demonstrations intended to deceive Lee and give him the impression that the army was turning his right with the intention of either moving on Richmond or crossing the James River above City Point.[541]

Hancock's corps followed, moving south toward the James. Burnside set out next on the road to Jones's Bridge, twenty miles below Cold Harbor, followed by Wright.

By dawn the next day, the Army of the Potomac was moving south in one of the most daring strategic military maneuvers in American history.[542]

Early that morning, rebel troops discovered the empty Union trenches in front of Cold Harbor. Grant had vanished. The Army of the Potomac—more than 115,000 men—had marched away so quietly that Confederate pickets didn't even know they were gone.

For the first time since the Army of the Potomac crossed the Rapidan, Lee didn't know where it was.

Lee was mystified when Southern patrols reported the empty trenches. Had Grant retreated to Washington? Had he moved south to lure him into a hasty move in pursuit? Would Grant double back and try to get into his rear? For the moment, the Southern commander had no idea.

With his cavalry off chasing Sheridan, Lee had no way of knowing the exact location of the Union army—just as Grant had intended. The pressing threat, Lee understood, was to Richmond, only ten miles away. Uncertain of Grant's location, Lee believed he had no choice but to guard the capital. He ordered the Army of Northern Virginia across the Chickahominy to cover the approaches to Richmond.[543]

All the while, the bulk of Grant's army was far to the south.

ON THE BANKS OF THE JAMES

Hancock's corps reached the river at Wilcox's Landing on the afternoon of June 13, passing the plantation once owned by ex-president John Tyler.[544] Wright's and Burnside's corps arrived the next day. The Union troops had marched up to fifty miles in the scorching Virginia heat, each soldier carrying a heavy pack filled with ammunition and rations.[545]

After weeks of nearly nonstop brutal fighting, Meade's infantrymen found themselves marching across open country with no enemy patrols to worry about. With the nightmare of Cold Harbor behind them, they realized Grant was setting them up for a strategic, decisive blow against Lee.[546]

At its narrowest, ten miles east of City Point, the James River was seven hundred yards wide. It had a tidal range of four feet. No one knew whether a 2,100-foot pontoon bridge could ride out that kind of buckling rise and fall.

No army had ever built a pontoon bridge more than a thousand feet long.

Grant took the greatest risk of his military career—and perhaps of the entire war—when he allowed his army to be divided for an extended period of time as they crossed this formidable obstacle. If Lee discovered the location of the Army of the Potomac, he could move in force to destroy large numbers of the Northern troops in detail. With such a victory, he could even the odds and possibly destroy Lincoln's chances for reelection.

Another danger was the Confederate flotilla at Richmond, including three ironclads with long-range, heavy-caliber guns. From their position, the ships could shell the steamers that carried the infantry across the river. Or they could send fire ships downstream to wreck the pontoon bridge. For two days and one night, the Army of the Potomac would be divided and vulnerable to attack.

No one in the history of war had ever moved a force of 115,000 men across a tidal river so close to the guns of enemy naval forces.[547] Grant was risking everything—the Overland Campaign, Lincoln's reelection, possibly the war itself. The stakes could not have been higher.

General Grant set out from his camp near Old Cold Harbor on the night of June 12. Although there was moonlight, the dust rose in such dense clouds that the troops could not see more than a short distance, making the march exceedingly tedious and uncomfortable. He reached Wilcox's Landing on the night of June 13 and went into camp on the north bank of the James.[548]

That evening a much more relaxed Grant lounged on a blanket near a campfire. Assistant Secretary of War Charles Dana, on the other hand, paced back and forth, complaining angrily about the loss of some baggage wagons that had capsized while crossing the Chickahominy swamplands. Working himself into a frenzy, Dana declared that this mishap was "evidently a piece of damn folly."

Somewhat amused, the lieutenant general rose and pulled a burning stick from the fire to relight his pipe. "If we have nothing worse than this ..." Nothing more needed to be said, and Grant returned to his blanket.[549]

~

FROM *PERSONAL MEMOIRS*

The material for a pontoon bridge was already at hand and the work of laying it was commenced immediately, under the super-intendence of Brigadier-General [Henry Washington] Benham, commanding the engineer brigade. On the evening of the 14th the crossing commenced, Hancock in advance, using both the bridge and boats.[550]

~

Engineers completed construction of the pontoon bridge, attaching cables and ropes to ocean-going schooners anchored upstream for stability. They worked with such efficiency that they finished just before midnight.[551] Now the work of the engineers would be tested to see if a 2,100-foot bridge across a river with a four-foot tidal range[552] could withstand the ocean currents or the wind gusts sweeping inland from Chesapeake Bay.[553]

This was Ulysses S. Grant in his prime. He had deceived the South's finest general by withdrawing his forces as the enemy slept. He had exposed the Army of the Potomac to danger of piecemeal destruction and yet at the same time set them in motion to accomplish the possible destruction of the enemy.

"Our forces will commence crossing the James today," Grant wired Halleck. "The enemy show no sign of having brought troops to the south side of Richmond. I will have Petersburg secured, if possible, before they get there in much force. Our movement from

Cold Harbor to the James River has been made with great celerity and so far without loss or accident."

Admiral Samuel Phillips Lee—Robert E. Lee's cousin, who had remained loyal to the Union—moved his fleet into position on the river and assisted in ferrying the troops. Hancock's corps, which Grant wanted to cross first, boarded the navy ships that shuttled back and forth all night to transport the troops. Before daylight on the morning of June 15, Hancock's entire infantry had been transported to the south side of the James, along with four batteries of artillery.[554]

Once on the other side of the river, Hancock fanned out and moved his forces into position to establish a bridgehead around Windmill Point, acting as a shield for the rest of the army.

At 7:00 a.m. on June 15, President Lincoln sent a dispatch to General Grant: "I have just received your dispatch of 1 p.m. yesterday. I begin to see it. You will succeed. God bless you all. A. Lincoln."[555]

The sky on that fateful morning was a cloudless blue as the troops approached the river. Steamers waiting at the shore greeted the soldiers with short blasts on their whistles. At the pier, bands played martial tunes to keep spirits high—although soldiers were instructed to march out of step as they crossed to keep the bridge from swaying.[556]

Grant rode to a hill near the riverbank on the north side of the James to watch the grand procession—a line of blue stretching for twenty-five miles. Clasping his hands behind his back, the commanding general of all the armies of the United States drank in the mesmerizing scene below him. Banners snapped in the breeze coming off the river, steam rose from the vessels, and the sun reflected off the ripples of the river, the cannon, and thousands of gun barrels.

Colonel Porter described the magnificent scene: "A fleet of transports covered the surface of the water below the bridge, and gunboats floated lazily upon the stream, guarding the river above. Mingled with these sounds were the cheers of the sailors, the shouting of the troops, the rumbling of wheels, and the shrieks of steam-whistles. The calmly flowing river reflected the blue of the heavens, and mirrored on its surface the beauties of nature that bordered it. The rich grain was standing high in the surrounding fields. The harvest was almost ripe, but the harvesters had fled.

"It was a matchless pageant that could not fail to inspire all beholders with the grandeur of achievement and the majesty of military power," Porter wrote. "The man whose genius had conceived and whose skill had executed this masterly movement stood watching the spectacle in profound silence."

For once General Grant's cigar remained unlit.

"After a time he woke from his reverie," Porter recalled, "mounted his horse, and gave orders to have headquarters ferried across to the south bank of the river."[557]

Nearby Union gunboats kept a watchful eye on any threatening enemy movements. At the same time that soldiers and equipment were ferried from north to south, an enormous herd of cattle swam across the river under the watchful eyes of the quartermasters.[558] The approaches to the river on both banks were covered with troops moving briskly to their new positions or waiting patiently to cross. Remarkably, not one man, one animal, or one vehicle was lost in the crossing.[559]

As he watched with wonder the crossing of the massive Army of the Potomac, Assistant Secretary of War Dana breathlessly wired Stanton: "All goes on like a miracle."[560]

The muffled sound of cannon far off to the north announced that Warren's corps and Wilson's cavalry at the other end of the column continued to hold Lee in check and in confusion.[561] By midnight of June 16 the army, all the trains, the artillery, and the herds of cattle had been safely transferred to the south side of the James. The only casualties were those that occurred as Warren's corps and the cavalry held off the enemy.[562]

Lee still had no idea that Grant's army had slipped across the James. The operation was so successful one Confederate general later dubbed it "the most brilliant stroke in all the campaigns of the war."[563]

Confederate General Edward Porter Alexander described how the rebels could have attacked and annihilated the isolated Fifth Corps on the afternoon of June 13 had they known they were part of a grand ruse. "The only trouble about that was that we were entirely ignorant of the fact that it was isolated. On the contrary ... Warren's corps had taken up its line so near to Riddell's Shop as to give us the idea that it was the advance corps of Grant's whole army pushing toward Richmond on the road from Long Bridge."[564]

In permitting Grant to cross the James, Lee in fact was completely deceived—first by Sheridan and his cavalry, next by Warren's corps, and ultimately by Grant's ingenious strategy and direction. "Thus the last, and perhaps the best chances of Confederate success," General Alexander lamented, "were not lost in the repulse of Gettysburg, nor in any combat of arms. They were lost during the three days of lying in camp believing that Grant was hemmed in by the broad part of the James below City Point, and had nowhere to go but to come and attack us."

When the truth became known, Lee burst out at his subordinates in one of the rare cases where his anger was vented: "Stonewall Jackson would never have permitted it!"[565]

THE GATES OF PETERSBURG

~

FROM *PERSONAL MEMOIRS*

After the crossing had commenced, I proceeded by steamer to Bermuda Hundred to give the necessary orders for the immediate capture of Petersburg.[566]

~

Grant's army was now poised to strike at Petersburg, a city the Confederacy could not afford to lose. The Federals were prepared to launch a blow with a ten-to-one advantage in numbers.[567]

General William F. Smith confronted the strong rebel fortifications east of Petersburg with eighteen thousand soldiers. Behind miles of parapets, ditches, tangled abatis, and well-placed cannons was Confederate General Pierre Beauregard with fewer than 2,500 men. As Smith approached with General Hancock's Second Corps not far behind, Lee was just learning that the Federals were at the gates of Petersburg. He did not yet believe Beauregard's frantic dispatches and did nothing to support him.

It appeared Grant's strategic move across the James had been a glorious success. Lee had left the Southern door to the Confederate capital unlocked and relatively unguarded. Smith and Hancock could now secure the fruits of victory by taking Petersburg, then moving on to Richmond.

Chapter Nineteen

Capturing the General

General Grant was nearly exhausted. He had set a breakneck pace for himself as he worked to finish his memoirs—a schedule that many healthy writers would have difficulty maintaining. But the general was racing against his own demise. By mid-March his body had grown significantly weaker, and each day he sensed the urgency more acutely.

The pain in his throat was relentless, eased only by applications of cocaine water during the day and doses of morphine in the evening. Many nights he remained wide awake as he reclined in his chair, unable to sleep due to pain or the sensation of choking. He knew time was running out, and worried that the second volume of his memoirs might remain unfinished.

Since Christmas, he had experienced a season of relative strength and clarity of mind. But as Dr. Douglas had warned, he was regressing into a difficult physical and emotional state. This relapse slowed the pace of his writing and brought on another bout of depression.

Although he wrote less in the following weeks, he continued to plot out the content of the second volume. He hoped to pick up where he left off when his health improved, and then move forward to Appomattox.[568]

Both Doctors Douglas and Shrady recognized Grant's decline but still believed it was important for him to focus on the memoirs as he was able. "When he forced himself to write or dictate he was thus able to distract his attention from his condition," Shrady recalled. "Hence every encouragement was given him to do as he pleased in such regard." Grant often remarked to his doctors that his book was destined to be his salvation as well as that of his family. "Thus he would sit and write when most men would have been abed and under the influence of an anodyne," Shrady marveled.[569]

During that time, Grant received a timely tribute from an unknown artist. The meeting resulted in a piece of art that would be revered for years to come.

THE ARTIST AND HIS MENTOR

One evening, the fledgling sculptor Karl Gerhardt appeared unannounced at the home of his patron, Mark Twain. Gerhardt joined Twain in the library of his lavish Hartford home to show him a small bust he had been crafting in clay from a photograph of General Grant.

Four years earlier, Gerhardt had appeared both unannounced and unknown at the door of Samuel Clemens, asking him to come to his home to view a sculpture he had recently completed. Amused and curious, Clemens followed Gerhardt to his home and was surprised and mildly shocked to find a life-size sculpture of the artist's wife, Josie, nude to the waist. Clemens was so impressed with the work he asked painter James Wells Champney and prominent sculptor John Quincy Adams Ward to evaluate Gerhardt's work. They both gave positive reviews, so Clemens and his wife decided to finance Gerhardt's art education in Paris.

Clemens was about to discover if his investment had paid off.

"I was the more irritated for the reason that I had never seen a portrait of General Grant—in oil, water-colors, crayon, steel, wood, photography, plaster, marble or any other material, that was to me at all satisfactory," Twain explained. "Therefore, I could not expect that a person who had never even seen the general could accomplish anything worth considering in the way of a likeness of him."

But when Gerhardt uncovered the bust, Twain's misgivings disappeared. "The thing was not correct in its details, yet it seemed to me to be a closer approach to a good likeness of General Grant than any one which I had ever seen before."

The sculptor had brought it to Twain, hopeful that he would show it to a member of the general's family who could point out its chief defects for correction. Twain was hesitant. "I could not venture to do that, for there was a plenty of people to pester these folks without me adding myself to the number."

But one glance at the bust instantly changed his mind. "I said I would go to New York in the morning and ask the family to look at the bust and that he must come along to be within call in case they took enough interest in the matter to point out the defects."[570]

They arrived at the general's house at one o'clock the next afternoon. Twain left Gerhardt and the bust in the parlor on the first floor and climbed the stairs to see the family. As he approached the top of the staircase, he had second thoughts. "For the first time, the thought came into my mind, that perhaps I was doing a foolish thing, that the family must of necessity have been pestered with such matters as this so many times that the very mention of such a thing must be nauseating to them. However, I had started and so I might as well finish."

With a knock on the door, Twain entered Grant's anteroom, where he was greeted by Colonel Fred Grant, Mrs. Jesse Grant, and Dr. Douglas. He explained that he had brought a young artist with him who had been working on a small bust of the general from a photograph. He was waiting downstairs. "I wished they would look at it, if they were willing to do me the kindness," Twain explained.

The idea excited Jesse Grant's wife, Elizabeth. "Is it the artist who made the bust of you that is in *Huckleberry Finn?*" Twain answered yes. With great animation, Elizabeth responded, "How good it was of you, Mr. Clemens, to think of that!"

In his inimitable style, Twain described his surprise and delight at this unexpected reception. "She expressed this lively gratitude to me in various ways until I began to feel somehow a great sense of merit in having originated this noble idea of having a bust of General Grant made by so excellent an artist. I will not do my sagacity the discredit of saying that I did anything to remove or modify this impression that I had originated the idea and carried it out to its present state through my own ingenuity and diligence."

"How strange it is," Elizabeth continued, "only two nights ago I dreamed that I was looking at your bust in *Huckleberry Finn* and thinking how nearly perfect it was, and then I thought that I conceived the idea of going to you and asking you if you could not hunt up that artist and get him to make a bust of father!"

"Things were going on very handsomely!" Twain recorded with delight.[571]

Julia had stepped into the room and overheard the conversation. She immediately suggested that Gerhardt step in to look at the general.[572] Happily, Twain went downstairs to fetch Gerhardt who carried the bust upstairs and uncovered it. All of the family present marveled at the excellence of the likeness and the cross fire began. "I was sure his nose was so and so, and, I was sure his forehead was so and so," and "Don't you think his head is so and so?"

The family discussed the details and then checked themselves, begging Gerhardt's pardon for criticizing his work. He graciously replied that their criticisms were exactly what he wanted. Gerhardt begged them to go on. The general's wife said that in that case they would be glad to point out what seemed to them inaccuracies, but that he must not take their speeches as being criticisms of his art at all.

They found two inaccuracies: in the nose and the forehead. All were agreed that the forehead was wrong, but there was a lively dispute about the nose. Some of those present contended that the nose was nearly right—the others argued that it was distinctly wrong.

While the controversy raged concerning the nose and the forehead, Fred's wife, Ida, entered and joined the entertainment. Each of the three ladies disappeared, one by one for a few minutes, then returned with a handful of photographs and hand-painted miniatures of the general.

Julia knelt on the ottoman to get a clearer view of the bust and the others stood about her—all talking over each other. Finally, the general's wife said, hesitatingly, "If Mr. Gerhardt could see the general's nose and forehead himself, that would dispose of this dispute at once. The general is in the next room—would Mr. Gerhardt mind going in there and making the correction himself?"

Of course Gerhardt was delighted at this suggestion. Within a few minutes, Grant astonished everyone when he entered the room, wrapped in his shawl and supporting himself in a somewhat unsure way on his cane. Twain introduced Mr. Gerhardt to the general. Grant said he could sit on the sofa if it would be for the advantage of the artist.

Julia objected, saying he might catch cold. Showing a slight look of disappointment, he turned and started back to the other room. But at the door, he stopped and asked, "Then can't Mr. Gerhardt bring the clay in here and work?"

"This was several hundred times better fortune than Gerhardt could have dreamed of,"Twain exclaimed. "He removed his work to the general's room at once. The general stretched himself out in his chair, but said that if that position would not do, he would sit up. Gerhardt said it would do very well, indeed; especially if it were more comfortable to the sitter than any other would be."[573]

The ladies removed Grant's woolen skater cap and discussed the curve of his nose and the prominence of his forehead. They made him turn this way and that way to see different views and profiles of his features.

"He took it all patiently," Twain remembered, "and made no complaint. He allowed them to pull and haul him about in their own affectionate fashion without a murmur. Mrs. Fred Grant, who is very beautiful and of the most gentle and loving character, was very active in this service and very deft with her graceful hands in arranging and re-arranging the general's head for inspection and repeatedly called attention to the handsome shape of his head."

The general's wife placed him in various positions, none of which satisfied her, and finally she went to him and said, "Ulys! Ulys! Can't you put your feet to the floor?" He did so at once and straightened himself up.

"During all this time, the general's face wore a pleasant, contented and, I should say, benignant aspect, but he never opened his lips once," Twain observed. "The general's hands were very thin, and they showed, far more than did his face, how his long siege of confinement and illness and insufficient food had wasted him."

After fifteen minutes with the general and his family, Gerhardt announced that he could correct the defects now. "A table for the bust was moved in front of him," Twain explained. "The ladies left the room. I got a book."[574]

"The general watched Gerhardt's swift and noiseless fingers for some time with manifest interest in his face," Twain recalled, "and no doubt this novelty was a valuable thing to one who had spent so many weeks that were tedious with sameness and unemphasized with change or diversion. By and bye, one eyelid began to droop occasionally."[575]

Just as Grant was nearly asleep, Adam Badeau burst into the room, interrupting the nap. Like the others, he complimented the sculptor on the excellence of the likeness. He carried some sheets of the manuscript in his hand. "I've been reading what you wrote this morning, General, and it is of the utmost value; it solves a riddle that has puzzled men's brains all these years and makes the thing clear and rational."[576]

Grant nodded his thanks and Badeau exited, leaving the artist to his work and the general to his rest.

After a few moments, Harrison came in to attend to the general, also waking him from his slumber. The valet remained for a while, watching Gerhardt work, then smiled and cried out with great zeal: "That's the general! Yes, sir! That's the general! Mind! I tell you! That's the general!"

When Terrell left, the room became silent again, and Grant drifted into a deep sleep. "For two hours he continued to sleep tranquilly," Twain remembered, "the serenity of his face disturbed only at intervals by a passing wave of pain. It was the first sleep he had had for several weeks uninduced by narcotics."[577]

Gerhardt worked for those few silent hours, perfecting a true American masterpiece.

"To my mind this bust, completed at this sitting, has in it more of General Grant than can be found in any other likeness of him that has ever been made since he was a famous man," Twain later wrote. "I think it may rightly be called the best portrait of General Grant that is in existence. It has also a feature which must always be a remembrancer to this nation of what the general was passing through during the long weeks of that spring. For, into the clay image went the pain which he was enduring but which did not appear in his face when he was awake. Consequently, the bust has about it a suggestion of patient and brave and manly suffering which is infinitely touching."[578]

The experience was a welcome diversion of fun and family bonding in the midst of the long goodbye. Sadly, the tranquility was not to last.

The teamwork at 3 East Sixty-Sixth Street that had been effective since the previous autumn was showing signs of strain. Friction had developed between Grant's son Fred and his hired editor, Adam Badeau. Fred felt that Badeau treated both him and his father with condescension in the editing process. But worse than that, he was beginning to believe that Badeau increasingly acted as if they were working on his own book rather than General Grant's.[579]

This growing conflict increased the family's stress as they helplessly watched their beloved father and husband descend into what appeared to be the valley of the shadow of death.

Chapter Twenty

AT DEATH'S DOORWAY

MARCH 1865—NEW YORK CITY

As Grant's health declined rapidly in March, Dr. Douglas changed his opinion on the general's writing endeavors and concluded that the sudden turn for the worse in Grant's condition was brought about by the consistent strain of the writing. Another contributing factor was Grant's lack of sleep. Douglas noted these factors in his diary:

> January 28: The general had, at this time, more neuralgia in the head; interfering with his work upon his memoirs, which up to this date had occupied him quite assiduously. He had to intermit his labors more frequently, and this added to his trouble, for he was very anxious to complete his work, upon which he was constantly engaged.
>
> February 2: Suffered much last night. Great pain in right ear. Did not sleep until six in the morning, then at intervals until noon.
>
> March 17: Bad night. A report that the general had died during the night. In the morning both Doctor Barker and myself were visited by reporters to ascertain the correctness of the report. Neither knew anything concerning it.[580]

On March 4, as *The New York Times* story about Grant's decline still reverberated across the country, Doctor Barker wrote a memorandum to Doctor Shrady, giving him some history. "I do not believe that Doctor Douglas ever used the word *cancer* in connection with the case. We have always spoken of it as Epithelioma, of a malignant type probably. It was greatly improved for a time by the local treatment of Doctor Douglas, and the local condition was manifestly improving, until the moral shock (failure of the bill to pass Congress) broke down his general system."

At this time, two new figures became regular fixtures at the Grants' house. With the marked decline in the general's health, a male nurse named Henry McSweeny was hired to assist in caring for the general around the clock. Then at the invitation of Julia, Grant also began receiving frequent visits from their pastor, Reverend John Philip Newman of the Central Methodist Episcopal Church of New York City.[581]

Newman had been the pastor of the Metropolitan Church in Washington, where Ulysses and Julia attended services during Grant's presidency.[582] Newman had also been appointed chaplain of the Senate in 1869, a position he held until 1874. But while he rubbed shoulders with official Washington, his strongest supporter was Julia Grant, who admired his sermons and valued his pastoral friendship. Newman was in California when he learned of Grant's illness. "A great sufferer is passing away," he confided to his diary. He cut his visit short and returned to New York to be with Ulysses and Julia.[583]

Like most public figures, Newman did not shy away from publicity. As he went in and out of the Grant home, he stopped and answered the reporters' questions. "Prayers," Newman told them, "hundreds of thousands of prayers, were keeping Grant alive."

Grant told friends that he did not care how much praying went on at Sixty-Sixth Street as long as it made Julia feel better.[584] "Although strictly reverential, he was not what might be called an enthusiastically devout Christian," Dr. Shrady observed of Grant's religious leanings.[585]

While Mark Twain sometimes harrumphed at Newman's statements of faith, Shrady discerned the friendship and trust that existed between Grant and his pastor. "When the Rev. Dr. Newman, his pastor and friend, called to pray with him, he was always pleased to see him, would be the first to kneel to the devotional exercise, and afterward would always in a quiet and humble way converse with his spiritual adviser on spiritual affairs. There could be no doubt of a great bond of sympathy between these two men, who, from long association, understood each other perfectly."

"Grant's respect for religion was quite consistent with his high moral attributes," Shrady later wrote. "It has been most truly said of him that he was never profane or vulgar. His friends and intimates can bear ample testimony to this commendable part of his private character. He had promised his mother never to utter an oath, and he had faithfully kept his word."[586]

Although Grant expressed firm belief in Christianity, Dr. Shrady came to believe he was somewhat a fatalist. "Often, in speaking of his malady, he would say: 'It was to have been.' His was a Christianity that taught him to submit to whatever might come. Religion supported him on one side, and philosophy on the other."[587]

THE DEPOSITION

On March 26, Grant did not feel strong enough to work on his book, so instead he took a short ride in Central Park with Dr. Douglas and Matias Romero. The New York District Attorney, Elihu Root, was prosecuting James D. Fish of the Marine Bank, who was on trial as a coconspirator for embezzlement in the failure of Grant & Ward. Grant had decided to give a deposition that night and, possibly, the general wished to conserve his energy.[588]

Grant's doctors had agreed that he was strong enough to give his statement, so lawyers for both the federal government and Fish's defense conducted the examination at 3 East Sixty-Sixth Street. The lawyers found Grant seated in an armchair near a hickory-wood fire, wearing his woolen skater's cap and a dressing gown.

Fish was not present for the hearing. Already serving time for theft in the Grant & Ward swindle, he now faced additional charges for violating national banking embezzlement laws. In addition to the lawyers and Grant's doctors, those present at the deposition included reporters from *The New York Times* and the *New-York Tribune*, as well as Buck Grant and his brother Fred.

Grant testified for forty-five minutes as a stenographer recorded his comments, which would be read in full later during the trial. While he did not hesitate to denounce the crimes of Fish and Ward, he contritely admitted his failure to give proper oversight to the company's financial dealings. He admitted that he had never thoroughly examined the books, although he occasionally looked over the monthly statements.

The defendant's counsel, Edwin B. Smith, asked whether the general had, previous to the failure of Grant & Ward, "any mistrust on your part in respect to Mr. Ferdinand Ward?"

"I am sorry to say that I did not," Grant replied. "I had no mistrust of Mr. Ward the night before the failure, not the slightest. It took me a day or two to believe it was possible that Ward had committed the act he had."

The most important thing for the government's lawyers to establish was that Grant had not, as some had alleged, been involved in obtaining favorable treatment by dealing in government contracts. On that matter, Grant was rock solid:

> There is nothing wrong in being engaged in government contracts more than in anything else, unless made wrong by the acts of the individual, but I had been President of the United States, and I did not think it was suitable for me to have my name connected with government contracts. I did not think it was any place for me.

After taking Grant's deposition, the lawyers lingered to talk with the general. Expressing deep regret at his affliction, they offered him their good wishes. "You're certainly looking remarkable well," Edwin Smith said.

"I don't know about that," responded the general with a slight shake of the head. "I am conscious that I am a very sick man."[589]

Grant seemed under no strain during the deposition, although he sometimes winced in pain as he slowly articulated his words due to terrible mouth and throat soreness. But later that evening, he experienced a choking fit of such violence that he had to be sedated. Dr. Douglas doused his throat with cocaine water and administered morphine, but Grant still suffered through a sleepless night. Douglas was convinced the stress of being examined by the lawyers was to blame.[590]

As the disease progressed, morphine injections were increasingly needed to permit the general to sleep, and brandy injections were given to increase his heart rate. Hemorrhages relieved the congestion but weakened the patient. Drops of digitalis were given to strengthen the heart, but Grant could not live indefinitely under such a regimen.[591]

THE GROWING CRISIS

Grant woke the next morning and continued his work, but the deposition had weakened him and another choking fit followed that evening. These attacks took place every evening for the next few days, causing increasing alarm in the family. Once again, Grant faced his greatest fear—choking to death.

Several more violent coughing spells succeeded in the next few days, each one leaving him weaker. The doctors and family members feared for his life.[592]

Dr. Douglas added more ominous notes to his diary:

> March 29: When I returned from my night visit, I had not noticed anything particularly alarming, but I had hardly reached my room, when I was aroused by a message from Colonel Grant, stating that his father wished me to come to him at once. We found the general much agitated from an accumulation of mucus in the throat. ... The threat was immediately relieved of the accumulation of mucus, and soon after (the apprehension of dreaded suffocation having subsided) the general fell into a quiet slumber, which lasted several hours.[593]

On March 29, the general awoke gasping, as he couldn't clear his throat secretions. As before, he was overtaken with violent coughing. Two hours passed before the doctors arrived, and Grant's family feared he might not survive the attack.

At 5:00 a.m., reporters on deathwatch across the street saw the lights come on in the library and then one by one in other rooms throughout the house. Suddenly, Harrison burst through the front door and hailed a cab. He eventually returned with Dr. Shrady. Moments later, Dr. Douglas also appeared.

After more tense moments, Harrison once again emerged and jumped in the waiting taxi. He traveled downtown to the St. Cloud Hotel to gather Reverend Newman and Buck.[594] When they arrived, the doctors immediately gave the general injections of brandy and ammonia to dislodge objects wedged in his throat. This brought temporary relief, but then he underwent another terrifying episode two hours later.

As the doctors once again worked to bring relief, Grant cried out in a strangled voice, "I can't stand it! I am going to die!" The physicians applied chloroform to quiet him and ease the pain.

"The hurried call for Dr. Douglas and myself at the time of his first choking spell so alarmed the reporters on watch in the street that they gave currency to the probability that the general was in a very critical condition and that his death might be expected at any hour," said Dr. Shrady.[595]

The next day, Señor Romero spoke to reporters. "The truth is the disease has gotten away from the doctors. It is possible he may die tonight and at the very best he cannot live ten days. As soon as the disease reaches a vital point, it will create a hemorrhage. As he is too weak, he cannot expectorate the blood and will choke to death."[596]

Dr. Shrady also gloomily informed the press: "It is doubtful if the general's health could stand another choking attack."[597]

The growing crisis came to a climax on April 1, as Dr. Douglas noted in his diary:

> April 1 – midnight: After partaking of nourishment (following a severe coughing spell and pain due to accumulated secretions) the general appeared to be sleeping, but the almost imperceptible movement of the respiration, and the feebleness of the heart's action ... made me so solicitous that ... about 4 a.m. I aroused Dr. Shrady who was sleeping in the adjoining room. [598]

The moment everyone feared seemed to have arrived as Grant appeared to be approaching death. With all the signs pointing in that direction, the family was summoned to the bedside. For the first time, Mrs. Grant, who had refused to face the reality of her husband's demise, appeared to give up hope.

"There was warning of this possible condition during the previous day," Shrady remembered, "and it was deemed best that I should remain at the house in case any threatened change for the worse should show itself. While Dr. Douglas was watching the patient, I was hastily summoned from an adjoining bedroom by the startling announcement that the general was dying.

"The sufferer was evidently in an extremely weak condition. He was sitting in his chair as usual, with head bowed on chest, and was breathing in a labored way, feebly bidding farewell to his family, and striving to leave final directions regarding the completion of the second volume of his *Memoirs*. His voice was scarcely audible, and his sentences were interrupted by painful gaspings for breath."[599]

At Julia's request, Reverend Newman entered the sick room. General Grant had never been baptized, and Julia wanted the reassurance that this sacrament had taken place before he died. While Julia begged him to baptize her husband, Newman made his theological position clear to her. "I will baptize him if he is conscious. I cannot baptize an unconscious man."

"As I began to pray," Newman later recalled, "the general opened his eyes and looked steadily at me. As the physicians believed he could not live five minutes longer, I prayed that God would receive his departing soul. I then observed, 'General, I am going to baptize you.'"

Newman was standing behind the chair with a small silver bowl in hand, repeating in solemn tones: "Ulysses Simpson Grant, I baptize thee in the name of the Father, Son, and Holy Ghost." From the silver bowl, Rev. Newman gently applied some water to the general's brow. He followed these solemn words with a brief and appropriate prayer. The general slowly raised his eyes, and looking about him said, "I thank you, Doctor. I am much obliged to you. I had intended to have attended to this myself."[600] Mrs. Grant knelt by the side of her husband and called for everyone to pray. Newman led the family in the Lord's Prayer.

Dr. Douglas had prepared a syringe filled with the purest brandy in case the heart stopped beating. Shrady, who was monitoring Grant's weakening pulse, recognized the telltale signs of death. "Doctor," he said with alarm, "the syringe filled with brandy is upon the desk back of you." Douglas turned, took it up, and offered it to Shrady. "Use it, Doctor, if it is just as convenient to you." He did so, injecting the brandy into the general's right arm. Both doctors watched the faltering pulse.

"If you doctors know how long a man can live under water, you can judge how long it will take me to choke when the time comes," Grant said as they administered the potion.

The pulse did not improve, so a second injection was given, and, in a moment, the heart regained a more normal rhythm. "Throughout this time," Shrady remembered, "the general was conscious, spoke clearly when addressed and was the least perturbed of those present." The general then began to cough violently.

Grant's coughing fit worsened. To let the doctors do their work, Julia and Newman stood aside, horrified at the agony of what both were convinced were his last minutes.[601] Moments after the additional brandy went into his arm, he vomited a thick fistful of slimy diseased tissue.

With his throat cleared, the general breathed more easily. Relieved, Grant quickly fell into an exhausted sleep.[602] As the night progressed and Grant slept soundly, the doctors concluded that the crisis had passed.[603]

"During this affecting scene hypodermics of brandy were repeatedly administered," Shrady recalled, "and to the bystanders it appeared as if the sufferer had been almost miraculously snatched from death."[604]

A Turning Point

Beginning the next morning, Grant's health improved so dramatically that some thought the cancer diagnosis was false. This was a double victory for Grant, for he was well on his way to completing his memoirs. In addition to the completed first volume, he had chronicled the lesser known and more disputed phases of his early life and his war career. The writing that lay ahead concerned elements of his record that were already reasonably well known to the public.

At the bottom of the page on which the chapter on Chattanooga ends, there is a footnote, likely inserted by Mark Twain, that states: "From this point on this volume was written (with the exception of the campaign in the Wilderness, which had been previously written) by General Grant after his great illness in April, and the present arrangement of the subject matter was made by him between the 10th and the 18th of July 1885."[605]

Grant's resurgence of vitality astounded everyone, including those in the press, motivating both Douglas and Shrady to issue warnings that the disease was marked by an ebb and flow. Each recovery would be weaker than the one that had preceded it as the cancer continued to take its toll.[606]

A Final Easter: April 5, 1885

Easter Day that year dawned bright and clear as large crowds promenaded along Fifth Avenue. Many New Yorkers paused at the corner of East Sixty-Sixth Street to gaze concernedly at Grant's townhouse. From the bay window, Dr. Shrady observed the curious crowd mingling on the sidewalk below. Reporters and ordinary citizens gathered in front of the house. Some onlookers wept as they gazed up at Grant's window.

Noticing Shrady's interest in the scene, Grant grabbed his cane, shuffled to the window, and, screened by curtains, looked out over the crowd with equal curiosity. The general was much impressed by this evidence of good feeling. For a while, he stood silent at the window. The day before, he had received a friendly, conciliatory letter from Jefferson Davis, which gratified and touched him deeply. Backing away from the window, he paced the room, then sat by the fire, deep in thought.

After a while, Grant dozed off in his chair. During that time, a spring shower scattered the people on the street, leaving only the resolute reporters. By the time the general awoke, the rain had ceased, and the crowd grew larger than the earlier one. The police were kept busy clearing the street in front of the house for passing vehicles.

Shrady told him what had occurred during his nap, pointing out the interest manifested by all classes of citizens. Grant stood and shuffled back to the window. Looking down on the crowd below, he remarked, "Yes, I am very grateful for their sympathy." Returning to his seat by the fire, he was quiet again.

"Why not tell them so, General?" Shrady asked as he prepared to write the usual afternoon medical bulletin. He suggested that it would be good for him to express his gratitude to the people of the country, especially on Easter Sunday, when many churches had offered prayers on his account.

"Very well," said Grant.

Shrady urged that the bulletin be dictated in the first person, and signed by General Grant, so that it would appear as coming directly from him. To this suggestion, however, Grant objected, saying that it would be better coming from him indirectly.

To comply with such a wish and to give the document somewhat the character of a message from the sickroom, Shrady began by saying that General Grant had just awakened from a short nap and had expressed himself as feeling comfortable.

The general then dictated the following: "General Grant wishes it stated that he is very much touched by, and very grateful for, the sympathy and interest manifested for him by friends and by those"—here he stopped and thought for a moment, then continued—"who have not been regarded as such."[607]

Adam Badeau entered the room and cheered. "Splendid! Splendid! Stop right there, General Grant! I would not say another word."[608]

After another moment of reflection Grant added, "I suppose that will do."

Shrady signed the bulletin, giving the time as 5:15 p.m. The dispatch was immediately sent to the press-bureau on Madison Avenue and sent out over the wires.

As Shrady anticipated, the bulletin attracted the attention of the nation.

The Southern papers particularly had many kind comments regarding the statement and sympathized with the stricken commander. They made repeated references to the general's magnanimous terms when he accepted Lee's surrender at Appomattox and to other actions that reflected the sentiments of a high-minded, generous victor.

"With him war had a different definition from mere enmity," Shrady later observed. "It meant fidelity to a principle, not mere death, destruction, and humiliation of the opponent. The hand that had so valiantly held the sword was then open to all, 'whether heretofore friends or not.' The dying man had said, 'Let us have peace,' and posterity was destined to cherish the sentiment."[609]

A Cigar for Appomattox

Four days after Easter, the nation marked the twentieth anniversary of Robert E. Lee's surrender of the Army of Northern Virginia to Grant at Appomattox Court House. When Badeau reminded the general of the date, Grant sighed and remarked in a raspy voice, "Twenty years ago I had more to say. I was in command then."

"Even then it took a year to win," Badeau replied. "Perhaps you may win still."

That same day Julia received a telegram from Queen Victoria's lady-in-waiting:

> The Queen who feels deeply for you in your anxiety commands me to inquire after General Grant.
> Dowager Marchioness of Ely
> Aix-les-Bains

Fred cabled Julia's reply:

> Mrs. Grant thanks the Queen for her sympathy and directs me to say General Grant is no better.
> Colonel Frederick Grant[610]

Messages also arrived for Grant from veterans' organizations across the country, a gesture that pleased him greatly.

In a celebratory mood, Grant asked Dr. Shrady if he could have "one or two puffs" on a cigar.[611] Shrady saw so little harm in the pitiable request that he said there was no reason the general shouldn't enjoy one mild cigar. Grant eagerly reached up above the mantel and pulled a cigar out of an ornamental box. Settling into his leather chair, the old warrior lit the stogie and contentedly puffed away.

Neither Grant nor Shrady had thought to pull the shades, and the next day the *Journal* ran the headline: "Grant Smokes Again!"

The article angered Julia, who called it vile. She told Dr. Douglas that "there was no end to which the newsmen would not stoop." Sheepishly, Grant and Shrady nodded their heads in silent agreement.[612]

Around that time, Jesse Grant and his young daughter, Nellie, left the house to go on an errand. General Grant was standing at the time, looking out the second-story library window. When the crowd saw the general, several men lifted their hats. Every person was standing with their eyes raised toward the window. The child studied the scene with curiosity as she descended the front steps holding her father's hand. When she reached the sidewalk, she raised her head and followed the gaze of the crowd until she saw Grant in the window. "There's Grandpa," Nellie said, and with both hands blew him a kiss. The general blew one back.[613]

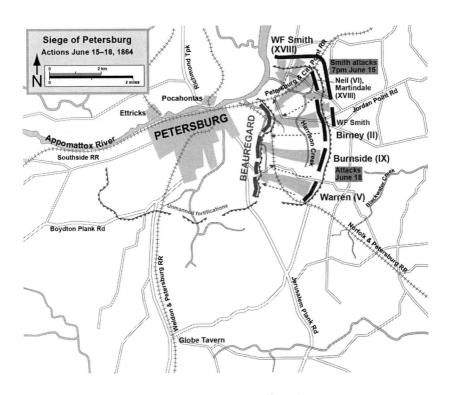

Chapter Twenty-One

PETERSBURG

JUNE 15, 1864—PETERSBURG, VIRGINIA

The arrival of spring and warmer temperatures brought back memories for Grant of the warm temperatures at his headquarters on the bluff at City Point, Virginia. The army had successfully crossed the James, and it was time for the troops under General William F. "Baldy" Smith to lead the way into Petersburg.

~

FROM *PERSONAL MEMOIRS*

Smith arrived in front of the enemy's lines early in the forenoon of the 15th, and spent the day until after seven o'clock in the evening in reconnoitering what appeared to be empty works. The enemy's line consisted of redans occupying commanding positions, with rifle-pits connecting them. To the east side of Petersburg, from the Appomattox back, there were thirteen of these redans extending a distance of several miles, probably three. If they had been properly manned they could have held out against any force that could have attacked them, at least until reinforcements could have got up from the north of Richmond.[614]

~

Grant's ingenious maneuvering after Cold Harbor had left Robert E. Lee in the dark. And it left the door to Petersburg wide open. The only Confederate officer who seemed to understand the danger was the Petersburg commander, General Beauregard. He had predicted Grant's movement in urgent telegraphs to General Lee on June 7 and 9. He continued sending telegraphic warnings in the following days, and when they were not heeded, he dispatched a personal emissary to Lee on June 14.

Still Lee did not act.

As the Federal troops began massing in front of his works at Petersburg, Beauregard continued to send dire reports and urgent requests for reinforcements on June 15 and 16. Lee continued to cover Richmond from the approach General McClellan had attempted in 1862. But Grant's forces were no longer there.

Confederate General Edward Porter Alexander shared his dismay at the Southern commander's decisions: "General Lee did not have a soldier there to meet him! Grant had gotten away from US completely & was fighting *Beauregard*. The Army of Northern Virginia had lost him, & was sucking its thumb by the roadside 25 miles away, & wondering where he could be!"[615]

In General John Fuller's words, "Lee had been completely out-generalled."[616]

Grant needed to strike at Petersburg before Lee could recover. Smith's Eighteenth Corps had been ordered to return to Petersburg after Cold Harbor. Because they had been with Butler's forces at Bermuda Hundred prior to this time, Smith's troops, numbering eighteen thousand men, knew the territory surrounding Petersburg and could serve as the lead in the new offensive. The Eighteenth Corps arrived in the area on the evening of June 14 and marched toward the Confederate trench line at Petersburg, six miles away. Beauregard had deployed most of his troops facing General Butler at Bermuda Hundred and could muster only a mixed assortment of twenty-five hundred soldiers, home guard, and convalescents to man the city's trenches.[617]

Grant ordered Smith to move forward under cover of darkness and then storm the Confederate works. General Smith approached Petersburg from the northeast in the summer heat. He was usually a vigorous commander, but on this day he became overly cautious. Spreading his cavalry out to his left to protect his flank, his soldiers overran the advanced picket lines, coming under fire from the Confederate artillery. From there, he formed his battle lines a quarter of a mile away from the powerful fortifications.[618]

Then Smith hesitated.[619] After suffering through the hell of Cold Harbor, the sight of seeming endless entrenchments stopped him cold. He may have remembered that reconnaissance had been sparse at Cold Harbor, so he insisted on inspecting the ground before him.[620] At this critical moment, Smith was weary from an all-night march and suffering from what he reported as "the effects of bad water, and malaria brought from Cold Harbor."[621]

The fortifications in front of him were some of the most impressive he had ever seen. No Federal general with recent memories of Cold Harbor was likely to attack without a careful examination of the ground before him. Although it would cause another delay, Smith was rightfully wary. He spent the better part of the afternoon reconnoitering under fire at considerable risk. Suffering from what may have been dysentery, he nearly fainted several times in the scorching Virginia heat.[622] He was also hindered by the lack of an engineer officer to help him.[623] His inspection of the enemy's defenses consumed an additional four hours.[624]

Smith discovered that on three sides of the city, miles of breastworks—twenty-four feet thick in places—protected the approaches. In front of the breastworks were ditches fifteen feet deep, enclosed by abatis snarled with felled trees. All along the line stood forts secured with cannon placed strategically to cover the open ground with a deadly cross fire. His troops had faced similar obstacles at Cold Harbor, yet the trenches were sparsely manned.[625]

As hours passed with no word, a nervous Grant wired Butler: "Have you any news from Petersburg?" He did not know that Hancock—using a faulty map and troubled by a severe thigh injury suffered at Gettysburg that had broken open again—was marching toward Petersburg with an uncharacteristic lack of urgency. Increasingly concerned, Grant wrote Butler again: "I have not yet heard a word of the result of the expedition against Petersburg."[626]

At four o'clock, Smith sent a note to Hancock, describing the situation: "If the Second Corps can come up in time to make an assault tonight after dark in vicinity of Norfolk and Petersburg railroad ... I think we may be successful." He warned Hancock this would be the last chance, because Lee was reportedly crossing troops farther up the James to reinforce the Petersburg garrison.

In his report, Hancock later complained that he "spent the best hours of the day on the 15th in marching by an incorrect map in search of a designated position which, as described, was not in existence or could not be found." Worst of all, he thought he was simply making a routine movement in which no special haste was called for.

Nobody had told Hancock that Petersburg was to be attacked that day.

Finally, after five o'clock, a courier from Grant's headquarters reached Hancock with a dispatch saying that Smith was assaulting the Petersburg fortifications and that Hancock must hurry forward to help him. Soon Smith's dispatch also arrived informing Hancock about a large-scale attack planned for that night. Hancock picked up the pace, and his two leading divisions pushed forward, although they were completely exhausted—like everyone else in both armies. But the soldiers' enthusiasm grew as word spread along the column that they were about to strike Lee's almost undefended underbelly.[627]

A Plan of Attack

During his reconnaissance, Smith discovered that opposite his center and left, where the high ground lined with forts jutted forward in a salient, there might an opening if heavy skirmish lines could charge with a rush after a sharp bombardment. Smith finally ordered such an attack.

Once again, faulty communication hindered the assault. No one informed Smith's chief of artillery that a fight was imminent. That officer had sent all the artillery horses off to be watered, causing yet another delay. Just before sundown, the guns were finally brought into action.[628] General Edward Winslow Hincks' African American infantrymen were the first to fight their way over the massive trenches, storming into the forts. In half an hour, the salient was gone, and the ridge to the south was covered with Black men in blue uniforms cheering and brandishing their weapons.

Once the Union infantry came within rifle range of the artillery positions, Confederate gunners fled to the rear rather than be shot dead at their cannons. Petersburg stood helpless before the Federal troops—though Smith didn't know it.[629] Union forces swept forward and easily overran the Confederate position, taking more than two miles of earthworks, five forts, sixteen large guns, and several hundred prisoners. As his men advanced, a bright moon illuminated their path. When Hancock finally arrived, thirty-five thousand Union troops faced the Confederates.[630]

"Petersburg was clearly at the mercy of the Federal commander, who had all but captured it," Beauregard wrote later.[631]

In his note to Hancock, Smith had spoken of making "an assault tonight, after dark," but when the twilight gave way to full darkness, Smith had second thoughts. General Hincks urged him to drive on ahead, saying that Petersburg could be taken, tonight, at once—the darkness would be no great problem because a moon was rising, and the few Confederates were terribly disorganized. But Smith, who was in the process of winning what could have been one of the most decisive and strategic battles of the war, lost his nerve.[632]

When Hancock arrived, he had little knowledge about the situation before him. Even with the moonlit night, he could not see the lay of the ground or the enemy defenses. For the moment, Smith was in command, and Hancock had been ordered to support him. The hour was late, both commanders were ailing, and all the soldiers were exhausted. After talking things over with Smith, Hancock placed himself and his troops at his disposal and asked for orders. Smith directed him to relieve the men of the Eighteenth Corps in the captured works and stand by to repel a probable Confederate counterattack.

The day's battle had ended, and the wide-open door began to swing shut.

From *Personal Memoirs*

Smith assaulted with the colored troops, and with success. By nine o'clock at night he was in possession of five of these redans and, of course, of the connecting lines of rifle-pits. All of them contained artillery, which fell into our hands. Hancock came up and proposed to take any part assigned to him; and Smith asked him to relieve his men who were in the trenches.

Next morning, the 16th, Hancock himself was in command, and captured another redan. Meade came up in the afternoon and succeeded Hancock, who had to be relieved, temporarily, from the command of his corps on account of the breaking out afresh of the wound he had received at Gettysburg. During the day Meade assaulted and carried one more redan to his right and two to his left. In all this we lost very heavily. The works were not strongly manned, but they all had guns in them which fell into our hands, together with the men who were handling them in the effort to repel these assaults.

Up to this time Beauregard, who had commanded south of Richmond, had received no reinforcements, except the division under General Robert Hoke from Drury's Bluff, which had arrived on the morning of the 16th; though he had urged the authorities very strongly to send them, believing, as he did, that Petersburg would be a valuable prize which we might seek.[633]

~

Thursday, June 16

General Beauregard was reinforced that evening, but not nearly as heavily as Smith believed. Confederate engineer details had been busy all night, improvising a new defensive line behind Harrison's Creek. On the morning of June 16, Beauregard made a desperate move, ordering General Bushrod Johnson's division to evacuate the trenches that sealed off the Federal position on Bermuda Hundred neck. Beauregard ordered him to march to Petersburg, leaving only pickets and skirmishers to hold the old line in front of General Butler.[634]

That morning, Grant rode forward to Petersburg to have a look for himself. He was immediately impressed by the strength of the defenses—thick earthworks, deep moats, sharpened tree branches, and tangled telegraph wires. On his return from the front, he met Meade on the road, and the two conferred while seated on their horses.[635] Grant enthusiastically told Meade, "Smith has taken a line of works stronger than we have seen in this campaign!"[636] Grant ordered that the attack be resumed, eager to take the city before Lee reacted.[637]

Inexplicably, Smith still did not attack, preferring to wait until yet more Union reinforcements arrived.

Becoming increasingly impatient at the Union delay, Grant instructed Burnside to bring his corps forward as quickly as possible and then ordered Meade to launch a full-scale attack on the Confederate position at 6:00 p.m. That evening, Hancock's corps struck hard, but Beauregard had deployed the troops brought over from Bermuda Hundred and was prepared for the attack. Once again the Union assault was uneven and loosely coordinated. Hancock and Burnside advanced aggressively, but Smith hung back, possibly still obsessed with the failure at Cold Harbor.

The Second Corps captured an additional stretch of Petersburg's outer defenses, giving the Federals a better position for a new attack the next day, while inflicting two thousand casualties. Burnside's men took an important redan, but at no point was there a breakthrough.[638] Warren was ordered to follow Burnside, while Wright brought up the rear.

News from Bermuda Hundred

Meanwhile, back at City Point, Grant received bright reports from Butler that the Confederates had all but abandoned their line on Bermuda Hundred neck. Butler's men had occupied the abandoned trenches. Troops had reached the Petersburg-Richmond Railroad and were beginning to dismantle it. Butler wrote that if reinforced, he could get between Lee and Beauregard to keep them separated.

Grant reflected on this possibility. With the big push coming up at Petersburg, he did not think he could mount a second major attack on the Confederate center. Wright and two divisions of his Sixth Corps would reach City Point that night. Grant told Butler that if things still looked promising the next morning, he would send Wright over to Bermuda Hundred.

In addition to his telegraphs, Beauregard also sent two colonels and a major as personal emissaries to convince Lee of the desperate nature of the situation. Lee initially rebuffed the two colonels, but the major convinced him that the broad representation of three Union corps among captured prisoners demonstrated that Grant indeed was across the James in strength.

Finally, about three days late, Lee realized that Grant had fooled him and that he was in danger of losing Petersburg, Richmond, and the war.[639]

The Federals at Bermuda Hundred had twenty-four hours of freedom, but they did not take advantage of it. On the night of June 16, Lee deployed troops in front of Butler's lines, drove the Federal advance guard away from the railroad, regained the abandoned trenches, and sent enough reinforcements to secure the ground by the time Wright's veterans arrived the next day. And so Butler's troops were sealed off again, out of the battle, just as if nothing had happened.

FRIDAY, JUNE 17

At Petersburg, Meade ordered Hancock and Burnside forward at dawn on June 17. One of Burnside's divisions seized a fortified hill near the line of the Norfolk & Petersburg Railroad—the spot Smith had chosen for the after-dark assault he decided not to make on June 15. Burnside captured four guns and six hundred prisoners, achieving what could have been a real breakthrough. But the division Burnside ordered up in support failed to get its orders and did not appear until after noon, and the opportunity was lost.

Warren was supposed to advance into almost empty country below the Confederate right, on the far side of a highway known as the Jerusalem Plank Road, but he was deterred by active Confederate skirmishers and long-range artillery fire. In the end, his corps achieved nothing of consequence.

Even with all the Union missteps, however, by the end of the day they had taken much of the Confederate line. Beauregard once more was desperately falling back to a new defensive line, a mile closer to Petersburg. He could retreat no further without withdrawing. That evening he notified Lee that he would hold on while he could, but if reinforcements did not speedily reach him, he would have to abandon Petersburg.[640]

In one of his finest moments during the war, Beauregard scrambled to organize a new inner defensive line to hold Petersburg until Lee arrived—if he ever did.[641]

JUNE 18

For the Federals, a few hours of opportunity remained—but sadly, they were not seized. Meade's soldiers moved forward cautiously at daybreak on June 18 and got into the trenches the enemy had left the previous night. Meade learned that the bulk of Lee's troops had not yet reached Beauregard, so he ordered an attack all along the line.[642] But at seven thirty that morning, the first of Lee's troops began unloading from train cars just behind the Confederate lines. Lee himself reached Petersburg by 11:00 a.m.[643]

At the hour appointed for the attack, each corps commander waited for his neighbor to go first. No concerted action was taken, and by then Lee had caught up with the Federals. Hard-marching veterans from the Army of Northern Virginia filed into the Petersburg trenches, and the odds against Beauregard shrank to manageable proportions. Disjointed Union attacks continued through the afternoon, costly in Yankee lives but completely ineffective.

At last, apparently almost beside himself, Meade angrily told his corps commanders that it was useless to try to coordinate their movements, so each general must attack when and as he could, without reference to what his neighbors were doing.[644]

The Army of the Potomac could go no further.

The exhausted Union soldiers had grown tired of blunt operations against an entrenched enemy. Lee and his army had appeared in full force in front of Petersburg.[645] By the afternoon of June 18, the opportunity was lost. The rebel trenches were held in full strength, and a successful frontal assault was out of the question.[646]

In late afternoon, Grant called off the attack. He had known when they left the Cold Harbor trenches that success depended on speed.[647] Now his forces were too worn down to take the initiative.

In the four days since crossing the James, Union losses totaled 11,386 killed, wounded, and missing,[648] evidence that the men in the ranks had fought as bravely as ever. Petersburg was invested by the Federals on the east, but the city, with its vital rail lines, remained in rebel hands.[649]

Recognizing his men's exhaustion, Grant bowed to their human limitations. "We will rest the men and use the spade for their protection until a new vein has been struck." There would be a siege, with Grant steadily extending his line westward to attack the railroads one by one.[650]

Since crossing the Rapidan on May 4, the Army of the Potomac had sacrificed sixty-five thousand men killed, wounded, or missing. This fearful toll far exceeded anything experienced in the past. Averse to more frontal assaults, Grant changed the war's character in Virginia, setting his men to work with pick and ax to construct defenses as expansive as those that guarded Petersburg. Whenever Grant extended his lines, Lee would have to match him.[651]

Like Lee, Grant understood that the outcome of the war was merely a question of time—provided the Northern people remained behind the war and Mr. Lincoln was reelected.[652]

From *Personal Memoirs*

During the 17th the fighting was very severe and the losses heavy; and at night our troops occupied about the same position they had occupied in the morning, except that they held a redan which had been captured by Potter during the day. During the night, however, Beauregard fell back to the line which had been already selected, and commenced fortifying it. Our troops advanced on the 18th to the line which he had abandoned, and found that the Confederate loss had been very severe, many of the enemy's dead still remaining in the ditches and in front of them.

If General Hancock's orders of the 15th had been communicated to him, that officer, with his usual promptness, would undoubtedly have been upon the ground around Petersburg as early as four o'clock in the afternoon of the 15th. The days were long and it would have given him considerable time before night. I do not think there is any doubt that Petersburg itself could have been carried without much loss; or, at least, if protected by inner detached works, that a line could have been established very much in rear of the one then occupied by the enemy. This would have given us control of both the Weldon and South Side railroads. This would also have saved an immense amount of hard fighting which had to be done from the 15th to the 18th, and would have given us greatly the advantage in the long siege which ensued.

I now ordered the troops to be put under cover and allowed some of the rest which they had so long needed.[653]

Chapter Twenty-Two

CONTINUE ON THIS LINE
ALL SUMMER

APRIL 1885—NEW YORK CITY

During the revival in Grant's health, Noble Dawson often transcribed enough material to fill twenty-five printed pages. The general rarely made a mistake in the dictation, and the corrections required less and less time. Twain concluded that the general had amassed enough material for the second volume and that if he passed away, Fred, Badeau, or both could complete the work.

Despite Grant's increased stamina, the pain in his throat was ever present, and he often experienced violent uncontrollable coughing spells. When Julia complained to Ulysses and to the doctors that the general was not getting enough rest, Grant kindly protested and continued writing. He was fully aware that his strength would continue to wane and his pain would increase. He must soldier on to complete the work that had become his primary focus.[654]

On April 4, the twentieth anniversary of Grant's occupation of Richmond, Dr. Douglas turned to him with a smile after an examination and declared: "General, we propose to keep to this line if it takes all summer." Grant responded with a smile and slight, painful laughter.

By the middle of April, as the days grew longer and warmer, Grant returned to his habit of reading several newspapers per day. He even attempted a little writing without the stenographer. He also astonished the family one day by joining them for lunch, eating some macaroni and cold mutton to everyone's delight.

Ex-senator Chaffee, Grant's good friend and Buck's father-in-law, was a frequent visitor. He was amazed at his friend's recovery and began to suspect the diagnosis of the physicians. He told reporters that Grant was coming along so well that perhaps the doctors might have been wrong. General Grant, in his opinion, did not have cancer, but had been suffering from an ulcerated throat. He thought the general might pull through.

The *New York World* fanned the flames of false hope: "The People rejoice that their great soldier Grant, whose death a syndicate of doctors led them to expect at any moment for the past five weeks, is now apparently on the high road to recovery."

When reporters asked Dr. Shrady for a comment, he said there was no reason to question the diagnosis. The disease was one of ups and downs, with a definite downward tendency. Everyone was glad for this respite, but the physicians knew it was only temporary.[655]

"Then came the suspicion that the doctors had given false reports," Dr. Shrady later wrote, "and that there had been a grave mistake in the diagnosis of the original disease. This was made probable by the fact that many of the distressing symptoms had disappeared for a time, and also by the anxious but ill-founded expectation that the general would ultimately recover, in spite of previous predictions.

"Once the difficulty in swallowing had so far disappeared that the patient ventured to indulge in solid food. He was so delighted with such an opportunity that while lunching on a mutton chop in his dining room, he felicitated himself on being able to surprise the reporters with his ability to perform what he considered a remarkable feat. But alas! this ability was short-lived."[656]

Shrady was also quite confident that the general fully understood the real nature of his malady and would not be given false hopes by these articles in the newspaper. "These attacks were not only abusive in the extreme," Shrady wrote, "but often-times they were positively libelous."[657]

One morning, when one of these articles had appeared in an editorial, General Grant asked Dr. Shrady how he felt after such a virulent attack on his professional character. Shrady answered that he and the team of doctors were certain their diagnosis was correct—despite the criticism in the press. Grant smiled and said that he was perfectly satisfied with the medical treatment of his case and that he was the person who most naturally was interested in the course taken.

Shrady then asked how Grant had treated the many newspaper criticisms to which he had been subjected in his long public career. The general said he had always been too busy with more important matters to notice "the vaporings of scribblers who were willing to give free and valueless lessons on matters of which they knew little or nothing. ... If a man assumes the responsibility of doing a thing," Grant continued, "he naturally does it his own way, and the result is the only proof, after all, that he may be right or wrong. One does the work, and the other does the guessing."[658]

Grant was indignant at the charge that there had been an error in diagnosis and asked that the facts be explained to the public in a long bulletin. This release was published after the general approved it.

The publication of this document had the desired effect of silencing further criticism on the subject. "This result was also in great part due to the care to state only the exact truth in all the bulletins," Shrady explained, "and to obtain a unanimity of opinion from the entire staff before publication was permitted."[659]

The anniversary of the war's end, along with the rising temperatures in New York City, took the general back to that earlier life-or-death struggle in the sweltering heat of Petersburg, Virginia. He picked up where he had left off with his account of the summer where the Union almost lost the war.

SUMMER 1864

The heavy casualties sustained by the Army of the Potomac since Grant took command had diminished public support for him by some in the North in 1864. But this did not affect the outlook of the delegates to the Republican National Convention, who met at the Front Street Theatre in Baltimore the week following Cold Harbor. The choice before them was clear—stay the course with Abraham Lincoln at the helm or splinter and pave the way for a so-called "peace candidate" to win in November. Republicans knew that the peace being offered by the other political parties would ensure the permanent division of the country and the establishment of the Confederacy as a separate slave-holding nation.

Lincoln was renominated without opposition.[660]

With Lincoln's support, the convention also adopted a platform whose chief plank was "an amendment of the Constitution as will positively prohibit African slavery in the United States."[661]

EARLY IS LATE

To relieve the pressure around Richmond, Lee dispatched General Jubal Early and the Second Corps of the Army of Northern Virginia to clear the Shenandoah Valley of Federal troops. He was then ordered to threaten Washington, DC, with the hopes that Grant would be forced to send troops north to defend the city and weaken his lines around Petersburg.

After defeating the Army of West Virginia under General David Hunter at the Battle of Lynchburg, Early turned east and headed toward the capital. As the rebels began their march on Washington, they were confronted by General Lew Wallace and a small Union force that slowed their progress at the Battle of Monocacy. This gave time for the arrival of General Horatio Wright, who had been dispatched by Grant with the Sixth and Nineteenth Corps.

When Early's forces finally attacked the outskirts of Washington at 3:00 p.m. on July 11, they were stopped cold. President Lincoln, his wife, Mary, and some other officials rode out to view the affair. Observing the fight from atop the Fort Stevens parapet, Lincoln came under fire, and a surgeon standing next to him was wounded. The president was quickly ushered away from danger. After a day of fighting, Early finally decided that Washington could not be taken without heavy losses. The Confederates withdrew that night and crossed the Potomac River on July 13 at White's Ferry.

Writing of the battle, Union veteran Elisha Hunt Rhodes declared:

We marched in the line of battle into a peach orchard in front of Fort Stevens, and here the fight began. For a short time it was warm work, but as the President and many ladies were looking at us, every man tried to do his best. Without our help the small force in the forts would have been overpowered. Jubal Early should have attacked earlier in the morning, but Early was late. —Elisha Hunt Rhodes, 1st Rhode Island Volunteers, July 12, 1864.[662]

General Wright set out in pursuit of Early on the afternoon of July 13, but when it was discovered that the rebels were across the Potomac, the Federal troops were called back.

BATTLE IN THE SHENANDOAH

To keep the Northern public on edge, Early ordered Brigadier General John McCausland to take twenty-eight hundred Confederate cavalrymen across the Pennsylvania line into the town of Chambersburg on July 30. Ordering the residents out of their homes, McCausland demanded $100,000 in gold or $500,000 in greenbacks; otherwise, he would retaliate for Union attacks in the South. When the residents failed to raise the ransom, McCausland ordered his men to burn the town. Flames destroyed more than five hundred structures, leaving more than two thousand homeless and one dead.[663]

For Grant, this was a line too far. He determined it was time to take action to end the Confederate use of the Shenandoah Valley as an avenue for raiding the North and supplying Lee. And Grant knew just the man for the job.

Grant dispatched feisty young General Philip Sheridan, along with a division of cavalry, to the Shenandoah Valley and then sent a wire to General Halleck in Washington. "Unless Gen. Hunter is in the field in person I want Sheridan put in command of all the troops in the field with instructions to put himself south of the enemy and follow him to the death. Wherever the enemy goes, let our troops go also. Once started up the valley they ought to be followed until we get possession of the Virginia Central Railroad."[664]

Lincoln saw the order two days later, and was so impressed with the strength of Grant's message that he wired his congratulations. At the same time, the president sent a fatherly word of advice:

> I have seen your dispatch in which you say, "I want Sheridan put in command of all the troops in the field with instructions to put himself south of the enemy and follow him to the death. Wherever the enemy goes, let our troops go also." This, I think, is exactly right as to how our forces should move, but please look over the dispatches you may have received from here, ever since you made that order, and discover if you can, whether there is any idea in the head of anyone here, of "putting our army South of the enemy" or of "following him to the death" in any direction. I repeat to you it will neither be done or attempted unless you watch it every day, and hour, and force it.[665]

The president was alerting Grant to opposition from Secretary of War Stanton to Sheridan's appointment. Both Stanton and Army Chief of Staff Halleck believed Sheridan, at thirty-three years of age, was too young for so important an assignment. They were also both opposed to leaving Washington uncovered to pursue Early. Lincoln knew they would do their best to undercut Sheridan.

Grant was grateful for the warning.[666]

As soon as he read the president's message, he ordered a boat to get up steam for a quick voyage to the capital. In Washington the next morning, Grant visited neither the White House nor the War Department but went straight to the railway station and caught a train to Monocacy Junction, headquarters of the Union forces from the Shenandoah to meet with General Hunter.[667]

When asked the location of the enemy troops, Hunter was unable to answer—he had no idea where the rebels were located. Grant was not impressed. To draw the Confederates out of their hiding place, Grant sent a trainload of soldiers four miles west of Harper's Ferry. Grant also ordered Hunter's cavalry and wagons to move west in search of Confederates and explained that Sheridan would command in the field.

~

FROM *PERSONAL MEMOIRS*

I told him that Sheridan was in Washington, and still another division was on its way; and suggested that he establish the headquarters of the department at any point that would suit him best, Cumberland, Baltimore, or elsewhere, and give Sheridan command of the troops in the field. The general replied to this, that General Halleck seemed so much to distrust his fitness for the position he was in that he thought somebody else ought to be there. He did not want, in any way, to embarrass the cause; thus showing a patriotism that was none too common in the army. There were not many major-generals who would voluntarily have asked to have the command of a department taken from them … I told him, "very well then," and telegraphed at once for Sheridan to come to the Monocacy, and suggested that I would wait and meet him there.[668]

~

Grant respected Hunter, but he agreed it was time for a change in this theater of warfare. He accepted Hunter's resignation and personally placed Sheridan in command of thirty thousand troops, charging him with clearing the Shenandoah Valley of Confederates.[669]

When Sheridan arrived in Monocacy the next day, Grant gave him his commission and told him he wanted Early driven from the valley and the Shenandoah made so desolate that the enemy would have no desire to return. "Eat out Virginia clear and clean … so that crows flying over it … will have to carry their provender with them."[670]

Grant then took decisive steps to stop the interference from Washington. To ensure that his orders were not countermanded, Grant told Sheridan to report directly to him, not to Halleck or the War Department. The lieutenant general made it clear that he had great confidence in Sheridan's judgment and would allow him to make critical command decisions on the battlefield—Grant's policy with all his generals.

The Northern commander then traveled to Washington to make these changes clear to the War Department. Meeting first with Halleck and then with Stanton, he deflected potential interference with his orders and reminded both men that he was in control of military affairs.

Grant's aide, Colonel Theodore S. Bowers, who accompanied the general to Washington, wrote afterward that "Grant now runs the whole machine independently of the Washington directory. Halleck has no control over troops except as Grant delegates it. He can give no orders and exercise no discretion."[671]

Returning to City Point, Grant immediately moved troops north of the James to keep Lee from reinforcing the Shenandoah.[672]

EXTENDING THE LINES

Throughout the summer, Grant continued to extend the Union lines around Petersburg westward with the goal of cutting off the Weldon Railroad—one of the vital lifelines over which Lee's army was receiving supplies from Weldon, North Carolina. In late June, the Union attack on the railroad was repulsed with a loss of three thousand troops. In August, Warren's Fifth Corps extended its line three miles to the west, took and fortified a position on the railroad, and then held on against a Confederate counterattack at the Battle of Globe Tavern. The Northern troops dug in, and after August 21, Confederates had to bypass that section of the railroad via a thirty-mile detour by wagon.[673]

Grant was slowly but surely cutting off Lee's supplies.

While many Northern newspapers and copperhead politicians criticized the casualty list and Grant's overall strategy, the lieutenant general remained steadfast, convinced that Federal victory would come if the Northern people remained resolute.

In mid-August, he wrote to his friend and political advocate Congressman Elihu Washburne: "The rebels have now in their ranks their last man. The little boys and old men are guarding prisoners, guarding rail-road bridges and forming a good part of their garrisons for intrenched positions. A man lost by them cannot be replaced. They have robbed the cradle and the grave equally to get their present force. Besides what they lose in frequent skirmishes and battles they are now loosing [sic] from desertions and other causes at least one regiment per day."[674]

In another strategic move, Grant recognized that prisoner exchanges were unwisely benefiting the Confederates, who were running low on manpower. On August 18, he wrote: "If we commence a system of exchanges which liberates all prisoners taken we will have to fight on until the whole South is exterminated. If we hold those caught they amount to no more than dead men. At this particular time to release all rebel prisoners [in the] North would insure Sherman's defeat and would compromise our safety here."

The next day he followed up on that idea. "We ought not to make a single exchange nor release a prisoner on any pretext whatever until the war closes. We have got to fight until the military power of the South is exhausted and if we release or exchange prisoners captured it simply becomes a war of extermination."

Lee's concerns expressed in an August 24 letter to the Confederate Secretary of War, James Seddon, confirmed Grant's views: "Unless some measures can be devised to replace our losses, the consequences may be disastrous. ... Without some increase of our strength, I cannot see how we are to escape the natural military consequences of the enemy's numerical superiority."[675]

A CRUEL SUMMER

Yet despite these strategic moves, in the view of most Northerners, Grant remained stuck in front of Petersburg, Sherman had not reached Atlanta, and Sheridan was just getting organized in the Shenandoah Valley. The hopes that had blossomed when the Overland Campaign began had been dampened by the massive loss of life.

The country was souring on the war, now in its fourth year, and Lincoln's prospects for election waned. In the summer of 1864,

Horace Greeley of the *New-York Daily Tribune* wrote, "Mr. Lincoln is already beaten. He cannot be elected. And we must have another ticket to save us from utter overthrow."[676]

Growing more convinced that he would not be reelected, Lincoln wrote a letter that summer and asked his cabinet to sign their names on the outside, sight unseen, to pledge their commitment to continue the fight to preserve the Union. The contents read: "This morning, as for some days past, it seems exceedingly probable that this Administration will not be re-elected. Then it will be my duty to so cooperate with the Government President elect, as to save the Union between the Election and the inauguration; as he will have secured his election on such ground that he cannot possibly save it afterwards."[677]

That same day, Lincoln wrote to a friend: "I am going to be beaten, and unless some great change takes place, badly beaten."[678]

Draft Riots and Unrest

At the same time, many in the North were resisting the draft, making it difficult for Grant to replace soldiers who were wounded or whose enlistments had expired.

Amid growing tensions, General Halleck wrote to Grant warning of possible draft riots in New York, Pennsylvania, Indiana, and Kentucky. Halleck thought it would be necessary to withdraw combat troops from around Richmond to quell the riots and maintain order. "Are not the appearances such that we ought to take in sail and prepare the ship for a storm?"

Grant could not have disagreed more. In his view, the riots were police work that should be left to the state governors and various local militias. "If we are to draw troops from the field to keep the loyal states in the harness it will prove difficult to suppress the rebellion in the disloyal states." If forced to move troops from Petersburg, Grant warned that Lee would be able to send soldiers to defend Atlanta, just as he had reinforced Bragg at Chickamauga the year before—and that "would insure the defeat of Sherman."

Grant dug in his heels and refused to compromise.

After reading Grant's reply on August 17, President Lincoln immediately telegraphed his approval. "I have seen your dispatch expressing your unwillingness to break your hold where you are. Neither am I willing. Hold on with a bull-dog grip, and chew and choke as much as possible."[679]

Reading the president's message at his City Point headquarters, Grant broke into loud laughter—something he seldom did. When surprised staffers asked what had amused him, he showed them the president's telegram. "The president has more nerve than any of his advisers," he said, then chuckled.[680]

Despite the dire predictions of naysayers, Lincoln and Grant would keep pounding until they were victorious.

SIGNS OF PROGRESS

At the same time in the Deep South, Admiral David Farragut attacked the harbor of Mobile, Alabama—the last major open port in the Gulf of Mexico. This was the only rail connection point between Alabama, Mississippi, and the rest of the Confederacy. On August 5, Farragut's naval forces moved into Mobile Bay with their commander lashed to the rigging due to a bad case of vertigo.[681]

When some of the ships hesitated after encountering mines floating in the water, Farragut cried out, "Damn the torpedoes— Full speed ahead," then whipped the rebel navy into submission. The victory gave a much-needed boost in morale for the Lincoln administration and Northern troops.[682]

Despite the Union victory, the Democrats' mood was upbeat at their national convention on August 29 in Chicago. Divided by issues of war and peace, they sought a strong candidate who could unify the party. The compromise was to nominate pro-war General George B. McClellan for president and anti-war Representative George H. Pendleton for vice-president. Pendleton, a close associate of the Copperhead Clement Vallandigham, balanced the ticket, since he strongly opposed the Union war effort. Many Democrats believed abolition posed an obstacle to peace, and they abhorred Lincoln's Emancipation Proclamation.

Those who called themselves "Peace" Democrats were having success by hammering away with the question of whether the war was worth the sacrifice already paid by so many families. As the presidential campaign heated up, many appeals became blatantly racist. Many Democrats asked whether it was worth shedding white blood to free Negro slaves.

Despite McClellan's pro-war position, the convention adopted a peace platform written by Vallandigham that renounced the war as an outright failure, demanded a "cessation of hostilities," called for a convention to restore peace, and reaffirmed states' rights.[683] The platform declared "after four years of failure to restore the Union by the experiment of war, justice, humanity, liberty and the public welfare demand" an end to the war "on the basis of the Federal Union of The States."[684]

~

FROM PERSONAL MEMOIRS

The convention, which had met and made its nomination of the Democratic candidate for the presidency, had declared the war a failure. Treason was talked as boldly in Chicago at that convention as ever it had been in Charleston.[685]

~

Meanwhile, George McClellan, back at his home in Orange, New Jersey, struggled to determine how to run as a War Democrat on a Peace Democrat platform.[686] At the same time, Abraham Lincoln worked to find a way to preserve the union even if he lost the election.

Chapter Twenty-Three

THE TURNING TIDE

SUMMER 1864—PETERSBURG, VIRGINIA

~

FROM *PERSONAL MEMOIRS*

We had our troops on the Weldon Railroad contending against a large force that regarded this road of so much importance that they could afford to expend many lives in retaking it; Sherman just getting through to Atlanta with great losses of men from casualties, discharges and detachments left along as guards to occupy and hold the road in rear of him; Washington threatened but a short time before, and now Early being strengthened in the valley so as, probably, to renew that attempt. It kept me pretty active in looking after all these points.[687]

~

SUMMER 1864

In the months after the siege at Petersburg began, Grant and his old West Point buddy, Quartermaster General Rufus Ingalls, transformed City Point from a quiet river village into a bustling Union port and staging area. Ingalls directed the building of enormous warehouses for the commissary, ordnance, and quartermaster departments. In addition, buildings were erected for various tradesmen and wagon repair shops. The bakery was a factory that churned out one hundred thousand loaves of bread a day. A depot field hospital was built that spread over two hundred acres, serving ten thousand patients.

The City Point wharf stretched more than a mile, housing up to seventy-five sailing ships and one hundred barges on a typical day. Four steamers a day connected City Point to Washington, DC. Ingalls built a twenty-one-mile railroad joining City Point and Petersburg, ensuring that the front lines were constantly supplied.[688]

Most people realized that the presidential election in November would be a referendum on the war. The presidential candidates had been chosen and their platforms clearly articulated; the public would decide whether to continue or to end the war.

Grant could see more clearly than almost anyone in Washington that, from the military point of view, the war was actually going well. Since the Virginia and Georgia campaigns had opened on May 4, the Confederacy had been placed under the kind of continuing strain it had not previously endured. Unlike the past, where Confederate leadership could move troops to a hot spot to reinforce the various armies, Grant's policy of unrelenting pressure kept the rebel armies separated. His strategy of divide and conquer was working. Something was bound to give.

Under Sherman's leadership, the first cracks appeared in Georgia.[689]

Because General Johnston had been unable to keep Sherman from crossing the Chattahoochee River and advancing to the outskirts of Atlanta, President Jefferson Davis relieved him of duty in mid-July, replacing him with General John Bell Hood. Grant had fought with Hood in the Mexican War. "I know very well," said Grant, "the chief characteristics of Hood. He is a bold, dashing soldier, and has many qualities of successful leadership, but he is an indiscreet commander, and lacks cool judgment. We may look out now for rash and ill-advised attacks."[690]

Confederate General Arthur M. Manigault remembered that "the army received the announcement with a very bad grace, and with no little murmuring."[691] Private Sam Watkins called Hood's appointment "the most terrible and disastrous blow that the South ever received," and described how fellow Army of Tennessee soldiers cried or deserted after the elevation of the "over-rated" Hood.[692]

Conversely, Hood's appointment brought joy in the Union command. John Schofield, Hood's West Point roommate, told Sherman that Hood was bold, rash, and courageous and would quickly hit Sherman "like hell." Sherman alerted his commanders to the risk of attack. "Each army commander will accept battle on anything like fair terms."[693]

Hood did just what Grant and Sherman expected, coming out from behind his entrenchments and fighting both valiantly and foolishly. Beginning on July 20, Hood launched frontal assaults on strong Union positions at Peach Tree Creek, then Decatur on July 22. On July 28, the Federal army defeated the Confederates at Ezra Church.

The results were so disastrous that on August 5, President Davis, who must have been having second thoughts, provided his newly appointed army commander with some ironic tactical advice: "The loss consequent upon attacking the enemy in his entrenchments requires you to avoid that if practicable."

With Atlanta in the crosshairs, the Yankees increased the artillery bombardment and cut the railroad lines going into the city. Early in August, Sherman assured Grant, "One thing is certain, whether we get inside of Atlanta or not it will be a used-up community when we are done with it." He brought the city under the continuous fire of siege guns and sent cavalry and infantry swinging out to west and south with orders to "make a circle of desolation around Atlanta."

During the preceding two months of the Atlanta campaign, Johnston had lost nine thousand men to Sherman's eleven thousand. In a little more than a week, Hood lost fourteen thousand casualties compared to Sherman's four thousand.

With Hood in command, the struggle for Atlanta became a horrific bloodbath. The hundred-day campaign had cost the Union thirty-two thousand casualties and the Confederates thirty-five thousand—almost three-fourths of these rebel casualties occurring after Hood succeeded Johnston. With Sherman's two-to-one troop advantage, the Southerners could not afford to trade casualties on this scale.[694]

While the Democrats in Chicago were nominating McClellan and composing a platform based on the assumption that the war was a failure, General Hood was forced to evacuate Atlanta to keep his troops alive. On August 31, Hood lost more than four thousand men at Jonesboro. Union forces now controlled all the railroads into Atlanta, cutting off Confederate supplies.[695]

On September 1, Hood blew up the munitions he could not carry out of Atlanta so they wouldn't fall into enemy hands. That night General Henry Warner Slocum's corps watched great lights flashing as repeated explosions rocked the city. On the morning of September 2, Slocum marched his men past abandoned fortifications and the wreckage left by fire and bombardment. As Northern troops entered Atlanta, the mayor officially surrendered the city. Soon after, Slocum sent the War Department the news in a telegram:

GENERAL SHERMAN HAS TAKEN ATLANTA

Later in the day, Sherman sent his own dispatch:

SO ATLANTA IS OURS, AND FAIRLY WON[696]

The Democratic convention had adjourned on August 31 in a mood of campaign euphoria. Only two days later, the bubble had burst. Secretary of State Seward declared, "Sherman and Farragut have knocked the bottom out of the [Democrats'] Chicago platform."[697]

Grant received the news on the evening of September 4, while seated in a camp chair in front of his headquarters tent, smoking a cigar and chatting with members of his staff. He read the official telegram announcing Sherman's victory aloud to the officers.[698] They greeted the announcement with cheers, and the news spread rapidly throughout the army.[699] Grant ordered Meade's and Butler's headquarters to have a hundred-gun salute fired from every battery that bore on the rebel works.[700]

Church bells rang across the land as they had not rung since Grant took Vicksburg. Lincoln proclaimed a day of thanksgiving and prayer.[701]

After his decisive victory in Atlanta, talk began in Washington of conferring the equal rank of lieutenant general on Sherman with the possibility of giving Sherman supreme command over Grant. Some Northern politicians and reporters accused Grant of loafing at City Point while others like Sherman were busy doing the fighting.

Sherman would have none of it.

The fiery commander immediately disavowed the talk as foolishness and wrote a heartfelt letter to his chief and his friend: "I would rather have you in command than anybody else, for you are fair, honest, and have at heart the same purpose that should actuate all. I should emphatically decline any commission calculated to bring us into rivalry."

Grant graciously replied, "No one would be more pleased at your advancement than I, and if you should be placed in my position and I put subordinate, it would not change our relations in the least. I would make the same exertions to support you that you have ever done to support me, and I would do all in my power to make our cause win."[702]

THE SHENANDOAH CAMPAIGN

~

FROM *PERSONAL MEMOIRS*

On the 15th of September I started to visit General Sheridan in the Shenandoah Valley. My purpose was to have him attack Early, or drive him out of the valley and destroy that source of supplies for Lee's army. I knew it was impossible for me to get orders through Washington to Sheridan to make a move, because they would be stopped there and such orders as Halleck's caution (and that of the Secretary of War) would suggest would be given instead, and would, no doubt, be contradictory to mine. I therefore, without stopping at

Washington, went directly through to Charlestown, some ten miles above Harper's Ferry, and waited there to see General Sheridan, having sent a courier in advance to inform him where to meet me.

When Sheridan arrived I asked him if he had a map showing the positions of his army and that of the enemy. He at once drew one out of his side pocket, showing all roads and streams, and the camps of the two armies. He said that if he had permission he would move so and so (pointing out how) against the Confederates, and that he could "whip them." Before starting I had drawn up a plan of campaign for Sheridan, which I had brought with me; but, seeing that he was so clear and so positive in his views and so confident of success, I said nothing about this and did not take it out of my pocket.[703]

~

September 15, 1864

After taking command in the Shenandoah, Sheridan and his troops went right to work, unleashing a swath of destruction in the valley, burning barns filled with hay and wheat, gathering livestock and horses, and then shipping them off to the Army of the Potomac.[704]

Despite these accomplishments, President Lincoln still expressed concern over Early and his forces. He asked Grant to reinforce Sheridan so he could attack Early and drive him out once and for all. Grant set out with these instructions in mind, but he also wanted Sheridan to destroy the two railroads and the canal to the west of Richmond that helped to supply Lee's army.[705]

When the two commanders sat down to discuss the situation, Sheridan outlined his plan of attack to Grant, tracing troop positions and lines of march on a map. This meeting took place on a Friday. Grant asked Sheridan how soon he could attack Early's forces, hoping they could get started by the following Tuesday. Sheridan was confident in his reply. "O yes," he responded, he "could be off before daylight on Monday."[706]

As the lieutenant general chatted with Sheridan, a sergeant standing guard outside complained about the presence of Grant.

"I hate to see that old cuss around. When that old cuss is around there's sure to be a big fight on hand."[707]

Grant gave Sheridan orders to attack. As soon as their conversation concluded, Grant set off on his return journey to City Point.[708]

On September 19, Sheridan attacked the rebels at Opequon Creek near Winchester, Virginia. After an all-day battle, the contest climaxed with a classic infantry charge that sent Confederate soldiers "whirling through Winchester," wrote Sheridan's chief of staff.[709] Northern troops suffered five thousand casualties compared with four thousand casualties on the Southern side. Yet despite the lower casualty rates, the battle hurt Early badly and drove him south.[710]

Grant had arrived at his headquarters on the night of Monday, September 19. News arrived the next day in a triumphant telegram from Sheridan: "I have the honor to report that I attacked the force of General Early on the Berryville pike at the crossing of Opequon Creek, and after a most stubborn and sanguinary engagement, which lasted from early in the morning until 5 o'clock in the evening, completely defeated him, and, driving him through Winchester, captured about 2,500 prisoners, 5 pieces of artillery, 9 army flags and most of the wounded."[711]

In typical style, Grant urged his victorious commander to capitalize on the victory: "Push your success and make all you can of it."[712]

Like Grant, Sheridan gave the rebels no rest, catching up to them three days later at Fisher's Hill on September 22. Again the Federals attacked, this time at a cost of only five hundred soldiers. Sheridan turned the tables on Early, imposing twelve hundred casualties.[713] He battered the rebel army with a shattering blow in the late-afternoon light, and only darkness saved it from total destruction.[714]

What was left of the Confederate Second Corps went stumbling up the valley toward Staunton.[715] Sheridan once again pursued with vigor, driving Early so far south that the Federals lost contact with both Grant and Washington, DC. This communications blackout brought renewed anxiety to the White House and the War Department.

To calm Lincoln's fears that Lee would reinforce Early in an attempt to destroy Sheridan, Grant assured the president that he would renew and intensify the attack on Lee to keep the rebel forces pinned down in front of Petersburg. On September 28, Grant directed General Edward Ord's Eighteenth and Major General David Birney's Tenth Corps to work with Brigadier General August V. Kautz's cavalry to threaten the rebels at the end of the line closest to Richmond.

Grant launched a simultaneous offensive on the Petersburg end of the siege lines, capturing the strategic Fort Harrison near Richmond. This action forced Lee to launch an unsuccessful counterattack against that fort, costing him dearly in men and supplies. Lee was forced to extend his lines three miles farther west of Petersburg, thinning his defenses by further spreading his dwindling troops. A few days later, Grant's soldiers used Spencer repeating rifles to repulse a Lee-directed assault along Darbytown Road.[716]

Grant knew the Union triumphs in the Shenandoah Valley were adding to the stranglehold on Lee's army. "Keep on," Grant exhorted Sheridan, "and your work will cause the fall of Richmond.[717] Your great victory wipes out much of the stain upon our arms by previous disasters in [the valley]."[718]

OCTOBER 1864

On October 7, Sheridan reported to Grant of having "destroyed over 2,000 barns filled with wheat, hay and farming implements, and 70 mills filled with flour and wheat.[719] This total-war strategy created a massive flight of residents from the Shenandoah Valley.[720] Production and the distribution of food and supplies for the Confederate army in that vital region ground to a halt.

Lee had to act.

Word came to Grant and Sheridan that the Southern commander had reinforced Early by sending him Joseph Kershaw's infantry division of three thousand men plus a cavalry brigade. With this added strength, Early moved against Sheridan on October 19, hoping to surprise him. After an all-night march through heavy fog, the rebels splashed through the waters of Cedar Creek as they approached the Yankees. At dawn, Confederate forces struck hard at Sheridan's men in a surprise attack, driving them back four miles and capturing twenty pieces of artillery.[721]

With Sheridan traveling back from a meeting in Washington, his second-in-command, Horatio Wright, led the Federal troops. Wounded in the face in the initial attack, with blood clotting his gray beard, Wright led valiantly, but soon Federal soldiers retreated in confusion. Believing they had won a great victory, Early's famished, poorly clad soldiers took advantage of an afternoon lull to plunder the abandoned Union camps.[722]

~

FROM PERSONAL MEMOIRS

Sheridan having left Washington on the 18th, reached Winchester that night. The following morning he started to join his command. He had scarcely got out of town, when he met his men returning in panic from the front and also heard heavy firing to the south. He immediately ordered the cavalry at Winchester to be deployed across the valley to stop the stragglers. Leaving members of his staff to take care of Winchester and the public property there, he set out with a small escort directly for the scene of battle. As he met the fugitives he ordered them to turn back, reminding them that they were going the wrong way. His presence soon restored confidence. Finding themselves worse frightened than hurt the men did halt and turn back. Many of those who had run ten miles got back in time to redeem their reputation as gallant soldiers before night.

When Sheridan got to the front he found General George Getty and General George Custer still holding their ground firmly between the Confederates and our retreating troops. Everything in the rear was now ordered up. Sheridan at once proceeded to intrench his position; and he awaited an assault from the enemy. This was made with vigor, and was directed principally against General

William Emory's corps, which had sustained the principal loss in the first attack. By one o'clock the attack was repulsed. Early was so badly damaged that he seemed disinclined to make another attack, but went to work to intrench himself with a view to holding the position he had already gained. He thought, no doubt, that Sheridan would be glad enough to leave him unmolested; but in this he was mistaken.[723]

~

Spurring his magnificent black Mississippi Morgan, Rienzi,[724] Sheridan raced toward the fighting. As he pressed ahead, he heard the noise growing louder and soon found the Valley Turnpike clogged with retreating Union soldiers at the south edge of Winchester.[725] He moved into the middle of his disorganized retreating men, waving his cap and urging them to turn back. "I rode to the crest of the elevation, and there taking off my hat, the men rose up from behind their barricade with cheers of recognition," Sheridan recalled.[726]

"About face, boys! Turn back," he cried out, wheeling his horse around in a circle so everyone could see and hear their commander. "I am going to sleep in that camp tonight or in hell!"[727]

They stopped and began to chant his name. "Cheers seemed to come from throats of brass," an officer said, "and caps were thrown to the tops of the scattering oaks. No more doubt or chance for doubt existed."

"God damn you!" Sheridan shouted. "Don't cheer me. Fight! We will lick them out of their boots!"

A colonel told Sheridan how glad the men were to see him. "Well, by God," said Sheridan, "I'm glad to be here!"[728]

Sheridan's words breathed new courage into his shaken soldiers, who turned and followed him back to the front lines. As he gathered the retreating troops and organized a counterattack, he met a twenty-one-year-old major, William McKinley—the future twenty-fifth president of the United States—who raced ahead, blaring that Sheridan had returned.[729]

When Sheridan arrived at the front, he found that Wright's troops were still holding firm in the Union center. Although wounded, Wright had worked to stabilize his men. Sheridan's army had been surprised and damaged, but they still maintained a three-to-two advantage in numbers.[730]

Riding along the line of battle, "Little Phil" reorganized the remainder of his army, and late in the afternoon led the troops forward in a dazzling counterattack.[731] With the cavalry leading the way, the Yankees attacked the rebels under the autumn sunset. Sheridan drove the enemy across Cedar Creek and completely routed the Southern soldiers.[732]

Confederate soldiers flung away their weapons as they fled.[733] Within a few hours victory was achieved, effectively ending Early's campaign and closing off the Shenandoah Valley from the Confederates for the rest of the war.[734]

~

FROM PERSONAL MEMOIRS

Early tried to rally his men, but they were followed so closely that they had to give way very quickly every time they attempted to make a stand. Our cavalry, having pushed on and got in the rear of the Confederates, captured twenty-four pieces of artillery, besides retaking what had been lost in the morning. This victory pretty much closed the campaigning in the Valley of Virginia. All the Confederate troops were sent back to Richmond with the exception of one division of infantry and a little cavalry. Wright's corps was ordered back to the Army of the Potomac, and two other divisions were withdrawn from the valley. Early had lost more men in killed, wounded and captured in the valley than Sheridan had commanded from first to last.[735]

~

At three o'clock on the afternoon of October 20, General Grant sat at his table in his tent, writing letters. Several members of the staff were seated in front of the tent discussing some anticipated movements. The telegraph operator rushed across the campground, stepped into the general's quarters, and handed him a dispatch. He read it over, and then came to the front of the tent, put on a very grave look, and said to the members of the staff: "I'll read you a dispatch I have just received from Sheridan." In a solemn tone, the general read the dispatch, which was dated 10:00 p.m. the previous night:

> I have the honor to report that my army at Cedar Creek was attacked this morning before daylight, and my left was turned and driven in confusion; in fact, most of the line was driven in confusion, with the loss of twenty pieces of artillery. I hastened from Winchester, where I was on my return from Washington, and joined the army between Middletown and Newtown, having been driven back about four miles.

Here the general looked up, shook his head solemnly, and said, "That's pretty bad, isn't it?"

A melancholy chorus replied, "It's too bad, too bad!"

"Now just wait till I read you the rest of it," added the general, with a perceptible twinkle in his eye:

> I here took the affair in hand, and quickly united the corps, formed a compact line of battle just in time to repulse an attack of the enemy's, which was handsomely done at about 1 p.m. At 3 p.m., after some changes of the cavalry from the left to the right flank, I attacked with great vigor, driving and routing the enemy, capturing, according to the last reports, forty-three pieces of artillery and very many prisoners. I do not yet know the number of my casualties or the losses of the enemy. Wagon-trains, ambulances, and caissons in large numbers are in our possession. Affairs at times looked badly, but by the gallantry of our brave officers and men disaster has been converted into a splendid victory. Darkness again intervened to shut off greater results.

By this time, Grant's staff members were beside themselves with delight. The general seemed to enjoy the bombshell he had thrown among the staff almost as much as the news of Sheridan's signal victory.[736] To celebrate Sheridan's victory, Grant ordered the armies at Petersburg to fire another hundred-gun salute, just as he had done when he received news of the fall of Atlanta. He immediately wrote to the War Department and urged them to make Sheridan brigadier general in the regular army.[737]

Both sides transferred most of their remaining troops to the Richmond and Petersburg front, and fighting in the Shenandoah came to an end. Sheridan's third and final major victory in the valley in just over a month further revived the spirits of Northerners and gave hope to those working for Lincoln's reelection.[738]

Cedar Creek caught the nation's attention and made a badly needed victory look miraculous. An air of finality hung over this triumph—and no one, North or South, could fail to see it.[739]

Lee was now so hard-pressed to hold Petersburg and Richmond that he could not reinforce Early again. There would be no more threats against Washington.[740]

THE 1864 PRESIDENTIAL ELECTION

NOVEMBER 1864

All predictions about the presidential race became obsolete with Farragut's capture of Mobile Bay, Sherman's march into Atlanta, and Sheridan's decisive victory in the Shenandoah Valley. The psychological effect of these victories echoed throughout the loyal states. The North was suddenly endued with the confidence of victory while the South faced the reality that the war was nearly lost. John C. Fremont, who had toyed with the idea of running against Lincoln, now abandoned his candidacy as Republicans fell into line behind the president. McClellan vocally disavowed the "peace plank" in the Democratic platform.[741]

Grant insisted that soldiers be allowed to vote in the election, even though some feared that this would work to the advantage of McClellan, beloved former commander of the Army of the Potomac. Although Grant believed the president's reelection essential to winning the war, he remained neutral and refused to say anything publicly that could be read as an endorsement of Lincoln. He also prohibited political speakers from either party to campaign in army camps.[742]

On November 8, polls opened across America. To everyone's relief, voting was done efficiently and quietly in the camps. Every soldier was allowed absolute freedom in the choice of candidates. General Grant strolled through some of the neighboring camps while the voting was going on and watched with interest how effectively the system for depositing the ballots worked.[743]

He and his staff sat up late around the campfire to await the results on election night. According to Brigadier General M. R. Morgan, commissary general at headquarters, Grant received reports from the headquarters telegraph operator and read them out for everyone to hear. Throughout the evening, he read telegram after telegram showing McClellan far ahead. Most of the officers who listened to him were Lincoln supporters, and some went off to bed dejected, convinced their candidate had lost.

Just after midnight as Grant prepared to go to bed, he confessed to those who had stayed up long enough to hear the result of the election that it had all been a hoax. Every report that came in, throughout the evening, had showed Lincoln in the lead.[744]

Lincoln's victory became clear on November 10. That night Grant telegraphed to Halleck: "Congratulate the President for me for the double victory. The election having passed off quietly, no bloodshed or riot throughout the land, is a victory worth more to the country than a battle won."[745]

Lincoln won nationally by what is, for presidential elections, a sizeable margin—55 percent to 45 percent. In the Electoral College, he won 212 votes to only 21 for McClellan.[746] Lincoln carried all but three states—Kentucky, New Jersey, and Delaware. Most significantly, a majority of the Union troops voted for their commander, including a large percentage of McClellan's old command, the Army of the Potomac.[747] A later analysis of absentee ballots in twelve states showed that Union soldiers helped to tip the scales toward Lincoln, favoring him with 78 percent of their votes versus 53 percent among civilian votes.[748]

The fact that the election was held at all set an important historical precedent. Before this, no country had ever held elections during such a pressing military crisis.[749]

As Lincoln and Grant hoped, the Confederacy gazed with dismay at the election results since its whole strategy had been to stir Northern fears and doubts with the hopes of defeating Lincoln at the polls.[750] Jefferson Davis refused to accept the fact that the game was up and insisted that Lincoln's reelection had changed nothing. But Southern hopes were dashed, and Confederate soldiers deserted in massive numbers. The writing was on the wall.[751]

The massive Southern defeat at Nashville in December was further proof that the Confederacy's days were numbered. After a delay due to an ice storm that covered the ground with a dangerous slippery glaze, Major General George Thomas finally attacked the troops of Confederate General John Bell Hood. In one of the most decisive victories of the war, Thomas, "The Rock of Chickamauga," routed Hood's army, effectively destroying it as a fighting force.

Perhaps the most glaring harbinger of the Confederacy's impending demise was General Sherman's ability to cross the heartland of Georgia virtually unopposed. After the defeat at Atlanta, his western army set out to do in Georgia what Sheridan had done in the Shenandoah Valley—confiscate or destroy all crops and livestock and demolish any means of supplying the rebel armies.

For nearly six weeks, nothing was heard from Sherman, who was far from any telegraphic communication. Then after cutting a swath of destruction across the Georgia countryside, Sherman emerged near Savannah on December 21.[752] Savannah had been one of the last major ports open to the Confederates. Sherman wired Lincoln with a holiday message: "I beg to present you, as a Christmas gift, the city of Savannah, with 150 heavy guns and plenty of ammunition, and also about 25,000 bales of cotton."[753]

With Lincoln's reelection, nearly everyone north and south recognized that it was only a matter of time before the war would be won as well. But they also knew that much more death and destruction lay ahead.

Chapter Twenty-Four

ENDING THE MATTER

JANUARY 1865—PETERSBURG, VIRGINIA

During the winter months, as the Union army was strengthened with manpower and refitted with equipment and ammunition, the Confederate army was evaporating. Nearly 40 percent of rebel soldiers east of the Mississippi had deserted during the fall and early winter.[754] By the end of 1864, less than half of the Confederacy's soldiers were present in their units.

Grasping at any possibility of victory, on January 19, 1865, the Confederate Congress appointed Lee commander in chief of all Confederate forces to the consternation of Jefferson Davis, who had served as US Secretary of War under President Franklin Pierce and did not like relinquishing control. In desperation, Lee ordered the troops of General Kirby Smith's Trans-Mississippi Army transferred to Virginia.

Lee did not wait long to countermand one of Davis's most controversial decisions. On February 22, Lee recalled General Joseph Johnston and ordered him to patch together the remnants of the western armies. Lee charged Johnston with the monumental task of stopping General Sherman.

Lee's recall order reflected the unrealistic expectations of Johnston's chances against Sherman's overwhelming forces: "Assume command of the Army of Tennessee and all troops in Department of South Carolina, Georgia, and Florida. Assign General Beauregard to duty under you, as you may select. Concentrate all available forces to drive back Sherman."[755]

At the same time, Lee's army continued to melt away. On February 25, the Southern commander wrote: "Hundreds of men are deserting nightly—at least a regiment a day, taking it throughout the army, by desertions alone."[756] The situation in the rebel army became so desperate around Petersburg and Richmond that in January, Lee and Davis agreed to exchange their African American prisoners—something they had sworn they would never do.

Referring to the new Southern law for conscripting boys from fourteen to eighteen, calling them junior reserves, and men from forty-five to sixty, calling them senior reserves, General Butler used the now common phrase that they were "robbing both the cradle and the grave."[757]

Sherman's and Sheridan's campaigns—along with the recent Union victory that closed Wilmington Harbor—had their intended effect. With all Southern ports closed to blockade runners, the scarcity of food and supplies not only affected Lee's army but also brought privations to the South's civilians. Soldiers in the trenches received desperate letters from home, begging them to leave the army and tend to their families.[758]

Grant was extremely eager to make the end come sooner rather than later. The way to ensure that was by keeping Lee's and Johnston's armies divided. Sherman would work to keep Johnston away from Virginia, and Grant would strive to keep Lee from swinging west and south to hook up with Johnston in North Carolina. If the Federals could keep these two rebel armies separated, then the end was truly in sight. If not, the war could go on and on.

The pressure on Grant was acute.

But the pressure on Lee was even greater, prompting him to ask the Confederate Congress to pass a bill allowing the recruiting of slaves into the army. "We must decide whether the Negro will fight for us, or against us," Lee wrote. Residents of Richmond were shocked to see a new Confederate battalion made up of slaves and White hospital convalescents marching up Main Street while a band played "Dixie."[759]

The Union cavalry also made progress, led by the fiery General Sheridan. Galloping through central Virginia, the Yankees tore up and twisted railroad ties back toward Lynchburg. A division continued on to the vital James River Canal to destroy locks, levies, and culverts. Mills, factories, grain silos, and anything else that could contribute to the Confederate war effort were destroyed as well.

Sheridan decided it would be best to fight his way along the railroad and canal as he moved as close to Richmond as possible. More than two thousand escaped slaves joined his column, assisting in the destruction of the railroad and the canal.

Publicly, Sheridan said he believed it best not to continue on to Lynchburg as Grant had ordered because the March rains had fallen in torrents, turning the roads into bogs and flooding the streams. The real reason Sheridan did not try to capture Lynchburg and push south to join Sherman is that he simply did not want to miss the action around Petersburg. Convinced the war was nearly over, Sheridan wanted his cavalry "to be in at the death."[760]

As the Federals tightened the vise on the rebels, General Grant had two choices: (1) hold Lee while Sherman mopped up the rest of the Confederate armies or (2) force Lee out of his entrenchments and destroy the remainder of the Army of Northern Virginia in open battle. Sheridan believed the second option was the best way to end the war, and he wanted to be in the thick of the action.

On March 22, 1865, Grant wrote to Sherman, who was then at Goldsboro, North Carolina:

> Since Sheridan's very successful raid north of the James, the enemy are left dependent on the Southside and Danville roads for all their supplies. These I hope to cut next week. His instructions will be to strike the Southside road as near Petersburg as he can, and destroy it so that it cannot be repaired for three or four days, and push on to the Danville road, as near to the Appomattox as he can get.
>
> From that point I shall probably leave it to his discretion either to return to this army, crossing the Danville road south of Burkesville, or go and join you, passing between Danville and Greensboro. When this movement commences I shall move out by my left, with all the force I can, holding present intrenched lines. I shall start with no distinct view, further than holding Lee's forces from following Sheridan. But I shall be along myself, and will take advantage of anything that turns up. If Lee detaches, I will attack; or if he comes out of his lines I will endeavor to repulse him, and follow it up to the best advantage.[761]

Sheridan was not at all happy with this development.

After reading Grant's instructions telling Sheridan to join Sherman, his chief of staff, James W. Forsyth, asked, "General, you are going to join Sherman?"

Sheridan answered with a firm no.

"How are you going to get out of it?" Forsyth responded. "This order is positive and explicit."

"I am not going to join Sherman," Sheridan repeated. "This campaign will end the war. I have been anxious for fear Lee would commence moving west before we could get to Grant's army. The Army of the Potomac will never move from its present position unless we join them and pull them out.

"The cavalry corps and the Army of the Potomac have got to whip Lee. If I obeyed these instructions and crossed the James and joined Sherman, the Army of the Potomac would rest where they are and Sherman, with our assistance, would close the war. If this should happen it would be disastrous to the country, for there would be no balance of power between the east and the west. This cavalry corps and the Army of the Potomac, of which it is a part, have got to wipe Lee out before Sherman and his army reach Virginia."[762]

Sheridan had made up his mind.

As the Federals tightened the noose, Lee knew his options were dwindling. He argued to Jefferson Davis that if he could force General Grant to shorten his lines, perhaps the rebels could escape around their right flank and join Johnston in North Carolina. If he could do this, the two armies could defeat Sherman and then turn and attack Grant. Davis did not want to abandon Richmond, but with Grant's stranglehold doing its work, Lee did not see any other choice.

Lee and Davis reluctantly agreed that Petersburg and Richmond could no longer be defended and that they must escape as soon as possible.

LINCOLN AT CITY POINT

As Grant completed his plans for the assault on Petersburg, he extended an unusual courtesy to President Lincoln, who had become a close friend. "Can you not visit City Point for a day or two? I would like very much to see you, and I think the rest would do you good."[763]

Lincoln immediately accepted Grant's offer.

On March 24, word arrived at headquarters that the president was on his way up the James aboard the *River Queen*. About nine o'clock that evening, the steamer approached the wharf, and General Grant, with some of his staff and Robert Lincoln, went down to the landing and met the president; Mrs. Lincoln; their youngest son, Tad; and several ladies who had come from Washington with the presidential party.

"It was after dark on the 24th when we reached City Point," recalled presidential guard William Crook. "It was a beautiful sight at this time, with the many-colored lights of the boats in the harbor and the lights of the town straggling up the bluffs of the shore, crowned by the lights from Grant's headquarters at the top.

"As soon as the River Queen was made fast to the wharf, General Grant with some members of his staff came aboard. They had a long consultation with the President, at the end of which Mr. Lincoln appeared particularly happy. General Grant had evidently made him feel that the end of the conflict was at hand, nearer than he had expected."[764]

The meeting was cordial but lasted a short time because Lincoln and his family were fatigued by the trip and decided to retire.

The next day, Grant offered the president the choice of his two favorite horses, Cincinnati and Jeff Davis. Lincoln selected the magnificent Cincinnati, the larger of the two and better suited to his tall frame. During his stay at City Point, Lincoln frequently rode Cincinnati around the camp.

"He was a good rider and greatly enjoyed this recreation," wrote War Department employee David Homer Bates. "When Grant went to the front to personally direct the general assault upon Lee's army along a line of over thirty miles, he left a trusted groom in charge of Cincinnati, so that if the movement should prove successful, the President might ride out to the front."[765]

"We had an opportunity of seeing one of the great centres of the war," presidential guard William Crook later recalled. "In Mr. Lincoln's estimation it was the critical point, and he had placed his lieutenant-general, the man in whom he had most faith, in charge. The Appomattox and the James come together at City Point. The harbor thus made is overhung with high bluffs. On the top of one bluff was a group of houses, which Grant and his staff used as headquarters."

"From higher ground in the vicinity could be seen the tents of Lee's army," Crooks chronicled. "It was a busy camp, and everything was in motion. Just west of our troops was the long, curved line of Lee's intrenchments, stretching from Petersburg, south of the James and fifteen miles from City Point, to Richmond, northwest of City Point and nearly double that distance."

"General Grant invited the president to take a ride to the front to visit with General Meade," Crook said. The group saw some lively skirmishing between the picket lines of the two forces while they were at General Meade's headquarters. "We were on a hill just east of where the troops were engaged; it was not more than a quarter of a mile away from the wood where the fighting was in progress. The President asked whether the position was not too close for the comfort of his party. When he was assured that there was no danger, he remained two hours watching the struggle, and turned away only when the firing ceased."[766]

March 25, 1865: Lee's Final Offensive

~

From Personal Memoirs

Early on the morning of the 25th the enemy assaulted our lines in front of the 9th corps (which held from the Appomattox River towards our left), and carried Fort Stedman, and a part of the line to the right and left of it, established themselves and turned the guns of the fort against us, but our troops on either flank held their ground until the reserves were brought up, when the enemy was driven back with a heavy loss in killed and wounded, and one thousand nine hundred prisoners. Our loss was sixty-eight killed, three hundred and thirty-seven wounded, and five hundred and six missing. General Meade at once ordered the other corps to advance and feel the enemy in their respective fronts. Pushing forward, they captured and held the enemy's strongly intrenched picket-line in front of the 2d and 6th corps, and eight hundred and thirty-four prisoners. The enemy made desperate attempts to retake this line, but without success. Our loss in front of these was fifty-two killed, eight hundred and sixty-four wounded, and two hundred and seven missing. The enemy's loss in killed and wounded was far greater.[767]

~

Lee hoped the predawn assault from his Petersburg lines on Fort Stedman would cause Meade to concentrate his troops in the midst of a panic allowing the main army to slip away into North Carolina.[768] So many Southern soldiers had been surrendering to their Northern counterparts that Lee decided to use this as a ruse to keep the Yankees off guard. Taking advantage of the soft-hearted Yankees, Confederate General Gordon sent his pickets forward during the night dressed as though they were ready to surrender. Instead, they captured the unsuspecting Union pickets along that portion of the sector without arousing the main line fifty yards in the rear.

At daylight, Gordon successfully stormed the main line.[769]

~

FROM *PERSONAL MEMOIRS*

Turning to the right and left they captured the fort [Stedman] and the battery, with all the arms and troops in them. Continuing the charge, they also carried Batteries Eleven and Twelve to our left, which they turned towards City Point.

Meade happened to be at City Point that night, and this break in his line cut him off from all communication with his headquarters. [General John] Parke, however, commanding the Ninth Corps when this breach took place, telegraphed the facts to Meade's headquarters, and learning that the general was away, assumed command himself and with commendable promptitude made all preparations to drive the enemy back. General [John C.] Tidball gathered a large number of pieces of artillery and planted them in rear of the captured works so as to sweep the narrow space of ground between the lines very thoroughly. [General John F.] Hartranft was soon out with his division, as also was General Orlando B. Willcox. Hartranft to the right of the breach headed the rebels off in that direction and they were driven back into the entrenchments which they had captured, and Batteries eleven and twelve were retaken by Willcox early in the morning.

Parke then threw a line around outside of the captured fort and batteries, and communication was once more established. The artillery fire was kept up so continuously that it was impossible for the Confederates to retreat and equally impossible for reinforcements to join them. They all, therefore, fell captives into our hands.[770]

~

The tide quickly turned and the Confederate attackers were driven back or surrounded by an immediate counterattack and deadly cross fire from every direction. Lee lost four thousand men, killed, wounded, or captured. Grant's army had lost only two thousand men.

The rebel attack on Fort Stedman was Lee's last offensive—and it was a flat failure.

MARCH 26, 1865: A MEETING WITH SHERIDAN

When he concluded his raid in central Virginia, Sheridan and his troops made their way back to the Army of the Potomac at Petersburg. On March 26, he left his troops in the field on the far-left flank of the Federal army and made his way across the muddy Virginia roads to meet with his commander at the City Point headquarters.

"Rawlins, in his enthusiasm, seized both of Sheridan's hands in his own, wrung them vigorously, and then went to patting him on the back," Horace Porter recalled. "Sheridan returned all the greetings warmly, and Rawlins now informed him that General Grant had made up his mind to send the cavalry through to join Sherman, destroying all communications as they went."

Sheridan was visibly irritated as he was ushered into Grant's little log cabin headquarters. Inside the cabin the general in chief showed Sheridan the written instructions to which Rawlins had referred. They directed him "to proceed with this cavalry around Lee's right, and then to move independently under other instructions."[771]

~

FROM PERSONAL MEMOIRS

I saw that after Sheridan had read his instructions he seemed somewhat disappointed at the idea, possibly, of having to cut loose again from the Army of the Potomac, and place himself between the two main armies of the enemy. I said to him: "General, this portion of your instructions I have put in merely as a blind"; and gave him the reason for doing so, heretofore described. I told him that, as a matter of fact, I intended to close the war right here, with this movement, and that he should go no farther.[772]

~

Grant explained that all of the talk about sending him to join Sherman was simply a diversion, inserted into the written record largely because of the "negotiate-now" peace party in the North. The Northern public had grown so eager to end the war, Grant explained, that unless the current Virginia campaign proved an unqualified success, "it would be interpreted as a disastrous defeat."[773] For that reason, he had stated, for the record only, that Sheridan might move south. Grant's notion was that if the move against Lee's flank and rear met with a repulse, the peace group would accuse the administration of having blundered into another defeat when it ought to be sitting quietly about a conference table.

If the army's move could be presented simply as a move to create close contact with Sherman, this criticism would not arise. Grant assured Sheridan that he need not worry. He did not intend to send him off on a tangent: "I mean to end the business here," the general in chief insisted.[774] Grant then elaborated, saying he "intended to close the war right here, with this movement, and that he should go no farther."[775]

Hearing this news, Sheridan's dark face brightened. Slapping his hand on his leg, Sheridan exclaimed, "I am glad to hear it, and we can do it." Saying his goodbyes, Sheridan mounted his grand horse and set off back to his troops, ready to help Grant bring the war to a conclusion.[776]

MARCH 27, 1865—A VISIT WITH SHERMAN

At the same time, Sherman was coincidentally planning his own trip to City Point. Fresh off his "March to the Sea" from Atlanta to Savannah, he had continued his slash-and-burn tactics up through the Carolinas and appeared to be on the verge of linking up with Grant. Desiring a parley with his boss, Sherman wrote to Grant that he might visit "for a day or two, before diving into the bowels of the country again," and that "in one more move" they could "checkmate" Southern commander Robert E. Lee.[777] Sherman then traveled nearly 100 miles to the North Carolina coast, where he hopped on a captured Confederate blockade runner, the *Russia*, which whisked him up to City Point by the afternoon of March 27.

General Grant and some of his staff welcomed him on the City Point wharf. They greeted each other, clasping arms and smiling.

"How d' you do, Sherman!" Grant cried out.

"How are you, Grant!" Sherman replied.

Horace Porter said they stood on the steps next to the dock, with their hands locked in a cordial grasp, uttering earnest words of familiar greeting. "Their encounter was more like that of two school-boys coming together after a vacation than the meeting of the chief actors in a great war tragedy."[778]

For the next hour, Sherman shared stories of his march through Georgia with Grant and several other officers around a campfire. Finally Grant interrupted. "I'm sorry to break up this entertaining conversation, but the President is aboard the *River Queen*, and I know he will be anxious to see you. Suppose we go and pay him a visit before dinner."[779] The two men walked back down the steps of the bluff to the wharf where they spent the next hour speaking with President Lincoln.

The following morning, Sherman and Grant, joined by Admiral Porter, boarded the *River Queen* and climbed to the upper saloon for what one Union officer described as an "informal interchange of views between the four men who held the destiny of the nation in their hands."[780]

Grant briefed the president on his latest military maneuvers and expressed his desire to prevent Lee from uniting with Johnston's army in North Carolina. The three commanders expected at least one more major battle. Lincoln understood the military necessity of battles but reiterated that there had been "blood enough shed."[781] Grant agreed but said it seemed impossible to avoid one last major engagement.

Sherman next turned the conversation to reconstruction of the South, with Lincoln responding that rebel soldiers would be allowed to return to their homes as soon as they laid down their arms. He even implied that he would not punish Jefferson Davis, provided the Confederate president left the country.

That afternoon, Sherman departed for North Carolina. He later wrote of the president: "Of all the men I have met, he [Lincoln] seemed to possess more of the elements of greatness, combined with goodness, than any other."[782]

VICTORY AT FIVE FORKS

The failed attack at Fort Stedman convinced Grant the time had come to press his advantage. He ordered General Edward Ord and General Phil Sheridan to move three divisions from the far right to the far left of the Union lines, beginning March 29. The movement, Grant said, was intended "for the double purpose of turning the enemy out of his present position around Petersburg, and to insure the success of the cavalry under General Sheridan in its efforts to reach and destroy the South Side and Danville railroads."[783]

Before he left to oversee what he hoped would be the final battle of the war, Grant stood in the cabin door at City Point, where he held his wife and kissed her tenderly. From that time until the end of the war, he risked the same deadly and dangerous exposure as the rest of his men. Julia bore the parting bravely, although Horace Porter noted that "her pale face and sorrowful look told of the sadness that was in her heart."[784]

President Lincoln then joined the small group of officers and walked with them down to the railroad station. The little group of men walked slowly along the platform, and then, stopping at the rear of the train, the president gave General Grant and every member of the staff a cordial handshake. As the train was about to start, the officers all raised their hats respectfully. The president returned the salute and said in a voice broken with feeling he could not hide: "Good-bye, gentlemen. God bless you all! Remember, your success is my success."[785]

Grant had full confidence in Sheridan's abilities, so he decided that the cavalry would lead the final push against Lee. Sheridan's optimism sparked Grant to downplay staff misgivings about conditions of roads and weather and to give orders for the movement of the Army of the Potomac against Lee's left flank.

As the rain poured down in torrents on the night of March 29, Grant sent a revealing telegraph to Sheridan: "I feel now like ending the matter, if it is possible to do so, before going back. I do not want you, therefore, to cut loose and go after the enemy's roads at present. In the morning, push around the enemy, if you can and get on to his right rear. The movements of the enemy's cavalry may, of course, modify your action. We will all act together as one army until it is seen what can be done with the enemy."[786]

Sheridan galloped back to join his command at Dinwiddie Court House and move them out to the location Grant had ordered. The ever-watchful Lee comprehended Grant's plans immediately and sent the cavalry led by his nephew, Fitzhugh Lee, along with five brigades of Pickett's infantry. This order moved more than ten thousand Confederates outside the bulk of the Southern fortifications, making them vulnerable to Union attack.

After an initial clash, Sheridan was pushed back by this superior force. He gave ground slowly, without any breaks in rank. "The men behaved splendidly. I will hold out at Dinwiddie Court House until I am compelled to leave," Sheridan reported to headquarters that night.

Instead of trying to cut the lifelines of Lee's army, Grant decided to strike directly at the army itself, seeking a final, decisive victory. Both Parke and Wright reported to headquarters that the forces opposing them seemed to be thinned out to the breaking point. They both believed they could assault successfully.

Despite the optimistic outlook of these generals, the rain continued to fall in sheets. Horses and mules sank into the mire. The army was forced to lay down corduroy roads to move forward with the artillery and wagon trains.[787] Transporting supplies to Sheridan's forces seemed impossible. Grant seriously considered ordering Sheridan to leave a force to hold Dinwiddie Court House and then lead the rest of his men back for food and forage. But Sheridan objected. On the evening of March 30, he slogged back to headquarters to argue his point. Along the way, Sheridan's horse went to its knees in the mud with every step.

As soon as Sheridan dismounted, Chief of Staff John Rawlins and Colonel Horace Porter asked him about the situation on the extreme left. Sheridan assured them he could beat the rebel cavalry and crush Lee's right if he had some infantry.

"I can drive in the whole cavalry force of the enemy with ease, and if an infantry force is added to my command, I can strike out for Lee's right, and either crush it or force him to so weaken his intrenched lines that our troops in front of them can break through and march into Petersburg." As he paced up and down, Sheridan "chafed like a hound in the leash."[788]

Sheridan said forage would be no problem. He could haul it out if he had to set every man to work corduroying roads. "I tell you, I'm ready to strike out tomorrow and go to smashing things."[789]

Porter told Sheridan that this was the kind of talk they liked to hear at headquarters. He explained that while General Grant felt no great apprehension, it would do his heart good to listen to words like these. But Sheridan objected to sharing his views with the general in chief without first receiving an invitation from him.

"Then we resorted to a stratagem," Porter wrote. "One of us went into the general's tent, and told him Sheridan had just come in from the left and had been telling us some matters of much interest, and suggested that he be invited in and asked to state them." Grant asked that they let Sheridan into his tent so that he could discuss this news with him.[790]

When Sheridan entered the tent, Grant and Rawlins were discussing the situation. Sheridan repeated his views to the lieutenant general and the conversation continued.

Soon several staff members entered the tent, and Sheridan, saying he was cold and wet, stepped out to the campfire. The general in chief remarked that he wanted to have some words with Sheridan in private before parting. Ingalls told them his tent was vacant if they wanted to talk in private. Grant and Sheridan entered and discussed the strategy for the coming offensive. Over the next twenty minutes, they came to a definite understanding of what Sheridan needed to do.[791]

Badeau reported that Sheridan "talked so cheerily, so confidently, so intelligently of what he could do, that his mood was contagious," and Grant's spirits revived. "We will go on," he informed Sheridan, ordering him to seize Five Forks. "You will assume command of the whole force sent to operate with you, and use it to the best of your ability to destroy the force which your command has fought so gallantly today."[792]

"I was glad to see the spirit of confidence with which he was imbued," Grant later wrote. "Knowing as I did from experience, of what great value that feeling of confidence by a commander was, I determined to make a movement at once. Orders were given accordingly."[793]

Exiting the tent, Sheridan mounted his horse, waved goodbye to the headquarters staff, and splashed off to prepare for the offensive against Pickett.[794]

THE BATTLE OF FIVE FORKS

Grant ordered Warren to move his entire corps west to support Sheridan in a strike on Pickett. As soon as he was ordered to reinforce Sheridan, Warren had told Meade that he would have to build a replacement bridge over Gravelly Run, which was too deep to wade across due to the recent rains.

That forty-foot bridge was not completed until 2:00 a.m.

During the night, Pickett had learned of the approach of Warren's infantry, which threatened to isolate him, and he withdrew from Dinwiddie Court House to a more secure line at Five Forks. During that movement, Pickett received a forceful message from Lee: "Hold Five Forks at all hazards. Protect road to Ford's Depot and prevent Union forces from striking the Southside Railroad. Regret exceedingly your forced withdrawal, and your inability to hold the advantage you gained."

Pickett and Fitzhugh Lee had enough men to hold off the Yankee cavalry, but not enough strength if Sheridan's troops were reinforced by a Federal army corps. They were now miles away from the main Confederate army with no chance of reinforcements.[795]

Sheridan was unaware of Warren's difficulties in building the bridge and wading through the mud-clogged roads. The Union's cavalry commander had wanted to attack immediately but was forced to delay until all Warren's troops arrived, which did not occur until 11:00 a.m. on April 1. Sheridan's anger and frustration toward Warren continued to rise throughout the day.

What the slow-moving Warren did not comprehend was that Grant and Meade were also upset at his recent lackluster performance. Grant believed this engagement could possibly end the war. He needed a quick-moving commander like Sheridan, who could act spontaneously to defeat the Confederates. Sadly, Warren was not that kind of leader. And on that day, his indecision would cost him.

While Sheridan made final preparations for his attack, he was joined by Colonel Babcock of General Grant's staff, who carried with him a message from the lieutenant general. Grant gave Sheridan complete control in the field. If he did not think Warren was capable of swift action at this critical time, Sheridan was authorized to relieve him of his command.[796]

There was also surprising incompetence on the part of Confederate commanders at such a critical time. The fish were spawning in the Virginia rivers, and a hungry General Pickett joined some of his fellow officers for a shad bake more than a mile in the rear of the rebel lines. Although Pickett had advised Lee of his situation and requested a diversionary action, in a shockingly irresponsible move, he and Fitzhugh Lee left the front lines and joined Major General Thomas L. Rosser at his fishing hole feast behind Hatcher's Run. Fitzhugh Lee attended the shad bake even after being advised that Union cavalry had driven back the Confederate horsemen between Five Forks and the rest of the Army of Northern Virginia.[797]

Pickett and Lee left without telling anyone where they might be found or when they would return. Pickett also failed to assign anyone to be in command during his absence. His other cavalry division commander, Rooney Lee, did not even know Pickett had left the area.

A few hours after Pickett left, rebel scouts observed the Yankee Fifth Corps moving into position on their left. Confederate division commander Thomas Mumford sent a courier in search of Pickett and Lee to inform them that the Federal infantry attack was imminent. But the courier was unable to find either officer, so when the Union soldiers attacked, no Confederate general was in overall command.

When the courier finally tracked them down and delivered the news of the battle, Pickett ordered Rosser to send two men to determine what might be happening at Five Forks, with one following the other by several hundred yards to prevent both from falling captive should they be intercepted. Within minutes, Pickett and his cavalry generals heard gunfire and watched Federal cavalry dash from the woods to seize the first courier. The second courier wheeled around and galloped back to Pickett, shouting, "Woods full of 'em, sir! They've got behind the men at Five Forks, too!"

Pickett mounted his horse and raced toward Five Forks only to find the way blocked by Union infantry from Crawford's division. Riding with his head bent down behind his horse's neck, Pickett dashed through a hail of Federal bullets to finally reach his command. He arrived in time to see his troops disintegrate.[798]

On the Union side, Horace Porter rode back and forth across the battlefield acting as Grant's eyes and ears. Porter reported on Warren's painfully slow movement that day. "The required formation seemed to drag, and Sheridan, chafing with impatience and consumed with anxiety, became as restive as a racer struggling to make the start. He made every possible appeal for promptness."[799]

Most of Sheridan's ten thousand cavalry had dismounted and manned the attacking Union line, taking the brunt of the rebel defenders' fire. Warren's twelve thousand troops came in on the left flank of Pickett's infantry. Because of an erroneous map and faulty reconnaissance, Warren's troops were misaligned and joined the fight only after changing direction.[800]

Porter rode to the front with Sheridan and Warren at the head of Romeyn B. Ayres's division, which was on the left. Ayres encountered the Southern forces at four o'clock and gave the order for an assault against Pickett's entrenched line. "Ayres threw out a skirmish-line and advanced across an open field which sloped down gradually toward the dense woods just north of the White

Oak Road," Porter recalled. "He soon met with a fire from the edge of these woods, a number of men fell, and the skirmish-line halted and seemed to waver.

"Sheridan now began to exhibit those traits which always made him a tower of strength in the presence of an enemy," wrote Porter. Spurring his magnificent horse, Rienzi, Sheridan dashed along in front of the line of battle from left to right, shouting words of encouragement to every regiment. "Come on, men," he cried; "go at 'em with a will! Move on at a clean jump, or you'll not catch one of 'em. They're all getting ready to run now, and if you don't get on to them in five minutes they'll every one get away from you! Now go for them!"[801]

Pointing to the enemy he proclaimed, "The cowardly scoundrels can't fight such brave men as mine. Kill that infernal skulker."[802]

Just then a man on the skirmish line was struck in the neck, and blood spurted as if the jugular vein had been cut. "I'm killed!" he cried and dropped to the ground. "You're not hurt a bit!" Sheridan countered. "Pick up your gun, man, and move right on to the front." The stricken soldier was so inspired by his commander that he snatched up his musket and rushed forward a dozen paces before he fell to the ground, never to rise again.

The line of weather-beaten Yankee veterans moved down the slope toward the woods near Pickett's command. "The roads were muddy, the fields swampy, the undergrowth dense," said Porter. Rienzi plunged forward across the swampy ground, "dashing the foam from his mouth and the mud from his heels."[803]

As the troops moved forward over the boggy ground, they were pushed back in confusion by a heavy fire from the angle. As bullets whizzed past him, and men fell wounded and killed in scores, Sheridan rushed into the midst of the broken lines, crying out, "Where is my battle-flag?"[804] The sergeant who carried it rode up, and Sheridan seized the crimson-and-white standard. Waving the war-torn banner above his head, he cheered on the men.

"Bullets were now humming like a swarm of bees about our heads," Porter remembered, "and shells were crashing through the ranks. A musket-ball pierced the battle-flag; another killed the sergeant who had carried it; another wounded an aide, Captain McGonnigle, in the side; others struck two or three of the staff-officers' horses. All this time Sheridan was dashing from one point of the line to another, waving the flag, shaking his fist, encouraging, entreating, threatening, praying, swearing, the true personification of chivalry, the very incarnation of battle.

"Ayers, with drawn saber, rushed forward once more with his veterans, who now behaved as if they had fallen back only to get a 'good ready,' and with fixed bayonets and a rousing cheer dashed over the earthworks, sweeping everything before them, and killing or capturing every man in their immediate front whose legs had not saved him."

Sheridan spurred Rienzi up to the angle, and with a bound the animal carried his rider over the earthworks, landing among a line of prisoners who had just thrown down their arms and were crouching close to the breastworks.[805] As other rebels tried to escape, Sheridan shouted to the Federal infantrymen, "See the sons of bitches run! Give them hell, boys!"[806]

Sheridan's cavalry and Warren's infantry destroyed Pickett's command at Five Forks, killing or wounding more than five hundred rebels and taking thousands of prisoners.[807] The Yankees captured six cannon and thirteen battle flags, at a loss of only eight hundred of their own troops.[808] The Federals had turned Lee's right flank and opened the way for the South Side Railroad to be taken.[809]

Some of the surrendering Confederates called out, "Wha' do you want us all to go to?" Hearing this, Sheridan's rage turned to humor and he had a continuing conversation with the "Johnnies" as they filed past. "Go right over there," he said to them, pointing to the rear. "Get right along, now. Oh, drop your guns; you'll never need them anymore. You'll all be safe over there. Are there any more of you? We want every one of you fellows."[810]

~

FROM *PERSONAL MEMOIRS*

My hope was that Sheridan would be able to carry Five Forks, get on the enemy's right flank and rear, and force them to weaken their centre to protect their right so that an assault in the centre might be successfully made.[811]

It was dusk when our troops under Sheridan went over the parapets of the enemy. The two armies were mingled together there for a time in such manner that it was almost a question which one was going to demand the surrender of the other. Soon, however, the enemy broke and ran in every direction; some six thousand prisoners, besides artillery and small-arms in large quantities, falling into our hands. The flying troops were pursued in different directions, the cavalry and 5th corps under Sheridan pursuing the larger body which moved north-west.

This pursuit continued until about nine o'clock at night, when Sheridan halted his troops.[812]

~

Porter was so excited about the decisive victory that he rode straight back to Grant's headquarters to share the news—"so rapidly that I reached headquarters at Dabney's Mill before the arrival of the last courier I had dispatched." As Porter rode into Grant's camp, he found the officers gathered around a blazing campfire, with Grant "wrapped in a long blue overcoat and smoking his usual cigar." Not waiting to dismount, Porter shouted the news from horseback. All the officers except Grant cheered and leapt to their feet, shook hands, and threw their hats in the air.

"For some minutes there was a bewildering state of excitement," wrote Porter, "and officers fell to grasping hands, shouting, and hugging each other like school-boys. The news meant the beginning of the end, the reaching of the 'last ditch.' It pointed to peace and home. Dignity was thrown to the winds."

In his enthusiasm, Porter leapt from his horse, rushed up to the general in chief, and clapped him on the back with his hand—"to his no little astonishment, and to the evident amusement of those about him."[813]

General Adam Badeau wrote that Porter "came up with so much enthusiasm, clapping the general in chief on the back, and otherwise demonstrating his joy, that the officer who shared his tent rebuked him that night for indulging too freely in drink at this critical juncture. But Porter had tasted neither wine nor spirits that day. He was only drunk with victory."[814]

General Grant asked his usual question: "How many prisoners have been taken?"

Porter was happy to report that the prisoners from this battle were estimated at more than five thousand. After listening to Porter's description of Sheridan's work, the general walked into his tent and by the light of a flickering candle started writing orders. Finishing several dispatches, he handed them to an orderly to be sent over the field wires.

Grant then emerged from his tent and joined the group around the campfire, remarking in his usual unruffled manner, "I have ordered a general assault along the lines."[815]

~

From Personal Memoirs

I then issued orders for an assault by Wright and Parke at four o'clock on the morning of the 2d. I also ordered the 2d corps, General Humphreys, and General Ord with the Army of the James, on the left, to hold themselves in readiness to take any advantage that could be taken from weakening in their front. ... I had ordered the assault to take place at once, as soon as I had received the news of the capture of Five Forks. The corps commanders, however, reported that it was so dark that the men could not see to move, and it would be impossible to make the assault then. But we kept up a continuous artillery fire upon the enemy around the whole line including that north of the James River, until it was light enough to move, which was about a quarter to five in the morning.[816]

~

Sheridan had struck a devastating blow, and Grant knew Lee would have to abandon Petersburg and Richmond. Grant ordered a concerted attack on the entire Petersburg front beginning at first light the next morning. It was time to end the matter.

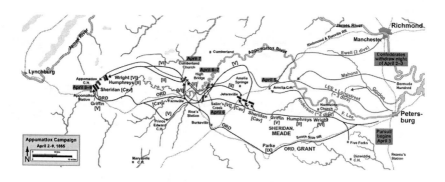

Map by Hal Jespersen, www.cwmaps.com © Hal Jespersen.
All rights reserved. Used with permission.

Chapter Twenty-Five

IF THE THING IS PRESSED

APRIL 1865—PETERSBURG AND RICHMOND, VIRGINIA

~

FROM *PERSONAL MEMOIRS*

During the night of April 2nd our line was intrenched from the river above to the river below. I ordered a bombardment to be commenced the next morning at five a.m., to be followed by an assault at six o'clock; but the enemy evacuated Petersburg early in the morning.[817]

~

After Grant ordered the assault, the corps commanders sent back enthusiastic soldierly replies, making it clear to the lieutenant general that they were prepared for the impending onslaught. Ord said he would go into the enemy's works "as a hot knife goes into butter." Wright sent word that when he started in he would "make the fur fly." He predicted, "If the corps does half as well as I expect, we will have broken through the rebel lines in fifteen minutes from the word 'go.'"[818]

Understanding the daunting fortifications and obstacles faced by these men and their troops, Grant was pleased with the fighting spirit of these messages. "I like the way Wright talks; it argues success. I heartily approve."[819]

The men in the trenches had faced similar enemy fortifications at Spotsylvania and Cold Harbor. As many of them had done at Cold Harbor, they took scraps of paper, wrote their names and home addresses, and pinned them to their uniforms, making it easier for burial details to identify their bodies and notify the folks at home.

At 4:45 a.m., a streak of gray cut across the heavens, revealing the outline of Confederate uniforms in the trenches across the battlefield. The artillery had been firing sporadically through the night, keeping the Southern soldiers awake and afraid. As dawn broke, the all-out assault commenced with the thunder of hundreds of cannons shaking the ground like an earthquake. The charge was ordered, and Northern troops groped and stumbled in the near darkness as they emerged from their rifle pits. They rushed forward to the enemy works with hearty shouts, and, as they navigated the maze of rebel obstructions, they came face-to-face with enemy rifle fire.

For the veterans, the battle seemed like a repeat of the Bloody Angle, Cold Harbor, and the earlier assaults at Petersburg. Confederate infantry released a shower of lead across the treacherous slopes. Years of combat had taught the Yankees that veteran rebels knew how to take a position where they could do the most killing. That kind of soldier could hold good trenches against five times their own numbers. That lesson was about to be reinforced.

Wright's corps lost 1,100 men in fifteen minutes. The first wave of Parke's men was mowed down, just as they had been in the initial assault at Cold Harbor.

Then everything changed. The Confederate resistance crumbled, and the Yankees pushed on an open door. Grant's theory that Lee had to weaken his center to fight against Sheridan on his far right proved true. Federal troops poured over the rebel works, taking trench after trench.

Southern troops that survived the onslaught surrendered in waves. Wright's men hit a thin part of the Confederate line on the west side of Petersburg where they overwhelmed the rebel defenders in hand-to-hand combat. Soon a wall of bluecoats stormed over the parapet, taking scores of prisoners and seizing enemy cannon.

Pushing past the defenses, Wright's men broke the enemy line in two. One brigade moved in to occupy the enemy trenches, while the rest of the corps turned to the left and continued mopping up Confederate troops all the way to Hatcher's Run. There they met Ord's troops, who had also made a breakthrough after a frontal assault.[820]

Inside the trenches, a raucous celebration erupted with troops so entangled that none of the commanders knew who was who. Soldiers threw their caps in the air and shouted like it was New Year's Eve.

General Grant had remained at headquarters, awaiting the result of the assault in a place where he could easily communicate with the commanders and from which he could give general directions. At a quarter past five, news started to stream across the telegraph wires. Wright was first to respond, reporting that he had carried the enemy's line in his front and was pushing in. Next came news that Parke had captured the outer works, seizing twelve pieces of artillery and eight hundred prisoners.

At 6:40 a.m. the general wrote a telegram with his own hand to Mr. Lincoln at City Point: "Both Wright and Parke got through the enemy's line. The battle now rages furiously. Sheridan, with his cavalry, the Fifth Corps, and Mile's division of the Second Corps, which was sent to him since one this morning, is now sweeping down from the west. All now looks highly favorable. Ord is engaged, but I have not yet heard the result in his front."[821]

~

From Personal Memoirs

At that hour Parke's and Wright's corps moved out as directed, brushed the abatis from their front as they advanced under a heavy fire of musketry and artillery, and went without flinching directly on till they mounted the parapets and threw themselves inside of the enemy's line. Parke, who was on the right, swept down to the right and captured a very considerable length of line in that direction, but at that point the outer was so near the inner line which closely enveloped the city of Petersburg that he could make no advance forward and, in fact, had a very serious task to turn the lines which he had captured to the defense of his own troops and to hold them; but he succeeded in this.

Wright swung around to his left and moved to Hatcher's Run, sweeping everything before him. The enemy had traverses in rear of his captured line, under cover of which he made something of a stand, from one to another, as Wright moved on; but the latter met no serious obstacle. As you proceed to the left the outer line becomes gradually much farther from the inner one, and along about Hatcher's Run they must be nearly two miles apart. Both Parke and Wright captured a considerable amount of artillery and some prisoners—Wright about three thousand of them.

In the meantime Ord and Humphreys, in obedience to the instructions they had received, had succeeded by daylight, or very early in the morning, in capturing the intrenched picket-lines in their front; and before Wright got up to that point, Ord had also succeeded in getting inside of the enemy's intrenchments. The second corps soon followed; and the outer works of Petersburg were in the hands of the National troops, never to be wrenched from them again. When Wright reached Hatcher's Run, he sent a regiment to destroy the South Side Railroad just outside of the city.[822]

~

THE FALL OF RICHMOND

Sheridan captured the last rail line into Petersburg from the south, while the Second, Sixth, and Ninth Corps fought their way through the main Confederate battle line. The first row of Southern entrenchments fell under the juggernaut, then the second. The outnumbered and overwhelmed rebel troops fell back to Petersburg's inner defenses.[823]

The Army of the James streamed into Petersburg through the northern entrance, while parts of the Army of the Potomac swept in from the other side with Meade and Grant out in front. Trying to squeeze through two bridges at the other end of the city was the rear guard of Lee's retreating forces. At that moment, they were sitting ducks for Grant's artillery fire. The lieutenant general, whom so many had called a "butcher," refused to fire on these helpless men. "At all events I had not the heart to turn the artillery upon such a mass of defeated and fleeing men," Grant later wrote, "and I hoped to capture them soon."[824]

That same morning, as Jefferson Davis sat in his regular pew at St. Paul's Episcopal Church in Richmond, an usher quietly tiptoed down the aisle in the middle of the service and handed him a telegram from Lee. "I see no prospect of doing more than holding our position here till night," Lee informed Jefferson Davis. "I am not certain that I can do that. If I can I shall withdraw tonight north of the Appomattox. I advise that all preparations be made for leaving Richmond tonight."[825]

Davis immediately rose and rushed from the church, followed, one-by-one, by members of the government and the military. The congregation was dismissed with the notice that there would be no evening service. The rebel government departed from Richmond by train about two o'clock in the afternoon.[826]

After a siege of 293 days, holding on, as Lincoln said, with a bulldog grip, Grant forced the Confederates to abandon Petersburg and Richmond on the same day.[827] The war had become a footrace.

A RACE TO APPOMATTOX

The Confederates retreated toward Burkeville along the Richmond & Danville Railroad, forty miles to the west. This was the location of the last remaining rail link to North Carolina and the forces of Joseph E. Johnston, nearly a hundred miles to the south.

It was Grant's turn to put himself in the place of his opponent to determine what General Lee would do. At Burkeville, the Richmond & Danville crossed the South Side Railroad, which went on to Lynchburg. Lee desperately needed food and forage to strengthen his starving troops. These supplies were ordered to Burkeville, either from Lynchburg or Danville, but Grant and the Federals were now closer to Burkeville than Lee was.[828]

Grant not only planned to follow Lee's army but also to get his cavalry in front of the rebels and cut them off to stop their move toward Johnston in North Carolina. Time was of the essence.

Lee had an eight-hour head start, but Sheridan's fast-moving cavalry and five infantry corps were in hot pursuit. Sheridan—"the inevitable," as the enemy now called him—was in advance, the

Union army racing westward on a parallel route with the Confederates.[829]

Meade's and Wright's corps followed Sheridan, while Ord with the Army of the James pressed on for Burkeville along the line of the Southside Railroad. Parke took up the rear, guarding the railroad itself.

Grant had been with President Lincoln, who had met him in Petersburg, awaiting news on the fall of Richmond. The general in chief felt he could wait no longer and set out to meet his troops, promising to keep the president informed of developments.

As they pursued the rebels, Union troops captured Sutherland Station on the South Side Railroad, four miles east of Five Forks.[830] Grant arrived there after leaving Petersburg and found General John Gibbon and his soldiers tearing up tracks while awaiting orders. As Gibbon approached, a courier came pounding down the road with a dispatch for the Northern commander. Grant read the note and then told Gibbon unemotionally, "Weitzel entered Richmond this morning at half past eight."

All the soldiers within earshot began cheering and sharing the news. The celebration moved down the line of soldiers. "I am sorry I did not get this information before we left the President. However I suppose he has heard it by this time," Grant said stoically. "Let the news be circulated among the troops as rapidly as possible."[831]

Gibbon rode forward to the head of his troops and ordered them to move out toward Burkeville. As he watched the columns depart, Grant penned a note for Sherman, updating him on the big breakthrough at Petersburg, Lee's retreat, and the fall of Richmond. He told his comrade that he would try to head off the Confederates at Burkeville. He cautioned that if Lee got past him, "you will have to take care of him with the force you have for a while." If, however, Grant beat Lee to Burkeville and pushed him toward Lynchburg, "there will be no special use in you going any farther into the interior of North Carolina."[832]

Grant added the telling words: "Rebel armies are now the only strategic points to strike at."[833]

Seeking Something to Eat

Grant rode forward with Ord's Army of the James while Meade, who had become quite ill, rode for part of the day in an ambulance with the Army of the Potomac. That night General Grant camped at Wilson's Station on the South Side Railroad, twenty-seven miles west of Petersburg. A Confederate railroad engineer who had been taken prisoner reported that Jefferson Davis and his cabinet had passed through Burkeville heading south the previous morning.[834]

Lee had telegraphed ahead to order food and forage to be delivered to Amelia Court House on the Richmond & Danville Railroad. His army had shrunk to thirty-five thousand as they approached the rail depot where trains stood waiting for them. Due to a bureaucratic blunder in Richmond, the train cars were filled with ammunition, but no food or forage. The extra ammunition was of little use as the pack animals were too weak to pull it.

Lee was forced to call a halt while his commissary staff scrounged through the depleted countryside for what food they could find. A precious day was lost by the rebels.

On the morning of April 5, what was left of the Army of Northern Virginia moved south but soon discovered that Sheridan's dismounted troopers had blocked the route. Not far behind them were three corps of Union infantry.

Lee immediately changed course, veering west and heading for Farmville, eighteen miles away on the South Side Railroad. Here he hoped to draw food and supplies from Lynchburg before continuing his effort to join Johnston.[835]

That evening Grant made camp halfway between Nottoway and Burkeville on a wagon road that ran parallel to the South Side Railroad. As the staff prepared to bunk down for the night, some alert soldiers from the headquarters escort dashed toward a dark figure emerging from the nearby woods. Colonel Porter recognized the man, who was dressed in a full Confederate uniform, and called the men off.

"How do you do, Campbell," Porter greeted the startled messenger. Campbell said he had just ridden hard from Sheridan's camp with a dispatch for General Grant. Reaching into his mouth he pulled out a small folded piece of tin foil, opened it, and pulled out a sheet of tissue paper. He handed the note to General Grant who had just ridden up on his horse, Jeff Davis.[836]

An intense debate had grown that day between Sheridan and Meade as to how to proceed in the morning. Meade wanted to dig in, wait for morning, and then advance on Amelia Court House and attack Lee there. Sheridan's scouts had reported that Lee's wagons and some of his guns were already moving west on the road out of Amelia Court House, and he suspected that the entire army would follow at first light.

What neither Meade nor Sheridan knew was that Lee had already begun a forced march that evening, driving his starving infantry forward in a desperate race for survival.

This was no time for an argument. Sheridan understood General Grant's leadership style well enough to know he would likely lean in the direction of hot pursuit. Going over Meade's head, Sheridan sent the tinfoil-encased message to the lieutenant general: "I wish you were here yourself. I feel confident of capturing the Army of Northern Virginia if we exert ourselves. I see no escape for Lee."[837]

After reading the dispatch, Grant called for his charger, Cincinnati. As he waited for the horse to be saddled, he stood in the road and wrote a dispatch for General Ord, informing him that he was joining Sheridan and Meade. Mounting his fresh horse, Grant told Campbell to lead the way. The scout responded that there was no way to avoid skirting close to the enemy lines and asked if they could have a cavalry escort. As there were none nearby, the general said he would risk it with his mounted escort of fourteen men.[838]

After a harrowing ride, Grant rode up to Sheridan's pickets shortly after 10:00 p.m. The men were shocked to see the general in chief ride in from the darkness at that hour. The cavalry was catching some much-needed sleep as Grant and his small party rode through camp. Roused by the neighing horses, the men looked up in astonishment as Grant rode by.

"Why, there's the old man. Boys, this means business!"

"Great Scott! The old chief's out here himself. The rebs are going to get busted tomorrow, certain."

"Uncle Sam's joined the cavalry sure enough. You can bet there'll be lively times here in the morning."[839]

Grant finally reached Sheridan's headquarters in Jetersville, where aides toiled by candlelight while the cavalry commander slept in an elevated loft. Informed of Grant's arrival, Sheridan climbed down the ladder and greeted the lieutenant general.

The cavalry commander ordered his staff to supply Grant and his aides with a dinner of beef, chicken, and coffee. As Grant sat at the table, Sheridan pulled out a map and pointed to the position of the enemy.

"Lee is in a bad fix," Grant agreed. "It will be difficult for him to get away."

"Damn him," Sheridan raged. "He can't get away."

As Sheridan suspected, Grant was inclined to agree with him. "My judgment coincided with Sheridan's," Grant later confided. "I felt we ought to find Lee, wherever he was, and strike him. The question was not the occupation of Richmond, but the destruction of the army."[840]

With Sheridan at his side, Grant rode over to Meade's headquarters, arriving just after midnight. Discussing the matter with the ailing commander, Grant did not countermand Meade's orders for an advance on Amelia Court House. Instead, he suggested that Meade should be prepared to follow in case Lee changed course with a flank march.

Sure enough, Meade discovered the flank march early the next morning. He immediately wheeled his three corps about and sent them off in the same direction with Sheridan's cavalry in the lead, firing on Lee's flank throughout the day.

Lee's sluggish troops marched as hard as they could, suffering from little food and no sleep the previous night. Now Humphrey's infantry also began biting at their heels as they caught up to the exhausted Confederate column. The rebels had to stop to fight off the encroaching Yankees. Lee's line grew longer and longer as the troops at the front pulled away from their beleaguered comrades in the rear.[841]

Weariness, hunger, and bewilderment overwhelmed the Southern soldiers, along with anxiety about their families back home. As they pursued the Confederates, Federal troops found what seemed like a small forest of abandoned muskets. Hundreds of them with bayonets attached were stuck upside-down in the ground, butt ends upward, where exhausted rebel troops had abandoned their weapons—and the rebel army.[842]

A South Carolinian remembered, "The Confederacy was considered as 'gone up' and every man felt it his duty, as well as his privilege, to save himself. ... The army was so crushed by the defeats of the last few days, that it straggled along without strength, and almost without thought. So we moved on in disorder, keeping no regular column, no regular pace ... there were not many words spoken. An indescribable sadness weighed upon us."[843]

Many of these troops disappeared into the forest to start the long, painful journey back home. Some remained with the army, unarmed now and almost useless, but still trying to keep up with their trusted commander, General Lee.

APRIL 6, 1865: THE BATTLE OF SAILOR'S CREEK

~

FROM *PERSONAL MEMOIRS*

The armies finally met on Sailor's Creek, when a heavy engagement took place, in which infantry, artillery and cavalry were all brought into action. Our men on the right, as they were brought in against the enemy, came in on higher ground, and upon his flank, giving us every advantage to be derived from the lay of the country. Our firing was also very much more rapid, because the enemy commenced his retreat westward and in firing as he retreated had to turn around every time he fired. The enemy's loss was very heavy, as well in killed and wounded as in captures. Some six general officers fell into our hands in this engagement, and seven thousand men were made prisoners. This engagement was commenced in the middle of the afternoon of the 6th, and the retreat and pursuit were continued until nightfall, when the armies bivouacked upon the ground where the night had overtaken them.[844]

~

Sheridan and General Wright isolated this corps of Confederate infantry under General Richard S. Ewell at Sailor's Creek, a muddy ford half a dozen miles from Farmville. Sheridan dismounted his troopers and led them, along with two divisions of Wright's Sixth Corps, against the crippled rebels. The Confederates put up slight resistance, and then collapsed in exhaustion. The Union forces inflicted more than two thousand casualties while taking seven thousand prisoners—a quarter of Lee's army. They also captured most of Lee's wagon train.[845]

Sitting astride his trusted horse, Traveller, Lee watched the remnants of two of his corps being taken prisoner in the valley below. "My God! Has the army dissolved?" he exclaimed in bewilderment.[846]

That night Sheridan made his report to Grant. "I attacked them with two divisions of the Sixth Army Corps and routed them handsomely, making a connection with the cavalry. I am still pressing on with both cavalry and infantry. Up to the present time we have captured Generals Ewell, Kershaw, Barton, Corse, DeBose [DuBose] and Custis Lee, several thousand prisoners, 14 pieces of artillery with caissons and a large number of wagons. If the thing is pressed I think Lee will surrender."[847]

The president, who was monitoring all telegraph messages, speedily endorsed Sheridan's proposal: "Let the thing be pressed. A. Lincoln."[848]

THE BLACK THURSDAY OF THE CONFEDERACY

Lee had won the race to Farmville, where he finally found rations for his men in waiting railcars. He planned to move to the north side of the Appomattox, delaying the Union pursuit by destroying all the bridges. Then he would strike west for Lynchburg, only three days' march away, where he could feed and refit his army in preparation for the drive south to link up with General Joe Johnston.

The Confederates had only partially removed the rations when Union Colonel Theodore Read arrived in Farmville with a small force of nine hundred men. Read had been sent to burn the vital High Bridge over the Appomattox River—standing 126 feet tall with a span of 2,500 feet, and carrying the South Side Railroad— and a smaller wagon bridge far below. Read arrived too late to burn the bridges as most of the Confederate Army had already crossed, but he realized his mission was to do what he could to protect this vital bridge so the Union Army could maintain its pursuit of Lee.

Read's men bravely and stubbornly gave battle, doing everything they could to protect the bridge until both he and Colonel Francis Washburn were mortally wounded. Nearly every officer in Read's small unit was either killed or wounded in the pitched battle, and the entire raiding party was taken prisoner. Despite the valiant resistance of Read's troops, the remainder of the Confederate army crossed and began setting torches to the bridges. But the sacrifice of Read and his men was far from vain. They held the rebels in place at this vital point long enough for Union infantry to arrive. Although a few spans of the high bridge collapsed in flames, the Yankees extinguished the fires set to the lower wagon bridge, allowing the Union forces to cross the Appomattox and continue the pursuit.

This brave sacrifice likely shortened the war by several days—if not more.

An exasperated Lee ordered the railcars, still mostly filled with food, moved west toward Appomattox Station.[849] Lee lost twelve precious hours fighting off this threat from Read and his men and was unable to continue his retreat until after dark. Most of the rations at Farmville went uneaten, and instead of a reprieve, the Southern army was forced to make yet another grueling night march.[850] It was, as historians have written, the "Black Thursday of the Confederacy."[851]

At the same time, Grant rode along with the Union columns of men racing forward on foot. He was greeted with hopeful remarks from the troops along the way:

"Cavalry's gi'n out, general. Infantry's going to crush the rest of the mud."

"We've marched nigh twenty miles on this stretch, and we're good for twenty more if the general says so!"

"We're not straddlin' any horses, but we'll get there all the same."

The general raised his hat in acknowledgment of the cheers, and gave a pleasant nod to the men who addressed him.[852]

A little before noon, General Grant and his staff arrived at Farmville. He rode up to the village hotel, a charming brick building. He dismounted and made his headquarters on the large front porch. News came that General George R. Crook with his cavalry and Humphreys with his infantry had crossed to the north side of the river and confronted Lee's army. Colonel Porter was sent to assess the situation and report back to General Grant.

Porter returned to general headquarters after dark and confirmed the news of the fighting. Orders were soon given to Wright's corps to cross the river and support the Union forces engaged there. "Notwithstanding their long march that day," Porter recalled, "the men sprang to their feet with a spirit that made everyone marvel at their pluck."

In the dark, Wright's troops spied the general in chief on the porch, watching them with pride as they marched past. The troops then sent Grant a message of affection. The men lit bonfires on the sides of the street and created improvised torches with straw and pinecones. The regiment's band started to play as the men waved their torches and banners. Muskets and hats were swung into the air. One regiment broke forth with the song "John Brown's Body," and soon the whole division was singing and shouting the chorus.[853]

John Brown's body lies a-mouldering in the grave
John Brown's body lies a-mouldering in the grave
John Brown's body lies a-mouldering in the grave
His soul's marching on!

Glory, glory, hallelujah!
Glory, glory, hallelujah!
Glory, glory, hallelujah!
His soul's marching on!

The night march had become a spontaneous grand review, with General Grant puffing on his cigar and occasionally doffing his hat to the cheering soldiers. This was Grant's army—and Grant was indisputably their general in chief.

CORRESPONDENCE BETWEEN TITANS

In the course of the evening, a Confederate prisoner named Dr. Smith, a native Virginian captured at Sailor's Creek, requested a meeting with General Grant. They had known each other in the regular army. Smith was a relative of General Ewell, and he wanted to inform Grant of a conversation from the previous night. According to Smith, Ewell told him that the Southern cause was lost when the Union forces had crossed the James River. "He considered that it was the duty of the authorities to negotiate for peace then, while they still had a right to claim concessions," Smith reported, adding that "now they were not in condition to claim anything."[854]

Ewell told Dr. Smith that for every man killed now, somebody would be responsible—and it would be little better than murder. He could not tell what General Lee would do, but he hoped that Lee would surrender his army at once.

News also came to headquarters from Sheridan. He had discovered that the railcars filled with General Lee's provisions had arrived at Appomattox Station. Sheridan had sent a portion of his cavalry ahead with orders to capture these vital supplies, if possible, before Lee could reach them.

The combination of these two reports convinced General Grant that the time had come to reach out to General Lee with an appeal for surrender. The defeat of the Southern army was inevitable, and Grant wanted the war to end with the fewest lives lost as possible.[855] He sent his appeal for peace from the Farmville Hotel.

Headquarters Armies of the U. S. A.,
5 P.M., April 7, 1865

General R. E. Lee,
Commanding C. S. A.

The results of the last week must convince you of the hopelessness of further resistance on the part of the Army of Northern Virginia in this struggle. I feel that it is so, and regard it as my duty to shift from myself the responsibility of any further effusion of blood by asking of you the surrender of that portion of the Confederate States army known as the Army of Northern Virginia.

U. S. Grant,
Lieutenant-General

He entrusted this message to Brigadier General Seth Williams, who had been Lee's adjutant at West Point and had become Grant's inspector general. As Williams set off to deliver the message, Grant settled down to wait.

Williams nearly lost his life carrying Grant's message through the lines, and his orderly was shot. Grant decided to remain in Farmville and was given a room in the hotel where, he was told, Lee had slept the previous night.

Having received Grant's letter from General Williams, Lee wrote a reply within an hour. The answer was taken by a circuitous route to avoid the firing along the line and reached Grant after midnight.

April 7, 1865.

General: I have received your note of this date. Though not entertaining the opinion you express of the hopelessness of further resistance on the part of the Army of Northern Virginia, I reciprocate your desire to avoid useless effusion of blood, and therefore, before considering your proposition, ask the terms you will offer on condition of its surrender.

R. E. Lee
General

Before leaving Farmville the next day, Grant dispatched the following reply through General Williams, who again braved the battle zone and carried the letter to Humphrey's front. From there it was delivered to General Lee.

April 8, 1865.

General R. E. Lee,
Commanding C. S. A.

Your note of last evening, in reply to mine of the same date, asking the conditions on which I will accept the surrender of the Army of Northern Virginia is just received. In reply I would say that, peace being my great desire, there is but one condition I would insist upon—namely that the men and officers surrendered shall be disqualified for taking up arms against the Government of the United States until properly exchanged. I will meet you, or will designate officers to meet any officers you may name for the same purpose, at any point agreeable to you, for the purpose of arranging definitely the terms upon which the surrender of the Army of Northern Virginia will be received.

U. S. Grant,
Lieutenant-General[856]

After issuing further instructions to Ord and Sheridan, Grant crossed to the north side of the Appomattox. The sun was bright and the spring weather pleasant. This part of Virginia had not been ravaged by the war. As the men marched onward, their spirits rose. When Grant overtook Meade, he gave an uncharacteristic greeting, referring to the general as "Old Fellow."

Both officers were in miserable physical shape. For days, Meade had been suffering with chills and a fever. He had made a good part of this march lying in an ambulance. Grant was stricken with a blinding headache and hardly able to stay in the saddle.[857]

Grant conferred with Meade as they rode with his columns. Encouraging reports came in from the various fronts throughout the day. That night headquarters was established at Curdsville in a large white farmhouse a few hundred yards from Meade's camp. After eating dinner with Meade, the ailing Grant returned to his headquarters to try to get some sleep.

~

FROM *PERSONAL MEMOIRS*

I was suffering very severely with a sick headache, and stopped at a farmhouse on the road some distance in rear of the main body of the army. I spent the night in bathing my feet in hot water and mustard, and putting mustard plasters on my wrists and the back part of my neck, hoping to be cured by morning.[858]

~

Grant was under tremendous pressure at this pivotal juncture, and it affected him physically. Lee was approaching the supplies sent by railroad at Appomattox Station while Grant's supply base was far in the rear. Grant knew he only had one day to close the contest before he would need to retreat and feed his own army. Lee, in turn, knew that if his army could survive another day, he might push farther west to Lynchburg where he could refit and feed his army. From there he could seek a haven in the Virginia or Tennessee mountains and eventually find a way to connect with Johnston.[859]

The stress on Grant was overwhelming.

At the same time, Lee gathered his top generals for an informal council of war in the woods. Seated on saddles and blankets, the officers listened as Lee read Grant's letter asking for the surrender of the Army of Northern Virginia. Still resolute, Longstreet answered sharply, "Not yet."[860]

At the farmhouse, the ailing General Grant lay down on a sofa in the sitting room on the left side of the hall, while the staff officers bunked on the floor in the room opposite.

At about midnight, they were wakened by Colonel Charles A. Whittier of Humphreys's staff, who brought the expected letter from Lee. Rawlins took the message and stepped across the hall to the door of General Grant's room. "He hesitated to knock," Porter later wrote, "not wishing to awake the commander if he were asleep, and opened the door softly and listened a moment to ascertain whether he could judge by any sound how the chief was resting. Soon the general's voice was heard saying 'Come in; I am awake. I am suffering too much to get any sleep.' I had in the mean time brought a lighted candle, and now stepped into the room with it. The general, who had taken off only his coat and boots, sat up on the sofa and read the communication."

Lee's reply was a suggestion to meet Grant, but not with a view to surrender the Army of Northern Virginia. "In mine of yesterday, I did not intend to propose the surrender of the Army of Northern Virginia, but to ask the terms of your proposition," Lee wrote defiantly. "To be frank, I do not think the emergency has arisen to call for the surrender of this army."

Grant shook his head in dismay. "It looks as if Lee still means to fight. I will reply in the morning." After making a few more comments, Grant lay down again on the sofa. Rawlins and Porter expressed hope that the general might still be able to get some sleep, and then retired from the room.[861]

April 9, 1865: Date of Destiny

At about four o'clock on the morning of April 9, Porter looked in on Grant to see how he was feeling and found the room empty. Walking out the front door, he saw the general pacing in the yard in agony, holding both hands to his head. Grant had had very little sleep and was still suffering the most excruciating pain.

At 4:30 a.m., they were joined by some of the other staff and walked over to General Meade's headquarters to drink some coffee. This brought slight relief to the general in chief, and before he set out for the day, he wrote a reply to General Lee:

> I am equally anxious for peace with yourself, and the whole North entertains the same feeling. The terms upon which peace can be had are well understood. By the South laying down their arms they will hasten that most desirable event, save thousands of human lives, and hundreds of millions of property not yet destroyed. Sincerely hoping that our difficulties may be settled without the loss of another life.[862]

After finishing his note, he mounted Cincinnati and rode forward toward the south side of the Appomattox. On that fair spring day, small buds from the apple trees emerged from limbs along the road. Some members of his staff implored the general to ride in the covered ambulance, but Grant refused.

In his communication with his generals, Grant added a warning: "I do not think Lee means to surrender until compelled to do so."[863]

Sheridan had sent Custer with his cavalry division galloping to Appomattox Station to get west of Lee's supply trains. At the same time, the head of Lee's army had reached Appomattox Court House, just a few miles away. Griffin and Ord had made an all-night march, hoping to join Sheridan's cavalry at the vital Appomattox crossroads. Sheridan believed that if they came up promptly "we will perhaps finish the job in the morning."[864]

Lee's army was trapped between the Appomattox and James Rivers, with the Union army in his front and rear. Sheridan's cavalry had captured the train cars filled with rebel rations at Appomattox Station and effectively blocked any farther advance by the Army of Northern Virginia. At the same time, Griffin and Ord were advancing rapidly toward Appomattox.[865]

Lee had no place else to go, but he was determined to try to break out.

Chapter Twenty-Six

COMPOSITION ENTIRELY MY OWN

APRIL 27, 1885—NEW YORK CITY

As the temperatures warmed in New York City, flowers emerged in Central Park and leaves once again unfurled on the trees. The general's weight had fallen from more than 200 pounds to 146 pounds, so he was always bundled as if it were winter. Grant celebrated his sixty-third birthday on April 27 by receiving a number of friends throughout the day. During the mild spring day, he enjoyed two rides in Central Park accompanied by Julia, Nellie, and Buck in Senator Chaffee's carriage.

The *Times* reported on the festivities: "The perfume of flowers filled his house from early morning. Many callers left them with their cards, while messengers and expressmen, similarly laden, kept the bell ringing often until well into the afternoon."[866] A larger crowd than usual gathered outside the house to pay their respects to the general on his birthday.

Andrew Carnegie sent General Grant a large basket of sixty-three red roses surrounded by an assortment of spring flowers. Julia used the lavish floral arrangement to decorate the dinner table for the birthday dinner she planned. Another beautiful bouquet arrived from Grant's former secretary of state, Hamilton Fish, and his wife, which added to the decorations.

At six thirty that evening, Mark Twain, General Sherman, Reverend Newman and his wife, and Adam Badeau joined the immediate family for the celebration.

"The family and guests had entered the dining room when the general came down stairs," the *Times* article continued. "He was joyfully greeted and seemed very happy. In the centre of the table 63 tapers were aflame amid banks of flowers. The mantelpiece and windows were also bright and redolent with flowers. Dinner occupied about two hours, the general sitting through it and relishing as much as any one the pleasantries of the event."[867]

After Grant's recent remarkable recovery, the press had somewhat relaxed their vigil across the street. The general's name almost disappeared from the front page of most papers for a time.[868] Gradually, he had regained some physical strength. His mind and purpose had remained clear throughout, but the pain remained. Even so, he was determined to live long enough to finish the book; after that, he could say goodbye.[869]

As Doctors Douglas and Shrady had warned, the disease was still there, and it was growing. This recovery was only temporary.

ENCOURAGEMENT FROM A FRIEND

Galley proofs of the first volume had been completed, and Mark Twain was reading through them, providing minor edits. He told Webster that his marks could be transferred to the copy regularly sent to Colonel Fred Grant. "My marks will not be seriously important, since they will concern grammar & punctuation only."[870]

"There is much more that I could do if I was a well man," Grant told Clemens apologetically. "I do not write quite as clearly as I could if well."[871]

Fred Grant noticed that his father fought depression as he struggled to complete his book amid the unrelenting pain and weariness. He suggested to Twain that a little encouragement might help his father at this critical time.

Twain was amazed by the request. "I was as much surprised as Columbus's cook could have been to learn that Columbus wanted his opinion as to how Columbus was doing his navigating."[872]

Mark Twain was more than happy to oblige, and he repeated to the birthday guests his observation that Grant's writing was comparable with Caesar's Commentaries, in their "clarity of statement, directness, simplicity, manifest truthfulness, fairness and justice toward friend and foe alike, soldierly candor and frankness, and soldierly avoidance of flowery speech." These volumes qualify, Twain continued, as "the best purely narrative literature in the language."[873]

Grant was overjoyed at Twain's kind words—just the friendly encouragement he needed to press on. He was ready to take up the work again and push ahead to completion.

Twain's attention then shifted to the projected sales of the book. Dozens of his canvassers reported that public response to Grant's book surpassed even Twain's optimistic sales projections.[874] By late May, Twain could confirm more than one hundred thousand orders for the two-volume boxed sets. At this rate, Twain estimated that three hundred thousand sets would eventually be sold. Production went into overdrive as the publishing company lined up twenty presses and seven binderies to meet the demand.[875]

Grant spent considerable time adding to his unfinished manuscript "and expressed himself as feeling strong enough to take up the work where he left it more than a month ago." Despite the never-ending pain, Grant worked with continued dedication, ever aware of the ticking clock. He dictated or wrote until exhausted, napped for a while, and then continued when he awoke. Grant's stenographer, Noble Dawson, was amazed at the general's remarkable memory for facts and events.[876]

A FINAL BETRAYAL

Just as Grant began the final push to the end, a disturbing story appeared in the *New York World* on April 29 with the scandalous report that the general was not writing his own book.

In the "National Capital Gossip" column, the Washington correspondent wrote the following:

> Another false idea of Gen. Grant is given out by some of his friends, and that is that he is a writer. He is not a writer. He does not compose easily. Writing for him is a labor. The work upon his new book about which so much has been said is the work of Gen. Adam Badeau.

Gen. Grant I have no doubt has furnished all of the material and all of the ideas in the memoirs as far as they have been prepared, but Badeau has done the work of composition. The most that Gen. Grant has done upon the book has been to prepare the rough notes and memoranda for its various chapters.

Grant's greatness as a soldier should not be obscured by foolish misrepresentation. He was not a man who could chain himself down to a desk to write. He had always been a man of action. He is so great that he can well afford to have the exact truth told about him.[877]

Grant was outraged, but in his normal fashion he kept his emotions in check. Mark Twain, on the other hand, exploded, calling the *World* "that daily issue of unmedicated closet paper." He exhorted Grant to bring a lawsuit that would "cripple—yes, disable—that paper financially."[878] To everyone's relief, no other newspaper stooped to dignify the false report, and Twain soon relented.

The general handled the matter in his own direct fashion. He wrote a letter to Charles L. Webster & Co., intended for the press. He quoted the pertinent statements in the *World*'s story about the book and commented on them briefly. "The composition is entirely my own," he declared. It was true, as stated, that he had furnished all the material and all the ideas for the memoirs. But he had also "done the entire work of composition and preparing notes, and no one but myself has ever used one of such notes in any composition."[879]

He pointed out that it was to the interest of the publisher to correct the false report, "which places me in the attitude of claiming the authorship of a book which I did not write, and it is also injurious to you who are publishing and advertising such book as my work."[880]

Fred also issued a statement to the press to counter the story. "My father is dictating the Appomattox Campaign," he explained. "And from his dispatches and other data is enabled to give a perfectly straight and lucid account to a stenographer."[881]

Speaking to Doctor Douglas, Grant insisted that he desired that the book be as accurate as possible. And he insisted on doing the work himself so that "the authorship would be clearly mine."[882]

General Grant was shocked, therefore, when on the heels of the infamous report in the *World*, Adam Badeau handed him a letter on May 2, then turned and left the room without a word. The letter demanded more money for his services and brazenly suggested that Grant could not finish the book without him: "for you have neither the physical strength nor the habits of mind yourself to make the researches to verify or correct your own memory. If you cannot yourself finish the work, nobody can do it fitly but me."[883]

Badeau said he felt degraded that instead of dealing directly with Grant, he was forced to take copy from a stenographer and "piece and prepare and connect the disjointed fragments into a connected narrative."[884] He called this work "the merest literary drudgery, such as I would never consent to do for any one but you. ... I desire the fame of my own book, not of yours. Yours is not, and will not be, the work of a literary man, but the simple story of a man of affairs and of a great general; proper for you, but not such as would add to my credit at all."[885]

In Badeau's mind, the more he helped with the general's memoirs, the more he was destroying his own reputation as Grant's historian. Badeau knew from Twain's reports that Grant's book would have "a circulation of hundreds of thousands," while his own three-volume work on Grant's military career would likely be overshadowed, or even forgotten. To compensate for this potential loss, Badeau demanded $1,000 a month, paid in advance, until the work was done, and afterward 10 percent of the entire profits. [886]

Grant was stunned. Fred found him pacing back and forth in his room. Removing Badeau's letter from a drawer, Grant gave it to his son. "Read this and tell me what you think of it."[887] Like his father, Fred was incensed. But he was also outraged at the insolence of this man who had advanced his career mostly by the kindness and generosity of Ulysses S. Grant.

Grant had always taken pride in his writing, and so his eleven-page reply to Badeau on May 5 was blistering. "... You and I must give up all association as far as the preparation of any literary work goes which is to bear my signature," the general began. He assured Badeau that he could find many people to perform the task of editing who would find it neither drudgery nor degrading.[888]

He answered Badeau's long letter paragraph by paragraph. His book, he believed, would not supplant Badeau's but rather enhance it. As to the drudgery of connecting disjointed fragments into a connected narrative, which Badeau found so distasteful, "I do not admit that disjointed nature of the matter you speak of, except of that part I wrote after I became so ill that I could write but little at a time.

"To be frank, I do not believe the work would ever be done by you in case of my death while $1,000 per month was coming in." Grant called Badeau petulant and quarrelsome. "... And you are overbearing even to me at times, and always with those for whom you have done or are doing literary work."[889]

Grant predicted that Badeau would have become so arrogant that "there would have been a rupture between you and my family before many days had elapsed." He rejected Badeau's demand for 10 percent of the profits as preposterous. "This would make you a partner with my family as long as the book found a sale."[890]

The general also offered a defense of his writing ability: "I have only to say that for the last twenty-four years I have been very much employed in writing. As a soldier I wrote my own orders, directions and reports. They were not edited nor assistance rendered. As President I wrote every official document, I believe, bearing my name. ... All these have been published and widely circulated. The public has become accustomed to them and my style of writing. They know that it is not even an attempt to imitate either a literary [or classical style] and that it is just what it is pure and simple and nothing else."[891]

Badeau's response confirmed all that Grant had written to him. "You look upon my assistance as that of an ordinary clerk or literary hack; I thought I was aiding you as no one else could in doing a great work."[892] With that, Adam Badeau packed his belongings and moved out of 3 East Sixty-Sixth Street, never to communicate with Ulysses S. Grant again.

Coming at that time in his illness, with the memoirs still unfinished, Julia felt the Badeau letter represented "the most cruel blow" her husband could have received.[893]

Perhaps it was stress caused by Badeau's treachery or merely the resurgence of the disease, but beginning in May 1885, Dr. Douglas made frequent references to the general's sleeplessness in his diary.

> The night was not a good one; not that there was much pain, but a restlessness which deprived him of sleep, so that he had not good, continuous sleep till toward daylight. At one time during the night he requested to be furnished with paper and a pencil. They were brought to him reluctantly, and after writing for some time, he laid them aside of his own accord. The activity of his brain under the renewal of work the last few days is the probable cause of this insomnia, the result of "cerebral exaltation."

Douglas later added on the opposite page:

> Since writing the above, I have learned that at this period the general was very much exercised by occurrences which greatly disturbed his mind, and that the writing in the night which I supposed to be due to the preparing of further notes for his book was in relation to a *question of authenticity* of the part already prepared. This was what he was engaged upon in the middle of the night when he called for paper and pencil, and his decision as to how to meet this question in fairness and truth being made, he dismissed the annoyance from his mind and yielded to sleep.

From the diary on May 3 Douglas wrote:

> With this continued restlessness however, came some pain, and an increase in the fullness of the neck. It was suggested that the general should rest more and give over the preparations of the materials of his book, and the authentication of dates, to his son, the Colonel, and that for the present, or until he was stronger, he should not attempt the weaving of the narrative.[894]

Douglas worried that Grant was overexerting himself, and the doctor knew the consequences could be dire. "Unless the general conserves his strength he will be unable to finish the *Memoirs*."

Even in the midst of the controversy with Badeau, Grant had worked diligently on the second volume. "In two days General Grant has dictated 50 pages of foolscap," Mark Twain wrote in amazement to his friend William Dean Howells. Despite this progress, the general's voice failed him on some days, and he continued dictation in a whisper. By the end of May, his strength waned again, and for several days he could do no work at all. Then he rallied and returned to the work whenever he was able.[895]

Dr. Shrady's admiration for the general also grew as he watched his struggle to complete the memoirs day by day. "Long accustomed to take his life in his hands and to face death in the emergencies of battle," Shrady later wrote of those harrowing days. "He was not one to manifest fear when the end seemed inevitable. He would often speak of it with a calmness that could not be shaken. He was simply living each day by itself in the hope that there would be no distressful struggle at the last."[896]

FINAL TOUCHES

By this time, the tumor on the right side of Grant's throat, once the size of an egg, had grown twice as big. His voice grew weaker, at times nothing more than a whisper. And still he pressed on to finish his work.

On May 23, the *New-York Tribune* reported that "the story of the general's campaigns is about finished."[897]

That same day Grant realized that he had not written a dedication for the book. After some reflection, the general scratched out a simple tribute. "These volumes are dedicated to the American soldier and sailor." When Fred read the statement, he asked if his father meant only the soldiers and sailors who had fought for the North. To that, Ulysses replied: "It is a great deal better that it should be dedicated as it is ... as it is the dedication is to those we fought against as well as those we fought with. It may serve a purpose in restoring harmony."[898]

Chapter Twenty-Seven

MOUNT MCGREGOR

MAY 1885—NEW YORK CITY

Grant's health and vitality steadily waned through the early summer. Although the pain remained constant, he refused to stop his work on the memoirs. To provide encouragement, Samuel Clemens frequently called at the house. Following the advice of the ancient biblical proverb, "A merry heart doeth good like a medicine," Clemens gave Grant several doses per week, talking "cheerful nonsense" to the dying hero.[899]

One of the yarns he weaved for the general was a fable drawn from their proximity in Missouri at the beginning of the Civil War—Clemens fighting quite temporarily for the Confederates, and Grant fighting quite permanently for the Union. "I did not know that this was the future General Grant," Twain later wrote in his journal, "or I would have turned & attacked him. I supposed it was just some ordinary Colonel ... & so I let him go."[900]

The tall tale amused Grant, so Mark Twain continued to embellish it. "To-day talked with General Grant about his & my first Missouri campaign in 1861. ... He surprised an empty camp near Florida, Missouri, on Salt River, which I had been occupying a day or two before. How near he came to playing the devil with his future publisher!"[901]

Inside his fertile mind, Clemens's ranger days were easily transformed from reality into an entertaining blend of fact, fiction, and even fantasy. He even contemplated inserting Tom, Huck, and Jim into the account, scribbling a marginal note: "Union officer accosts Tom & says his name is US Grant." In the end, he decided against it.

By late May, Twain had completed a draft of "The Private History of a Campaign That Failed," and showed it to Grant. The story had the intended effect of lifting Grant's spirits and strengthening him for another day's work.[902] The finished version ran in the December issue of *The Century Magazine*.[903]

Since beginning work with stenographer Noble Dawson, Grant had dictated nearly all of volume two. At this point, he wanted to add some color to the book through his views of fellow commanders and thoughts of what the war ultimately meant for the nation, so the effort to complete his beloved book exacted an even greater physical toll. In the early part of his illness, Dr. Douglas had argued that Grant should write as much as possible to guard his mind from worrying, but since the general's health was clearly faltering, Douglas became concerned that the writing was hindering Grant from getting enough rest.

The cancer had spread into the back of the general's throat and into his jaw causing even more pain, which, in turn, kept him awake at night. Unable to sleep, Grant composed alone into the early morning hours when everyone else was in bed until he finally fell asleep from utter exhaustion.[904]

He still needed to write the revamped chapters on Appomattox, and, as always, he rallied when work was to be done.[905]

With the cancer slowly eating away at his tongue and mouth, Grant grew more feeble, and he appeared much older than his sixty-three years. His beard was fully white, and he could barely walk without support. Because he could not swallow food, he was literally starving to death.[906]

Eventually his voice left him completely, and he was forced to communicate by writing short notes to doctors, family, and friends. "I could do better," he wrote in one note to Twain, "if I could get the rest I crave."

Toward the end of May, Grant began the final phase of the book, writing for four to five hours each day on the end of the siege of Petersburg and Lee's retreat to Appomattox. He wrote without major revisions and on June 8 delivered the first draft of volume two to an astonished Mark Twain.[907]

A Move to the Mountains

Manhattan, with its stone and brick buildings, was like an oven in the summer. The air was filled with noxious odors and the toxic dust kicked up from thousands of horses continuously treading over their own dried droppings. The city was no place for someone in Grant's condition, and his family and physicians wanted to move him away from fierce heat and discomfort.

The family had suggested retiring to the cottage at Long Branch, which had been kept in Mrs. Grant's name. The doctors, however, did not think the blazing summer sun and the humid seacoast atmosphere would be healthy for the general.

After putting out the word, Fred Grant received an appealing offer from his father's friend, Joseph W. Drexel. He was a minor partner in the Hotel Balmoral near the tony Upstate New York resort town of Saratoga Springs. Known for its milder summer climate, especially in the surrounding mountains, Saratoga featured famous mineral waters and a thoroughbred racetrack. The charming town had become a favorite vacation spot for New York City residents desiring a break from the summer heat.

Drexel's hotel had recently opened at the peak of breezy Mount McGregor, which stood 1,100 feet above sea level. Nearby, between the hotel and the narrow-gauge train depot, Drexel had purchased a colorful roomy cottage—a small house, really—with a wide porch on two sides. He offered the cottage to the Grant family at no charge.[908]

Dr. Douglas and his family vacationed every summer in Saratoga Springs, and one day he commented that if he could find a place somewhere around Saratoga, that above all would be his choice for a summer home for the general. Douglas was pleasantly surprised when Fred Grant told him about the Drexel invitation. Douglas knew the mountain well and was thrilled with the location. "That is just the place I have been looking for. There is little heat there, it is on the heights, it is free from vapors, and above all, it is among the pines. The pure air is especially grateful to patients suffering as General Grant is suffering."[909]

Excited by the prospect of spending the summer on a wooded mountain, Grant told a reporter that he walked around his room after breakfast "getting himself in condition for long tramps through the woods after he got in the country."[910]

Taking care of business before leaving for the mountain, the general wrote to the Librarian of Congress, asking if he was "authorized to receive" the property that the Grants had given to William H. Vanderbilt as payment of their $150,000 debt to him. Grant identified this as including "the medal voted to me by Congress, and other trophies of the war and of my trip around the world." This collection of valuable and historical objects still remained crated up at 3 East Sixty-Sixth Street. "I will soon be leaving the city," Grant concluded, "and will be very glad to have it out of the house during the absence of myself and my family."

The medals and trophies were soon shipped off to the War Department in Washington, "to await the further action of Congress."[911]

VETERANS SALUTE THEIR COMMANDER

As preparations continued for the move to Mount McGregor, Grant suffered through a particularly bad episode on Memorial Day. He was lying in bed in terrible pain when he heard music and cheering from outside. Horace Porter, his trusted friend, was visiting with the general in chief as the military sounds echoed outside the open window.

Out on the street, men wearing the dark-blue uniforms and wide-brimmed hats of the Grand Army of the Republic moved as a unit down Fifth Avenue, with bands playing and the crowd cheering. As unit after unit came to Sixty-Sixth Street, they turned left off their usual route, passing in review before Grant's house.[912]

"Now he heard the sound of martial music," Porter remembered. "Then came the heavy, measured steps of moving columns, a step which can be acquired only by years of service in the field. He recognized it all now. It was the tread of his old veterans."

"With his little remaining strength he arose and dragged himself to the window. As he gazed upon those battle-flags dipping to him in salute, those precious standards bullet-riddled, battle-stained ... his eyes once more kindled with the flames that had lighted them at Shiloh, on the heights of Chattanooga, amid the glories of Appomattox."

Grant was now clearly visible as he stood in his second-story window and gazed down at his beloved "Boys in Blue." As each regiment passed, they performed a machine-like "eyes left" maneuver, turning their heads toward the general and taking off their hats to him as they marched passed. "... As those war-scarred veterans with uncovered heads and upturned faces for the last time looked upon the pallid features of their old chief, cheeks which had been bronzed by southern suns and begrimed with gun powder, were bathed in tears of manly grief.

"Soon they saw rising the hand which had so often pointed out to them the path of victory. He raised it slowly and painfully to his head in recognition of their salutations." After all the columns had passed, General Grant's hand fell heavily to his side. That would be his last military salute.[913]

A reporter from the *New-York Tribune,* stationed with the rest of the press across the street, witnessed the scene. "The old warrior stood at his post in the window, like a statue, looking toward the Park. Someone came up from behind and touched him, and he moved slowly away. The sight of the old soldiers, many of whom had been with him in the Wilderness, touched him deeply, and he sat thinking in his chair for a long time after the sound of the music had died away in the distance."[914]

In early June, when Grant suffered yet another day wracked with pain, the possibility of postponing the trip to Mount McGregor was raised. He quickly protested, "Now or never."[915]

By the middle of June, the swelling in the general's neck was so large that he had difficulty breathing. From "the great and injurious effect the heat seemed to have upon the general," the doctors advised the family to no longer postpone the trip to Mount McGregor. Grant was pleased and relieved by the decision.[916]

As they prepared to leave for the mountain, a concerned Grant asked Dr. Shrady to promise that he would find a way to be with him until the last moment. "So anxious was he that nothing should interfere with such an understanding, that he questioned me concerning my whereabouts and future plans in my necessary absences from Mount McGregor," Shrady remembered. "On learning that my summer home was at my farm on the Hudson, near Kingston, he was particular to learn how long it would take me to reach him in response to an urgent message."[917]

To master every detail of the trip, Grant drew the route on a piece of wrapping-paper, and smilingly styled it "a working plan of battle." A line was made across the river to Barrytown, a spur to Poughkeepsie, a straight course northward through Hudson, Albany, and Saratoga, and a slight detour to Mount McGregor. "The probable time between these places was duly indicated at proper points," Shrady recalled, "and the total added at the bottom of the sheet."[918]

JUNE 16, 1885: ASCENDING THE MOUNTAIN

At 7:00 a.m. on the morning of June 16, Ulysses S. Grant emerged from his home at 3 East Sixty-Sixth Street and shuffled slowly toward a waiting carriage. Having lost more than sixty pounds, he was a shell of his former self. His hair and beard were completely white. Despite rising summer temperatures, he stood bundled in a thick black coat, a black beaver-skin top hat with a five-inch crown, a white scarf, and bedroom slippers. Grant was accompanied by Julia, Fred and Ida, Nellie, five grandchildren, plus Noble E. Dawson, Harrison Terrell, Dr. Douglas, and nurse Henry McSweeny.[919]

His appearance shocked those who had not seen him for a while. When he adjusted his white scarf, a reporter thought his wrist looked skeleton-like. According to an account forwarded to the newspaper *The Daily Saratogian*, "The great malignant looking swelling under his right ear is a big as a man's two fists put together."[920]

Grant seemed to realize he was leaving his home forever. After being seated in the carriage, he turned and gave a sad look at the house, then waved a solemn farewell to a few bystanders and reporters gathered on the sidewalk.[921]

The carriage bore them to Grand Central Depot, where Grant, leaning on his cane, moved slowly toward the train. William Vanderbilt lent the Grant family his private car, which was emptied to make room for the general's two leather armchairs, allowing him to rest comfortably on the long, hot train ride. As the locomotive chugged upstate, small crowds gathered at stations and crossings and waved as he sped by.[922]

Harper's Weekly reported on the journey: "At station after station on the route knots of people were found gathered to wave greeting and godsend. At West Point he beckoned to Dr. Douglas and with a smile motioned toward the Military Academy … as though the sight were dear to him. Till the last outline of its surroundings had passed his gaze was fixed on the spot."[923]

As the train steamed up the line beside the Hudson River, temperatures rose to 105 degrees. Grant changed from his top hat and coat to one of his skating caps and a long linen duster.[924]

Arriving at Saratoga, Grant transferred to a narrow-gauge railroad car that would lift him to the summit of Mount McGregor. Fred moved the leather high-back chairs from one train to the other. The new engine slowly chugged up the side of the mountain, throwing cinders and smoke into the open-air car carrying the general and his family.

At 2:40 p.m., this second train reached the end of its line at a small platform atop Mount McGregor—where guests of the Hotel Balmoral exited and walked the remaining distance up a covered sloping walkway to the hotel, with porters following, carrying their luggage or pushing it on a cart. A hospital bed was placed on the platform to transport the general up the slope to the cottage. Grant refused to use it. Instead, using his cane, he struggled to make his way up the path on his own.

Passing under an arch composed of two poles with an over-head banner welcoming "Our Hero," he stumbled. Two muscular men from the Saratoga police department, Detective John Fryer and Constable James Minnick, had positioned themselves nearby with a large wicker chair. They carried it over to the general, who collapsed into it. The policemen then carried Grant the rest of the way to the steps of the cottage.

Thanking the officers, the general rose from the chair. Using his cane, he climbed the steps to the porch, where Mrs. Drexel stood waiting to greet him.[925] Mrs. Drexel led Ulysses, Julia, and the family into the house and gave them a quick tour. Retiring momentarily to his new bedroom, the general changed his clothes, and Harrison brushed the ashes from the train ride out of his beard and hair.

A *New York World* reporter sent to the mountain described the Drexels' mountain home. "The cottage is a modest-looking two-story frame building, decked out in a new coat of old gold paint with neat brown trimmings." There was a wide veranda on three sides, and the cottage was surrounded by pines, maples, and oaks. The family or reception room had been artistically papered and veneered, and the ceiling paper was "radiant with gold stars."

The general's first-floor sleeping room was furnished with a mahogany suite and wickerwork couch, rocker, and settee. Fred moved his father's leather high-back chairs to the center of this room. Julia occupied an adjoining room, just as she had at East Sixty-Sixth Street. Another door led to a room for Harrison and nurse Henry McSweeny, allowing them to be close by when Grant called on them.

Two windows opened into the general's room from the west. They had "double shades, one cream colored, the other black." The carpet was a delicate figured blue, and the paper was also of "a delicate mixed blue shade." There were six rooms on the second floor, reached by a staircase between the servants' and dining rooms.[926]

After cleaning up, Grant reappeared and slowly walked along the broad covered porch. He stopped several times, his hands on his hips, peering out at the different views, including one of the magnificent Hotel Balmoral. Once again wearing his black coat and top hat, he sank into the wicker armchair and peacefully "sat for hours until the mosquitoes drove him in."[927]

An Albany G.A.R. veteran, Sam Willett, had received permission from the Drexel family to stand guard at the foot of the porch steps to keep unwanted visitors away from the general. The Grants were grateful for this service, and soon grew fond of the affable veteran. Willett informed reporters that he would stay on duty until the general left the mountain. While firm in his resolve to let only authorized visitors past him up the path to the cottage, Willett spoke kindly to hotel visitors, local residents, and reporters who came to gaze at Grant. He was recruited from time to time as a playmate for the Grant grandchildren and Dr. Douglas's two little girls, although he never drifted too far from his post.[928]

Willett had served as a private in Company A, Sixteenth Heavy Artillery, New York State Volunteers. When he enlisted in 1863, he was forty-three years old, and he served until the end of the war. He joined up to keep an eye on his son Ebenezer, who was a private in the same company. In time, the elder Willett acted as his unit's unofficial chaplain. Willett had read of Grant's stay at Mount McGregor and decided that the family needed someone to shield his old general from the public.

Shortly before the Grants arrived, he set up an army tent ten yards away from the southern corner of the cottage, complete with a small wood stove and a washtub for doing his laundry. Wearing his G.A.R. uniform, he took up his post in front of the steps at the top of which Grant sat in a wicker armchair working on his book or reading the newspapers.[929]

Colonel Fred Grant was elated with the results of the trip and the alpine location. The general had borne the fatigue much better than anyone had anticipated, and Fred hoped his father would recover his speech fully and see all-around improvement. Dr. Douglas, however, warned the family and the reporters that nothing more than a temporary improvement could be expected: "the decay of vitality is slowly but steadily progressing."[930]

Grant was also quite pleased with the Drexel cottage. He hoped the change in atmosphere would restore his voice and vitality. "This new phase of the disease was a great discouragement to him," Dr. Shrady wrote, "and his main hope was that the balsamic air of the mountains might possibly have a soothing and healing effect upon his throat." Sadly, this did not prove to be the case. On the contrary, his voice almost permanently disappeared. "Most of the conversations I had with him on my visits to Mount McGregor were carried on by means of the pencil and pad that he always carried with him," Shrady remembered.[931]

A Test of Strength

On his first night at Mount McGregor, the temperature mercifully dropped to forty degrees, allowing Grant to sleep for ten hours. He rested comfortably curled up in his leather armchairs, undisturbed by lightning from a mountain thunderstorm that flashed in the skies.[932]

The following day Grant sat for a long time alone on the veranda of the cottage, seemingly lost in deep meditation. Informed of a nearby overlook on the side of the mountain, he determined to make a test of his strength by walking to see the magnificent view for himself.

Refreshed by his night's sleep and the mountain air, now at seventy degrees, he made the trek. Holding on to Harrison's arm with one hand and using his cane with the other, the general set off down the path through the pines. The trail of 150 yards brought them to the Eastern Overlook. This clearing provided a spectacular wide-angle panorama overlooking the Hudson Valley to the east, with the Saratoga Revolutionary War battlefield less than ten miles away. To the north, the Adirondack Mountains were visible, and the Catskills to the south.[933]

The Civil War hero seated himself on a wooden bench at the height and looked out across the valley to Saratoga. Below was the spot where Revolutionary War General Horatio Gates had once accepted the surrender of "Gentleman" Jonny Burgoyne of the British army. Grant took in the view for a long time, alone in his thoughts.[934] Then he stood to make the laborious upward climb back to the cottage on the arm of faithful Harrison.

The return trip was a grueling incline that severely weakened the general. Grant arrived at the Drexel home short of breath and haggard. Once inside he collapsed onto his armchairs and struggled to catch his breath. Again he meditated for a long while. Finally catching his breath, he asked Harrison to bring him a pencil and paper.

First, he wrote a message to Dr. Douglas, who was staying up the path at the hotel. Later that evening when Douglas walked down to check on the general, Grant gave him the note. "He handed me a folded paper," Dr. Douglas recalled, "giving it to me quietly in a rather furtive manner. It was written upon a pad of yellow colored paper."[935]

The note said:

> Since coming to this beautiful climate, and getting a complete rest for about ten hours, I have watched my pains, and compared them with those of the past few weeks. I can feel plainly that my system is preparing for dissolution in three ways; one by hemorrhage; one by strangulation, and the third by exhaustion. The first and second are liable to come at any moment to relieve me of my earthly sufferings. The time of the arrival of the third can be computed with almost mathematical certainty. With an increase of daily food, I have fallen off in weight and strength very rapidly for the last two weeks.
>
> There cannot be hope of going far beyond this period. All my physicians, or any number of them can do for me now, is to make my burden of pain as light as possible. I do not want any physician but yourself, but I tell you, so that if you are unwilling to have me go without consultation with other professional men, you can send for them. I dread them however, knowing that it means another desperate effort to save me, and more suffering.[936]

Next, Grant wrote his eldest son a note he titled "Memoranda for My Family." Colonel Fred tore open the family letter at once, and found it alarming. "I have given you the directions about all my affairs except my burial," it began, and then listed several options for his final resting place:

We own a burial lot in the cemetery at St. Louis and I like that city, as it was there I was married and lived for many years and there three of my children were born. We have also a burial lot in Galena, and I am fond of Illinois, from which state I entered the Army at the beginning of the war. I am also much attached to New York, where I have made my home for several years past, and through the generosity of the citizens I have been enabled to pass my last days without experiencing the pains of pinching want.[937]

Reading this, Fred told his father that the national expectation was that he would be buried in Washington. Grant responded by writing a tremendous understatement on a slip of paper. "It is possible that my funeral may become one of public demonstration." He added that he understood he might have no choice in the matter of where he would be buried. But Julia was his first priority, and he wanted to lie beside her forever if possible. "There is one thing I wish you and the family to insist upon and that is that wherever my tomb may be, a place shall be reserved for your mother."

Fred believed the time had come to share his father's wishes with his mother. Of course this conversation overwhelmed Julia, who could not bear the thought of losing her beloved "Ulys." After receiving this message from Fred, she seldom left her husband's side. When Grant dozed in his wicker chair on the porch or in his leather armchairs, she often sat beside him, holding his hand.[938]

In his letter to Dr. Douglas, Grant made it clear that he did not want any more desperate efforts to save him. They only meant more suffering. The walk to the overlook had been a test, and his body had failed it.[939]

Chapter Twenty-Eight

APPOMATTOX

That summer, Charles L. Webster & Co. issued a prospectus of Grant's *Personal Memoirs* to the subscription canvassers across the country and overseas. The publishing company intended to issue the first volume on December 1 and the second volume the following March. They announced that the first draft had been completed and mostly set in type.

The general, however, was not completely satisfied with his work. Mark Twain's firm had enlarged the book to contain the excess copy already written, but Grant still wanted to add, as Mark Twain said, "no end of little plums and spices."[940]

The biggest plum was his chapter on the surrender at Appomattox.

APRIL 1865—APPOMATTOX, VIRGINIA

~

FROM *PERSONAL MEMOIRS*

Sheridan sent Custer with his division to move south of Appomattox Station, which is about five miles south-west of the Court House, to get west of the trains and destroy the roads to the rear. They got there the night of the 8th and succeeded partially; but some of the train men had just discovered the movement of our troops and succeeded in running off three of the trains. The other four were held by Custer.

The head of Lee's column came marching up there on the morning of the 9th, not dreaming, I suppose, that there were any Union soldiers near. The Confederates were surprised to find our cavalry had possession of the trains. However, they were desperate and at once assaulted, hoping to recover them. In the skirmish that ensued they succeeded in burning one of the trains, but not in getting anything from it. Custer then ordered the other trains run back on the road towards Farmville, and the fight continued.[941]

~

APRIL 9, 1865

At the direction of Sheridan, General George Custer led his Union cavalry division pounding hard for Appomattox Station. He had received word from one of his scouts that four train cars loaded with supplies for Lee's army were waiting at the rail depot. Custer understood that these supplies meant life and another day to fight for Lee's army if they won this race, or death and defeat if they didn't.

Custer wisely ordered two of his regiments to swing around to the west to break the railroad tracks behind the trains so they could not return to Lynchburg. With the rest of his force, Custer galloped toward the station. The Union cavalry and the Confederate advance guard converged at nearly the same time. The well-fed, rested Federal troops attacked the weary, hungry rebels and utterly routed them. The Yankees not only captured two dozen artillery pieces and a wagon column, but they also captured the precious supply trains. Fearing another Sailor's Creek, the Confederates retreated back down the road toward Appomattox Court House.

Soon Sheridan arrived at Appomattox and ordered his men to follow the Confederate retreat and press the attack. Sensing victory was at hand, "Little Phil" did not sleep that night. He knew his cavalry wasn't strong enough to surround Lee's entire army, so he sent continued requests to both Grant and Ord for immediate support.[942]

"The necessity of getting Ord's column up was so obvious now that staff officer after staff officer was sent to him and to General Grant requesting that the infantry be pushed on," Sheridan remembered, "for if it could get to the front, all knew that the rebellion would be ended on the morrow."[943]

In his communication to Grant, Sheridan reported that his cavalry had taken a gun park loaded with reserve artillery and a considerable number of prisoners. He had dug in at the Lynchburg road, blocking Lee's escape. He knew Ord's Army of the James and Griffin's Fifth Corps followed close behind. "If they can get up tonight we will perhaps finish the job in the morning," Sheridan wrote.[944]

General Sheridan saw the noose tightening on Lee's army. His cavalry was directly in front of the rebels, blocking their westward movement. Meade and most of the Army of the Potomac was behind, blocking their retreat. And the rebels were also hemmed in on both sides by the James and Appomattox Rivers. Infantry from the Army of the James was coming up rapidly to reinforce Sheridan to the west, leaving Lee nowhere to turn. To Sheridan's great frustration, the night passed with no word from Ord or Grant. The cavalry commander knew his forces would have difficulty holding back a frontal attack by what was left of the Army of Northern Virginia.

Even though Lee's forces had dwindled to twelve thousand fighting men and sixty-one cannons, he ordered General John B. Gordon to make one final, desperate attempt to break through Sheridan's cavalry line.

Gordon hit Sheridan's dismounted troopers at dawn and pushed them back, which gave the rebels a glimmer of hope as they pushed westward. The Confederate soldiers' spirits rose when it appeared the Union troops were retreating, but their hearts sank when they reached the crest of the hill.

Just as the sun rose over Appomattox on that unseasonably cold, damp Palm Sunday, a wall of blue appeared out of the darkness fanning out behind the cavalry—General Ord and his Army of the James with thirty thousand men. Ord's infantry had marched all night and were bone tired. Yet as they trudged through the darkness, they understood their sacrifice could help to finally corner Lee.[945]

The day the Union boys had fought for so valiantly over the last four years had finally arrived.

Gordon and his men watched in shock as Ord's columns poured onto the battlefield. The rebels reflexively halted, then fell back toward Appomattox Court House. Gordon understood the hopelessness of the situation. At 7:30 a.m., he informed Lee that he could do nothing further.

Raising the White Flag

Sheridan was eager for a fight. This was the golden moment, and he did not want to let the rebels slip the trap. But as Custer and Wesley Merritt, Sheridan's second in command, were about to charge, news arrived that Lee had raised the white flag.[946]

When Grant's letter of the previous night reached Lee, the Confederate commander was in a much different frame of mind than he had been the previous day. Lee knew the rebels were both surrounded and greatly outnumbered. It became clear that further resistance was futile.

Lee gathered his senior officers and sought their counsel one final time. When one officer suggested to Lee that his army should disband and soldier on in guerrilla warfare, Lee rejected it as dangerous thinking. "We must consider the effect on the country as a whole. Already it is demoralized by four years of war. If I took your advice, the men would be without rations and under no control of officers. They would be compelled to rob and steal in order to live."[947] Southern rebels attacking from the mountains and forests "would become mere bands of marauders," Lee replied, "and the enemy's cavalry would pursue them and overrun many sections they may never [otherwise] have occasion to visit. We would bring on a state of affairs it would take the country years to recover from."[948]

Lee knew he had no other choice. "There is nothing left for me to do but go and see General Grant," Lee told the officers and staff, "and I would rather die a thousand deaths." Lee dressed in his best formal uniform and departed to meet Grant shortly before 9:00 a.m.[949]

When a rebel staffer commented on his apparel, Lee replied, "I have probably to be General Grant's prisoner, and thought I must make my best appearance."[950]

Lee was accompanied by an orderly bearing a flag of truce—a soiled white handkerchief tied to a stick—and by his military secretary, Lieutenant Colonel Charles Marshall, grandson of the former Chief Justice of the Supreme Court. The three horsemen had gone little more than half a mile when they met a Union officer, also under a flag of truce, bearing the message Grant had written that morning.

Lee, who had assumed the meeting he had requested the previous evening was still in place, was startled by Grant's reply. Lee's misgivings were heightened when he heard the rumble of artillery, marking Meade's advance, sounding from the rear.

At this point, the Southern commander had no alternative but to trust in providence and the mercy of Ulysses S. Grant. He dictated a message to be sent with all haste to the Northern commander. Lee signed the letter in a large, bold hand, and gave it to the Union officer. Then he sent Marshall forward to arrange a cease-fire while the message was being delivered.

Persuading the Union commanders to suspend the impending attack proved to be easier said than done. Both Meade and Sheridan were moving forward for what they knew would be the final assault of the war, and neither wanted to back off and risk allowing the rebel army to escape.

When the movements of the Union army and cavalry became clear, Lee wrote out a second message to Grant requesting a suspension of hostilities until the terms of surrender could be established. Marshall rode across the no-man's-land between the two armies under his simple flag of truce and handed the letter to General Meade. The commander of the Army of the Potomac reluctantly ordered an informal cease-fire until Lee could contact Grant.

At five minutes after eleven on Palm Sunday, the Union guns went silent.[951]

A Message of Peace

Traveling with his staff, Grant rode steadily down the road leading toward Appomattox Court House, swinging south of the place where Meade's troops were preparing to fight. Far to the west came the faint rumble of artillery fire.[952] Grant had ridden no more than a few miles when his entourage was overtaken near noon by a high-spirited officer from Meade's staff who galloped toward him, flapping his hat wildly and brandishing a sealed letter.

The slightest hint of a smile spread across Grant's face as he read the note. Turning to his chief of staff, John Rawlins, Grant requested that he read it aloud. As he complied, Rawlins's eyes flashed, and his voice resonated with solemn emotion:

~

FROM PERSONAL MEMOIRS

April 9, 1865.

GENERAL: I received your note of this morning on the picket-line whither I had come to meet you and ascertain definitely what terms were embraced in your proposal of yesterday with reference to the surrender of this army. I now request an interview in accordance with the offer contained in your letter of yesterday for that purpose.

R. E. LEE, General.[953]

~

"Well, how do you think that will do?" asked Grant, a full smile on his face.

"I think that will do," Rawlins answered joyfully.[954]

"No one looked his comrade in the face," wrote war correspondent Sylvanus Cadwallader. "Finally Colonel William Duff, chief of artillery, sprang upon a log and proposed three cheers. A feeble 'hurrah' came from a few throats when all broke down in tears."[955]

Grant later wrote of the moment: "When the officer reached me I was still suffering with the sick headache, but the instant I saw the contents of the note I was cured."[956]

Four years had passed since the rebels fired on Fort Sumter, and 344 days since Grant had crossed the Rapidan.

The officer had also carried a note from Meade saying that, at Lee's request, he had read the communication addressed to Grant, and in consequence of it had granted a short truce. As soon as he had read these letters, Grant dismounted, sat down on the grassy bank by the roadside, and asked for his dispatch book. He wrote the following reply to Lee:[957]

~

From *Personal Memoirs*

April 9, 1865.
    GENERAL R. E. LEE,
    Commanding C. S. Armies.
    Your note of this date is but this moment (11:50 A.M.) received, in consequence of my having passed from the Richmond and Lynchburg road to the Farmville and Lynchburg road. I am at this writing about four miles west of Walker's Church and will push forward to the front for the purpose of meeting you. Notice sent to me on this road where you wish the interview to take place will meet me.
    U. S. GRANT,
    Lieutenant-General.[958]

~

Grant handed the note to Colonel Orville Babcock, telling him to deliver it to Lee and to escort him to whatever meeting place the Southern commander chose. Babcock needed a fresh horse, so he delayed long enough to pull one from the wagon train. Joining another staff officer, Captain W. M. Dunne, he galloped toward Appomattox to deliver the fateful message.[959]

    Also bypassing Lee's army, Grant took the long, roundabout route along boggy lanes that spattered his already dirty uniform.

~

From *Personal Memoirs*

When I had left camp that morning I had not expected so soon the result that was taking place, and consequently was in rough garb. I was without a sword, as I usually was when on horseback in the field, and wore a soldier's [enlisted man's] blouse for a coat, with the shoulder straps of my rank to indicate to the army who I was.[960]

~

Thirty minutes later, Babcock found Lee sitting on a blanket atop a pile of fence rails, talking to General "Old Pete" Longstreet. Lee was greatly concerned, Longstreet later reported, that with the Confederate army surrounded, Grant might demand stiffer terms than what he had conveyed in his original letter. Old Pete did not think so. He reminded Lee that he had known Grant since they were cadets together at West Point. They had remained close friends until the outbreak of the war. He believed Grant was a man of honor and would impose only such terms as Lee himself would if the roles were reversed.

Lee stood to his feet as Babcock approached. The Union officer dismounted and respectfully handed him Grant's note. Babcock was struck by the fact that Lee was in full dress, wearing his best uniform, his boots highly polished. A red silk sash surrounded his waist, over which he had buckled a splendid sword with an ornate hilt and scabbard.

The contents of Grant's reply eased Lee's mind. Longstreet had been right. Grant would be gracious. Lee mounted Traveller and rode to the village of Appomattox Court House to meet Lieutenant Colonel Charles Marshall, who had been sent to secure a proper place for the meeting.

In the meantime, Marshall had found a first-floor parlor room in the house of Wilmer McLean that he believed would be suitable for the commanders.[961] By amazing coincidence, McLean had surrendered another home to General Beauregard to serve as his headquarters during the First Battle of Bull Run in 1861. In the midst of that contest, a shell exploded in McLean's kitchen, and he determined to move his family far beyond the reach of the two armies.[962]

Now the Southern commander would meet in McLean's front parlor to surrender his army to the Northern commander. General Lee and his aides arrived and made themselves comfortable in the parlor as they waited. Babcock met the Confederate leadership at the McLean house and sent an orderly off to inform General Grant of the location.

Arriving at Appomattox

At one o'clock, Grant and his staff rode up the main street of Appomattox Court House, with its rolling hills and half-dozen houses. The town was situated on rising ground, and beyond it the country slopes down into a broad valley. The enemy was seen with his columns and wagon trains covering the low ground. As he crested the hill, Grant could see his own cavalry, the Fifth Corps, and part of Ord's command holding the high ground to the south and west.

The hopelessness of the rebels' situation was evident to all.

Approaching the historic meeting, Grant became even more aware that his dress was not as formal as it should have been for such an occasion—his sword and clean clothing left far behind in his straggling baggage wagon.

"I had an old suit on," Grant told John Russell Young during their world tour, "without my sword, and without any distinguishing mark of rank, except the shoulder straps of a Lieutenant General on a woolen blouse. . . . I was afraid that Lee might think I meant to show him studied discourtesy by so coming—at least I thought so."[963]

Later, when asked what he was thinking as he approached this historic meeting with General Robert E. Lee, Grant replied honestly and simply: "My dirty boots and wearing no sword."[964]

Despite his mud-spattered boots and clothing, Ulysses S. Grant projected an air of confident authority as he approached the McLean house. This victory was his triumph. Some said the Northern commander was merely a butcher who wore down the Confederacy by sacrificing superior numbers and resources in a series of bloody battles. But these critics overlooked the fact that all the Union generals in chief before Grant had access to the same troop superiority and Northern resources, but they refused to bring them to bear.

General Grant had devised and deployed a strategy that coordinated all the Union forces, unleashing the strength of the United States—not against cities but against the armies of the Confederacy. He directed Federal forces in a manner that blocked the rebels from sending soldiers from one army to another to reinforce their weak points. He unleashed a "total warfare" strategy in places such as the Shenandoah Valley and the heart of Georgia to destroy civilian support of the military. And, as he had done so effectively in Vicksburg, Grant moved methodically to cut off supplies to the rebel armies by destroying railroads and canals.

Having directed Union forces to do these things, he held on with a bulldog grip—and he "chewed and choked," as Lincoln observed, until the rebels fell to their knees.

Following the advice of President Lincoln and Frederick Douglass, Grant not only utilized Black soldiers for manual labor and guard duty, but once they had proved themselves to him, he also placed them in combat to fight for their own freedom—and they made excellent soldiers. They understood from the day the rebels fired on Fort Sumter what the war was really about.

Brigadier General Joshua Lawrence Chamberlain, one of the heroes of Gettysburg, stood awestruck on the main street of Appomattox Court House as Grant trotted by. He described the scene: "Slouched hat without cord; common soldier's blouse, unbuttoned, on which, however, the three stars; high boots, mud-splashed to the top; trousers tucked inside; no sword, but the sword hand deep in the pocket; sitting his saddle with the ease of a born master, taking no notice of anything, all his faculties gathered into intense thought and mighty calm. He seemed greater than I had ever seen him, a look as of another world about him. No wonder I forgot altogether to salute him. Anything like that would have been too little. He rode on to meet Lee at the Court House."[965]

Grant approached Sheridan, Ord, and a group of officers who stood in the street, waiting to see what would happen next. Spying his cavalry commander among them with a satisfied expression on his flushed face, Grant asked, "How are you, Sheridan?"

"Little Phil" replied excitedly, "First-rate, thank you; how are you?"

"Is Lee over there?" asked Grant, pointing up the road, having heard a rumor that the Confederate commander was in that vicinity.

"Yes, he is in that brick house, waiting to surrender to you."

"Well, then, we'll go over."[966]

As Grant approached, Colonel Babcock's orderly was seen sitting on his horse in the street in front of the two-story brick house. He informed Grant that General Lee and Colonel Babcock had gone into the house half an hour earlier. Grant and the others entered the grounds by the gate and dismounted. In the yard, General Lee's fine gray horse, Traveller, stood next to a dark-colored mare belonging to Colonel Marshall. The orderly in gray watching over them had removed their bridles to let them eat the spring grass.

Hearing the clumping of boots coming up the steps, Babcock looked out the window and saw Grant ascending to the porch, followed by Sheridan, Ord, Rawlins, staff officer General Eli Parker, and assorted other staff officers. Babcock went to the door and escorted Grant inside, while the others waited on the porch.[967]

The two commanders stood in striking contrast. Lee in his bright clean uniform, with a sash and a jeweled sword, appearing as the patrician from the colonial past; Grant in his mud-spattered uniform, looking like the common American of the unknown future. Lee stood tall and erect; Grant was relatively short and slouched. Lee was the son of one of General Washington's top commanders in the Revolutionary War; Grant was the son of an unknown tanner from the western frontier.[968]

"Lee was tall, large in form, fine in person, handsome in feature, grave and dignified in bearing—if anything, a little too formal," Adam Badeau recorded of the encounter. "There was a suggestion of effort in his deportment, something that showed he was determined to die gracefully, a hint of Caesar muffling himself in his mantle."

The man who conquered this grand figure and his army couldn't have been more different. "Grant as usual was simple and composed, but with none of the grand air about him," Badeau remembered. "No elation was visible in his manner or appearance. His voice was as calm as ever, and his eye betrayed no emotion.

He spoke and acted as plainly as if he were transacting an ordinary matter of business."

"No one would have suspected that he was about to receive the surrender of an army, or that one of the most terrible wars of modern times had been brought to a triumphant close by the quiet man without a sword who was conversing calmly, but rather grimly, with the elaborate gentleman in grey and gold."[969]

General Grant stepped into the hall and Colonel Babcock opened the door of the room on the left. The general passed in as Lee arose and stepped forward. Grant extended his hand, saying respectfully, "General Lee." The two shook hands cordially.[970]

For the first time during the war, the two great commanders met face-to-face. And now the war was over.

Chapter Twenty-Nine

IT IS FINISHED

JUNE 21, 1885—MOUNT MCGREGOR, NEW YORK

Grant viewed each day as a providential gift, so he added final details to his memoirs as long as he was able. His most productive day was June 21, when he sat on his porch several hours, working with Noble Dawson.[971] The general had received the printed page proofs of Volume One, and he had the completed handwritten manuscript of Volume Two. Dawson read to him various sections from both volumes. From time to time, Grant interrupted Dawson to suggest a change—either insertions of a new sentence and paragraph, or the rearrangement of existing sections.

The next day, using a yellow legal pad and a pencil, he worked again, sitting on the porch in the wicker armchair with a writing board that ran from one arm of the chair to the other. Dr. Douglas asked General Grant after he had finished his work if he could talk in a louder key and he replied he could, but he spoke low "to economize his strength."

In the cool mountain air, his voice had rebounded a little. Grant sat with Dawson and completely rewrote his chapter on Lee's surrender at Appomattox. "During his last days, the general worked almost continually on his book," Dawson later remembered. "I saw that he was sinking fast and suffering intensely, and [I] worked all the time to try and ease his discomfort."[972]

Over the next few days, Colonel Fred, Buck, Jesse, or Dawson read the galley proofs to the general and collected the revision slips that he wrote. The room next to Grant's at the corner of the cottage, first intended for Mrs. Grant's use, was almost at once made into an office, while Julia moved upstairs. At night Fred or Dawson wrote the revisions into the proofs. Reporters noticed that the lights sometimes burned in the office for hours after the general had gone to bed. At times Fred and Dawson could be seen through the windows busy with charts and war records, from which they carefully verified the manuscript.[973]

In the midst of his work, Grant sometimes paused, short of breath, after an hour or so of dictation or editing. Then at the end of each pain-filled day, Grant's doctors provided some relief with cocaine water. They cleaned out his mouth and throat, which by evening became filled with phlegm and dead tissue. Grant usually waited until after he had completed his work for the day before taking any morphine.[974]

"It was interesting to watch this literary labor on the part of the great captain from the piazza of the hotel that looked down into the cottage," the New York Herald's reporter wrote, "and see how good an example in earnestness of purpose and concentration of thought this very sick man was setting to his able-bodied literary brethren. The common feeling often expressed is that General Grant never fought as well as he fights now. A clerical-looking man, who looked at him from a respectable distance, said that it was the most eloquent and suggestive sermon that he had ever met with."[975]

FINAL VISITATIONS

Guests of the Hotel Balmoral arrived daily on the busy little train or by carriage. For the most part, the visitors were respectful of the general's privacy and sympathetic to his suffering. Every day, long lines of people walked past the cottage, hoping to see the legendary figure. Now and then, Grant—sitting on the porch on sunny afternoons, writing or reading the newspapers—looked up and nodded or waved his hand.[976] If anyone got too close to the cottage, the kindly Sam Willett graciously shooed them away. Always polite to ladies, Grant sometimes tipped his hat if a collection of women walked past.

Thousands of Union army veterans made the pilgrimage to Mount McGregor to get one final glimpse of the great general sitting on the cottage porch, writing his memoirs. They solemnly filed past, sometimes alone or in small groups. Occasionally, the remain-

ing members of a particular regiment gathered in a military formation and marched up to the cottage, then stopped and snapped a
soldierly salute. When this took place, Grant always looked up from
his manuscript and acknowledged the men with a nod or a wave.[977]

In the evenings, the Grant family walked together up the inclined path to dine at the hotel. The general was often too weak to
join them, so he stayed at the cottage and attempted to eat some
soft fruit and drink tea or milk. Although the relatively new hotel
was not yet officially open for the summer season, reporters who
had watched the Grant home on East Sixty-Sixth Street used the
Balmoral's charming dining room as their headquarters. As a result,
the Grant family dined in one of the smaller private dining areas,
which looked out on the porch and the valley beyond.[978]

Grant kept a pad and pencil at his side, scribbling notes to family and doctors. "About an hour ago," he wrote to Dr. Douglas, "I
coughed up a piece of stringy matter about the size of a small liz-
ard." At times he experienced terrifying sensations of being strangled by thick ropes of phlegm.

"I have no desire to live," he scribbled to Reverend Newman
on one particularly difficult day. "But I do not want you to let my
family know this."[979]

One day, when he seemed to drift off into the twilight of death,
he suddenly awoke. "I was passing away peacefully and soon all
would have been over," he wrote. "It was like falling asleep."[980]

When Dr. Shrady arrived at Mount McGregor, he realized
Grant was fading fast, although there was at least a small chance
that he could live for several more months.[981] Believing this possible, he ordered Grant to stop using his voice—if even for a short
time.

"When I visited the general for the first time at Mount McGregor," Shrady recalled, "it was quite evident that he had grown weaker and that he had lost considerably in weight. This was in part due
to his difficulty in swallowing even the liquid food which, for obvious reasons, was his only form of nourishment. His voice at this
time, although not entirely gone, was guttural, of harsh tone, and

very indistinct, except when he used it in a deliberate and studied whisper. Even then he could not always make himself understood. He became much worried over this affliction, and was constantly hoping that it would grow less under the influence of the changed climate.

"In order to give every opportunity for improvement in such direction, he carefully avoided speaking as much as possible," Shrady later wrote, "and would often write on his pad in answering questions rather than otherwise run risk of a set-back. This practice made his remarks necessarily short, but always to the point. This was particularly evident in his replies to my questions, and showed his anxiety on many points and his desire to obtain all the necessary information regarding his physical condition at the time."[982]

"I do not suppose," Grant wrote in a note to him, "I will ever have my voice back again at all." Shrady made no comment.[983]

Shrady later wrote about a conversation he had with the general in those final days at Mount McGregor.

"How have you been doing, General?"

"I am having a pretty tough time, Doctor, although I do not suffer so much actual pain."

"What is the special difficulty?"

"My trouble is in getting my breath."

"How do you sleep?"

"Pretty well, although rarely more than an hour at a time."

To give some encouragement, Shrady remarked that the general looked stronger, notwithstanding his suffering. To this Grant answered in his trademark honest way: "I am growing lighter every day, although I have increased the amount of food. I have gained a little in strength since I came here."

"The air is doing you good, then?"

"I cannot at this moment get a breath through my nostrils."

"By and by I hope you will improve in that respect. What you need is restful sleep in this quiet place."

Grant told Shrady that for the past few nights Dr. Douglas had given him a small dose of morphine at bedtime, and then another dose an hour later. "Last night, however, he reduced the second dose, and I slept well."

Shrady asked about his progress on the book. "I have dictated only twenty pages since we have been here," Grant replied, "and written out with my own hand almost as much more. I have no connected account now to write. Occasionally I see something that suggests a few remarks."[984]

When Grant had trouble breathing that same evening, Shrady gave him morphine, although Grant objected. But he had no choice. Each day brought new coughing fits, which usually ended only when Grant, choking on his own blood, was able to vomit and clear his breathing passages. Shrady reassured the dying general that, while he was in deep discomfort in life, his death would be free of pain.[985]

Shrady observed that when the general was not engaged on his memoirs, he sat for hours on the porch, watching the crowds of sightseers who constantly milled about in front of the cottage.

"Many as they passed the porch would lift their hats in saluta-tion, whereupon the general would quietly and feelingly acknowl-edge the attention. These salutations, however, became so frequent that it was impossible to respond to them, it being generally under-stood that to do so would tire him unnecessarily.

"On one occasion a lady removed her bonnet and waved it in a most deferential manner. This action so appealed to the natural gallantry of the general that he duly acknowledged the courtesy by rising from his chair and lifting his own hat by way of graceful recognition."[986]

JUNE 25, 1885: THE BATH CHAIR

Grant's steadily increasing weakness did not allow him to walk very far. He ventured only short distances, and then always with some-one at his side to steady him.[987]

A welcome diversion came to the general in the form of a gift from Dr. Douglas to help him move around the mountainside more easily. On June 25 a "Bath chair" arrived by train. The contrap-tion—first developed to pull or push vacationers or invalids along the boardwalk at the English seaside town of the same name—had a slanting wicker chair set inside a tub-like wicker body, with two large wheels in the rear and a smaller one up front. The chair could be pulled from the front by means of a wooden tongue with a cross-piece, and pushed from the rear by a rod that was bolted across its back.

It was basically an English version of a rickshaw, enabling the general to travel with his family and some friends up the slightly steep pathway to the veranda of the hotel. Near noon the next day, settling himself into the chair, with the ladies of the family cheerfully walking along beside him and Harrison pulling, occasionally helped by others, Grant set off the short journey up the slope to the Balmoral.

The Daily Saratogian carried the eyewitness story: "When Harrison made a facetious reference to his having become a draught horse, the general smiled, and, drawing forth his pencil wrote the following: 'For a man who has been accustomed to drive fast horses this is a considerable come down in point of speed.' Reply was made that though there was less speed there was more safety."[988]

Grant humorously remarked that often before he had had a much faster horse, but probably no safer one, as he was certain that this animal could not run away uphill. The general joined audibly in the laughter.[989]

When they reached the Hotel Balmoral, the manager offered to carry the Bath chair up onto the veranda.[990] In an unexpected surge of energy, Grant stood and walked up the hotel steps by himself. The Bath chair was carried up the stairs, and he was wheeled up and down the covered piazza, two hundred feet long and twenty feet wide. The hotel boasted the same spectacular views he had seen from the Eastern Outlook.

Grant spent the afternoon sitting in this vehicle on the porch of the hotel as he read the newspapers. Later someone asked if this had been his best day since arriving at Mount McGregor. "Decidedly," Grant replied.[991]

Giving Thanks

A truly special and cherished moment during his stay at Mount Mc-Gregor came when a middle-aged man in dark suit, straw hat, and country shoes came strolling down the path toward the cottage, a broad smile on his face. Fred had invited Charles Wood of Lansingburgh, New York, for a visit—the veteran who had sent Grant $1,000 "on account" after the collapse of Grant & Ward "for services ending about April 1865."

The general received Wood while seated in his armchairs, still tired from his exertions the previous day. The aging veteran was a gracious guest. Knowing that Grant could not speak, he recounted his own time in the Union army, reviewed some of its battles, and then said goodbye—understanding that the general was easily tired by long visits.[992]

Wood carried with him a kind note from his old commander: "I feel very thankful to you for the kindness you did me last summer. I am glad to say that while there is much unblushing wickedness in this world, yet there is a compensating generosity and grandeur of soul. In my case I have not found that Republics are ungrateful nor are the people."[993]

June 28, 1885: Twain's Final Visit

Mark Twain received a telegram from General Grant asking him to come to Mount McGregor to discuss the final additions and edits he was making to *Personal Memoirs*. Twain arrived the next day at 8:00 p.m. Beginning early the next morning, he and Grant spent long hours working over page proofs. The general talked by slips of paper, many of which Twain took with him when he returned to Elmira, New York—his summer writing retreat.

Twain hoped to take a completed version of the memoirs at the end of this visit. All he received from Grant was a series of maps detailing his battles and campaigns. The general penciled, "If I could have two weeks of strength I could improve it very much. As I am, however, it will have to go as is, with verifications by the boys and by suggestions which will enable me to make a point clear here and there."[994] Although somewhat frustrated by the delay, Twain recognized that the more Grant labored on the manuscript, the better it became.

In one of his scribbled notes to Twain, Grant explained, "I have worked harder than if I had been well." He had finished his account of Lee's surrender, and was in the process of writing three short chapters and a chapter titled "Conclusion."[995] With Twain there, Grant wrote a new chapter assessing Lincoln, Stanton, and the major commanders.

As a result of reducing the Vicksburg article, the editors of The Century asked the general to insert transitional sentences. To make this new work for the magazine consistent with the copy in the book, the general needed the publisher's help. Mark Twain and Fred Grant accomplished this in one sitting, lasting from midnight until daybreak.

Grant expressed interest in the sales effort. "He asked me with his pencil, and evidently with anxious solicitude, if there was a prospect that his book would make something for his family," Clemens wrote later. "I said that the canvass for it was progressing vigorously, that the subscriptions and the money were coming in fast, that the campaign was not more than half completed yet, but that if it should stop where it was there would be two hundred thousand dollars coming to his family. He expressed his gratification, with his pencil."[996]

With Twain's assurances, Grant was confident the work itself would provide for Julia long after he had departed. More than 150,000 copies had already been ordered, and subscription agents still had to cover more than half the country. Financial success was certain.

JULY 1, 1885: NOT AS BAD AS THE OTHER

Although most of the work on the memoirs had concluded, Twain remained on the mountaintop to visit with Jesse Grant, who arrived that day. The previous day, James D. Fish of the Marine Bank

had been sentenced to seven years in prison for his part in the Grant
& Ward collapse. Twain joined Buck and Jesse in a discussion of the
verdict as Grant listened.

The judge in the case had remarked that except for his gray
hairs Fish should be serving a sentence seven times seven. Buck
responded that seven years was too short. Jesse cursed Fish. Twain,
summoning his bluest language, helped paint the picture of disdain.
The general took it all in impassively.[997]

"Buck Grant said the bitterest things about him he could frame
his tongue to," Twain remembered. "I was about as bitter myself.
The general listened for some time, then reached for his pad and
pencil and wrote *He was not as bad as the other*—meaning Ward. It
was his only comment. Even his *writing* looked gentle."[998]

After he made this observation, Grant looked off to the hills,
and the conversation about Fish promptly ended.

During Twain's visit, the general penned the five-hundred-
word preface.[999] Grant chose to begin his book with a quote from
Imitation of Christ, by fifteenth-century mystic Thomas à Kempis:[1000]

~

From *Personal Memoirs*

Man proposes and God disposes. There are but few important
events in the affairs of men brought about by their own choice.[1001]

~

At the end of his life, Grant seemed to reflect on the amazing doors
that opened to him and why that may have been so. He wrote to
Dr. Douglas along a similar vein: "It seems that one man's destiny
in this world is quite as much a mystery as it is likely to be in the
next. I never thought of acquiring rank in the profession I was ed-
ucated for; yet it came with two grades higher prefixed to the rank
of General officers for me. I certainly never had either ambition or
taste for political life; yet I was twice president of the United States.
If anyone had suggested the idea of my becoming an author, as they

frequently did, I was not sure whether they were making sport of me or not. I have now written a book which is in the hands of the manufacturers. I have already too many trades to be proficient in any," Grant said facetiously.[1002]

With the work nearly completed, Clemens said his farewell to Grant on July 2, knowing in his heart that he likely would never see the general again.

Adding to Book and Coffin

Certain that he did not have many more days, Grant wrote a letter of farewell to Julia. He could not bear to say this goodbye face-to-face. He took the note and placed it in his coat pocket to be found after his death. In it he confessed that he could sense the end was near. "For the last few days, although my suffering has not been as intense as heretofore, that my end is approaching rapidly I earnestly pray and desire. I am sure I never will leave Mt. McGregor alive. I pray God however that it may be spared to complete the necessary work upon my book. ... But for these considerations I would welcome the arrival of the 'Messenger of Peace', the earlier the better."[1003]

The process of communicating by the small slips of paper had become tedious. The mere effort of writing taxed his strength. But for Grant the book was not yet complete, so he soldiered on as well as he could.

On a cool day as he sat by the fire in the living room, the general had Dawson collect all the various slips of paper and notes he had written in recent days. After studying them for a time, he summoned the stenographer to him. "Then, as the proof sheets were slowly read over, he stopped the reading at different points and dictated short insertions." He refused to allow the pain and weariness to stop him from completing his work. Dawson estimated that the general dictated in a whisper enough material to add another ten printed pages to his book.[1004]

Completely exhausted from the day's exertions, that night the general wrote a whimsical note to Dr. Douglas after whispering a comment that could not be heard: "I said that I had been adding to my book and to my coffin. I presume every strain of the mind or body is one more nail in the coffin." He then explained his motivation for the day's work: "I have worked off all that I had notes of, and which often kept me thinking at night. I will not push to make more notes for the present."

Despite this bedtime promise, the next morning Grant sat in the parlor and once again wrote for nearly an hour "and revised some proof sheets of his book."[1005]

Grant shared with his friend and physician, Doctor Douglas, thoughts from what he was writing: "I have been writing up my views of some of our Generals and of the character of Lincoln and Stanton. I do not place Stanton as high as some people do. Mr. Lincoln cannot be extolled too highly."[1006]

In a state of exhaustion from the constant pain, Grant wrote to Douglas: "The fact is that I am a verb instead of a personal pronoun. A verb is any thing that signifies to be; to do; or to suffer. I signify all three."[1007]

THE LOVE OF A WIFE

Despite her best efforts, Julia could not persuade her husband to rest from his labors. "The general could not be induced to rest long on the piazza," she remembered. "He was so anxious about his book, so afraid of not being able to finish it. After sitting awhile with us, he would take out his little tablets and write, 'It is very pleasant to be here, but I must go to my writing or I fear my book will not be finished.' And so he wrote on and on."[1008]

Mary Robinson had spent most of her life as a slave on the Dent plantation. In an interview for the *Bismarck Daily Tribune*, she shared the story of one of Julia Grant's remarkable dreams. "One day—I'll never forget it as long as I live—Mrs. Grant was sitting in a large rocking chair talking to some of her relatives about family affairs and the financial troubles of her husband. Suddenly she said, 'We will not always be in this condition. Wait until Dudie (her nickname at the time for Ulysses) becomes president. I dreamed last night that he would be elected president.' Every one laughed at this as a capital joke."[1009]

In Grant's last days, Julia watched her suffering, struggling husband—a man who had been underestimated at every stage of his illustrious career—once again digging deep into that mysterious well of courage and tenacity to overcome this final struggle to make sure she and her children would be cared for after his death.

"General Grant," Julia wrote, "the savior of our Union, General Grant, commander-in-chief of 1,000,000 men, General Grant, eight years President of the United States, was writing, writing of his own grand deeds, recording them that he might leave a home and independence to his family. . . . He wrote on and on in his love's labor."[1010]

As her husband's condition worsened, the cocaine treatments he received to ease his pain became more frequent and less effective. "I feel worse this A.M. than I have for some time," he wrote to Douglas one day. "My mouth hurts me and cocaine ceases to give me the relief it once did. If its use can be curtailed I hope it will soon have its effect again."[1011]

July 10, 1885: Harmony and Good Feeling

Of all the friends who had stopped to pay their respects, one whom Grant most eagerly looked forward to seeing was his friend from the West Point days, General Simon Bolivar Buckner. To Dr. Douglas, he enthusiastically wrote: "General Buckner—Fort Donelson will be here on the next train. He is coming up especially to pay his respects."

Buckner was only a year younger than Grant, but he had just remarried and was returning with his young bride from a Niagara Falls honeymoon. It was Buckner who had rescued Grant with a loan in New York City, when the destitute and disgraced captain, after resigning from the army in California, needed money to get home to St. Louis. Then, after the surrender of Fort Donelson, their roles momentarily reversed. "Grant," Buckner remembered, "left the officers of his own army and followed me, with the modest manner peculiar to himself, in the shadow, and there he tendered me his purse."

"I have my full share of admiration and esteem for Grant," said Buckner. "It dates back to our cadet days. He has as many merits and virtues as any man I am acquainted with but he has one deadly defect. He is an incurable borrower and when he wants to borrow he knows of only one limit—he wants what you've got. When I was poor, he borrowed $50 of me; when I was rich, he borrowed 15,000 men."[1012]

Buckner had become a successful Kentucky newspaper editor and politician. He traveled to Mount McGregor with his new wife, Delia Claiborne Buckner. Mrs. Buckner later wrote, "The sole object of General Buckner's visit was to assure [Grant] that the southern people appreciated his magnanimity at Appomattox."[1013]

Grant was very pleased to see Buckner, who entered the sick room and office without his bride. He conversed with Buckner by means of a series of paper slips. "I appreciate your calling very highly," he wrote, then added, "You look very natural, except that your hair has whitened, and you have grown stouter."

After a pause during which Buckner apparently spoke, Grant replied on paper: "I am very glad to see you indeed; and allow me to congratulate you. I still read the papers, and saw a full account of your recent marriage." He slowly scribbled another line: "Is Mrs. Buckner at the house with you? I would be very glad to see Mrs. Buckner, if she can come in and see me as I am now."

The next slip was clearly for the new Mrs. Buckner. "I knew your husband long before you did. We were at West Point together, and served together in the Mexican war. I was with him on a visit to the top of Popocatépetl, the highest mountain in North America. Your husband wrote an account of that trip for publication at the time. I have just written my account, which will be published in my forthcoming book."

Before the Buckners left, Grant wrote his old friend a final, poignant thought: "I have witnessed since my sickness just what I have wished to see ever since the war—harmony and good feeling between the sections. I have always contended that if there had been nobody left but the soldiers we would have had peace in a year . . ."[1014]

"We may now well look forward to perpetual peace at home, and a national strength that will secure us against any foreign complications. I believe myself that the war was worth all it cost us, fearful as that was. Since it was over I have visited every state in Europe and a number in the East. I know, as I did not know before, the value of our inheritance."[1015]

As they departed, reporters followed Buckner and his wife down the sloping walkway to the railroad platform where they shouted for a statement before they boarded the train. Buckner said his visit was "purely personal," and that as a gentleman he could not very well discuss what had passed between him and Grant without the general's permission.

Arriving in New York City, Buckner learned that Grant did indeed think the tenor of their conversation had public import. Buckner shared some of the details of the visit, which then appeared in newspapers across the country.[1016]

Another soldier that received an especially warm welcome from Grant was Colonel John Eaton, who had been charged with relief and resettlement of Blacks during the war. Due to the growth of the tumor, Grant's face was shrouded by a cloth, and Eaton could see little of his features. Grant beckoned him closer with his fingers, then greeted his friend with a note. "I am very glad to see you. I should like to have you say something about our utilizing the Negroes down about Grand Junction, Tennessee. In writing on that subject for my book I had to rely on memory."[1017]

Eaton was amazed and moved that Grant had decided to devote space to the Union army's policy on escaped slaves and Black soldiers alongside the epic chronicle of his own military victories.[1018] The inclusion was yet another example of how Lincoln's views on the participation of African Americans in the national struggle had not only become Grant's views during the war but remained so for the rest of his life.

July 11, 1885: The Providential Extension

By the combined diligence of Grant, Dawson, Fred, Buck, and Jesse, the revised proofs for the first volume of the work were mailed to the publishers on July 11. This was a great relief to all, for everyone knew that the general's mind could not be quieted on that part of the book until it was beyond his reach. Dawson said later that on this date, "At last he had reached the end of all he could do," although "he had intended to have the whole read over to him and have revised it all."[1019]

To Dr. Douglas, Grant wrote the following:

> I am thankful for the providential extension of my time to enable me to continue my work. I am further thankful, and in a much greater degree thankful, because it has enabled me to see for myself the happy harmony which has so suddenly sprung up between those engaged but a few short years ago in deadly conflict.
>
> It has been an inestimable blessing to me to hear the kind expression towards me in person from all parts of our country; from people of all nationalities of all religions, and of no religion, of Confederate and National troops alike. ... They have brought joy to my heart if they have not effected a cure. To you and your colleagues I acknowledge my indebtedness for having brought me through the 'valley of the shadow of death' to enable me to witness these things.[1020]

Although he hoped he could live long enough to complete all the minor changes he wanted to make in *Personal Memoirs*, he told Douglas, "If it is within God's providence that I should go now I am ready to obey His call without a murmur."[1021]

Grant was so intent on finishing the second volume of his book that he gave instructions to his son that if he died and the manuscript was not ready for the printer, Fred should have his body embalmed and delay the funeral to complete the manuscript. "This is now my great interest in life," he wrote, "to see my work done."[1022]

JULY 17, 1885: MERELY A QUESTION OF TIME

Dr. Shrady stayed at the house, relieving Douglas for the night, and he and Grant had a long talk, the general writing his part of the conversation. "He came out on the porch about noon in his gown and blue skull cap," Shrady recalled. "A pillow at the back of his chair reached far above his head. A shawl, fastened to the pillow, covered the right side of his face and neck where the glandular swelling is. The swelling was further protected by a scarf which muffled him closely. The thermometer marked 80 degrees, but he was wrapped from waist to feet in a thick robe. While he was thus enjoying the air and sunshine a photographer got permission to go on the porch and level a camera on him. He sat out doors for nearly four hours altogether."[1023]

Shrady suggested that music might afford him some diversion. To the doctor's surprise, Grant shook his head, and wrote: "I do not know one tune from another. One time in traveling, when there were brass bands everywhere, and all playing the same tune, 'Hail to the Chief,' I remarked at last, with greatest innocence, that I thought I had heard that tune before."

"This frank admission," Shrady observed, "did not imply a personal dislike of music, but rather a lack of appreciation of its beauties; for on a previous occasion I recollect his saying that the playing of spirited and patriotic airs had a very marked effect upon men both before and after a battle.

"Notwithstanding his show of almost cheerfulness at times, he seemingly never lost sight of the final outcome of his disease. It was merely a question of time. After one of the many references to the subject, he significantly wrote his own sad comment: 'I am ready now to go at any time. I know there is nothing but suffering for me while I do live.'

"But," remarked I, "the newspapers should not be the highest authorities for such a prognostication." To this he wrote: "*The New York Times* has been killing me off for a year and a half. If it does not change, it will get [it] right in time."[1024]

Just before Shrady set out for the train to depart on July 18, Grant seemed quite anxious to know when he would come again, expressing the desire that the doctor be with him "at the last." Shrady assured him that he would surely be within call, little thinking at the time that the final summons would come so soon afterward.

"On shaking his hand as he sat in his usual position in his room, he pleasantly asked me in writing if he could do anything for me. I at once bethought myself to obtain his autograph. On his attempting to write with a pencil on his pad, I suggested that it be done with pen and ink, and brought an inkstand, pen, and blank visiting-card to his chair. He wrote his name and handed me the card. This was probably his last signature, as thereafter he evidently became too ill to make any attempt in that direction."[1025]

Before he left, Douglas pulled Shrady aside. "I fear the worst the day the general completes his book."[1026]

JULY 19, 1885: NEVER MORE WILLING TO GO

On the afternoon of July 19, Grant was seated as usual, bundled in his chair and making some final edits to the second volume of the memoirs. Dawson waited patiently, ready to render whatever assistance the general may require. Grant put down his pencil, smiled, and gazed over at the stenographer with a look of deep satisfaction. He looked back down at his paper for another moment and then handed it to Dawson. "The book is finished," he said with that old familiar gleam in his eye.

"I shall never forget his joy at the completion of his book," Dawson remembered. "He was so afraid in the last weeks that he couldn't finish or revise it."[1027] Grant told Dawson he had done all he was going to do. The stenographer remembered the joy with which the general informed his family and his physician that the task was done.

General Grant spent most of that day on the porch of the cottage sitting bundled up in his willow chair. He read the newspapers and altogether passed a restful and uneventful day.

That night Douglas told reporters the disease was not at the moment spreading, and weakness seemed to be the factor most to be considered. "Growing weaker day by day, as the general has been doing now for some days past, will inevitably lead to the end, and that is not very far off."

Several hours after finishing the book, Grant wrote his last message to Douglas: "After all that however the disease is still there and must be fatal in the end. My life is precious of course to my family and would be to me if I could entirely recover. There never was one more willing to go than I am.

"I know most people have first one and then another little something to fix up, and never quite get through. This was partially my case. I first wanted so many days to work on my book so the authorship would be clearly mine. It was graciously granted to me. ... Since then I have added as much as fifty pages to the book, I should think. There is nothing more I should do to it now, and therefore I am not likely to be more ready to go than at this moment."[1028]

"I should prefer going to enduring my present suffering for a single day without hope of recovery."[1029]

Suffering the searing pain and wrenching agony of throat cancer, Ulysses S. Grant had produced 336,000 words,[1030] completing the two volumes of *Personal Memoirs* in the course of one year. As he had so many times in his remarkable life, Grant once again overcame monumental obstacles to achieve something many people said he couldn't do—and, in the process, he created an American literary masterpiece.

In this, Grant's final triumph, he won the race with death to complete his memoirs and secure the financial fortunes of his wife and children. But he also showed the world once, and for all time, that he was much more than a simple Midwestern hack who got lucky. He victoriously restored his legacy as one of the greatest Americans of all time.

For Grant and his family, the end of writing meant the end of the struggle. The time had come for him to finally rest.

Chapter Thirty

8:08

July 1885—Mount McGregor, New York

In his final days, Ulysses wrote a comforting note to his son Fred, who often looked grief-stricken as he diligently cared for his father:

> You ought to feel happy under any circumstances. My expected death called forth expressions of the sincerest kindness from all the people of all the sections of the country. The Confederate soldier vied with the Union soldier in sounding my praise. The Protestant, the Catholic, and the Jew appointed days for universal prayer in my behalf. It looks as if my sickness has had something to do to bring about harmony between the sections. Apparently I have accomplished more while apparently dying than it falls to the lot of most men to be able to do.[1031]

July 20, 1885: Death Seemed to Seize Him

At four in the afternoon of Monday, July 20—the day after he finished his book—Grant wrote to Dr. Douglas: "What do you think of my taking the bath wagon and going down to overlook the south view?" Douglas conducted an examination, found the general's pulse normal and his color good, and agreed.

Grant had visited the Eastern Outlook on June 16, his first full day at Mount McGregor, and he longed to return to that scenic destination, with its wide-angled vista of the Adirondack foothills to the north, the Green Mountains of Vermont to the east, and the Catskills to the south.[1032] This time, Dr. Douglas insisted on coming along. Grant was helped down the steps and then bundled up with a blanket over his lap in the Bath chair. Harrison pulled from the front, while Douglas, Fred, and Sam Willett took turns pushing the bar bolted across the back.

The trip was enjoyable at first, but both doctor and patient had miscalculated his strength. Unlike the first visit to the overlook—when Grant sat and gazed for several moments over the lush, historic valley below—this time he arrived pale, exhausted, and wheezing. Alarmed, Dr. Douglas allowed everyone only a few minutes' rest before the party turned to head back to the cottage.

Although the group intended to limit the general's suffering by taking a shortcut, the route they chose was blocked by a platform the railway used for storing tons of coal. The road back to the cottage continued on the other side of this obstacle. Gasping for breath, Grant was forced to climb out of the Bath chair while the others carried it over the platform. Using his cane, and steadied by Fred, the general struggled around the edges of this irregular pile of coal, occasionally having to go up and down a little valley. When he arrived on the other side, Grant fell back into the chair, completely exhausted.

Everyone was anxious to get back home as soon as possible. The general had been animated and talkative when the outing began, but he had become limp and listless.

Noticing that Grant "was very pale," Douglas and the others took him around to the side of the cottage, "where the steps were few." With the assistance of Fred and the male nurse, Henry McSweeny, the general entered his own room, struggling to breathe.[1033] "He was carried into the drawing room and death seemed to seize him," said Reverend Newman. "We gathered around him and I prayed for him."[1034] Grant sank into his leather armchairs and slipped into a fitful sleep.

"When he arrived at the cottage, he took to his sleeping chair for the night," Shrady later wrote, "and had his usual restless endeavor to compose himself. At 10 p.m. he fell into a sleep of exhaustion and fortunately remained at rest for fully eight hours."

"The trip should not have been made," Douglas told reporters late in the evening, "but we were all at fault for allowing it."[1035]

July 21, 1885: I Wish No One to Be Disturbed

Waking the next morning, Grant appeared weaker than ever. The weather was also uncomfortable, the thermometer hovering around eighty-five degrees. Exhausted and listless, Grant drifted in and out of sleep for most of the day.

Douglas was eating lunch at the hotel when the family sent him word that Grant appeared to be increasingly weak and confused.[1036] The general was uncomfortable and had difficulty breathing, so Douglas administered two small doses of morphine. Concerned for the patient's comfort, McSweeny suggested they move him to a more airy room.

As his leather armchairs were moved, Grant swayed uneasily on his feet. With a trembling step, the general walked from one room to the other while his pillows were readjusted. During this time, he "minutely directed that all his manuscripts and literary effects should be duly cared for and safely packed," Shrady observed, "as all his work was finished in such directions. Alas! All work was soon to be done forever!"[1037]

The hotel manager sent down an ingenious piece of furniture for the suffering commander—a long desk that could be opened up and expanded into a bed. This was placed in a corner of the room under a framed print of Abraham Lincoln. A few feet beyond the foot of the bed was a window, kept open, its lace curtain moving slightly in the breeze.[1038]

Grant remained clearly conscious, fully aware of what transpired. Hearing the voices of his family on the porch at 10:00 p.m., the concerned husband and father whispered, "There's no earthly reason for you to sit up.[1039] Tell them to retire. I wish no one to be disturbed on my account."[1040]

July 22, 1885: The General Surrenders

Early the next morning, Dr. Douglas gave an impromptu medical update to the reporters gathered around the cottage. The *New-York Tribune* reporter telegraphed a story from the Balmoral, stating that

Douglas "said that the patient was in critical condition and he would hazard no prediction, even of the night."[1041]

From the Balmoral, Douglas sent word to the famous surgeon, Dr. H. B. Sands, to come as quickly as possible. He also reached out to Buck and his wife, Fannie, who made plans to arrive at three the next afternoon on a special train.

At noon, the porcelain clock sitting on the mantel in the big parlor began to strike, rousing the general from sleep. When it had finished, Grant wrote a note to Fred: "Fix the clock right. It only struck eleven."[1042] At the urging of his family and doctors, the general tried to eat some food. After a few swallows, he was struck by a violent coughing fit and pushed the food away. He also shook his head at a glass of wine. Then he began hiccupping and could not stop.

Doctors Shrady and Sands arrived by special train on the afternoon of July 22. As the three physicians discussed the state of their patient, Douglas said he feared a heavy dose of morphine would submerge him forever. He decided to administer two minimal doses, which seemed to bring some comfort. Several times Grant got up and sat on the bed while the pillows on the leather armchairs were refreshed. Then he returned to the chairs and continued to doze.

Ulysses revived a little toward dusk and shuffled into the parlor, where he sat beside Julia, holding her hand for a few moments. He quickly grew tired and gestured that he wanted to go lie down again. Julia helped him back to his room and onto his chairs.

There was no question in Douglas's mind that Grant was dying. He administered two hypodermics of brandy, which temporarily steadied the flickering pulse. At that time, the general was still conscious, seated in the cushioned chairs he had occupied continuously, night and day, for months. However, in his exhaustion he asked to be moved to the bed.[1043]

The general was surrendering. His sons transferred him from the leather chairs to the bed. For the first time in many months, the general lay on the bed supine. Julia sat beside him, mopping his brow, never releasing his hand, staring sadly into his face. She, Nellie, the three sons, their wives, Harrison, McSweeny, and the three doctors waited by the bedside.[1044] Slipping in and out of his lucid state, Grant realized he was surrounded by those dearest to him. The mood was one of quiet grief.

Douglas wrote in his diary: "At 7 p.m., while I was seated at the dinner table at the hotel, Harrison came for me, saying that the general had suddenly become weaker. I immediately hastened to the cottage, and found that the general had been transferred from the chair to the bed, which had hastily been prepared for him, and was then lying on his back, a position I had not seen him occupy at any time during his sickness."[1045]

As dusk gave way to darkness, the doctors noticed what they called "a sinking spell"—the result of increasing weakness. Shrady sketched the scene. "A temporary unconsciousness showed itself, and then a troubled, fretful sleep. During one of the wakeful spells, Mrs. Grant asked Rev. Newman to offer a prayer. The general looked appreciatively at the preacher, and apparently in his mute way understood the solemn significance of the ceremony. It was the last prayer to fall on the ears of the one for whom the earnest supplication was being made.

"The clergyman knelt beside the sick chair, and the family stood around it with bowed heads. When it was over, the general looked with a kindly smile to his friend and feebly and feelingly returned the gentle hand-grasp."[1046]

Observing that Grant's "pulse was much weaker and faster," Douglas gave him a "hypodermic of brandy," which "in ten minutes I again repeated." Working in consultation with Shrady and Sands, he wrote, "We all recognized that the end was very near. Every one about the cottage remained up, expecting the end at any moment."

"As the hours grew on," Douglas wrote, "the symptoms of dissolution grew. The respiration quickened, the pulse became small and very frequent, the respiration shallower and quicker, the pulse too frequent to be counted."

Fred asked his father if he was in pain. Quite audibly, Grant said, "No," but his head slumped to one side. Standing next to the bed, Fred put his arm under a pillow, and kept that under his father's head. When Fred asked his father if he wanted anything, Grant replied, "Water." The nurse, McSweeny, placed a wet towel against his mouth.[1047]

JULY 23, 1885: A GENTLE FALLING TO SLEEP

This vigil went on past midnight. Rev. Newman said of the scene: "Mrs. Grant has been sitting with the general. When she speaks to him he opens his eyes. She says little and bears up wonderfully." Other than that, the room remained silent.

At some time after midnight, Douglas encouraged everyone to go to their rooms, in the cottage or at the hotel. Heading up to the hotel himself, he left McSweeny with the unconscious Grant and told the nurse to summon him if there were a change.[1048]

Waking after a few hours of sleep, Douglas took a walk in the cool morning air. "At sunrise, I walked up to the brow of the hill in front of the hotel, just as the first rays of the new day shot over the mountains in the East, and illuminated the valley upon which the general had looked when he took the ride only three days before." Douglas walked down the covered path and returned to the cottage where he found Ulysses S. Grant nearing death.

"Going to the bedside, I found the rhythm of the heart had been so rapid and irregular that the pulse could not be counted," Douglas wrote. "The blue discoloration about the nails presaging approaching dissolution. About seven, Dr. Sands having come down from the hotel, Dr. Shrady and myself met him upon the piazza, and while we were then discussing the situation, Henry came hurriedly out from the parlor, and said that a sudden change had come over the general's features; he thought he was dying. I immediately went in, and confirmed this opinion by my own observations, and sent Henry at once to summon such members of the family as were temporarily absent."[1049]

Fred's nine-year-old daughter, Julia Grant, was with the family and described the somber scene: "As we opened our nursery door and stepped into the hall Harrison rushed across it from my parents to my grandmother's door and knocked there, having left the first door thrown wide open. ... I saw my father throw on his jacket—probably he had been asleep in shirt and trousers, ready for any emergency. ... He rushed out of his bedroom and passed us without seeing us at all, taking the staircase faster than I could imagine his doing. My mother was moving about rapidly, putting on her things, also, and across the hall from grandmamma came a sob, and 'I'm coming,' in reply to Harrison's quick knock."[1050]

In his final moments of life, Grant rested peacefully, surrounded by his loving family.

"Grandmama was crying quietly and was seated by his side," Julia later wrote. "She had in her hands a handkerchief and a small bottle, perhaps of cologne, and was dampening my grandfather's brow. His hair was longer and seemed to me more curled, while his eyes were closed in a face more drawn than usual and much whiter. Beads of perspiration stood on the broad forehead, and as I came forward, old Harrison gently wiped similar drops from the back of the hand which was lying quietly on the chair arm. My father sat at the opposite side from Grandmama, and the doctor and nurse stood at the head, behind the invalid."[1051]

Grant had already told his lifelong friend and former pastor from Galena, Reverend John Heyl Vincent, "I am ready to go. No Grant ever feared death. I am not afraid to die."[1052]

A few hushed moments passed in silence. Julia still held the hand of her Ulys—her Victor. Colonel Grant stroked his father's brow. The general opened his eyes and glanced about him, looking into the faces of all and lingering for a moment as he met the tender gaze of his beloved Julia. Then there was the appearance of falling into a gentle sleep. He lay motionless as everyone looked on.

Ulysses S. Grant was dead. The end of his life had been so quiet and graceful that, Dr. Douglas said, "To be sure it had terminated, we waited a minute. Then looking at my watch, I found it was precisely eight."

The New York Times wrote: "Mrs. Grant could not believe it until the Colonel, realizing the truth, kneeled at the bedside clasping his father's hand. Then she buried her face in her handkerchief."

Later, she wrote of that dark day: "He finished his book about July the nineteenth. His work was done, and to our dismay he grew rapidly weaker and weaker, and on the morning of July the twenty-third, he, my beloved, my all, passed away, and I was alone, alone."[1053]

"It was the calm death he had hoped for," Shrady reflected, "a gentle and gradual falling to sleep. The weary, anxious night had passed, the rays of the morning sun stole quietly into the death-chamber; but at last there was another morning for him, another light, glorious, infinite, immortal."[1054]

As everyone dispersed to their rooms, Fred Grant lingered next to his father. Then he stood and walked over to the clock on the mantel, whose face gave the time as 8:08. He stopped the clock at that moment. It has remained fixed at that time ever since.[1055]

News immediately raced across the nation by telegraph. As planned, church bells and fire bells in every town and city were rung every thirty seconds for exactly thirty-one minutes—sixty-three peals for sixty-three years.[1056]

Fred unexpectedly discovered several items in the pockets of his father's robe, including a ring Julia had given Ulysses many years before. It had come loose when the general's fingers shrank, and he had hidden it in his clothing. Another item was a lock of Julia's hair entwined with a lock of Buck's that he had carried with him in Oregon and California. Fred also found the pencil the general had used to complete *Personal Memoirs*.

And then there was the letter he had written to Julia fourteen days before:

> My Dear Wife:
> There are some matters about which I would like to talk but I cannot. The subject would be painful to you and the children, and, by reflex, painful to me also. When I see you and them depressed I join in the feeling.

I have known for a long time that my end was approaching with certainty ... the end is not far off. ... My will disposes of my property. ... I have left with Fred a memorandum giving some details of how the proceeds of my book are to be drawn from the publisher.

Look after our dear children and direct them in the paths of rectitude. It would distress me far more to hear that one of them could depart from an honorable, upright and virtuous life than it would to know that they were prostrated on a bed of sickness from which they were never to rise alive. They have never given us any cause for alarm on this account, and I trust they never will.

With these few injunctions and the knowledge I have of your love and affection and the dutiful affection of all our children, I bid you a final farewell, until we meet in another and, I trust, better world. You will find this on my person after my demise."[1057]

Grant's body had shrunk to a mere ninety pounds.[1058] A local funeral director named Ebenezer Holmes placed Grant's remains in his patented ice coffin to preserve the body before it decayed in the summer heat. Undertaker Stephen Merritt then arrived to complete the embalming process.[1059]

A death mask was fitted by Karl Gerhardt, Mark Twain's friend who had done the sculpture of Grant that his family liked so much.

Instead of a military uniform, Grant was dressed in attire befitting a two-term president—a Prince Albert suit of black broadcloth, his feet covered in white stockings and black patent leather slippers. A white linen standing collar covered his neck, graced with a black bow tie. There were no military decorations—no swords or sashes—they had all been donated to the Smithsonian Institution in Washington as part of the settlement of his loan with William Vanderbilt.[1060]

Fred slipped around his father's shrunken finger the ring Julia had given him.[1061] The Colonel lifted his father's right hand and placed it across his breast and arranged the left arm by his side. Then the casket's heavy plate glass top was screwed into place and Grant's remains were covered with an American flag.[1062]

A Final Resting Place

Soon after Grant's death, General Phil Sheridan wired, informing the family that they could bury the general in the park surrounding the Soldier's Home in Washington. At the same time, the governor of Ohio reached out to promise that the legislature would provide a site at either Point Pleasant or Georgetown.[1063] Many people called for the general to be buried at Arlington National Cemetery. Even Galena, Illinois, made an offer to have Grant interred in their city.

Remembering his father's final preference for a site in New York City, Fred wired Mayor William Grace. The mayor sent Chief Clerk W. L. Turner to Mount McGregor to inform the family that the City Board of Aldermen had voted to appropriate a site in one of the public parks.

Julia wanted the general to be buried in Central Park, near their home on East Sixty-Sixth Street. But by 1885, Central Park was well established, having been acquired by the city in 1856. Local residents did not want to add a mausoleum to the popular attraction.

Mayor Grace suggested an alternative at the "prominent height" and natural beauty of the relatively new Riverside Park in the Claremont area on Riverside Drive. The area extended northward from Eighty-Sixth Street, gradually ascending a high bluff that ended at 122nd. The bluff plummeted rapidly to the Hudson River below, presenting a view of the Palisades stretching north and the Jersey piers and railroad terminals to the south.[1064]

On July 27, Fred and Jesse Grant left Mount McGregor for a meeting with the mayor of New York City to tour several possible interment sites. The small delegation included trusted family and friends, including General Porter, General Sherman, and former Colorado senator Jerome B. Chaffee.

The group visited several sites in the city, including Central Park and Riverside Park. As Mayor Grace anticipated, the group considered Central Park too crowded and noisy, but all of them approved of Riverside Park.[1065]

"Mother takes Riverside Park," wired Fred.

The entire family agreed that Riverside Park would be the ideal resting place. In a widely published letter written to the Mayor of New York City, Julia Grant indicated her strong support of that city as the final resting place of her husband. "Riverside was selected by myself and my family as the burial place of my husband, General Grant. First, because I believed that New York was his preference. Second, it is near the residence that I hope to occupy as long as I live, and where I will be able to visit his tomb often." She believed the location would be convenient for many Americans to visit. And most important for her, she would be given a final resting place next to her beloved Ulys.[1066]

As flags flew at half-mast across the nation, the Grant family conducted their own funeral at Mount McGregor—the only service Julia attended. Although it was intended to be a small affair among close friends, word got out to the public, and thousands attended.[1067]

Mark Twain entered the debate about General Grant's final resting place in a letter to *The Sun*: "We should select a grave which will not merely be in the right place now, but will still be in the right place 500 years from now," he maintained. "How does Washington promise as to that? ... But as long as American civilization lasts New York will last." In answer to the objection that New York was not "national ground," Mark Twain responded resolutely, "Wherever General Grant's body lies, that is national ground."[1068]

Chapter Thirty-One

A SOLDIER'S FAREWELL

Lower Manhattan had not been invaded since the days of the American Revolution. But on August 8, 1885, as the streets and windows reflected the moonlight, ferries began arriving at Battery Park, carrying soldiers from Governor's Island—American soldiers, prepared to take their place in the largest funeral procession in the history of New York City. The brick streets and stone walls reverberated with the sounds of boots and horses moving into position to begin the day's solemn and somber parade.

With the first glimmer of light peeking over the Atlantic horizon, another army—all civilians—began walking across the Brooklyn Bridge to Manhattan.[1069] Tens of thousands took the footway over to Manhattan. On the western side of the island, ferries from Hoboken and Jersey City were crowded with guests journeying from as far away as Washington, DC.

Every available passenger train had been scheduled for duty in and around New York City by the Pennsylvania, the Central, the New Haven, and the Harlem River Railroads. Most of the trains were so long they required two locomotives. The New York Elevated passenger trains transported more than six hundred thousand spectators that day.[1070]

The United States Army had commandeered every horse from every stable in Manhattan for the military escort. The government hired every cab, and then went on to borrow as many carriages as it could from city residents.

Hundreds of bright sailboats had anchored in the Hudson River so people could watch the funeral through binoculars or spyglasses—from Stevens Point in upper Manhattan around to the Narrows on the East River.

Below the bluff at Riverside Park, five US Navy warships waited at anchor on the Hudson, including the flagship of Admiral Jouett, the *Despatch*. Behind it were the *Omaha*, the *Swatara*, the *Alliance*, and the *Powhatan*, which had been Commodore Matthew Perry's flagship when he landed at Nagasaki, Japan, in 1853. At the end of the line, in a place of honor, was the revenue cutter, the *U. S. Grant*.

Following navy tradition, at dawn the bo'sun piped "all hands on deck," which began the ceremony of "cockbilling the yards," the mariners' sign of grief—the "yards" being the spars that support the sails. At the command "sway," the foreyard of each ship was lowered to port, and then the main yards to starboard. There they were made fast, and the colors were dipped to half-mast. The sailors were all dressed in mourning garb—white cap, white jacket, and black trousers.[1071]

Throughout Manhattan, residents heard the steady clip-clop of the horses' hooves along with the cadence of marching men, as soldiers and police surrounded City Hall.

Military units from across America assembled on their assigned streets. On that day, twenty years after the surrender at Appomattox, some units found themselves placed next to regiments that had been enemies in the war. On Broome Street in downtown, men of the Virginia State Guard lined up beside the First Massachusetts Infantry. Their forebears had fought bloody battles against each other at first and second Bull Run.[1072]

The number of former Confederate soldiers present made an impression on onlookers. "It was quite a sight to see the Stonewall Brigade march up Fifth Avenue with their drums marked Staunton, Virginia," observed one mourner. "They wore the grey, with a black and brass helmet. There were several companies of Virginia and Southern troops."

Contingents of Black veterans were also liberally represented, along with eighteen thousand veterans of the Grand Army of the Republic.[1073]

Mayor William R. Grace led a delegation up the City Hall steps that included members of the Grant family—minus Julia, who remained secluded in mourning at Mount McGregor. They were followed by a contingent of ministers and the honorary pallbearers named by President Cleveland—including General William T. Sherman, Lieutenant General Philip Sheridan, Admirals David Dixon Porter and John L. Worden, Vice-Admiral Stephan T. Rowan, Hamilton Fish, George Boutwell, Senator John A. Logan, George Jones, Oliver Hoyt,[1074] and Rabbi E. B. M. Browne.[1075]

The public expected close comrades like William T. Sherman and Philip H. Sheridan to serve as honorary pallbearers. But in the twenty years since the Civil War, Ulysses S. Grant had become a symbol of North and South reconciliation. Julia Grant insisted that two Confederate generals be added to balance their Federal counterparts. The Grant family chose Generals Joseph Johnston and Simon Buckner for that honor.

The men of the Grand Army Guard grasped the silver bars on either side of the casket, carried it down the steps of City Hall, and carefully placed it on the catafalque. Also standing on the steps, the Liederkranz Society sang Schubert's *"Geisterchore"*—the song of spirits over the water—and the "Pilgrim's Chorus" from Tannhauser. The funeral hearse, covered by a black canopy, was led by twenty-four black horses, each attended by an African American groom. Each horse was draped in black; each groom was dressed in broadcloth and wearing a black silk hat.[1076]

Reverend Newman led nine other ministers down to the sidewalk. Behind them came Doctors Douglas, Shrady, and Sands, wearing wide mourning sashes of black and white.

An African American coachman, Albert Hawkins, drove the hearse. He had chauffeured Grant as secretary of war and later as president. He had stayed on at the White House and asked President Cleveland for the honor of driving General Grant to his final resting place.[1077]

General Hancock served as escort commander. He wore a gold-trimmed admiral's hat and knee-length coat; his chest glittered with a gold sash. Hancock, mounted on a splendid black charger, rode to the front of twenty other generals on horseback at the head of the parade.[1078] He was followed by the mounted members of his staff and eight brigadiers, including Fitzhugh Lee, the grandson of Lighthorse Harry and the nephew of Robert E. Lee. The gold helmets with white plumes, gold epaulets, white gauntleted gloves, and shiny medals all seemed incandescent as they reflected the bright morning sun.[1079]

Riding spirited horses, the generals maneuvered themselves into line in order of seniority. The army was experimenting with new uniforms, some officers wearing fore 'n' aft gold-trimmed hats like those worn by admirals. Others wore a belted tunic and a German-style steel helmet, with either a spike or white plume. Medals glistened on the chest of every officer.

At 9:30 a.m., all was in readiness for the procession to be underway. General Hancock raised a white-gauntleted hand and thrust it to the north, his strong voice crying out, "Forward March!" Behind the escort, the David's Island Military Band stepped off, playing Beethoven's "*Marche Funèbre*." After them came the West Point Corps of Cadets, the clergymen, and the hearse. In the custom of formal military funerals, a soldier marched beside the coffin, leading a riderless horse with boots reversed in the stirrups.[1080]

At the moment of Hancock's order, a signal flashed from Western Union to St. Paul's and Trinity Church, then to the city's other churches so that the sound of tolling bells filled the air. That sound echoed across the country as sextons in many states received the electronic signal to sound their church bells.[1081]

As the funeral parade moved forward from City Hall, the procession flowed with flawless precision. Uniformed soldiers filling fifty side streets, east and west of Broadway, waited patiently for the escort commander to pass and then fell into their assigned place. Armed troops, carrying weapons reversed in the traditional manner, preceded the catafalque.

Detachments of sailors wore blue uniforms with white leggings and hats. Then came a marine division in white trousers, blue coats with yellow epaulets, and white caps with black brims. There were National Guard regiments and brigades from every state that had fought for the Union. Black "Buffalo Soldiers" from the southwest followed Pennsylvania Zouaves in red pantaloons. These were followed by the governor's footguards from Connecticut in colorful uniforms with crisscrossed white chest belts.

When the last of the soldiers had joined the line at noon, the command stretched for two and one-half miles. The men marched with fixed bayonets, a river of gleaming steel spikes moving in lockstep.[1082]

The funeral procession was a marvel of military drill and precision. In all, sixty thousand armed men paraded the length of the city.

The catafalque was flanked by an honor guard, followed by carriages filled with the pallbearers.[1083] President Grover Cleveland shared a carriage drawn by six bay horses with Secretary of State Thomas Francis Bayard. Ex-Presidents Rutherford B. Hayes and Chester A. Arthur were directly behind. Members of the Supreme Court followed. The carriages of the governors were arranged in the order in which their states had entered the union.

From City Hall, spreading southeast and west were eighteen thousand men of the Grand Army of the Republic led by Major General Dan Sickles. Carriages for disabled veterans lined the length of Canal Street three abreast. Even a complement of the "Old Guard"—soldiers mustered out before the Civil War began—marched in bearskin caps, white coats, and blue trousers.

Mayor William Grace led a contingent of carriages that followed the soldiers, filled with eight thousand civil and municipal dignitaries from across America. Delegations from various societies and fraternities made up the tail of the massive cortege.

Nearly two hundred fife and drum corps and musical units marched in the line, playing funeral dirges such as "Nearer My God to Thee," Sullivan's "Lost Chord," and Beethoven's "Hymn to Night." Some of the bands also played Civil War era songs and marches, including Rudolph Aronson's "Memorial March," composed especially for this occasion.[1084]

The line of march stretched half the length of Manhattan—up Broadway from City Hall to Fourteenth Street, west to Fifth Avenue, north up to Fifty-Seventh Street, again west to Broadway, which traverses Manhattan at an angle, north again to Seventy-Second Street, then west to Riverside Drive, proceeding north to the temporary tomb at 122nd Street.

"Broadway moved like a river," one spectator observed, "a river into which many tributaries were poured. There was one living mass choking the thoroughfare from where the dead lay in state to the grim gates at riverside open to receive him. From 14th Street to the top of the hill, pavements, windows, curbs, steps, balcony, and housetops were teeming with mourners. All walls and doorways were a sweep of black."[1085]

More than a million and a half spectators jammed the streets, sitting on window ledges and statues, climbing up trees, occupying the porches of empty houses, straddling the tops of lampposts and telephone poles, and crowding dangerously onto rooftops. It was the largest funeral in the history of New York City—bigger even than the funeral for Abraham Lincoln. By early afternoon, people were backed up along the bluffs above the Hudson River.[1086]

Mark Twain watched the funeral pageant for five hours from his office windows on Fourteenth Street at Union Square.[1087] Fifty years old, Twain was at the peak of his powers when Ulysses S. Grant died.[1088] He considered the publishing of *Personal Memoirs of Ulysses S. Grant* as one of his greatest accomplishments.[1089] "I think his book kept him alive several months," Twain wrote when he heard the news of Grant's death. "He was a very great man and superlatively good."[1090]

Amid the tens of thousands watching the somber event from offices and homes, one man stood in another window next to a police officer, hidden behind smoked glasses—Ferdinand Ward, the self-confessed most hated person in America. With his trial approaching, he had bribed a shady cop to allow him to leave the Ludlow Street Jail to view the funeral.

Delusional to the end, Ward never admitted to committing a crime and believed that he and Grant had remained friends. "Our friendship never changed through all the period of stress and trouble," he later told a reporter, "but remained until the time of his death."

Grant's family and friends knew better. "Wall Street killed him," Sherman told the press. "There isn't any doubt about it. He would have been alive today, if he hadn't fallen into the hands of Ward and those fellows."[1091]

Windows of large warehouses along the way had been cleared of goods so spectators could look out from them. From myriad balconies, proper ladies viewed the procession through lorgnettes. Countless gentlemen wore watch chains with a "Grant" pennant, while ladies donned "Grant" medallions sold at stores such as Bloomingdale's.[1092]

The only considerable delay on the funeral route came when the catafalque could not pass under the elevated railway structure at Seventy-Second Street and had to make a detour of several blocks.[1093] When Hancock's escort broke on the knoll at Riverside and Seventy-Second Street, they saw the massive naval vessels floating in the Hudson below.

By midafternoon, the funeral cortege reached Riverside Park and the small temporary brick tomb at Riverside Drive and 122nd Street. Hancock ordered "Route March," and the men shifted their weapons more comfortably. The tail end of the procession did not arrive until just before 5:00 p.m. when the burial service was scheduled to begin.[1094]

The service included a public ceremony, singing, and prayer. Then to the strains of Chopin's "Funeral March," Hancock ushered the honorary pallbearers into the temporary tomb—a small, simple brick structure facing the Hudson River, covered by a barrel arch with a cross on top at the front. A large iron *G* hung on the front gate.

The honor guard carried the casket from the catafalque into the tomb, where they laid it on two steel beams supported at each end by blocks of marble. Sherman stood at the head of Grant's casket, as Reverend Newman offered a final benediction. Reporters noted that pallbearers Johnston, Sherman, Sheridan, and Buckner—with their heads collectively bent—were solemn and tearful. Flowers were placed on the casket.[1095]

"God of battles," Hancock spoke forcefully, "Father of all. Amidst this mournful assembly we seek Thee with whom there is no death."[1096]

The American flag that had been on Grant's coffin was folded by the burial detail into a triangle. An officer somberly presented it to Colonel Frederick Grant. An enlisted man placed a simple wreath made by Grant's granddaughter, Julia, on top of her grandfather's coffin. Everyone filed out of the tomb, and a soldier closed and locked the metal gates.[1097]

A sailor with a semaphore flag signaled the warships in the Hudson. Their guns let loose a final 21-gun cannonade salute to General and President Ulysses S. Grant.

A bugler paced alone to the center of the tomb as every soldier came to ramrod attention. He placed the gleaming instrument to his lips and reverently played "Taps"—the same tune that floated over Grant's army camps at dusk during the war.[1098] As the notes rang out above the hushed crowd, William Tecumseh Sherman, saluting his fallen friend and standing at rigid attention, silently wept.[1099]

~

FROM *PERSONAL MEMOIRS*

The cause of the great War of the Rebellion against the United States will have to be attributed to slavery. For some years before the war began it was a trite saying among some politicians that "A state half slave and half free cannot exist." All must become slave or all free, or the state will go down. I took no part myself in any such view of the case at the time, but since the war is over, reviewing the whole question, I have come to the conclusion that the saying is quite true.[1100]

This war was a fearful lesson, and should teach us the necessity of avoiding wars in the future.[1101]

It is possible that the question of a conflict between races may come up in the future, as did that between freedom and slavery before. The condition of the colored man within our borders may become a source of anxiety, to say the least. But he was brought to our shores by compulsion, and he now should be considered as having as good a right to remain here as any other class of our citizens.[1102]

I feel that we are on the eve of a new era, when there is to be great harmony between the Federal and the Confederate. I cannot stay to be a living witness to the correctness of this prophecy; but I feel it within me that it is to be so. The universally kind feeling expressed for me at a time when it was supposed that each day would prove my last, seemed to me the beginning of the answer to "Let us have peace."[1103]

POSTSCRIPT

The two-volume set of *Personal Memoirs of U. S. Grant* was published by Mark Twain's firm, Charles L. Webster & Company, shortly after Grant's death in 1885. The ten thousand agents spread across the country followed a sales manual written by Twain, encouraging them to use "the Bull Run voice" and to "keep pouring hot shot" into the customers until they made their purchase.[1104] Mark Twain dubbed this "the vastest book enterprise the world has ever seen."[1105]

Altogether, the literary marketing army sold more than 312,000 two-volume sets of *Personal Memoirs of Ulysses S. Grant* at prices from $3.50 to $12, depending on the binding—624,000 books total. Each copy included a facsimile of a handwritten note from Grant himself.

Seven months after her husband's death, Twain presented Julia Grant with the largest single royalty in the history of publishing up to that time: $200,000. In the end, she received nearly $450,000— equal to more than ten million dollars today. No previous book had ever sold so many copies in such a short period of time. Grant's book rivaled the popularity of another nineteenth-century sensation, *Uncle Tom's Cabin*.[1106]

Charles L. Webster & Company cleared $200,000 on the first edition, and $50,000 on each of two subsequent editions, published in 1892 and 1894.[1107] *Personal Memoirs* became a treasure of American literature and is recognized as one of the enduring masterpieces of military autobiography.[1108]

The money earned from the great success of the book secured Julia's widowhood. She used a portion to pay off $187,900 of Grant & Ward debts that bore the general's endorsements. Julia Grant continued to live in Washington and New York and she traveled frequently through Europe. She lent her energies to the cause of women's suffrage and befriended Varina Davis, the widow of Jefferson Davis.[1109] Julia also devoted herself to her twelve grandchildren.

HONORS FOR THE GENERAL

"Out of the hubbub of the war Lincoln and Grant emerge, the towering majestic figures," wrote Walt Whitman. Observing how these two men rose from obscurity to the highest office in the land, Whitman believed their lives demonstrated how people lifted from the lower classes of American society could overcome all obstacles in a climb to greatness. "I think this is the greatest lesson of our national existence so far."[1110]

During his illness, a tremendous outpouring of sympathy and respect for Ulysses S. Grant poured in from across America, North and South.

African American churches across the country held "meetings of sorrow" that eulogized Grant as a champion of the Fifteenth Amendment and the fight against the Ku Klux Klan. George M. Arnold, an African American leader from Washington, DC, wrote to Fred Grant asking him "to let General Grant know how the Colored people of this country feel towards him, how they love, honor, and pray for him."[1111]

Frederick Douglass eulogized Grant as "a man too broad for prejudice, too humane to despise the humblest, too great to be small at any point. In him the Negro found a protector, the Indian a friend, a vanquished foe a brother, an imperiled nation a savior."[1112]

At the time of his death, *The Jewish Record,* a Philadelphia newspaper, wrote of Grant: "None will mourn his loss more sincerely than the Hebrew, and ... in every Jewish synagogue and temple in the land the sad event will be solemnly commemorated with fitting eulogy and prayer."[1113]

Speaking of the man who had been his friend at West Point, who fought by his side in Mexico, and who was married to his cousin, General James Longstreet declared that Ulysses S. Grant "was the truest as well as the bravest man that ever lived."

The former Confederate general recalled the moment he saw Grant at Appomattox: "The first thing that General Grant said to me when we stepped inside, placing his hand in mine, was, 'Pete, let us have another game of brag ...'"—a card game they had played together as fellow soldiers during the Mexican War—...'to recall the days that were so pleasant.' Great God! I thought to myself, how my heart swells out to such magnanimous touch of humanity. Why do men fight who were born to be brothers?"[1114]

When asked by a reporter who was the greatest Northern general, Longstreet did not hesitate: "Grant—incomparably the greatest."[1115]

During Grant's illness, telegrams arrived from Jefferson Davis, the sons of Robert E. Lee, and the sons of Albert Sidney Johnston.[1116] The editor of South Carolina's *News and Courier* wrote at the time of Grant's death: "Had his life ended but a few years since, the mourning for the great leader would have been more or less sectional in its manifestation. Dying as he now dies, the grief is as widespread as the Union."[1117]

THE GENERAL GRANT NATIONAL MEMORIAL

Julia could not bring herself to attend the massive funeral in New York City, saying that it would only add to her sorrow. But she was seated on the grandstand on her husband's seventy-fifth birthday, April 27, 1897, for the dedication of his ornate tomb. On that cool spring day, more than one million people gathered as President William McKinley and General Horace Porter presided over the dedication of the General Grant National Memorial. In time, the neo-classical structure would come to be known simply as "Grant's Tomb."

Sitting atop a hill on the north end of Manhattan's Riverside Park, 270 feet above the Hudson River, the massive 160-foot granite and marble tomb was an architectural masterpiece, designed to inspire awe.[1118] The project was financed by public contributions—and leading the fundraising drive was the lawyer Richard T. Greener, the first Black graduate of Harvard College. In 1892, Horace Porter took over as president of the Grant Monument association and led the drive to finish the fundraising and begin construction. When completed, Grant's Tomb became the largest mausoleum in North America.

President William McKinley gave a short, gracious tribute during the dedication: "A great life never dies. Great deeds are imperishable; great names immortal. General Grant's services and character will continue undiminished in influence, and advance in the estimation of mankind so long as liberty remains the corner-stone of free government and integrity of life the guaranty of good citizenship."[1119]

When Julia Grant died of heart failure in 1902 at age seventy-six, she was laid to rest next to her beloved "Ulys." They lay encased in red granite sarcophagi at the center of the open structure.

Grant's tomb quickly became New York's number one tourist destination.[1120] The mausoleum became a sacred pilgrimage destination for Union veterans and their families from all over the country. Many thousands gathered for regularly scheduled ceremonies on Grant's birthday, Memorial Day, and the Fourth of July. Presidents and other prominent politicians selected the spot for speeches and important announcements. Foreign dignitaries visited frequently to pay their respects. Until 1916, it attracted five to six hundred thousand people annually, more visitors than even the Statue of Liberty. It maintained extremely high levels of visitation through the 1920s.[1121]

"The tomb is not a mere building," National Park historian David M. Kahn said of Grant's final resting place. "It is a monument, and as such it embodies the spirit and ideals of the American people at a particular point in history. The mammoth and costly building in a very real sense symbolizes an entire generation's feeling not just about Grant, but about the Civil War and the role every foot soldier played in it."[1122]

In 1900, Vice President Theodore Roosevelt shared his thoughts regarding Grant's place in the American pantheon: "As the generations slip away, as the dust of conflict settles, and as through the clearing air we look back with keener wisdom into the nation's past, mightiest among the mighty dead loom the three great figures of Washington, Lincoln, and Grant. There are great men also in the second rank; for in any gallery of merely national heroes Franklin and Hamilton, Jefferson and Jackson, would surely have their place. But these three greatest men have taken their place among the great men of all nations, the great men of all time."[1123]

Walt Whitman saved his more poetic admiration for Ulysses S. Grant for his book, *Specimen Days*:

> What a man he is! What a history! What an illustration—his life—of the capacities of that American individuality common to us all. .... He proves how an average western farmer, mechanic, boatman, carried by tides of circumstances, perhaps caprices, into a position of incredible military or civil responsibilities ... may steer his way fitly and steadily through them all, carrying the country and himself with credit year after year—command over a million armed men—fight more than fifty pitch'd battles—rule for eight years a land larger than all the kingdoms of Europe combined—and then, retiring, quietly (with a cigar in his mouth) make the promenade of the whole world, through its courts and coteries, and kings and czars and mikados ... as phlegmatically as he ever walk'd the portico of a Missouri hotel after dinner ... Seems to me it transcends Plutarch. How those old Greeks, indeed, would have seized on him! A mere plain man—no art, no poetry. ... A common trader, money maker, tanner, farmer of Illinois—general for the republic ... in a war of attempted secession—President following, (a task of peace, more difficult than the war itself)—nothing heroic, as the authorities put it—and yet the greatest hero. The gods, the destinies, seem to have concentrated upon him.[1124]

ACKNOWLEDGMENTS

I want to thank John Marszalek, Executive Director of the Ulysses S. Grant Presidential Library at Mississippi State University. Thanks also to his helpful and courteous staff and colleagues—David S. Nolen, Ryan P. Semmes, Eddie Rangel, and Kate Salter Gregory.

I'm most grateful for the assistance and encouragement from Ben Kemp, Operations Manager at the U. S. Grant Cottage State Historical Site on Mount McGregor in Wilton, NY. Ben was not only helpful with fact-checking, photographic information, and overall encouragement, but he also stepped up to write the eloquent, moving foreword. I'm also grateful to the excellent, friendly staff at Grant Cottage. My daughter, Margo, and I visited the cottage in the summer of 2018 and enjoyed the informative tour, museum, and bookshop.

I'm also thankful for the assistance and support from Greg Roberts, Curator of the U.S. Grant Birthplace, Point Pleasant, Ohio, and the Village Administrator in New Richmond, Ohio. Thanks also to Jim Godburn, Education Specialist at Sailor's Creek Battlefield Historical State Park in Rice, Virginia.

Thanks to the project manager for my last three books, Ann Tatlock, who has been a source of encouragement and strength through this long journey. Thanks also to my editor with the eagle eye, Denise Loock. Thanks to the support team at Iron Stream Media/LPC Books: John Herring, Bradley Isbell, Shonda Savage Whitworth, Kim McCulla, Tina Atchenson, Ramona Pope Richards, Cindy Sproles, and Eddie Jones. Thanks to my agent, Del Duduit, for his support and encouragement. Thanks to the staff and leadership at Inspiration Ministries. Special thanks for the support of my colleagues on the Digital team, in particular Michael Black, Greg Bentley, Bernard Baker, John Ferrell, and Willie Mangum.

My interest in the final two years of Ulysses S. Grant's life began sometime in the 1990s when I first viewed *The Civil War* by Ken Burns. I am thankful for Ken Burns, along with writers Ric Burns and Geoffrey C. Ward, whose work set me on this path of discovery. Living in Virginia at that time, I began a tradition of visiting Civil War battlefields, which continues to this day.

My thanks and gratitude to the amazing battlefield guides and expert staff at the battlefields, museums, national parks, and historical sites I have visited on this journey. For the complete list of the sites, visit https://www.vonbuseck.com/single-post/us-grant-sites-visited.

Thanks to my parents, Clem and Carol Buseck, for their ongoing love and support. Thanks to my siblings for their encouragement and support over the years—Barbie MacFarland, Dawn Buseck, Sean von Buseck, and Erin Staaf. I also thank my children, Aaron and Julie, David, and Margo for their unending love, assistance, and encouragement. My kids have traveled with me to many of these historic sites, but most importantly, they have traveled on the journey to make these stories known through books, articles, and film. With much love and gratitude.

NOTES

Chapter One: World Tour

[1] Perrett, Geoffrey, *Ulysses S. Grant: Soldier & President* (New York: Modern Library–Random House, 1999/1997), 453–454.

[2] McClure, James Baird, *Stories, Sketches and Speeches of General Grant at Home and Abroad: In Peace and in War* (Chicago: Rhodes & McClure, Publishers, 1879), 162.

[3] Brier, Bob, *Cleopatra's Needles: The Lost Obelisks of Egypt* (London: Bloomsbury Publishing, 2016), 159–160.

[4] McClure, *Stories*, 162.

[5] Chernow, Ron, *Grant* (New York: Penguin Press, 2017), 871–872.

[6] Brands, H. W., *The Man Who Saved the Union: Ulysses Grant in War and Peace* (New York: Doubleday–Random House, 2012), 583.

[7] Young, John Russell, *Around the World with General Grant* (Baltimore: The Johns Hopkins University Press, 2002/1879), 111–115.

[8] Young, *Around the World*, 118–121.

[9] Chernow, *Grant*, 872.

[10] Brands, *The Man*, 583–584.

[11] Chernow, *Grant*, 872.

[12] Young, *Around the World*, 122–123.

[13] Brands, *The Man*, 584.

[14] Young, *Around the World*, 154–155.

[15] Brands, *The Man*, 584–586.

[16] Young, *Around the World*, 157.

[17] Chernow, *Grant*, 874–875.

[18] Young, *Around the World*, 158.

[19] Chernow, *Grant*, 243.

[20] Chernow, *Grant*, 243.

[21] Chernow, *Grant*, 243.

[22] Young, *Around the World*, 158.

[23] Fellman, Michael, *Introduction* in Young, John Russell, *Around the World with General Grant* (Baltimore: The Johns Hopkins University Press, 2002/1879), 186.

[24] Young, *Around the World*, 215–216.

[25] Grant, Julia, *Memoirs*, Edited by John Y. Simon (New York: G. Putnam's Sons, 1975), 268.

[26] Young, *Around the World*, 371–373.

[27] Dukes, Sabrina, "General Grant National Memorial (Grant's Tomb)," *Riverside Park Conservancy*, February 8, 2013, https://riversideparknyc.org/places/general-grant-national-memorial-grants-tomb/.

[28] Chernow, *Grant*, 861.

Chapter Two: Grant & Ward

[29] Chernow, *Grant,* 900.

[30] Twain, Mark, *Autobiography of Mark Twain, Volume 1*, Edited by Harriet Elinor Smith (Berkeley, CA: University of California Press, 2010), 483.

[31] White, Ronald C., *American Ulysses* (New York: Penguin Random House, 2016), 623.

[32] Moser, Rick, "American Ulysses tries to set the record straight on the Civil War general," *Chicago Tribune,* October 21, 2016, https://www.chicagotribune.com/entertainment/books/ct-books-1030-american-ulysses-grant-ronald-white-20161020-story.html.

[33] White, *American Ulysses,* 623.

[34] White, *American Ulysses,* 624–625.

[35] Grant, Julia, *Memoirs,* 323.

[36] Perrett, *Ulysses S. Grant,* 466.

[37] Chernow, *Grant,* xvii.

[38] Perry, Mark, *Grant and Twain* (New York, Random House, 2004), xx–xxi.

[39] Green, Horace, *General Grant's Last Stand* (New York: Charles Scribner's Sons, 1936), 271.

[40] Goldhurst, Richard, *Many Are the Hearts: The Agony and the Triumph of Ulysses S. Grant* (New York: Readers Digest Press, 1975), 14–15.

[41] Green, *General,* 272.

[42] Perry, *Grant and Twain*, xx–xxi.

[43] Goldhurst, *Many,* 14–15.

[44] Firstladies.org, "First Lady Biography: Julia Grant," www.firstladies.org/biographies/firstladies.aspx?biography=19.

[45] Perry, *Grant and Twain*, xx–xxi.

[46] Lynghaug, Fran, *The Official Horse Breeds Standards Guide* (Stillwater, MN: Voyageur Press, 2009), 70. https://www.google.com/books/edition/The_Official_Horse_Breeds_Standards_Guide/myQBSVVEhagC?hl=en&gbpv=1&dq=The+stallion+he+call+Leopard,+and+the+Barb,+he+named+Linden+Tree&pg=PA70&printsec=frontcover.

[47] Huntington, Randolph, *"Leopard" and "Linden," General Grant's Arabian Stallions* (Philadelphia: J. B. Lippincott Company, 1885), https://www.wiwfarm.com/LEOPARD_AND_LINDEN.htm.

[48] Simon, John Y., *The Papers of Ulysses S. Grant, Volume 31, January 1–July 23, 1883–1885* (Carbondale, Illinois: Southern Illinois University Press, 2009), XVII.

[49] White, *American Ulysses,* 629.

[50] Grant, Julia, *Memoirs,* 326–327.

[51] Shrady, George F., MD, "General Grant's Last Days," *The Century Magazine,* 411.

52 Grant, Julia, *Memoirs*, 327–328.
53 Flood, Charles Bracelen, *Grant's Final Victory* (Cambridge, MA: Da Capo Press, 2011), 11–13.
54 Goldhurst, *Many*, 3.
55 Flood, *Grant's Final*, 11–13.
56 Smith, Jean Edward, *Grant* (New York: Simon and Schuster, 2001), 620.
57 Chernow, *Grant*, 921.
58 Flood, *Grant's Final*, 11–13.
59 Chernow, *Grant*, 921–922.
60 Flood, *Grant's Final*, 13.
61 Goldhurst, *Many*, 7–8.
62 Chernow, *Grant*, 922–923.
63 Goldhurst, *Many*, 7–8.
64 Goldhurst, *Many*, 7–8.
65 Chernow, *Grant*, 922–923.
66 Goldhurst, *Many*, 8.
67 Flood, *Grant's Final*, 20.
68 Goldhurst, *Many*, 8.
69 Chernow, *Grant*, 922–923.
70 Simon, *The Papers*, Volume 31, 147.
71 Simon, *The Papers*, Volume 31, 146–147.
72 Grant, Julia, *Memoirs*, 328.
73 Flood, *Grant's Final*, 41–42.
74 Perry, *Grant and Twain*, xxix–xxx.
75 Flood, *Grant's Final*, 43–44.
76 Green, *General*, 8–9.
77 Chernow, *Grant*, 922–923.
78 Flood, *Grant's Final*, 44.
79 Flood, *Grant's Final*, 43.

CHAPTER THREE: STUNG

80 Chernow, *Grant*, 928.
81 Perry, *Grant and Twain*, 55–56.
82 Badeau, Adam, *Grant in Peace* (Hartford, CT: S.S. Scranton & Company, 1887), 555.
83 Green, *General*, 276.
84 Perry, *Grant and Twain*, 55–56.
85 Chernow, *Grant*, 929.
86 Flood, *Grant's Final*, 56–57.
87 Green, *General*, 277.
88 Grant, Julia, *Memoirs*, 328.
89 Flood, *Grant's Final*, 45–47.

[90] Grant, Julia, *Memoirs*, 328–329.

[91] Grant, Julia, *Memoirs*, 329.

[92] Pitkin, Thomas M., *The Captain Departs: Ulysses S. Grant's Last Campaign* (Carbondale, Illinois: Southern Illinois University Press, 1973), 10–11.

[93] Green, *General,* 277.

[94] Green, *General,* 277.

[95] Perry, *Grant and Twain*, 57.

[96] Flood, *Grant's Final,* 47.

[97] Flood, *Grant's Final,* 57–58.

[98] Chernow, *Grant,* 929.

[99] Johnson, Robert Underwood, *Remembered Yesterdays*, 210–213, quoted in Thomas M. Pitkin, *The Captain,* 11.

[100] Green, *General,* 36.

[101] Flood, *Grant's Final,* 57–58.

[102] Chernow, *Grant,* 929.

[103] Simon, *The Papers,* Volume 31, 175.

[104] Flood, *Grant's Final,* 59.

[105] Perry, *Grant and Twain*, 57–58.

[106] Flood, *Grant's Final,* 59.

[107] Perry, *Grant and Twain*, 58.

[108] Green, *General,* 279.

[109] Green, *General,* 279.

[110] White, *American Ulysses*, 635.

[111] Perry, *Grant and Twain*, 59.

[112] Perry, *Grant and Twain*, 58–59.

[113] Green, *General,* 282.

[114] Grant, Julia, *Memoirs*, 328–329.

[115] Flood, *Grant's Final,* 75.

[116] Green, *General,* 283.

[117] Green, *General,* 279.

CHAPTER FOUR: SHILOH

[118] Green, *General,* 279.

[119] Grant, Ulysses S., *Personal Memoirs of Ulysses S. Grant* (New York: Barnes & Noble Books, 2005. Originally published by Charles L. Webster and Company, New York, 1885), 186.

[120] Green, *General,* 53.

[121] Perrett, *Ulysses S. Grant,* 187–188.

[122] Green, *General,* 55.

[123] Perrett, *Ulysses S. Grant*, 189.

[124] Grant, Ulysses, *Personal Memoirs*, 190.

[125] Chernow, *Grant,* 201.

[126] Grant, Ulysses, *Personal Memoirs*, 197.

[127] Perrett, *Ulysses S. Grant*, 193.

[128] Chernow, *Grant*, 203.

[129] "Battle of Shiloh," Wikipedia, Wikimedia Foundation, https://en.wikipedia.org/wiki/Battle_of_Shiloh.

[130] Burns, Ken, "Episode Two: A Very Bloody Affair—1862," *The Civil War*, PBS Video, 1990.

[131] Daniel, Larry J. "General Albert Sidney Johnston's Death at Shiloh," *Shiloh: Voices of the Civil War* (New York: Time-Life Books, Quoted in *Tennessee4Me.org*), 1996, http://www.tn4me.org/sapage.cfm/sa_id/26/era_id/5/major_id/5/tnailer.xml.

[132] Burns, "A Very Bloody," 1990.

[133] Bonekemper, Edward H., *Grant and Lee: Victorious American and Vanquished Virginian* (Washington: Regnery History, 2012), 58.

[134] Grant, Ulysses, *Personal Memoirs*, 190.

[135] Perrett, *Ulysses S. Grant*, 196.

[136] Grant, Ulysses, *Personal Memoirs*, 193.

[137] Bonekemper, *Grant and Lee*, 61.

[138] Grant, Ulysses, *Personal Memoirs*, 194.

[139] Green, *General*, 56.

[140] Beauregard, Pierre Gustave. *War of the Rebellion: Serial 010 Page 0384 KY., TENN., N. MISS., N. ALA., AND SW. VA.* Chapter XXII, Ohio State University EHistory, https://ehistory.osu.edu/books/official-records/010/0384.

[141] Grant, Ulysses, *Personal Memoirs*, 194.

[142] Chernow, *Grant*, 205.

[143] Chernow, *Grant*, 205.

[144] Perrett, *Ulysses S. Grant*, 198.

[145] Perrett, *Ulysses S. Grant*, 198.

[146] Grant, Ulysses, *Personal Memoirs*, 205.

CHAPTER FIVE: OPPORTUNITY OF THE CENTURY

[147] Pitkin, *The Captain*, 11.

[148] Perry, *Grant and Twain*, 62–63.

[149] Green, *General*, 281.

[150] Perry, *Grant and Twain*, 62–63.

[151] Grant, Julia, *Memoirs*, 328–329.

[152] Flood, *Grant's Final*, 62.

CHAPTER SIX: VICKSBURG

[153] Perry, *Grant and Twain*, 61–63.

[154] Simon, *The Papers*, Volume 31, 177.

[155] Flood, *Grant's Final*, 69.

[156] Welles, Gideon, "Admiral Farragut and New Orleans: with an account of the origin and command of the first three naval expeditions of the war," *The Galaxy, v. 12*, 669–683, 817–832 (November and December 1871), https://babel.hathitrust.org/cgi/pt?id=ucl.$b201039;view=1up;seq=685.

[157] Bonekemper, *Grant and Lee*, 213.

[158] Bien, Madeleine, "Vicksburg is the Key," National Park Foundation. https://www.nationalparks.org/connect/blog/vicksburg-key.

[159] Townsend, Timothy, "Lincoln, Grant, and the 1864 Election," National Park Service, www.nps.gov/liho/learn/historyculture/lincolngrant.htm.

[160] Wert, Jeffry D. "Crossing The Mississippi," History.net, July 2006, https://www.historynet.com/crossing-the-mississippi.htm.

[161] Badeau, Adam, *Military History of Ulysses S. Grant from April 1861 to April 1865, Volume 1*, 184, http://www.perseus.tufts.edu/hopper/text?doc=184&fromdoc=Perseus%3Atext%3A2001.05.0259.

[162] Grant, Ulysses, *Personal Memoirs*, 256–257.

[163] Bonekemper, *Grant and Lee*, 214.

[164] Bonekemper, *Grant and Lee*, 214–215.

[165] Green, *General*, 71.

[166] Bonekemper, *Grant and Lee*, 215.

[167] Green, *General*, 71.

[168] Perrett, *Ulysses S. Grant*, 253.

[169] Grant, Ulysses, *Personal Memoirs*, 267.

[170] Grant, Ulysses, *Personal Memoirs*, 267.

[171] Chernow, *Grant*, 259–260.

[172] Smith, *Grant*, 238.

[173] Grant, Ulysses, *Personal Memoirs*, 269.

[174] Bonekemper, *Grant and Lee*, 223.

[175] Perrett, *Ulysses S. Grant*, 254.

[176] Green, *General*, 74.

[177] History.com Editors, "Siege of Vicksburg," History.com, November 9, 2009, https://www.history.com/topics/american-civil-war/vicksburg-campaign.

[178] Green, *General*, 79.

[179] Grant, Ulysses, *Personal Memoirs*, 295–296.

[180] Brands, *The Man*, 239.

[181] Green, *General*, 79.

[182] Brands, *The Man*, 239.

[183] Perrett, *Ulysses S. Grant*, 263–264.

[184] Chernow, *Grant*, 279.

[185] Grant, Ulysses, *Personal Memoirs*, 317.

[186] Perrett, *Ulysses S. Grant*, 263–264.

[187] Perrett, *Ulysses S. Grant*, 264.

[188] Green, *General*, 75.

[189] Smith, *Grant*, 256.

[190] Chernow, *Grant,* 289.

[191] Grant, Ulysses, *Personal Memoirs*, 317.

[192] Flood, Charles Bracelen, *Grant and Sherman: The Friendship That Won the Civil War* (New York: Macmillan, 2005), 184.

[193] Perrett, *Ulysses S. Grant*, 265.

[194] Waugh, Joan, *U. S. Grant: American Hero, American Myth* (Chapel Hill, NC: UNC Press, 2009), 66.

CHAPTER SEVEN: IS IT CANCER?

[195] Flood, *Grant's Final,* 81.

[196] Pitkin, *The Captain,* 11.

[197] Perry, *Grant and Twain*, 62–63.

[198] Green, *General,* 283.

[199] Green, *General,* 283.

[200] Green, *General,* 286–287.

[201] Flood, *Grant's Final,* 83–84.

[202] Green, *General,* 286–287.

[203] Perry, *Grant and Twain,* 66.

[204] Flood, *Grant's Final,* 83–84.

[205] Perry, *Grant and Twain,* 66.

[206] Perry, *Grant and Twain*, 65–66.

[207] Perry, *Grant and Twain*, 67–68.

[208] Waugh, *U. S. Grant*, 175.

[209] Pitkin, *The Captain,* 24–25.

[210] Green, *General,* 288.

[211] Perry, *Grant and Twain*, 66–67.

[212] Grant, Julia, *Memoirs*, 328–329.

[213] Perry, *Grant and Twain*, 66–67.

[214] Pitkin, *The Captain,* 25.

[215] Perry, *Grant and Twain*, 68.

[216] Flood, *Grant's Final,* 86–87.

[217] Pitkin, *The Captain,* 32.

[218] Shrady, "Last Days," 103–104.

[219] Perry, *Grant and Twain*, 69.

[220] Shrady, "Last Days," 416.

[221] Simon, *The Papers,* Volume 31, 211.

[222] Perrett, *Ulysses S. Grant,* 471.

[223] Flood, *Grant's Final,* 83.

[224] Perry, *Grant and Twain*, 76–77.

[225] Flood, *Grant's Final,* 83.

[226] Perry, *Grant and Twain*, 76–77.

[227] White, *American Ulysses*, 639.

[228] Chernow, *Grant,* 934.

[229] Flood, *Grant's Final,* 87–88.

[230] Flood, *Grant's Final,* 87–88.

[231] Perry, *Grant and Twain*, 76–77.

[232] Flood, *Grant's Final,* 87–88.

[233] White, *American Ulysses*, 639.

[234] Shrady, "Last Days," 411.

[235] White, *American Ulysses*, 639.

[236] Perry, *Grant and Twain*, 79.

[237] Badeau, *Grant in Peace*, 427–428.

[238] Flood, *Grant's Final,* 87–88.

[239] Chernow, *Grant,* 931.

[240] Perry, *Grant and Twain*, 80–81.

[241] Chernow, *Grant,* 933.

[242] Shrady, "Last Days," 411.

[243] Chernow, *Grant,* 933.

[244] Green, *General,* 76.

CHAPTER EIGHT: MARK TWAIN

[245] Flood, *Grant's Final,* 99.

[246] Twain, *Autobiography,* 77–78.

[247] Twain, *Autobiography,* 78.

[248] Twain, *Autobiography,* 78.

[249] Powers, Ron, *Mark Twain: A Life* (New York: Free Press–Simon & Schuster, 2005), 492–493.

[250] Twain, *Autobiography,* 78–79.

[251] Twain, Mark, *Mark Twain's Autobiography, Volume 1* (Project Gutenberg of Australia). http://gutenberg.net.au/ebooks02/0200551h.html.

[252] Powers, *Mark Twain,* 493.

[253] Flood, *Grant's Final,* 101.

[254] Chernow, *Grant,* 935.

[255] Green, *General,* 290.

[256] Flood, *Grant's Final,* 98.

[257] Brands, *The Man,* 610.

[258] Flood, *Grant's Final,* 101.

[259] Brands, *The Man,* 623–624.

[260] Powers, *Mark Twain,* 492–493.

[261] Flood, *Grant's Final,* 101–102.

[262] Brands, *The Man,* 623–624.

[263] Flood, *Grant's Final,* 101.

[264] Chernow, *Grant,* 935–936.

[265] Simpson, *The Papers,* 237.

CHAPTER NINE: WINTER OF DISCONTENT
[266] Chernow, *Grant,* 933.
[267] Badeau, *Grant in Peace,* 427.
[268] Simon, *The Papers,* Volume 31, 266.
[269] Flood, *Grant's Final,* 89.
[270] Flood, *Grant's Final,* 117–118.
[271] Perry, *Grant and Twain,* 122.
[272] Perry, *Grant and Twain,* 123.
[273] Perry, *Grant and Twain,* 123.
[274] Shrady, "Last Days," 102–103.
[275] Shrady, "Last Days," 106–107.
[276] Shrady, "Last Days," 106–107.
[277] Shrady, "Last Days," 284.
[278] Flood, *Grant's Final,* 117–118.
[279] Chernow, *Grant,* 933–934.
[280] Badeau, *Grant in Peace,* 429–430.
[281] Flood, *Grant's Final,* 118.
[282] Green, *General,* 296–297.
[283] Samet, Elizabeth D., "Moral Courage and the Civil War," *The American Scholar*, September 3, 2019. https://theamericanscholar.org/moral-courage-and-the-civil-war/.
[284] Chernow, *Grant,* 632.
[285] Chernow, *Grant,* 708.
[286] Chernow, *Grant,* 709.
[287] Chernow, *Grant,* 795.
[288] Chernow, *Grant,* 795.
[289] Shrady, "Last Days," 278–279.
[290] Green, *General,* 296–297.

CHAPTER TEN: THREE STARS
[291] Grant, Ulysses, *Personal Memoirs*, 383.
[292] Brands, *The Man,* 279.
[293] Green, *General,* 113–114.
[294] Mr. Lincoln's White House, "The Generals and Admirals: Ulysses S. Grant (1822-1885)" http://www.mrlincolnswhitehouse.org/residents-visitors/the-generals-and-admirals/generals-admirals-ulysses-s-grant-1822-1885/.
[295] Flood, *Grant's Final,* 28.
[296] Grant, Julia, *Memoirs,* 126–127.
[297] Blumberg, Arnold, "Grant Takes D.C.," Warfarehistorynetwork.com, https://warfarehistorynetwork.com/2018/12/21/grant-takes-d-c/.

[298] Chernow, *Grant,* 340.

[299] Chernow, *Grant,* 340.

[300] Catton, Bruce, *Grant Takes Command* (Edison, NJ: Castle Books—Book Sales Inc., 2000), 124.

[301] Green, *General,* 116–117.

[302] Chernow, *Grant,* 341.

[303] Chernow, *Grant,* 341.

[304] Catton, *Command,* 125–126.

[305] Perrett, *Ulysses S. Grant,* 296.

[306] Porter, Horace, *Campaigning with Grant* (New York: Time Life Books, 1981, Reprinted from The Century Company, 1897), 19.

[307] Porter, *Campaigning,* 21.

[308] Catton, *Command,* 125–126.

[309] Chernow, *Grant,* 342.

[310] Grant, Julia, *Memoirs,* 128.

[311] Catton, *Command,* 125–126.

[312] Grant, Ulysses, *Personal Memoirs,* 383–384.

[313] Catton, *Command,* 127.

[314] Grant, Julia, *Memoirs,* 127.

[315] Chernow, *Grant,* 343.

[316] Brands, *The Man,* 186.

[317] Porter, *Campaigning,* 14–16.

[318] Porter, *Campaigning,* 16.

[319] Catton, *Command,* 128.

[320] Smith, *Grant,* 292.

[321] Chernow, *Grant,* 345.

[322] Grant, Ulysses, *Personal Memoirs,* 384–385.

[323] Porter, *Campaigning,* 29.

[324] Smith, *Grant,* 292.

[325] Chernow, *Grant,* 346.

[326] Catton, *Command,* 153.

[327] Porter, *Campaigning,* 22.

[328] Catton, *Command,* 143.

[329] Green, *General,* 122.

[330] White, *American Ulysses,* 328–329.

[331] Simon, John Y., *The Papers of Ulysses S. Grant, Volume 10: January 1-May 31, 1864* (Carbondale, Illinois: Southern Illinois University Press, 1982), 253.

[332] Smith, *Grant,* 302.

[333] Smith, *Grant,* 302.

[334] Smith, *Grant,* 302–303.

[335] Burns, Ken, "Episode Six: The Valley of the Shadow of Death—1864," *The Civil War,* PBS Video, 1990.

[336]   Catton, *Command*, 159.

[337]   Green, *General,* 123.

[338]   Grant, Ulysses, *Personal Memoirs*, 104.

CHAPTER ELEVEN: GRANT AND LEE

[339]   Flood, *Grant's Final,* 115.

[340]   Grant, Ulysses, *Personal Memoirs*, 416.

[341]   Porter, *Campaigning*, 35–37.

[342]   Grant, Ulysses, *Personal Memoirs*, 633.

[343]   Porter, *Campaigning*, 37–38.

[344]   Chernow, *Grant,* 366.

[345]   Porter, *Campaigning*, 46–47.

[346]   Bonekemper, *Grant and Lee,* 289.

[347]   Smith, *Grant*, 314.

[348]   Porter, *Campaigning*, 42.

[349]   Porter, *Campaigning*, 43–44.

[350]   Grant, Ulysses, *Personal Memoirs*, 641.

[351]   Porter, *Campaigning*, 44.

[352]   Catton, *Command*, 184–185.

[353]   Brands, *The Man,* 298.

[354]   Chernow, *Grant,* 278–279.

[355]   Smith, *Grant,* 314–315.

[356]   Porter, *Campaigning*, 48–51.

[357]   Bonekemper, *Grant and Lee,* 290.

[358]   Grant, Ulysses, *Personal Memoirs*, 428.

[359]   Catton, *Command*, 189.

[360]   Bonekemper, *Grant and Lee,* 293.

[361]   Catton, *Command*, 191–192.

[362]   Chernow, *Grant,* 382.

[363]   Chernow, *Grant,* 382.

[364]   Catton, *Command*, 193.

[365]   Porter, *Campaigning*, 72–73.

[366]   Catton, *Command*, 193.

[367]   Bonekemper, *Grant and Lee,* 293–294.

[368]   Catton, *Command*, 193.

[369]   Porter, *Campaigning*, 45.

[370]   Smith, *Grant*, 318.

[371]   Porter, *Campaigning*, 53–54.

[372]   Perrett, *Ulysses S. Grant,* 313–314.

[373]   Wert, Jeffry, *The Sword of Lincoln: The Army of the Potomac* (New York: Simon & Schuster, 2005), 338.

CHAPTER TWELVE: THE WILDERNESS, DAY TWO

[374] Grant, Ulysses, *Personal Memoirs*, 432.

[375] Wert, *The Sword,* 340.

[376] Porter, *Campaigning*, 57.

[377] Chernow, *Grant,* 380.

[378] Porter, *Campaigning*, 59.

[379] White, *American Ulysses*, 335.

[380] White, *American Ulysses*, 335–336.

[381] Porter, *Campaigning*, 61.

[382] Bonekemper, *Grant and Lee,* 295.

[383] Grant, Ulysses, *Personal Memoirs*, 431.

[384] Mackowski, Chris, and White, Kristopher D., *Forgotten Casualty: James Longstreet Wounded in the Wilderness: Part Two*, EmergingCivilWar.com, May 6, 2014, https://emergingcivilwar.com/2014/05/06/forgotten-casualty-james-longstreet-wounded-in-the-wilderness-part-two/.

[385] White, *American Ulysses*, 335–336.

[386] Porter, *Campaigning*, 62.

[387] Bonekemper, *Grant and Lee,* 295.

[388] Porter, *Campaigning*, 62–63.

[389] White, *American Ulysses*, 335–336.

[390] Porter, *Campaigning*, 65.

[391] Porter, *Campaigning*, 63.

[392] Green, *General,* 127.

[393] Perrett, *Ulysses S. Grant,* 311.

[394] Porter, *Campaigning*, 63–64.

[395] Bonekemper, *Grant and Lee,* 295–296.

[396] Porter, *Campaigning*, 70–71.

[397] Porter, *Campaigning*, 70–71.

[398] Bonekemper, *Grant and Lee,* 296.

[399] Smith, *Grant,* 337–338.

CHAPTER THIRTEEN: BY THE LEFT FLANK

[400] Grant, Ulysses, *Personal Memoirs*, 434.

[401] Smith, *Grant,* 337–338.

[402] Porter, *Campaigning*, 76.

[403] Porter, *Campaigning*, 78.

[404] Smith, *Grant,* 337–338.

[405] Wert, *The Sword,* 344–345.

[406] Catton, *Command,* 208.

[407] Smith, *Grant,* 337–338.

[408] Bonekemper, *Grant and Lee,* 298.

[409] Perrett, *Ulysses S. Grant,* 314.

[410] Porter, *Campaigning*, 78–79.
[411] Catton, *Command*, 208–209.
[412] Brands, *The Man,* 300–301.
[413] Smith, *Grant*, 337–338.
[414] Wert, *The Sword,* 344–345.
[415] Porter, *Campaigning*, 78–79.
[416] Bonekemper, *Grant and Lee,* 298.
[417] Grant, Ulysses, *Personal Memoirs*, 438.
[418] Porter, *Campaigning*, 83.
[419] Catton, *Command*, 211.
[420] Catton, *Command*, 217.
[421] Porter, *Campaigning*, 90.
[422] Catton, *Command*, 235.
[423] Simon, *The Papers,* Volume 10, 422.

Chapter Fourteen: The Book Contract

[424] Simon, *The Papers,* Volume 31, 250–251.
[425] Flood, *Grant's Final,* 123.
[426] Grant, Julia, *Memoirs*, 328
[427] Flood, *Grant's Final,* 127–128.
[428] Chernow, *Grant*, xix.
[429] Shrady, "Last Days," 279–280.
[430] Flood, *Grant's Final,* 127–128.
[431] Shrady, "Last Days," 279–280.
[432] Green, *General,* 299–300.
[433] Twain, *Autobiography,* 80.
[434] Brands, *The Man,* 623–624.
[435] Twain, *Autobiography,* 82.
[436] Twain, *Autobiography,* 82–84.
[437] Perry, *Grant and Twain*, 138–139.
[438] Green, *General,* 293.
[439] Green, *General,* 293-294.
[440] Twain, *Autobiography,* 83–84.
[441] Twain, *Autobiography,* 82.
[442] Twain, *Autobiography,* 84.
[443] Twain, *Autobiography,* 84.
[444] Perry, *Grant and Twain*, 138–139.
[445] Pitkin, *The Captain,* 27.
[446] Perrett, *Ulysses S. Grant*, 472.
[447] Twain, *Autobiography,* 81–82.
[448] Flood, *Grant's Final,* 129–130.
[449] Perry, *Grant and Twain*, 141.

[450] Perrett, *Ulysses S. Grant,* 472.

[451] Perrett, *Ulysses S. Grant,* 472.

[452] Perry, *Grant and Twain*, 141.

[453] Flood, *Grant's Final,* 130–131.

[454] Twain, *Autobiography,* 84.

[455] Perry, *Grant and Twain*, 162.

[456] Simon, *The Papers*, Volume 31, 293–294.

CHAPTER FIFTEEN: COLD HARBOR

[457] Shrady, "Last Days," 106–107.

[458] Shrady, "Last Days," 106–107.

[459] Chernow, *Grant,* xxi.

[460] Grant, Ulysses, *Personal Memoirs*, 465.

[461] Grant, Ulysses, *Personal Memoirs*, 469.

[462] Catton, *Command*, 258.

[463] Spangenberger, Phil, "The Yankee 'Sixteen Shooter,'" *True West Magazine*, Truewestmagazine.com/the-yankee-sixteen-shooter/.

[464] Catton, *Command*, 258.

[465] Bonekemper, *Grant and Lee,* 307–308.

[466] Waugh, *U. S. Grant,* 86–87.

[467] Porter, *Campaigning*, 174–175.

[468] Smith, *Grant*, 363–364.

[469] Bonekemper, *Grant and Lee,* 309.

[470] Burns, "The Valley," 1990.

[471] Catton, *Command*, 264.

[472] Porter, *Campaigning*, 175.

[473] Grant, Ulysses, *Personal Memoirs*, 473.

[474] Porter, *Campaigning*, 176–177.

[475] Perrett, *Ulysses S. Grant,* 330–331.

[476] Burns, "The Valley," 1990.

[477] Porter, *Campaigning*, 177.

[478] Perrett, *Ulysses S. Grant,* 331.

[479] History.com Editors, "Battles of Cold Harbor," History.com, December 2, 2009, www.history.com/topics/american-civil-war/battles-of-cold-harbor.

[480] Burns, "The Valley," 1990.

[481] Porter, *Campaigning*, 179.

[482] Smith, *Grant*, 363–364.

[483] Burns, "The Valley," 1990.

[484] Burns, "The Valley," 1990.

[485] Green, *General,* 144.

[486] Chernow, *Grant,* 406.

[487] Perrett, *Ulysses S. Grant,* 332.

[488] Grant, Ulysses, *Personal Memoirs*, 477.

[489] Bonekemper, *Grant and Lee,* 307–308.

[490] Catton, *Command*, 270.

[491] Waugh, *U. S. Grant,* 86–87.

[492] Grant, Ulysses, *Personal Memoirs*, 473.

[493] Brands, *The Man,* 308.

CHAPTER SIXTEEN: RACE WITH DEATH

[494] Pitkin, *The Captain,* 25–26.

[495] Pitkin, *The Captain,* 26–27.

[496] *The NewYork Times* Editors, "Sinking into the Grave," *The NewYork Times*, March 1, 1885. https://newspaperarchive.com/new-york-times-mar-o1-1885-p-2/.

[497] *The NewYork Times* Editors, "Sinking into the Grave."

[498] Chernow, *Grant,* 937–938.

[499] Pitkin, *The Captain,* 34–35.

[500] Flood, *Grant's Final*, 133.

[501] Shrady, "Last Days," 413.

[502] Shrady, "Last Days," 414.

[503] Shrady, "Last Days," 414.

[504] Flood, *Grant's Final*, 133.

[505] White, *American Ulysses*, 641.

[506] Goldhurst, *Many*, 154–155.

[507] Perry, *Grant and Twain*, 153–154.

[508] Flood, *Grant's Final*, 141–142.

[509] Shrady, "Last Days," 110.

[510] Flood, *Grant's Final,* 89–90.

[511] Shrady, "Last Days," 110–111.

CHAPTER SEVENTEEN: THE GENERAL RETURNS

[512] Goldhurst, *Many,* 166–167.

[513] Green, *General,* 298.

[514] Goldhurst, *Many,* 167.

[515] White, *American Ulysses*, 641.

[516] Flood, *Grant's Final,* 40.

[517] Goldhurst, *Many,* 167.

[518] Goldhurst, *Many,* 169.

[519] Flood, *Grant's Final*, 135–136.

[520] Perry, *Grant and Twain*, 157–159.

[521] Flood, *Grant's Final,* 135–136.

[522] Goldhurst, *Many,* 167.

[523] Goldhurst, *Many,* 171.

[524] Perry, *Grant and Twain*, 159–160.

[525] Flood, *Grant's Final,* 135–136.

Chapter Eighteen: Crossing the James
[526] Grant, Ulysses, *Personal Memoirs,* 479.
[527] Porter, *Campaigning,* 35–37.
[528] Green, *General,* 145–146.
[529] Porter, *Campaigning,* 172–173.
[530] Catton, *Command,* 276.
[531] Melton, Brian C., *Robert E. Lee: A Biography* (Santa Barbara, CA: ABC-CLIO, 2012), 110.
[532] Porter, *Campaigning,* 172–173.
[533] Green, *General,* 145–146.
[534] Bonekemper, *Grant and Lee,* 314.
[535] Porter, *Campaigning,* 189–190.
[536] Catton, *Command,* 278.
[537] Porter, *Campaigning,* 190.
[538] Smith, *Grant,* 369–370.
[539] Grant, Ulysses, *Personal Memoirs,* 648.
[540] Smith, *Grant,* 370.
[541] Porter, *Campaigning,* 194–195.
[542] Perrett, *Ulysses S. Grant,* 333.
[543] Smith, *Grant,* 370.
[544] Smith, *Grant,* 370.
[545] Chernow, *Grant,* 411–412.
[546] Catton, *Command,* 282.
[547] Perrett, *Ulysses S. Grant,* 334.
[548] Porter, *Campaigning,* 195–197.
[549] Catton, *Command,* 282.
[550] Grant, Ulysses, *Personal Memoirs,* 483–484.
[551] Chernow, *Grant,* 411–412.
[552] Bonekemper, *Grant and Lee,* 314.
[553] Chernow, *Grant,* 411–412.
[554] Porter, *Campaigning,* 198.
[555] Smith, *Grant,* 372.
[556] Smith, *Grant,* 373.
[557] Porter, *Campaigning,* 199–200.
[558] Chernow, *Grant,* 411–412.
[559] Smith, *Grant,* 373.
[560] Bonekemper, *Grant and Lee,* 315.
[561] Perrett, *Ulysses S. Grant,* 335–336.
[562] Catton, *Command,* 284.
[563] Chernow, *Grant,* 411–412.

[564] Bonekemper, *Grant and Lee,* 314.

[565] Green, *General,* 148.

[566] Grant, Ulysses, *Personal Memoirs*, 651.

[567] Catton, *Command,* 284.

CHAPTER NINETEEN: CAPTURING THE GENERAL

[568] Perry, *Grant and Twain*, 165.

[569] Shrady, "Last Days," 415.

[570] Twain, *Autobiography,* 87–88.

[571] Twain, *Autobiography,* 88.

[572] Green, *General,* 300–301.

[573] Twain, *Autobiography,* 88–89.

[574] Green, *General,* 300–301.

[575] Twain, *Autobiography,* 90.

[576] Green, *General,* 300–301.

[577] Twain, *Autobiography,* 90.

[578] Twain, *Autobiography,* 90.

[579] Flood, *Grant's Final,* 90.

CHAPTER TWENTY: AT DEATH'S DOORWAY

[580] Green, *General,* 106–109.

[581] Flood, *Grant's Final,* 141.

[582] Pitkin, *The Captain,* 34.

[583] Perry, *Grant and Twain*, 178–179.

[584] Flood, *Grant's Final,* 141–142.

[585] Shrady, "Last Days," 276.

[586] Shrady, "Last Days," 275–276.

[587] Shrady, "Last Days," 28.

[588] Pitkin, *The Captain,* 33.

[589] Flood, *Grant's Final,* 143–144.

[590] Pitkin, *The Captain,* 33.

[591] Green, *General,* 301–303.

[592] Pitkin, *The Captain,* 34.

[593] Green, *General,* 109.

[594] Goldhurst, *Many,* 181.

[595] Shrady, "Last Days," 416.

[596] Goldhurst, *Many,* 181.

[597] Chernow, *Grant,* 940.

[598] Green, *General*, 109.

[599] Shrady, "Last Days," 416.

[600] Green, *General,* 110.

[601] Flood, *Grant's Final,* 145–146.

[602] Flood, *Grant's Final*, 145–146.

[603] Perry, *Grant and Twain*, 181.

[604] Shrady, "Last Days," 416.

[605] Grant, Ulysses, *Personal Memoirs*, 369.

[606] Goldhurst, *Many*, 181.

[607] Shrady, "Last Days," 417–418.

[608] Chernow, *Grant*, 940–941.

[609] Shrady, "Last Days," 419.

[610] Goldhurst, *Many*, 182.

[611] Flood, *Grant's Final*, 149.

[612] Goldhurst, *Many*, 183.

[613] Goldhurst, *Many*, 183.

Chapter Twenty-One: Petersburg

[614] Grant, Ulysses, *Personal Memoirs*, 486–487.

[615] Gallagher, Gary W., *Fighting for the Confederacy: The Personal Recollections of General Edward Porter Alexander* (Chapel Hill, NC: UNC Press, 2000), 422.

[616] Fuller, General John, *The Generalship of Ulysses S. Grant* (New York: Dodd, Mead and Company, 1929), 289. https://archive.org/stream/generalshipofuly010523mbp/generalshipofuly010523mbp_djvu.txt.

[617] Smith, *Grant*, 373–374.

[618] Catton, *Command*, 286.

[619] Smith, *Grant*, 374.

[620] White, *American Ulysses*, 366.

[621] Catton, *Command*, 286.

[622] Perrett, *Ulysses S. Grant*, 336.

[623] Catton, *Command*, 286.

[624] Smith, *Grant*, 374.

[625] White, *American Ulysses*, 367.

[626] White, *American Ulysses*, 367.

[627] Catton, *Command*, 287–288.

[628] Catton, *Command*, 286–287.

[629] Perrett, *Ulysses S. Grant*, 337.

[630] White, *American Ulysses*, 367.

[631] Smith, *Grant*, 374.

[632] Catton, *Command*, 288–289.

[633] Grant, Ulysses, *Personal Memoirs*, 487.

[634] Catton, *Command*, 290.

[635] White, *American Ulysses*, 369.

[636] Perrett, *Ulysses S. Grant*, 338.

[637] White, *American Ulysses*, 369.

[638] Smith, *Grant*, 374–375.

[639] Bonekemper, *Grant and Lee,* 316.

[640] Catton, *Command*, 293.

[641] White, *American Ulysses*, 369.

[642] Catton, *Command*, 293.

[643] White, *American Ulysses*, 369.

[644] Catton, *Command*, 293.

[645] Chernow, *Grant,* 412–413.

[646] Smith, *Grant*, 375.

[647] White, *American Ulysses*, 369.

[648] Smith, *Grant*, 375.

[649] Smith, *Grant*, 375.

[650] Porter, General Horace, "Campaigning with Grant," *The Century Magazine* (New York: The Century Magazine, Volume 53, 1897), 830.

[651] Chernow, *Grant,* 412–413.

[652] Smith, *Grant*, 376.

[653] Grant, Ulysses, *Personal Memoirs*, 487–488.

Chapter Twenty-Two: Continue on this Line All Summer

[654] Perry, *Grant and Twain*, 173–174.

[655] Pitkin, *The Captain,* 35.

[656] Shrady, "Last Days," 55.

[657] Shrady, "Last Days," 55.

[658] Shrady, "Last Days," 55–56.

[659] Shrady, "Last Days," 56.

[660] Smith, *Grant*, 366.

[661] White, *American Ulysses*, 363.

[662] Rhodes, Elisha Hunt, *All for the Union*, edited by Robert Hunt Rhodes (New York: Orion Books, 1985), 170–171.

[663] "Battle of Monocacy," Wikipedia, Wikimedia Foundation, https://en.wikipedia.org/wiki/Battle_of_Monocacy.

[664] Green, *General,* 158.

[665] Lincoln, Abraham, *The Collected Works of Abraham Lincoln, Volume 7* (Cabin John, MD: Wildside Press, 2008), 476.

[666] Smith, *Grant*, 379–380.

[667] Smith, *Grant*, 379–380.

[668] Grant, Ulysses, *Personal Memoirs*, 499–500.

[669] Bonekemper, *Grant and Lee,* 339.

[670] Grant, Ulysses S., "Letter to Henry W. Halleck, July 14, 1864." Encyclopedia Virginia, January 2, 2015. https://www.encyclopediavirginia.org/Letter_from_Ulysses_S_Grant_to_Henry_W_Halleck_July_14_1864.

[671] Smith, *Grant*, 379–380.

[672] Bonekemper, *Grant and Lee,* 339.

[673] Bonekemper, *Grant and Lee,* 339–340.

[674] Bonekemper, Edward H., *Ulysses S. Grant: A Victor, Not a Butcher* (Washington: Regnery Publishing, Oct 11, 2010), 201.

[675] Bonekemper, *Grant and Lee,* 336–337.

[676] Berry, Stephen, *House of Abraham: Lincoln and the Todds, a Family Divided by War* (New York: Houghton Mifflin Harcourt, 2009), 171.

[677] Bonekemper, *Grant and Lee,* 335.

[678] McPherson, James M., *Battle Cry of Freedom* (Oxford: Oxford University Press, 1988), 771.

[679] Thomas, Benjamin, *Abraham Lincoln: A Biography* (Carbondale, Illinois: Southern Illinois University Press, 2008), 441.

[680] Smith, *Grant,* 381–382.

[681] Burns, Ken, "Episode Seven: Most Hallowed Ground—1864," *The Civil War,* PBS Video, 1990.

[682] Bonekemper, *Grant and Lee,* 342.

[683] Chernow, *Grant,* 441.

[684] White, *American Ulysses,* 382.

[685] Grant, Ulysses, *Personal Memoirs,* 505.

[686] Bonekemper, *Grant and Lee,* 335.

CHAPTER TWENTY-THREE: THE TURNING TIDE

[687] Grant, Ulysses, *Personal Memoirs,* 503.

[688] White, *American Ulysses,* 366.

[689] Bonekemper, *Grant and Lee,* 288.

[690] Green, *General,* 161.

[691] Bonekemper, *Grant and Lee,* 329.

[692] Watkins, Sam, *Co. Aytch* (New York: Collier Books–Macmillan Publishing Co., 1962), 178.

[693] Bonekemper, *Grant and Lee,* 329–330.

[694] Bonekemper, *Grant and Lee,* 330–331.

[695] Bonekemper, *Grant and Lee,* 330.

[696] Catton, *Command,* 359.

[697] Bonekemper, *Grant and Lee,* 342.

[698] Catton, *Command,* 359.

[699] Chernow, *Grant,* 442.

[700] Catton, *Command,* 359.

[701] Smith, *Grant,* 383.

[702] Green, *General,* 151.

[703] Grant, Ulysses, *Personal Memoirs,* 503–504.

[704] Chernow, *Grant,* 443–444.

[705] Chernow, *Grant,* 444.

[706] Grant, Ulysses, *Personal Memoirs*, 504.

[707] Chernow, *Grant*, 444.

[708] Grant, Ulysses, *Personal Memoirs*, 504.

[709] Chernow, *Grant*, 445.

[710] Bonekemper, *Grant and Lee*, 340.

[711] Catton, *Command*, 364.

[712] Chernow, *Grant*, 445.

[713] Bonekemper, *Grant and Lee*, 340.

[714] Chernow, *Grant*, 445.

[715] Smith, *Grant*, 385-386.

[716] Bonekemper, *Grant and Lee*, 341.

[717] Chernow, *Grant*, 445.

[718] Smith, *Grant*, 385.

[719] Smith, *Grant*, 385–386.

[720] Chernow, *Grant*, 445.

[721] Chernow, *Grant*, 445.

[722] Catton, *Command*, 379.

[723] Grant, Ulysses, *Personal Memoirs*, 510.

[724] Smith, *Grant*, 385–386.

[725] White, *American Ulysses*, 385.

[726] Chernow, *Grant*, 445.

[727] White, *American Ulysses*, 385.

[728] Ward, Geoffrey C., Ken Burns, and Ric Burns, *The Civil War: An Illustrated History* (New York: Knopf, 1992), 333.

[729] White, *American Ulysses*, 385.

[730] Catton, *Command*, 379–380.

[731] Smith, *Grant*, 385-386.

[732] White, *American Ulysses*, 385.

[733] Chernow, *Grant*, 446.

[734] White, *American Ulysses*, 385.

[735] Grant, Ulysses, *Personal Memoirs*, 511.

[736] Porter, *Campaigning*, 307–308.

[737] Catton, *Command*, 364.

[738] Bonekemper, *Grant and Lee*, 341.

[739] Catton, *Command*, 379–380.

[740] Perrett, *Ulysses S. Grant*, 347.

[741] Chernow, *Grant*, 442.

[742] Perrett, *Ulysses S. Grant*, 351.

[743] Porter, *Campaigning*, 324.

[744] Catton, *Command*, 383.

[745] Porter, *Campaigning*, 324.

[746] Perrett, *Ulysses S. Grant*, 351.

[747] History.com Editors, "Abraham Lincoln Reelected," History.com, November 13, 2009, https://www.history.com/this-day-in-history/lincoln-reelected.

[748] Chernow, *Grant,* 452–453.

[749] History.com Editors, "Abraham Lincoln."

[750] Chernow, *Grant,* 452–453.

[751] Bonekemper, *Grant and Lee,* 338–343.

[752] American Battlefield Trust Editors, "Sherman's March to the Sea," battlefields.org, https://www.battlefields.org/learn/articles/scorched-earth.

[753] History.com Editors, "Sherman Presents Lincoln with a Christmas Gift," History.com, November 13, 2009, https://www.history.com/this-day-in-history/sherman-presents-lincoln-with-a-christmas-gift.

Chapter Twenty-Four: Ending the Matter

[754] Borritt, Gabor S., *Why the Confederacy Lost* (Oxford: Oxford University Press, 1993), 74.

[755] Johnston, Joseph E., "My Negotiations with General Sherman," JSTOR Digital Library, 2, https://www.jstor.org/stable/pdf/25101089.pdf.

[756] Robertson, James, Jr., "Desertion," Radio IQ, July 30, 2019, https://www.wvtf.org/post/desertion#stream/0

[757] Grant, Ulysses, *Personal Memoirs*, 560.

[758] Bonekemper, *Grant and Lee,* 353.

[759] Burns, Ken, "Episode Eight: War Is All Hell—1865," *The Civil War*, PBS Video, 1990.

[760] Chernow, *Grant,* 488.

[761] Sherman, William T., *The Personal Memoirs of William T. Sherman* (New York: Literary Classics of the United States, 1990), 408.

[762] Green, *General,* 195.

[763] Catton, *Command*, 433.

[764] Mr. Lincoln and Friends Editors, "The Officers: Ulysses Grant," MrLincolnandfriends.org, http://www.mrlincolnandfriends.org/the-officers/ulysses-grant/.

[765] Mr. Lincoln and Friends Editors, "The Officers: Ulysses Grant."

[766] Mr. Lincoln and Friends Editors, "The Officers: Ulysses Grant."

[767] Grant, Ulysses, *Personal Memoirs*, 692–693.

[768] Green, *General,* 184–185.

[769] Green, *General,* 184–185.

[770] Grant, Ulysses, *Personal Memoirs*, 563–564.

[771] Porter, *Campaigning*, 411.

[772] Grant, Ulysses, *Personal Memoirs*, 566.

[773] Chernow, *Grant*, 487.

[774] Catton, *Command*, 437.

[775] Chernow, *Grant,* 487.

[776] Catton, *Command,* 437.

[777] Greenspan, Jesse, "Lincoln, Grant, and Sherman Huddle Up 150 Years Ago," History.com, March 26, 2015. https://www.history.com/news/lincoln-grant-and-sherman-huddle-up-150-years-ago.

[778] Porter, *Campaigning,* 417–418.

[779] Porter, *Campaigning,* 419.

[780] Porter, *Campaigning,* 423.

[781] Greenspan, Jesse, "Lincoln, Grant, and Sherman Huddle Up."

[782] Greenspan, Jesse, "Lincoln, Grant, and Sherman Huddle Up."

[783] Grant, *Memoirs,* 690.

[784] Porter, *Campaigning,* 425.

[785] Green, *General,* 188–189.

[786] Catton, *Command,* 440.

[787] Chernow, *Grant,* 489.

[788] Porter, *Campaigning,* 428–429.

[789] Catton, *Command,* 440–441.

[790] Thompson, Robert, "Two Days in April: The Battle of Five Forks," American Battlefield Trust, https://www.battlefields.org/learn/articles/two-days-april-battle-five-forks.

[791] Porter, *Campaigning,* 428–429.

[792] Chernow, *Grant,* 489–490.

[793] Thompson, "Two Days."

[794] Porter, *Campaigning,* 428–429.

[795] Catton, *Command,* 444.

[796] Catton, *Command,* 444.

[797] Bonekemper, *Grant and Lee,* 363–364.

[798] Thompson, "Two Days."

[799] Porter, *Campaigning,* 436.

[800] Bonekemper, *Grant and Lee,* 364.

[801] Porter, *Campaigning,* 437.

[802] Chernow, *Grant,* 490.

[803] Porter, *Campaigning,* 437–438.

[804] Porter, *Campaigning,* 439.

[805] Porter, *Campaigning,* 439.

[806] Wert, Jeffry D., *Custer: The Controversial Life of George Armstrong Custer* (New York: Simon and Schuster, 2015), 218.

[807] Bonekemper, *Grant and Lee,* 365.

[808] Wert, *The Sword,* 401.

[809] Bonekemper, *Grant and Lee,* 365.

[810] Green, *General,* 199–200.

[811] Grant, Ulysses, *Personal Memoirs,* 567.

[812] Grant, Ulysses, *Personal Memoirs*, 570–571.

[813] Porter, *Campaigning*, 442–443.

[814] Green, *General,* 199–200.

[815] Porter, *Campaigning*, 442–443.

[816] Grant, Ulysses, *Personal Memoirs*, 571.

Chapter Twenty-Five: If the Thing Is Pressed

[817] Grant, Ulysses, *Personal Memoirs*, 574.

[818] Tyler, Mason Whiting, and C. Stephen Badgley, *Recollections of the Civil War* (New York: G. Putnam's and Sons, 1912), 275–276.

[819] Badeau, Adam, *Military History of Ulysses S. Grant: From April, 1861, to April, 1865,Volume 3* (New York: D. Appleton, 1881), 504.

[820] Catton, *Command*, 446–447.

[821] Porter, *Campaigning*, 444–445.

[822] Grant, Ulysses, *Personal Memoirs*, 571–572.

[823] Smith, *Grant*, 395.

[824] Chernow, *Grant*, 493.

[825] Phifer, Mike, "End Game at Appomattox," Warfarehistorynetwork.com, December 23, 2018, https://warfarehistorynetwork.com/2018/12/23/end-game-at-appomattox/.

[826] Catton, *Command*, 452–453.

[827] White, *American Ulysses*, 402–403.

[828] Catton, *Command*, 449.

[829] Johnson, Robert Underwood and Clarence Clough Buel, *Battles and Leaders of the Civil War*, *Volume 4* (New York: The Century Company, 1887), Perseus Digital Library. http://www.perseus.tufts.edu/hopper/text?doc=Perseus%3Atext%3A2001.05.0046%3Achapter%3D16.107.

[830] Bonekemper, *Grant and Lee,* 365.

[831] Porter, *Campaigning*, 452.

[832] Catton, *Command*, 450.

[833] Porter, *Campaigning*, 453.

[834] Porter, *Campaigning*, 453.

[835] Smith, *Grant*, 397–398.

[836] Porter, *Campaigning*, 454.

[837] Catton, *Command*, 452.

[838] Porter, *Campaigning*, 455.

[839] Porter, *Campaigning*, 456.

[840] Chernow, *Grant,* 497.

[841] Catton, *Command*, 452–453.

[842] Catton, *Command*, 453.

[843] Wert, *The Sword,* 405–406.

[844] Grant, Ulysses, *Personal Memoirs*, 586.

845 Smith, *Grant*, 397–398.
846 Wert, *The Sword*, 405–406.
847 Catton, *Command*, 454.
848 Chernow, *Grant*, 498.
849 Bonekemper, *Grant and Lee*, 369.
850 Catton, *Command*, 455.
851 Smith, *Grant*, 397–398.
852 Porter, *Campaigning*, 457.
853 Porter, *Campaigning*, 458.
854 Porter, *Campaigning*, 459.
855 Porter, *Campaigning*, 459.
856 Porter, *Campaigning*, 459–461.
857 Catton, *Command*, 459.
858 Grant, Ulysses, *Personal Memoirs*, 592.
859 Chernow, *Grant*, 501.
860 Smith, *Grant*, 400.
861 Porter, *Campaigning*, 463–464.
862 Calton, *Command*, 461.
863 Catton, *Command*, 460.
864 Sheridan, Philip, *Personal Memoirs of P. H. Sheridan*. Volume II, Part 5. https://www.gutenberg.org/files/4362/old/orig4362-h/p5.htm.
865 Bonekemper, *Grant and Lee*, 369.

Chapter Twenty-Six: Composition Entirely My Own

866 Flood, *Grant's Final*, 168.
867 Flood, *Grant's Final*, 169.
868 Pitkin, *The Captain*, 35.
869 Green, *General*, 303.
870 Pitkin, *The Captain*, 37.
871 Simon, *The Papers*, Volume 31, 390.
872 Chernow, *Grant*, 947.
873 Pitkin, *The Captain*, 37.
874 Perry, *Grant and Twain*, 194.
875 Chernow, *Grant*, 948.
876 Chernow, *Grant*, 939.
877 Pitkin, *The Captain*, 37–38.
878 Chernow, *Grant*, 943.
879 Simon, *The Papers*, Volume 31, 347–348.
880 Pitkin, *The Captain*, 40.
881 Perry, *Grant and Twain*, 197.
882 Green, *General*, 37.
883 Pitkin, *The Captain*, 41.

884 Pitkin, *The Captain,* 40–41.

885 Chernow, *Grant,* 944.

886 Pitkin, *The Captain,* 40–41.

887 Chernow, *Grant,* 944.

888 Chernow, *Grant,* 944.

889 Simon, *The Papers,* Volume 31, 353–354.

890 Pitkin, *The Captain,* 41–42.

891 Simon, *The Papers.* Volume 31, 355–356.

892 Chernow, *Grant,* 945.

893 Chernow, *Grant,* 944.

894 Twain, Mark, "The Private History of a Campaign That Failed," *The Century Magazine,* Volume XXXI, December 1885), 192, https://babel.hathitrust.org/cgi/pt?id=md39015035091274&view=1up&seq=208.

895 Pitkin, *The Captain,* 43–44.

896 Shrady, *"Last Days,"* 415.

897 Pitkin, *The Captain,* 44.

898 Flood, *Grant's Final,* 182.

CHAPTER TWENTY-SEVEN: MOUNT MCGREGOR

899 Twain, Mark, *Mark Twain's Notebook,* Edited by Albert Bigelow Paine (New York: Harper & Brothers, 1906), https://archive.org/stream/in.ernet.dli.2015.176144/2015.176144.Mark-Twains-Notebook_djvu.txt.

900 Braswell, Sean, "How Ulysses S. Grant and Mark Twain Rescued Each Other's Fortunes," May 22, 2020, https://www.ozy.com/true-and-stories/how-ulysses-s-grant-and-mark-twain-rescued-each-others-fortunes/330133/.

901 Paine, Albert Bigelow, *Mark Twain: A Biography* (New York: Harper & Brothers, 1912), 811.

902 Twain, Mark, *The Writings of Mark Twain, Volume XV* (New York: Mark Twain Company, 1917–1892), xi. https://archive.org/stream/marktworkswrite15twairich/marktworkswrite15twairich_djvu.txt.

903 Twain, Mark, "The Private History."

904 Perry, *Grant and Twain,* 202–203.

905 Green, *General,* 310.

906 Perry, *Grant and Twain,* 207.

907 Perry, *Grant and Twain,* 202–203.

908 Chernow, *Grant,* 948–949.

909 Pitkin, *The Captain,* 59.

910 Chernow, *Grant,* 948–949.

911 Flood, *Grant's Final,* 11.

912 Flood, *Grant's Final,* 185.

913 Flood, *Grant's Final,* 186.

914 Flood, *Grant's Final,* 185–186.

915 Chernow, *Grant,* 948.
916 Pitkin, *The Captain,* 61.
917 Shrady, "Last Days," 79.
918 Shrady, "Last Days," 79–80.
919 Chernow, *Grant,* 948–949.
920 Flood, *Grant's Final,* 188.
921 Shrady, "Last Days," 419.
922 Chernow, *Grant,* 948–949.
923 Green, *General,* 307.
924 Flood, *Grant's Final,* 189.
925 Flood, *Grant's Final,* 190–191.
926 Pitkin, *The Captain,* 61–62.
927 Flood, *Grant's Final,* 190–191.
928 Pitkin, *The Captain,* 65.
929 Flood, *Grant's Final,* 195–196.
930 Pitkin, *The Captain,* 64.
931 Shrady, "Last Days," 419–420.
932 Flood, *Grant's Final,* 192.
933 Green, *General,* 310.
934 Perry, *Grant and Twain,* 210.
935 Green, *General,* 309.
936 Marszalek, John F., *The Best Writings of Ulysses S. Grant* (Carbondale, Illinois: Southern Illinois University Press, 2015), 195.
937 Flood, *Grant's Final,* 194.
938 Flood, *Grant's Final,* 195.
939 Pitkin, *The Captain,* 64.

CHAPTER TWENTY-EIGHT: APPOMATTOX

940 Pitkin, *The Captain,* 45.
941 Grant, Ulysses, *Personal Memoirs,* 591.
942 Brands, *The Man,* 363–364.
943 Sheridan, Philip Henry, *Personal Memoirs of P. H. Sheridan, General United States Army, Volume 2* (New York: C. L. Webster, 1888), 191.
944 Smith, *Grant,* 401.
945 Brands, *The Man,* 363–364.
946 Brands, *The Man,* 363–364.
947 Smith, *Grant,* 401.
948 Chernow, *Grant,* 502–504.
949 Smith, *Grant,* 401–402.
950 Burns, "War Is All," 1990.
951 Smith, *Grant,* 402.
952 Catton, *Command,* 461.

[953] Grant, Ulysses, *Personal Memoirs*, 593.

[954] Richardson, Albert D., *A Personal History of Ulysses S. Grant* (Hartford, CT: American Publishing Company, 1885), 490. https://archive.org/stream/personalhistoryo01lcrich/personalhistoryo01lcrich_djvu.txt.

[955] Cadwallader, Sylvanus, *Three Years With Grant: As Recalled by War Correspondent* (New York: Knopf Doubleday Publishing Group, 2013). https://books.google.com/books?id=0VSFAAAAQBAJ&printsec=frontcover&source=gbs_ge_summary_r&cad=0#v=onepage&q&f=false.

[956] Grant, Ulysses, *Personal Memoirs*, 594.

[957] Porter, *Campaigning*, 467.

[958] Grant, Ulysses, *Personal Memoirs*, 594.

[959] Catton, *Command*, 462.

[960] Grant, Ulysses, *Personal Memoirs*, 596.

[961] Smith, *Grant*, 403.

[962] Burns, "War Is All," 1990.

[963] Young, *Around the World*, 455–456.

[964] Ross, Ishbel, *The General's Wife: The Life of Mrs. Ulysses S. Grant* (New York: Dodd, Mead & Company, 1959, Internet Archive), 58. https://archive.org/stream/generalswifethe1010870mbp/generalswifethe1010870mbp_djvu.txt.

[965] Chamberlain, Joshua Lawrence, *The Passing of the Armies* (Gettysburg, PA: Stan Clark Military Books, 1994/1915), 246–247.

[966] Porter, *Campaigning*, 469–470.

[967] Smith, *Grant*, 403–404.

[968] Catton, *Command*, 464.

[969] Brands, *The Man,* 366.

[970] Porter, *Campaigning*, 472.

CHAPTER TWENTY-NINE: IT IS FINISHED

[971] Perry, *Grant and Twain*, 219–220.

[972] Perry, *Grant and Twain*, 219–220.

[973] Pitkin, *The Captain,* 66–67.

[974] Flood, *Grant's Final,* 197–198.

[975] Pitkin, *The Captain,* 66.

[976] Pitkin, *The Captain,* 65.

[977] Perrett, *Ulysses S. Grant,* 476.

[978] Perry, *Grant and Twain*, 209–210.

[979] Chernow, *Grant,* 950.

[980] Chernow, *Grant,* 949.

[981] Perry, *Grant and Twain*, 223–224.

[982] Shrady, "Last Days," 420.

[983] Simon, *The Papers,* Volume 31, 381.

[984] Shrady, "Last Days," 423.

[985] Perry, *Grant and Twain*, 223–224.

[986] Shrady, "Last Days," 420.

[987] Shrady, "Last Days," 420.

[988] Goldhurst, *Many,* 218.

[989] Shrady, "Last Days," 420.

[990] Goldhurst, *Many,* 218.

[991] Flood, *Grant's Final,* 201.

[992] Perry, *Grant and Twain,* 221.

[993] Flood, *Grant's Final,* 208.

[994] Goldhurst, *Many,* 219–220.

[995] Flood, *Grant's Final,* 203–204.

[996] Brands, *The Man,* 629.

[997] Goldhurst, *Many,* 220.

[998] Twain, *Autobiography,* 83–84.

[999] Goldhurst, *Many,* 219–220.

[1000] Perrett, *Ulysses S. Grant,* 476.

[1001] Grant, Ulysses, *Personal Memoirs*, 5.

[1002] Simon, *The Papers,* Volume 31, 414–415.

[1003] Simon, *The Papers,* Volume 31, 416.

[1004] Perry, *Grant and Twain,* 225.

[1005] Pitkin, *The Captain,* 67.

[1006] Simon, *The Papers,* Volume 31, 404.

[1007] Flood, *Grant's Final,* 202.

[1008] Grant, Julia, *Memoirs,* 331.

[1009] Fay, John, "Reminiscences of Grant," *Bismarck Daily Tribune*, Bismarck, North Dakota, Sunday, October 2, 1887. https://libguides.css.edu/ld.php?content_id=10102489.

[1010] Grant, Julia, *Memoirs,* 331.

[1011] Simon, *The Papers,* Volume 31, 384.

[1012] Goldhurst, *Many,* 224–225.

[1013] White, *American Ulysses*, 650.

[1014] Simon, *The Papers,* Volume 31, 423.

[1015] Simon, *The Papers,* Volume 31, 424.

[1016] Goldhurst, *Many,* 224–225.

[1017] Simon, *The Papers,* Volume 31, 434.

[1018] Chernow, *Grant,* 951–952.

[1019] Pitkin, *The Captain,* 85.

[1020] Simon, *The Papers,* Volume 31, 403.

[1021] Simon, *The Papers,* Volume 31, 403.

[1022] Chernow, *Grant,* 952.

[1023] Pitkin, *The Captain,* 68.

[1024] Shrady, "Last Days," 426.

1025 Shrady, "Last Days," 427.

1026 Perry, *Grant and Twain*, 225.

1027 Perry, *Grant and Twain*, 225.

1028 Simon, *The Papers*, 437.

1029 Green, *General*, 10.

1030 Chernow, *Grant*, 952.

Chapter Thirty: 8:08

1031 Simon, *The Papers*, Volume 31, 392–393.

1032 Chernow, *Grant*, 954.

1033 Flood, *Grant's Final*, 222–223.

1034 Chernow, *Grant*, 954.

1035 Pitkin, *The Captain*, 90–91.

1036 Flood, *Grant's Final*, 223–224.

1037 Shrady, "Last Days," 427-428.

1038 Flood, *Grant's Final*, 223–224.

1039 Flood, *Grant's Final*, 223–224.

1040 Goldhurst, *Many*, 227–228.

1041 Flood, *Grant's Final*, 224.

1042 Flood, *Grant's Final*, 223–224.

1043 Shrady, "Last Days," 429.

1044 Goldhurst, *Many*, 229.

1045 Flood, *Grant's Final*, 225.

1046 Shrady, "Last Days," 429.

1047 Flood, *Grant's Final*, 225–226.

1048 Flood, *Grant's Final*, 226.

1049 Flood, *Grant's Final*, 227.

1050 Flood, *Grant's Final*, 227.

1051 Cantacuzène, Julia, *My Life Here and There* (Austria: C. Scribner's Sons, 1921), 52.

1052 Chernow, *Grant*, 954.

1053 Grant, Julia, *Memoirs*, 331.

1054 Shrady, "Last Days," 429.

1055 Flood, *Grant's Final*, 229.

1056 Perrett, *Ulysses S. Grant*, 478.

1057 Simon, *The Papers*, Volume 31, 387–388.

1058 Kemp, Ben, "A Necessary Undertaking," U.S. Grant Cottage State Historic Site, https://www.grantcottage.org/blog/2019/7/29/a-necessary-undertaking.

1059 Chernow, *Grant*, 954.

1060 Waugh, *U. S. Grant*, 229–230.

1061 Flood, *Grant's Final*, 235.

[1062] Waugh, *U. S. Grant,* 229–230.

[1063] Goldhurst, *Many,* 233–234.

[1064] Goldhurst, *Many,* 234.

[1065] Waugh, *U. S. Grant,* 273.

[1066] Waugh, *U. S. Grant,* 281.

[1067] Ben Kemp, U.S. Grant Cottage Historic Site Operations Manager, correspondence with the author, February 2021.

[1068] Powers, *Mark Twain,* 503–504.

Chapter Thirty-One: A Soldier's Farewell

[1069] Flood, *Grant's Final,* 243.

[1070] Goldhurst, *Many,* 238–239.

[1071] Goldhurst, *Many,* 239.

[1072] Flood, *Grant's Final,* 243.

[1073] Chernow, *Grant,* 956–957.

[1074] Waugh, *U. S. Grant,* 242.

[1075] Chernow, *Grant,* 956–957.

[1076] Waugh, *U. S. Grant,* 398.

[1077] Goldhurst, *Many,* 240–241.

[1078] Flood, *Grant's Final,* 244.

[1079] Goldhurst, *Many,* 240–241.

[1080] Flood, *Grant's Final,* 243–244

[1081] Waugh, *U. S. Grant,* 242.

[1082] Goldhurst, *Many,* 242–243.

[1083] Waugh, *U. S. Grant,* 243.

[1084] Goldhurst, *Many,* 242–243.

[1085] Goldhurst, *Many,* 240–241.

[1086] Waugh, *U. S. Grant,* 243.

[1087] Chernow, *Grant,* 958.

[1088] Powers, *Mark Twain,* 504.

[1089] Chernow, *Grant,* 958.

[1090] Chernow, *Grant,* 954.

[1091] Chernow, *Grant,* 957.

[1092] Goldhurst, *Many,* 240–241.

[1093] Chernow, *Grant,* 956–957.

[1094] Waugh, *U. S. Grant,* 245.

[1095] Waugh, *U. S. Grant,* 245–246.

[1096] Goldhurst, *Many,* 244.

[1097] Flood, *Grant's Final,* 247.

[1098] Chernow, *Grant,* 956–957.

[1099] Flood, *Grant's Final,* 247.

[1100] Grant, Ulysses, *Personal Memoirs,* 626.

[1101] Grant, Ulysses, *Personal Memoirs*, 627.

[1102] Grant, Ulysses, *Personal Memoirs*, 630.

[1103] Grant, Ulysses, *Personal Memoirs*, 632.

POSTSCRIPT

[1104] Chernow, *Grant,* 937.

[1105] Chernow, Ron, "On the Literary Wheelings and Dealings of Ulysses S. Grant and Mark Twain," Literary Hub, October 17, 2017. https://lithub.com/ on-the-literary-wheelings-and-dealings-of-ulysses-s-grant-and-mark-twain/.

[1106] Chernow, *Grant,* 953.

[1107] Goldhurst, *Many,* 257.

[1108] Powers, *Mark Twain,* 504.

[1109] Chernow, *Grant,* 958.

[1110] Chernow, *Grant,* 955.

[1111] Chernow, *Grant,* 937.

[1112] Achenbach, Joel, "U.S. Grant was the great hero of the Civil War but lost favor with historians," *Washington Post,* April 24, 2014, https://www. washingtonpost.com/national/health-science/us-grant-was-the-great-hero-of-the-civil-war-but-lost-favor-with-historians/2014/04/24/62f5439e-bf53-11e3-b574-f8748871856a_story.html?noredirect=on.

[1113] Chernow, *Grant,* 956.

[1114] Longstreet, General James, "Confederate General James Longstreet discusses his friendship with Grant," *The New York Times,* July 24, 1885, Grant Homepage Editors, granthomepage.com/intlongstreet.htm.

[1115] Cozzens, Peter, "The War Was a Grievous Error: General Longstreet speaks his mind," History.net, https://www.historynet.com/war-grievous-error. htm.

[1116] Chernow, *Grant,* 937.

[1117] Waugh, *U. S. Grant,* 252.

[1118] Waugh, *U. S. Grant,* 262.

[1119] Finan, Patrick, "McKinley participates in Grant's tomb dedication," *The Tribune Chronicle,* Warren, Ohio, April, 17, 2017. https://www.tribtoday. com/news/local-news/2017/04/mckinley-participates-in-grants-tomb-dedication/.

[1120] Chernow, *Grant,* 957–958.

[1121] Waugh, *U. S. Grant,* 262.

[1122] Waugh, *U. S. Grant,* 301.

[1123] Ulysses S. Grant Homepage Editors, "Grant's Genius," Ulysses S. Grant Homepage, granthomepage.com/grantgenius.htm.

[1124] Whitman, Walt, *Specimen Days* (Philadelphia: Rees Welsh and Company, 1882), https://www.bartleby.com/229/1200.html.

Bibliography

Achenbach, Joel. "U.S. Grant was the great hero of the Civil War but lost favor with historians." *Washington Post*, April 24, 2014. https://www.washingtonpost.com/national/health-science/us-grant-was-the-great-hero-of-the-civil-war-but-lost-favor-with-historians/2014/04/24/62f5439e-bf53-11e3-b574-f8748871856a_story.html?noredirect=on.

American Battlefield Trust. "Sherman's March to the Sea." https://www.battlefields.org/learn/articles/scorched-earth

Badeau, Adam, *Military History of Ulysses S. Grant from April 1861 to April 1865, Volume 1*. https://www.perseus.tufts.edu/hopper/text?doc=Perseus%3Atext%3A2001.05.0259%3Achapter%3D7%3Apage%3D184.

———. *Military History of Ulysses S. Grant from April 1861 to April 1865, Volume 3*. New York: D. Appleton, 1881.

———. *Grant in Peace*. Hartford, CT: S.S. Scranton & Company, 1887. https://archive.org/details/grantinpeacefro01badegoog/page/n8/mode/2up.

Beauregard, Pierre Gustave. *War of the Rebellion*. Serial 010 Page 0384 KY.,TENN.,N. MISS.,N. ALA.,AND SW. VA. Chapter XXII. Ohio State University EHistory. https://ehistory.osu.edu/books/official-records/010/0384.

Berry, Stephen. *House of Abraham: Lincoln and the Todds, a Family Divided by War*. New York: Houghton Mifflin Harcourt, 2009.

Bien, Madeleine. "Vicksburg is the Key." *National Park Foundation*. https://www.nationalparks.org/connect/blog/vicksburg-key.

Blumberg, Arnold. "Grant Takes D.C." *Warfarehistorynetwork.com*. https://warfarehistorynetwork.com/2018/12/21/grant-takes-d-c/.

Bonekemper, Edward H. *Grant and Lee: Victorious American and Vanquished Virginian*. Washington: Regnery History, 2012.

———. *Ulysses S. Grant: A Victor, Not a Butcher*. Washington: Regnery Publishing, October 11, 2010.

Borritt, Gabor S. *Why the Confederacy Lost*. Oxford: Oxford University Press, 1993.

Brands, H.W. *The Man Who Saved the Union: Ulysses Grant in War and Peace*. New York: Doubleday–Random House, 2012.

Braswell, Sean. "How Ulysses S. Grant and Mark Twain Rescued Each Other's Fortunes." *Ozy.com*, May 22, 2020. https://www.ozy.com/true-and-stories/how-ulysses-s-grant-and-mark-twain-rescued-each-others-fortunes/330133/.

Brier, Bob. *Cleopatra's Needles: The Lost Obelisks of Egypt*. London: Bloomsbury Publishing, 2016.

Burns, Ken. "Episode Two: A Very Bloody Affair—1862." *The Civil War*. Arlington, VA: PBS Video, 1990.

———. "Episode Six: The Valley of the Shadow of Death—1864." *The Civil War*. Arlington, VA: PBS Video, 1990.

———. "Episode Seven: Most Hallowed Ground—1864," *The Civil War*. Arlington, VA: PBS Video, 1990.

———. "Episode Eight: War Is All Hell—1865." *The Civil War*. Arlington, VA: PBS Video, 1990.

Cadwallader, Sylvanus. *Three Years with Grant: As Recalled by War Correspondent*. New York: Knopf Doubleday Publishing Group, 2013.

Cantacuzène, Julia. *My Life Here and There*. New York: Charles Scribner's Sons, 1921.

Catton, Bruce. *Grant Takes Command*. Edison, NJ: Castle Books–Book Sales Inc., 2000.

Chamberlain, Joshua Lawrence. *The Passing of the Armies*. Gettysburg, PA: Stan Clark Military Books, 1994/1915.

Chernow, Ron. *Grant*. New York: Penguin Press, 2017.

———. "On the Literary Wheelings and Dealings of Ulysses S. Grant and Mark Twain." *Literary Hub*, October 17, 2017. https://lithub.com/on-the-literary-wheelings-and-dealings-of-ulysses-s-grant-and-mark-twain/.

Cozzens, Peter. "The War Was a Grievous Error: General Longstreet speaks his mind." *History.net*. https://www.historynet.com/war-grievous-error.htm.

Daniel, Larry J. "General Albert Sidney Johnston's death at Shiloh." *Shiloh: Voices of the Civil War*. (New York: Time-Life Books, Quoted in Tennessee4Me.org), http://www.tn4me.org/sapage.cfm/sa_id/26/era_id/5/major_id/5/tnailer.xml.

Fay, John. "Reminiscences of Grant." *Bismarck Daily Tribune*, October 2, 1887. https://libguides.css.edu/ld.php?content_id=10102489.

Fellman, Michael, and John Russell Young. "Introduction," *Around the World with General Grant*. Baltimore: The Johns Hopkins University Press, 2002/1879.

Finan, Patrick. "McKinley participates in Grant's tomb dedication." *The Tribune Chronicle,* Warren, Ohio, April 17, 2017. https://www.tribtoday.com/news/local-news/2017/04/mckinley-participates-in-grants-tomb-dedication.

Firstladies.org. "First Lady Biography: Julia Grant." www.firstladies.org/biographies/firstladies.aspx?biography=19.

Flood, Charles Bracelen. *Grant's Final Victory*. Cambridge, MA: Da Capo Press, 2011.

———. *Grant and Sherman: The Friendship That Won the Civil War*. New York: Macmillan, 2005.

Fuller, General John. *The Generalship of Ulysses S. Grant*. New York: Dodd, Mead and Company, 1929. https://archive.org/stream/generalshipofuly010523mbp/generalshipofuly010523mbp_djvu.txt.

Gallagher, Gary W. *Fighting for the Confederacy: The Personal Recollections of General Edward Porter Alexander*. Chapel Hill, NC: UNC Press, 2000.

Goldhurst, Richard. *Many Are the Hearts: The Agony and the Triumph of Ulysses S. Grant*. New York: Reader's Digest Press, 1975.

Grant, Julia, *Memoirs*. Edited by John Y. Simon. New York: G. Putnam's Sons, 1975.

Grant, Ulysses S. "Letter to Henry W. Halleck (July 14, 1864)." *Encyclopedia Virginia*, January 2, 2015. https://www.encyclopediavirginia.org/Letter_from_Ulysses_S_Grant_to_Henry_W_Halleck_July_14_1864.

———. *Personal Memoirs of Ulysses S. Grant*. New York: Barnes & Noble Books, 2005. Originally published by Charles L. Webster and Company, New York, 1885.

Green, Horace. *General Grant's Last Stand*. New York: Charles Scribner's Sons, 1936.

Greenspan, Jesse. "Lincoln, Grant and Sherman Huddle Up, 150 Years Ago." History.com, March 26, 2015. https://www.history.com/news/lincoln-grant-and-sherman-huddle-up-150-years-ago.

History.com Editors. "Abraham Lincoln Reelected." History.com, November 13, 2009. https://www.history.com/this-day-in-history/lincoln-reelected.

———. "Battles of Cold Harbor." History.com, December 2, 2009. www.history.com/topics/american-civil-war/battles-of-cold-harbor.

———. "Sherman Presents Lincoln with a Christmas Gift." History.com, November 13, 2009. https://www.history.com/this-day-in-history/sherman-presents-lincoln-with-a-christmas-gift.

———. "Siege of Vicksburg." History.com, November 9, 2009. https://www.history.com/topics/american-civil-war/vicksburg-campaign.

Huntington, Randolph. *"Leopard" and "Linden," General Grant's Arabian Stallions*. Philadelphia: J. B. Lippincott Company, 1885. https://www.wiwfarm.com/LEOPARD_AND_LINDEN.htm.

Johnson, Robert Underwood. *Remembered Yesterdays*. Boston: Little, Brown, and Company, 1923. https://babel.hathitrust.org/cgi/pt?id=md39015018031156&view=1up&seq=9.

Johnson, Robert Underwood and Clarence Clough Buel. *Battles and Leaders of the Civil War, Volume 4*. New York: The Century Company, 1887. Perseus Digital Library. http://www.perseus.tufts.edu/hopper/text?doc=Perseus%3Atext%3A2001.05.0046%3Achapter%3D16.107.

Johnston, Joseph E. *My Negotiations with General Sherman*, 2. https://www.jstor.org/stable/pdf/25101089.pdf.

Kemp, Ben, "A Necessary Undertaking," U.S. Grant Cottage State Historic Site, https://www.grantcottage.org/blog/2019/7/29/a-necessary-undertaking.

————. U.S. Grant Cottage Historic Site Operations Manager, correspondence with the author, February 2021.

Lincoln, Abraham. *The Collected Works of Abraham Lincoln, Volume 7*. Cabin John, MD: Wildside Press, 2008.

Longstreet, General James. "Confederate General James Longstreet discusses his friendship with Grant." GrantHomePage.com, *New York Times*, July 24, 1885. granthomepage.com/intlongstreet.htm.

Lynghaug, Fran. *The Official Horse Breeds Standards Guide*. Stillwater, MN: Voyageur Press, 2009, p. 70. https://www.google.com/books/edition/The_Official_Horse_Breeds_Standards_Guide/myQBSVVEhagC?hl=en&gbpv=1&dq=The+stallion+he+call+Leopard,+and+the+Barb,+he+named+Linden+Tree&pg=PA70&printsec=frontcover.

Mackowski, Chris, and Kristopher D. White. "Forgotten Casualty: James Longstreet Wounded in the Wilderness: Part Two." *EmergingCivilWar. com*, May 6, 2014. https://emergingcivilwar.com/2014/05/06/forgotten-casualty-james-longstreet-wounded-in-the-wilderness-part-two/.

Marszalek, John F. *The Best Writings of Ulysses S. Grant*. Carbondale, Illinois: Southern Illinois University Press, 2015.

McClure, James Baird. *Stories, Sketches and Speeches of General Grant at Home and Abroad: In Peace and in War*. Chicago: Rhodes & McClure, Publishers, 1879.

McPherson, James M. *Battle Cry of Freedom*. Oxford: Oxford University Press, 1988.

Melton, Brian C. *Robert E. Lee: A Biography*. Santa Barbara, CA: ABC-CLIO, 2012.

Moser, Rick. "American Ulysses tries to set the record straight on the Civil War general." *Chicago Tribune*, October 21, 2016. https://www.chicagotribune.com/entertainment/books/ct-books-1030-american-ulysses-grant-ronald-white-20161020-story.html.

Mr. Lincoln & Friends Editors. "The Officers: Ulysses S. Grant (1822-1885)" MrLincolnandfriends.org. http://www.mrlincolnandfriends.org/the-officers/ulysses-grant/.

Mr. Lincoln's White House. "The Generals and Admirals: Ulysses S. Grant (1822-1885)." http://www.mrlincolnswhitehouse.org/residents-visitors/the-generals-and-admirals/generals-admirals-ulysses-s-grant-1822-1885/.

The New York Times Editors. "Sinking Into the Grave." The New York Times, March 1, 1885. https://newspaperarchive.com/new-york-times-mar-o1-1885-p-2/.

Paine, Albert Bigelow. Mark Twain: A Biography. New York: Harper & Brothers, 1912.

Perrett, Geoffrey. Ulysses S. Grant: Soldier & President. New York: Modern Library–Random House, 1999/1997.

Perry, Mark. Grant and Twain. New York, Random House, 2004.

Phifer, Mike. "End Game at Appomattox." Warfarehistorynetwork. com, December 23, 2018. https://warfarehistorynetwork.com/2018/12/23/end-game-at-appomattox/.

Pitkin, Thomas M. The Captain Departs: Ulysses S. Grant's Last Campaign. Carbondale, Illinois: Southern Illinois University Press, 1973.

Porter, Horace. Campaigning with Grant. New York: Time-Life Books, 1981, Reprinted from The Century Company, 1897.

———. "Campaigning with Grant." The Century Magazine. New York: The Century Magazine, Volume 53, 1897.

Powers, Ron. Mark Twain: A Life. New York: Free Press–Simon & Schuster, 2005.

Rhodes, Elisha Hunt. All for the Union. Edited by Robert Hunt Rhodes. New York: Orion Books, 1985.

Richardson, Albert D. A Personal History of Ulysses S. Grant. Hartford, CT: American Publishing Company, 1885, 490. https://archive.org/stream/personalhistoryo01lcrich/personalhistoryo01lcrich_djvu.txt.

Dukes, Sabrina. "General Grant National Memorial (Grant's Tomb). Riverside Park Conservancy, February 8, 2013. https://riversideparknyc.org/places/general-grant-national-memorial-grants-tomb/.

Robertson, James. "Desertion," Radio IQ, July 30, 2019. https://www. wvtf.org/post/desertion#stream/0.

Ross, Ishbel, *The General's Wife: The Life of Mrs. Ulysses S. Grant*. New York: Dodd, Mead & Company, 1959. https://archive.org/stream/generals-wifethel010870mbp/generalswifethel010870mbp_djvu.txt.

Samet, Elizabeth D. "Moral Courage and the Civil War," *The American Scholar*, September 3, 2019. https://theamericanscholar.org/moral-cour-age-and-the-civil-war/.

Sheridan, Philip Henry. *Personal Memoirs of P. H. Sheridan, General United States Army, Volume 2*. New York: C. L. Webster, 1888.

―――. *Personal Memoirs of P. H. Sheridan*, Volume II, Part 5. www.gutenberg.org/files/4362/old/orig4362-h/p5.htm.

Sherman, William T. *The Personal Memoirs of William T. Sherman*. New York: Literary Classics of the United States, 1990.

Shrady, George F. M.D. "General Grant's Last Days." *The Century Magazine*, July 1908.

Simon, John Y. *The Papers of Ulysses S. Grant, Volume 10: January 1–May 31, 1864*. Carbondale, Illinois: Southern Illinois University Press, 1982.

―――. *The Papers of Ulysses S. Grant, Volume 31: January 1–July 23, 1883–1885*. Carbondale, Illinois: Southern Illinois University Press, 2009.

Smith, Jean Edward. *Grant*. New York: Simon and Schuster, 2001.

Spangenberger, Phil. "The Yankee 'Sixteen Shooter.'" *True West Magazine*. Truewestmagazine.com/the-yankee-sixteen-shooter/.

Thomas, Benjamin. *Abraham Lincoln: A Biography*. Carbondale, Illinois: Southern Illinois University Press, 2008.

Thompson, Robert. "Two Days in April: The Battle of Five Forks." *American Battlefield Trust*. https://www.battlefields.org/learn/articles/two-days-april-battle-five-forks.

Townsend, Timothy. "Lincoln, Grant, and the 1864 Election." *National Parks System*. www.nps.gov/liho/learn/historyculture/lincolngrant.htm.

Twain, Mark. *Autobiography of Mark Twain, Volume 1*. Edited by Harriet Elinor Smith. Berkeley, CA: University of California Press, 2010.

―――. *Mark Twain's Autobiography, Volume 1*. Project Gutenberg of Australia. http://gutenberg.net.au/ebooks02/0200551h.html.

―――. *Mark Twain's Notebook*. Edited by Albert Bigelow Paine. New York: Harper & Brothers, 1906. https://archive.org/stream/in.ernet.dli.2015.176144/2015.176144.Mark-Twains-Notebook_djvu.txt.

―――. "The Private History of a Campaign That Failed." *The Century Magazine*, Volume XXXI, December, 1885. https://babel.hathitrust.org/cgi/pt?id=md39015035091274&view=1up&seq=208.

————. *The Writings of Mark Twain, Volume XV*. New York: Mark Twain Company, 1917–1892. https://archive.org/stream/marktworkswrite15t-wairich/marktworkswrite15twairich_djvu.txt.

Tyler, Mason Whiting, and Stephen C. Badgley. *Recollections of the Civil War*. New York: G. Putnam's and Sons, 1912.

Ulysses S. Grant Homepage Editors. "Grant's Genius." *Ulysses S. Grant Homepage*. granthomepage.com/grantgenius.htm

Ward, Geoffrey C., Ken Burns, and Ric Burns. *The Civil War: An Illustrated History*. New York: Knopf, 1992.

Watkins, Sam. *Co. Aytch*. New York: Collier Books–Macmillan Publishing Co., 1962.

Waugh, Joan. *U. S. Grant: American Hero, American Myth*. Chapel Hill, NC: UNC Press, 2009.

Welles, Gideon. "Admiral Farragut and New Orleans: with an account of the origin and command of the first three naval expeditions of the war." *The Galaxy, v. 12*, November and December, 1871. https://babel.hathitrust.org/cgi/pt?id=ucl.$b201039;view=1up;seq=685.

Wert, Jeffry D. *Custer: The Controversial Life of George Armstrong Custer*. New York, Simon and Schuster, 2015.

————. *The Sword of Lincoln: The Army of the Potomac*. New York: Simon & Schuster, 2005.

White, Ronald C. *American Ulysses*. New York: Penguin Random House, 2016.

Whitman, Walt. *Specimen Days*. Philadelphia: Rees Welsh and Company, 1882. https://www.bartleby.com/229/1200.html.

Wikipedia Editors. "The Battle of Monocacy." Wikipedia.org., Wikimedia. https://en.wikipedia.org/wiki/Battle_of_Monocacy.

————. "Battle of Shiloh." Wikipedia.org., Wikimedia. https://en.wikipedia.org/wiki/Battle_of_Shiloh.

Young, John Russell. *Around the World with General Grant*. Baltimore: The Johns Hopkins University Press, 2002/1879.

PHOTO CREDITS

1. "Ulysses S Grant as Brigadier General, 1861.jpg," photo. Reprinted from Wikimedia Commons. Public domain in the United States. https://commons.wikimedia.org/wiki/File:Ulysses_S_Grant_as_Brigadier_General,_1861.jpg.

2. "John_Aaron_Rawlins_-_Brady-Handy.jpg," photo. Reprinted from Wikimedia Commons. Public domain in the United States. https://commons.wikimedia.org/wiki/File:John_Aaron_Rawlins_-_Brady-Handy.jpg.

3. "William-Tecumseh-Sherman.jpg," photo. Reprinted from Wikimedia Commons. Public domain in the United States. https://commons.wikimedia.org/wiki/File:William-Tecumseh-Sherman.jpg.

4. "George_Meade_-_Brady-Handy.jpg," photo. Reprinted from Wikimedia Commons. Public domain in the United States. https://commons.wikimedia.org/wiki/File:George_Meade_-_Brady-Handy.jpg.

5. "Horace_Porter_-_Brady-Handy.jpg," photo. Reprinted from Wikimedia Commons. Public domain in the United States. https://commons.wikimedia.org/wiki/File:Horace_Porter_-_Brady-Handy.jpg.

6. "Winfield_Scott_Hancock.jpg," photo. Reprinted from Wikimedia Commons. Public domain in the United States. https://commons.wikimedia.org/wiki/File:Winfield_Scott_Hancock.jpg.

7. "Philip_Sheridan_01009a_restored.jpg," photo. Reprinted from Wikimedia Commons. Public domain in the United States. https://commons.wikimedia.org/wiki/File:Philip_Sheridan_01009a_restored.jpg.

8. "Mark_Twain_1871-02-07.jpg," photo. Reprinted from Wikipedia.org. Public domain in the United States. https://en.wikipedia.org/wiki/Mark_Twain#/media/File:Mark_Twain_1871-02-07.jpg.

9. "Julia_Grant_-_Brady-Handy.jpg," photo. Reprinted from Wikimedia Commons. Public domain in the United States. https://commons.wikimedia.org/wiki/File:Julia_Grant_-_Brady-Handy.jpg.

10. "Ulysses_Grant_and_Family_at_Long_Branch,_NJ_by_Pach_ Brothers,_NY,_1870.jpg," photo. Reprinted from Wikimedia Commons. Public domain in the United States. https://commons. wikimedia.org/wiki/File:Ulysses_Grant_and_Family_at_Long_ Branch,_NJ_by_Pach_Brothers,_NY,_1870.jpg.

11. "Frederick_Dent_Grant_and_his_wife.jpg," photo. Reprinted from Wikimedia Commons. Public domain in the United States. https://commons.wikimedia.org/wiki/File:Frederick_Dent_ Grant_and_his_wife.jpg.

12. "Ulysses_S._Grant_Jr._cph.3a38515.jpg," photo. Reprinted from Wikimedia Commons. Public domain in the United States. https://commons.wikimedia.org/wiki/File:Ulysses_S._Grant_ Jr._cph.3a38515.jpg.

13. "Mrs._Algernon_Sartoris_(Nellie_Grant)_LCCN2017893285_ (cropped).jpg," photo. Reprinted from Wikimedia Commons. Public domain in the United States. https://commons.wikimedia. org/wiki/File:Mrs._Algernon_Sartoris_(Nellie_Grant)_ LCCN2017893285_(cropped).jpg.

14. "Jesse_R._Grant,_youngest_son_of_President_Ulysses_S._Grant. jpg," photo. Reprinted from Wikimedia Commons. Public domain in the United States. https://commons.wikimedia.org/wiki/ File:Jesse_R._Grant,_youngest_son_of_President_Ulysses_S._ Grant.jpg.

15. "George Frederick Shrady," photo. Reprinted from Internet Archive —Archive.org. Public domain in the United States (copyright in the name of Dr. Shrady's wife, Hester Ellen Cantine Shrady, expired in 1986, seventy years after her death in 1916). File:https://ia800200.us.archive.org/BookReader/ BookReaderImages.php?zip=/0/items/generalgrantslas00shra/ generalgrantslas00shra_jp2.zip&file=generalgrantslas00shra_ jp2/generalgrantslas00shra_0018. jp2&id=generalgrantslas00shra&scale=1&rotate=0. https:// archive.org/details/generalgrantslas00shra/page/n19/mode/2up.

16. "Dr. John Hancock Douglas," found in the rare book, *Seven-Mile Funeral Cortege of Genl. Grant in New York Aug. 8, 1885*. CALL #421255. File: digital/collection/p16003coll6/id/887. The Huntington Library, San Marino, California. This book and image

are in the public domain. https://hdl.huntington.org/digital/collection/p16003coll6/id/887.

17. "Members of Family with Dr. John Hancock Douglas at Mt. McGregor in June 1885." Digital Id: cph 3c27588 //hdl.loc.gov/loc.pnp/cph.3c27588. Library of Congress, Prints & Photographs Division, Reproduction Number LC-USZ62-127588 (b&w film copy neg.). Library of Congress Control Number 2001695553. https://www.loc.gov/resource/cph.3c27588/.

18. "US_Grant_in_1885.jpg," photo. Reprinted from Wikimedia Commons. Public domain in the United States. https://commons.wikimedia.org/wiki/File:US_Grant_in_1885.jpg.

INDEX

M

Mackay, John: 26
Manigault, Arthur M.: 269
Markoe, T. M.: 87
Marine National Bank: 27, 28, 31,
  32, 33, 34, 234, 364
Marshall, Charles: 348, 349, 352,
  355
Martindale, John H.: 184
McCausland, John: 260
McClellan, George B.: 131, 214,
  216, 246, 266, 267, 271, 280,
  281
McDowell, Irvin: 131
McLean, Wilmer: 352, 353
McCook, Alexander M.: 57
McKinley, William: 277, 397, 398
McPherson, James B.: 57, 68, 71, 72,
  75, 76, 78
McSweeny, Henry: 233, 338, 340,
  376, 377, 379, 380
Meade, George G.: 120, 121, 123,
  124, 130, 131, 132, 135, 136,
  137, 139, 140, 142, 146, 149,
  150, 151, 152, 154, 156, 159,
  161, 162, 180, 184, 185, 215,
  218, 250, 251, 252, 253, 271,
  288, 289, 290, 297, 298, 309,
  311, 312, 313, 314, 321, 322,
  323, 347, 349, 350
Merritt, Stephen: 383
Merritt, Wesley: 348
Metropolitan Church: 233
Metropolitan Opera: 30
Mexican Southern Railway: 29, 35
Mexican War: 61, 67, 91, 121, 126,
  269, 369, 397
Military Pension (Pension): 22, 24,
  204, 205, 207, 209,
Minnick, James: 340

Missionary Ridge: 116
Mobile, Alabama: 124, 266, 280
Monocacy Junction: 259, 261, 262,
Morgan, J. Pierpont: 26
Morphine: 166, 225, 235, 236, 358,
  360, 361, 377, 378
Mount McGregor: 333, 335, 336,
  337, 338, 339, 341, 342, 343,
  357, 358, 359, 360, 362, 363,
  369, 375, 384, 385, 388
Mount Zion: 16
Mumford, Thomas: 298

N

Napoleon: 25, 27, 63
National Guard: 389
Nelson, William "Bull": 50, 57
Neuralgia: 90, 93, 196, 232
New Cold Harbor: 179
New Orleans, Louisiana: 67
New York City: 24, 26, 28, 29, 30,
  31, 32, 38, 41, 83, 90, 95, 103,
  105, 128, 165, 168, 173, 177,
  196, 198, 200, 201, 204, 225,
  227, 232, 233, 234, 240, 256,
  258, 325, 333, 335, 344 368,
  370, 384, 385, 386, 391, 397,
  398
New York District Attorney: 234
New York Herald: 11, 99, 358
New York State: 35, 165, 168, 206,
  265, 325, 327, 335, 341, 357,
  358, 363, 368, 375
New York State Assembly: 206
New York State Volunteers: 341
New York Times: 119, 177, 197, 198,
  205, 232, 234, 325, 372, 382
New York World: 196, 257, 327,
  328, 329, 340

If you enjoyed this book, you will love ...